GO AHEAD

10

Go Ahead 10

für die Jahrgangsstufe 10 an sechsstufigen bayerischen Realschulen

erarbeitet von	John Eastwood, Street, Somerset
	Klaus Berold, Kulmbach
	Elke Zahn, Bayreuth
	Jane Eastwood und Deirdre Watchorn (*Unit 1, Text 2*)
unter beratender Mitarbeit von	Gerlinde Eberhardt, Traunreut
	Werner Epp, Kempten
	Gisela Fiedler, Nürnberg
	Günter Geiß, Weiden
	Renate Grieshaber, Kempten
	Renate Heidemeier, Eichstätt
	Konrad Huber, Maisach
	Jürgen Kanhäuser, Rain
	Reinhold Schnell, Frickenhausen
Verlagsredaktion	Stefanie Gröne, Katja Hartmann
Projektleitung	Helga Holtkamp
redaktionelle Mitarbeit	Shefali Mehta (*Unit 4*), Ellie Robertson, Claire Ross, Cecile Rossant, Fritz Preuss
Design und Layout	David Graham (*Units*), James Abram (*Anhänge*)
Bildredaktion	Uta Hübner, Stefanie Gröne
zum Schülerbuch sind erhältlich	**Workbook, CDs**

Hinweise zu weiteren Bestandteilen im Lehrerhandbuch.
Bild-, Text- und Musikquellen auf Seite 176.

www.cornelsen.de

1. Auflage, 7. Druck 2012/06

Alle Drucke dieser Auflage sind inhaltlich unverändert und können im Unterricht nebeneinander verwendet werden.

Um die Wiederverwendbarkeit zu gewährleisten, darf in dieses Buch nicht hineingeschrieben werden.

© 2004 Cornelsen Verlag, Berlin
© 2012 Cornelsen Schulverlag GmbH, Berlin

Das Werk und seine Teile sind urheberrechtlich geschützt.
Jede Nutzung in anderen als den gesetzlich zugelassenen Fällen bedarf der vorherigen schriftlichen Einwilligung des Verlages.
Hinweis zu den §§ 46, 52a UrhG: Weder das Werk noch seine Teile dürfen ohne eine solche Einwilligung eingescannt und in ein Netzwerk eingestellt oder sonst öffentlich zugänglich gemacht werden.
Das gilt auch für Intranets von Schulen und sonstigen Bildungseinrichtungen.

Druck: Stürtz GmbH, Würzburg

ISBN 978-3-464-02853-7

 Inhalt gedruckt auf säurefreiem Papier aus nachhaltiger Forstwirtschaft.

CONTENTS / INHALT

Page Unit   What we learn in this unit

 THE OTHER SIDE OF THE WORLD

5	W & P	
6	Intro 1	Sit 1–2, Ex 1–3
8	Text 1	**Dreamtime**, Ex 4–7
10	List	Ex 8
11	Follow	Ex 9–11
12	Intro 2	Sit 3–4, Ex 12–14
14	Text 2	**The Kiwi Experience**, Ex 15–18
17	Com	**Feelings**, Ex 19–21
18	TYE	**The flying doctor**, 1–7
20	Read	**Grandmother**

Verb tenses (Rev)

Active – Passive (Rev)

2 FACT OR FICTION?

21	W & P	
22	Intro 1	Sit 1–2, Ex 1–4
24	Text 1	**Whiz-Kids**, Ex 5–8
26	List	Ex 9
27	Follow	Ex 10–12
28	Intro 2	Sit 3–4, Ex 13–15
30	Text 2	**The Eden Project**, Ex 16–20
33	Com	**Saying what you need**, Ex 21–22
34	TYE	**Predicting the future**, 1–5
36	Read	**The Hitchhiker's Guide to the Galaxy**

Participles – in relative clauses
            – in clauses of reason / time
            – used with a noun

Conditional sentences (Rev)
Conjunctions (Rev)

 FOREVER YOUNG

37	W & P	
38	Intro 1	Sit 1–2, Ex 1–3
40	Text 1	**From rock to rap**, Ex 4–6
42	List	Ex 7
43	Follow	Ex 8–9
44	Intro 2	Sit 3–4, Ex 10–11
46	Text 2	**Look what you did to me**, Ex 12–17
49	Com	**Hobbies and interests**, Ex 18–20
50	TYE	**Make love not war**, 1–5
52	Read	**How to Be Good**

to-infinitive / *ing*-form (Rev)

Preposition + *ing*-form (Rev)

three **3**

CONTENTS / INHALT

Page	Unit		What we learn in this unit

4 CANADIAN MOSAIC

53	W & P		
54	Intro 1	Sit 1–2, Ex 1–5	Adjectives and adverbs (Rev)
56	Text 1	An irritating person, Ex 6–10	Adverbs of degree (Rev)
58	List	Ex 11	
59	Follow	Ex 12, Song	
60	Intro 2	Sit 3–4, Ex 13–15	*shall I / shall we …?*
62	Text 2	In the middle of nowhere, Ex 16–21	Modals + *have* + past participle
65	Com	Suggestions, Ex 22–23	
66	TYE	The Inuit people, 1–5	
68	Read	Diary of a South African	

EXTRA PAGES

69	Unit 1	Danger from above
72	Unit 2	A whole new world
75	Unit 3	It's a conspiracy
78	Unit 4	Grey Owl

81		Song and Poems	
82	Read	Christmas in Hell	
84	Proj	Project page	
85	Rev	Revision exercises 1–17	
90	Read	Contemporary literature in the English language	
92		Dictionary work	Prüfungsvorbereitung – Wörterbuch
93		Translation practice	– Übersetzen
94		Speaking practice	– Sprechen
96		Pair work	Partnerübungen
97		Grammatical terms	Grammatikalische Fachausdrücke
100		Grammar	Grammatikanhang
120		Irregular verbs	Unregelmäßige Verben
122		English sounds	Erklärung der Lautschriftzeichen
123		Unit vocabulary list	Wörterverzeichnis
146		List of names	Liste der Namen
151		Geographical names	Länder und Nationalitäten
152		Index	Alphabetisches Wörterverzeichnis
174		Extra Pages vocabulary list	Wörterverzeichnis **Extra Pages**
175		Song / Poems vocabulary list	Wörterverzeichnis **Song / Poems**
175		Story vocabulary list	Wörterverzeichnis **Story**

Com = Communication   **Ex** = Exercise   **Follow** = Follow up   **Intro** = Introduction   **List** = Listening   **Proj** = Project
Read = Reading   **Rev** = Revision   **Sit** = Situation   **TYE** = Test your English   **W & P** = Words and pictures

4   four

UNIT 1
THE OTHER SIDE OF THE WORLD

WORDS AND PICTURES
02

Australia is not just a country, it's a whole continent. It's a land of great contrasts. There's the crowded south-east coast with the big cities of Sydney and Melbourne, and there's also the hot, dry outback with its huge empty spaces. There are 19 million people of mainly European origin, and there are 410,000 Aborigines, the first Australians. There's Sydney Opera House and the Harbour Bridge, and there are the magical colours of Uluru, the largest rock in the world. There are Christmas parties on the beach, there's football, rugby and cricket, and there are kangaroos and koala bears. But be careful – there are also seventy different kinds of poisonous snakes. And there are poisonous spiders such as the redback.

When the first European explorers reached what was to them a new continent, they called it the Great Southern Land. Now it's Australia or 'down under'. Australia became part of the British Empire, and even today the British Queen is also Queen of Australia. But there's nothing the Australians like better than beating the English at cricket or rugby.

At one time, Australians were mainly descendants of British and Irish immigrants, but nowadays they're much more of a mixture, with their origins in countries such as Italy, Greece, Lebanon and Vietnam.

five 5

Unit 1 **INTRODUCTION 1**

SITUATION 1
03

WELCOME TO JAKE'S HOME PAGE

WHO AM I? My name is Jake Roberts, I'm 16, and I live in Sydney, Australia. I go to South Sydney High School in Maroubra.
5 My girlfriend Ashleigh is a student there too.

I like basketball, weight training and surfing (in the sea as well as on the internet). Maroubra is a good beach
10 for surfing and not as crowded as the famous Bondi Beach just up the coast. I love riding the waves.

- more photos
- my school
  www.sthsydney-h.schools.nsw.edu.au
- **Aussie basketball**
  www.nbl.com.au
  www.basketball.net.au
  www.razorbacks.com.au
  www.sydneykings.com.au
- great surfing spots
  www.surfingaustralia.com
  www.globalsurfers.com

NEWS UPDATE It's pretty late. I've been e-mailing my friends most of the evening. I've also
15 visited a couple of chat rooms. I'm still sitting here at the computer and everyone else is in bed. It's a great feeling. Last night I went with Ashleigh to see a movie. She insisted on seeing 'Rabbit-Proof Fence', so I couldn't avoid it. She enjoyed it, but
20 I thought it was a bit GIRLIE and BORING. I'd been working hard at my weight training in the afternoon, and I was feeling pretty tired. I actually fell ASLEEP during the movie, but luckily Ashleigh didn't notice. I prefer Sylvester Stallone myself, more action. The new James Bond was also on, but we'd seen it before.

EXERCISE 1

Look again at Jake's home page and find examples of the verb tenses.

➡ Simple present
  I go to South Sydney High School.
1 Present perfect
2 Past perfect
3 Present progressive
4 Past progressive
5 Present perfect progressive
6 Past perfect progressive
7 There are several examples on the home page of one other tense. Which tense is it?

I like surfing the net. I've visited lots of websites today.

I'm just looking at this one. A friend told me about it yesterday.

➡ page 100-102

6 six

INTRODUCTION 1

SITUATION 2

Rabbit-Proof Fence is a film about the 'stolen generation' of children. Up to 1970, the government used to remove Aborigine and mixed-race children from their families. The children had to work for white people as servants or farm labourers. The idea was to make them part of white society.

The film tells the true story of Molly, Daisy and Gracie, three mixed-race girls who were removed from their families in Western Australia and taken to a school over 1,000 miles away to receive training as servants. The girls escaped from the school and made the long journey home on foot while the police were searching for them. They travelled through some remote parts of the outback. The fences which helped the girls to find their way had been put up to keep rabbits away from crops.

EXERCISE 2

 page 100-103

Complete the conversations. Use the correct form of the verbs.

1 Ashleigh is waiting for Jake outside a cinema. She is calling him on her mobile.
   Ashleigh Jake? Where are you?
   Jake Hi. I'm outside Central Station. I'll be with you in five minutes.
   Ashleigh Well, hurry up or we'll miss the film. I … (wait) outside the cinema for 20 minutes.
   Jake I'm already on my way. I … (walk) as fast as I can.

2 Matthew is playing a computer game, but his sister thinks it's her turn now.
   Jessica It's my turn on the computer now, Matthew.
   Matthew You'll have to wait. I … (play) this game.
   Jessica Oh, you … (always/say) that when it's my turn. You … (play) it since lunchtime.

3 Emma is telling Ashleigh that she saw her yesterday in Sydney.
   Emma We … (see) you yesterday afternoon outside the museum.
   Ashleigh Yes, I … (wait) for a bus.
   Emma We were in the car.
   Ashleigh Well, why … (you/not/stop) for me?
   Emma Oh, we … (go) in the other direction.

4 Michael is phoning his friend Jake.
   Michael I … (ring) earlier, but you … (switch) your phone off.
   Jake Sorry, I was at the beach. I … (surf). Then afterwards I … (forget) to listen to my messages.

5 Ashleigh is showing Rebecca some photos.
   Rebecca You … (look) very hot in this photo.
   Ashleigh That's because when Jake … (take) the photo, I … (just/finish) my training. I … (not/really/want) him to take it.

6 Jake and Ashleigh are sitting on the beach.
   Jake What's the time?
   Ashleigh I … (not/know). Actually, I … (lose) my watch. I … (have) it yesterday, but now I can't find it.
   Jake … (you/mean) the one that I … (give) you?
   Ashleigh Yes. I'm sorry, Jake.
   Jake I'll help you look for it.
   Ashleigh I … (already/look) everywhere.

EXERCISE 3

Put in the missing words.

Dick Morgan is an Aborigine. He … in an Aborigine community in the Northern Territory. He isn't too old to work yet, but he … had a job for a long time. Every week the government … him enough money to live on. Many Aborigines … problems with alcohol and … all their money on drink, but Dick's community is 'dry'.

When Dick was a young boy, a policeman … him away from his family. After some time at school he … as a farm labourer. But that was long ago. Nowadays, Dick often … about the past. For months now, he's … trying to find out about his origins. So far he … had any success. He still … know who his parents were.

seven 7

Unit 1 **TEXT 1**

Dreamtime

A long, long time ago Bulari rose from below the earth, came to the flat Australian continent and built the mountains and valleys. Then Kunapipi, 'the rainbow snake', dug out the earth to create the lakes and rivers. Bulari and Kunapipi are both Mothers of the Earth – like the gods who made the plants, the birds and all the other animals. The beginning of the world, the time long ago, is known to the first Australians as 'dreamtime'.

The dreamtime stories teach the Aborigines the rules for their society and their religion. They believe that the gods still live in the earth and in the trees, rivers and stones. The Aborigines are descendants of these gods, and so they have always treated nature with great respect. Although they hunted animals for food, they avoided damaging the Earth. No one can own the Earth, and so land cannot be bought and sold.

You have already seen that Australia is a fascinating nation of contrasts. One of these Australian contrasts is very unfortunate, and it's the one between the Aborigines and the immigrants who came later. When the British settled in Sydney in 1788, there were several hundred independent tribes – each with its own culture. The white settlers regarded the Aborigines as primitive people. In less than 200 years they had destroyed the Aborigine communities. Tens of thousands of Aborigines were killed by the settlers and by the diseases they brought with them, such as flu and smallpox. When they were driven from their land, the native people not only lost their homes, but also their culture and many of their dreamtime memories.

ABORIGINES

- Today there are 410,000 Aborigines, two per cent of the Australian population.
- The Aborigines have lived in Australia for at least 40,000 years and possibly more than 100,000 years.
- Aborigines were given equal rights in 1967.
- More than three-quarters of white children complete their school education, but only a third of Aborigine children do.
- On average, an Aborigine earns two-thirds of what a white person earns.
- A white Australian can expect to live 15-20 years longer than an Aborigine.

Cathy Freeman grew up with dreamtime stories. She was born on 16 February 1973 into a poor family in Mackay, on the Queensland coast. Her grandmother was a member of the 'stolen generation' who lived much of her life with strangers. Young Cathy was a marvellous runner, and she had a dream. As a teenager, she decided that she was going to win an Olympic gold medal. She trained till it hurt. Her exercises included twelve laps barefoot on grass – her family couldn't afford new running shoes. In the nineties, she became the nation's most popular and most successful athlete. She was young and beautiful, full of courage and ambition. In 1997 she became the world 400 metres champion and was named 'Australian of the Year'. Her career lasted until 2003, when she decided to give up international sport because she had lost the desire to compete.

At the time when Cathy became popular, white attitudes to Aborigines were slowly changing. In 1998 National Sorry Day was started, as a way of apologizing to the Aborigines for the way they had been treated. But two years later Prime Minister John Howard refused to apologize. He didn't think he was personally responsible for what earlier generations of settlers had done. However, it was another step forward when Cathy was chosen to light the Olympic flame at the 2000 Games in Sydney. In Australia she was a hero, and she carried the hopes of both black and white Australians.

8 eight

Ten days after lighting the flame, Cathy ran in the 400 metres final. Millions of Australians were
5 hoping she would do well. Cathy had to win! It took her 49.11 seconds to do just that, while 112,000 spectators cheered her as
10 loud as they could. Cathy felt enormous relief that she hadn't disappointed anyone.

She insisted on doing her victory
15 lap with two flags: the Australian flag and the Aborigine flag – which is black for the people, yellow for the sun and red for the land. The message of the two flags is that Aborigines should be Australians but that they should not
20 reject their background. Of course, the problems will not be magically solved because an Aborigine athlete won a gold medal. But through Cathy the situation of the first Australians has been brought to the world's attention. As young
25 Aborigines have said, 'Our stories must be told to people who have open hearts and open minds.'

TEXT 1

EXERCISE 4

Answer the questions.

1 What is 'dreamtime'?
2 What is the Aborigines' attitude to nature?
3 Was there a single Aborigine 'nation' in Australia when the Europeans invaded? Give a reason for your answer.
4 Why did the Aborigine population fall after the Europeans came to Australia?
5 Do Aborigines today have equal rights and opportunities? Give reasons for your answer.
6 How did Cathy Freeman train when she was a girl?
7 What is National Sorry Day?
8 What was the result of the women's 400 metres Olympic final in Sydney?
9 Why did Cathy carry two flags during her victory lap?
10 Cathy won a gold medal, but what else did she achieve in Sydney?

Unit 1 **TEXT 1**

EXERCISE 5

Find the missing words. They are all in the text.

▶ study → student, run → *runner*
▶ higher → lower, above → *below*
1 use → useful, succeed → ...
2 remember → forget, accept → ...
3 natural → nature, social → ...
4 kangaroo → animal, smallpox → ...
5 feel → heart, think → ...
6 happy → smile, sorry → ...
7 feel → feelings, remember → ...
8 down → up, fell → ...

EXERCISE 6

Read the sentences and discuss the questions about the verb forms.

1 The Aborigines believe that the gods live in nature.
 ~ Why *believe* and not *are believing*?
2 The Prime Minister refused to apologize for what other people had done.
 ~ Why *had done* rather than *did*?
3 When you phoned, I was watching the Olympics on TV.
 ~ Why *was watching* and not *watched*?
4 Hi. It's me. I'm running along the beach.
 ~ Why *I'm running*, and why not *I run*?
5 I'll be late home tomorrow because I'm training after school.
 ~ Why *I'm training* when no one is training at the moment?
6 Aborigines have been living in Australia for at least 60,000 years.
 ~ Why *have been living* rather than *live*?
7 The British settled in Sydney in 1788.
 ~ Why *settled*? Why not *have settled*?

Then say how you would express the meaning in German.

EXERCISE 7

Prime Minister John Howard refused to apologize to the Aborigines. Do you think he was right? Write an e-mail to him. Express your opinion in about 100 words and give your reasons. You can use some of these phrases.

Supporting Mr Howard
not your fault
not responsible
a long time ago
...

Against Mr Howard
treated very badly
put things right
an example to the nation
...

 ## EXERCISE 8

06-07 **Listening**

You are on a boat which is taking you on a cruise around Sydney Harbour. Listen to the guides. What they say is in two parts.

Part 1 (06)

Complete the sentences.

1 The site of the Sydney Opera House was once a garage where ... were kept.
2 The man who designed the opera house came from ... .
3 The building actually cost $... million.
4 It took ... years to build the opera house.
5 It wasn't completed until ... .
6 The first performance was of the opera ... by Prokofiev.

Part 2 (07)

Each of these sentences has an incorrect piece of information. Write down the correct word or phrase.

1 The Sydney Harbour Bridge joins central Sydney and West Sydney.
2 You get the best views if you cross the bridge on a train.
3 They started building the bridge from the middle.
4 People were worried that the fire might damage the bridge.
5 The bridge is made of concrete.
6 Someone who once worked on the bridge was Paul Hogan, the star of the film *Titanic*.

10 ten

FOLLOW UP

EXERCISE 9

Sometimes when you're speaking English, you may not know the word for what you want to say. You know the German word, but you don't know the English. When this happens, you can try to express the meaning in words you already know. Here are two examples.

> You think → Are there any (giftige) spiders in this area?
> You say → Are there any spiders that could kill you in this area?
>
> You think → I ran two (Runden) of the track.
> You say → I ran twice around the track.

Australian redback spider

Of course if you know the words, you can say it like this.

> You say → Are there any poisonous spiders in this area?
> You say → I ran two laps around the track.

Try to express the meaning in words you already know.

1 I wanted to avoid travelling in the (Hauptverkehrszeit).
2 Can you (empfehlen) a good restaurant?
3 There isn't any (Seife) in the bathroom.
4 That man is a (ehemaliger) Australian rugby player.
5 I need to buy some (Sonnenschutzmittel).
6 I bought these trousers at a (Kaufhaus) in Melbourne.
7 Did you (anprobieren) the trousers before you bought them?
8 Did you get a (Quittung) when you paid?

Then say the sentences with the words you didn't know before. They are all in this box. If you need to, check the meanings in a dictionary.

> department store • former • receipt • recommend
> • rush hour • soap • sun cream • try on

EXERCISE 10

There are a few words in English that are often shortened. For example, a message that encourages you to buy something is an *advertisement*. It can also be an *advert*.

Read each sentence and then find an alternative form (shorter or longer) for one of the words or phrases.

▶ His parents own a public house.
  His parents own a pub.
1 I took a photograph of the parade.
2 Most of us watched a film on the plane.
3 There's something wrong with this phone.
4 My bicycle has been stolen.
5 Unfortunately my friend has got influenza.
6 The students have to take a mathematics examination. (Change two words.)

EXERCISE 11

We also use abbreviations. For example, Canberra, the capital city of Australia, is known as the Australian Capital Territory or ACT. If you stay at a B&B, you get a bed and breakfast. What do these mean?

1 in the UK   7   an FBI agent
2 some FAQs   8   the teams in the NFL
3 a studio in LA   9   the BBC World Service
4 doing the D of E   10 the US government
5 a CD player   11 send your CV
6 working as a DJ   12 in the RAF

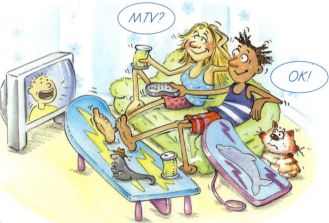

No one really knows where 'OK' comes from. One suggestion is that it is an abbreviation for 'orl korrect', a wrong spelling of 'all correct'.

eleven 11

Unit 1 **INTRODUCTION 2**

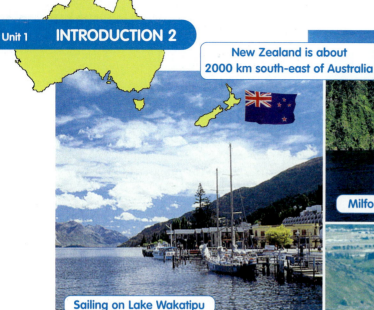

New Zealand is about 2000 km south-east of Australia

Milford Sound

Sailing on Lake Wakatipu

Paragliding over Queenstown

SITUATION 3

Mark is at a party in London when a young woman comes up to him and introduces herself.

Hannah Hi. I'm Hannah.
Mark Oh, hi. I'm Mark. Are you Australian?
Hannah I'm from New Zealand. I live in Auckland.
Mark Oh, really? I might go to New Zealand next year. I'm going to take some time off work and go to Australia with a friend, and we're thinking of visiting New Zealand too.
Hannah It's 'God's own country', so you couldn't go anywhere better. You'll have a great time.
Mark So where are the best places to go?
Hannah I guess most tourists go to Rotorua in the North Island or Queenstown in the South Island. Rotorua is where you can see the geysers.
Mark And Queenstown?
Hannah That's the main place for adventure sports, you know – bungee jumping, skydiving, paragliding, white-water rafting, that kind of thing. In fact, New Zealand is great for all outdoor activities – walking, mountain biking, sailing, skiing – you name it.
Mark Sounds great. I can't wait to get there. And what are you doing in England, Hannah?
Hannah I'm spending a year here. I'm working as a DJ for a local radio station. When I go home, I plan to train as a swimming instructor.

EXERCISE 12

Can you identify the activities?

➡ You get up to the top of a cliff or mountain.
   climbing

1 You jump from a high place with a rope around your feet.
2 You travel over the snow on long narrow pieces of metal or plastic.
3 You jump from a plane and fall through the air and then your parachute opens.
4 You fly through the air with a kind of sail above you.
5 You stand on a board and ride the waves as they come in.
6 You bounce up and down on a piece of strong material which throws you up in the air.

Describe what happens in these activities.

1 go-karting
2 white-water rafting
3 mountain biking
4 skating

12 twelve

INTRODUCTION 2

SITUATION 4

Mark is reading about Rotorua, a town on New Zealand's North Island.

This popular tourist destination is definitely worth a visit. It has hot springs, mud pools and geysers. The most famous geyser is called Pohutu, a Maori word which means 'big splash'. It's a spectacular
5 show as it shoots water up into the air at great speed, sometimes as high as 30 metres. The water in Rotorua is said to be very healthy, and you can swim in a thermal pool. Swimsuits and towels can be hired.

In Rotorua there's steam everywhere. You get the
10 feeling you're being followed – by the smell of rotten eggs. Some efforts have been made to remove the smell, but it doesn't seem likely that the problem will ever be solved. However, you soon get used to it, and it hasn't kept the tourists away. Tourism took off after the first European settlement had been established in the 19th century. Soon there was a
15 road and railway from Auckland, and visitors were being brought into the area.

Rotorua was first settled by Maoris about 650 years ago. Today there's still a Maori village with its church at the edge of Lake Rotorua and a meeting house where Maori concerts are held each evening.

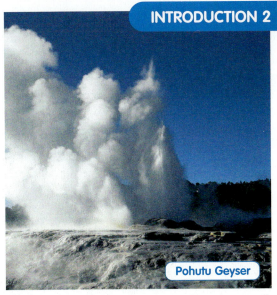
Pohutu Geyser

→ page 103-104

EXERCISE 13

Look again at the information about Rotorua and find examples of passive verbs in these tenses.

▶ Simple present
Maori concerts **are held** every evening.

1 Simple past
2 Present perfect
3 Past perfect
4 With *will*
5 With *can*
6 Present progressive
7 Past progressive

EXERCISE 14

Complete these two paragraphs about the Maoris. Put one word in each space.

The first Maoris arrived in New Zealand from Polynesia over a thousand years ago. They were not afraid to fight, and many battles and wars were … between the different tribes. Those who lost the
5 battle … often captured and used as slaves. Things got worse when the British arrived and brought guns with them because then many more Maoris were … or injured. Many also died of the diseases that had … brought by the white people. The Maoris'
10 traditional way of life was almost completely … .

In 1840 the British government agreed that the Maoris could have equal rights and could keep their land, but this promise … soon broken. Large amounts of land … taken from the Maoris. It wasn't until the 1970s and 1980s that the situation of the Maoris began to improve, and money was … to
15 a number of tribes whose land had … wrongly taken from them. More money … probably be paid in the future. Nowadays greater respect … shown to Maori language and culture than before. It should … recognized that New Zealand has had some success in its efforts to solve its race problems, and that the native people have been … less badly than in Australia.

Unit 1   TEXT 2

Skydiving

● The Kiwi Experience

Two friends, Jane and Deirdre, took a year off from their jobs in England and travelled round the world. During their trip, they spent a month in New Zealand. In the South Island they visited Queenstown, the adventure capital of the country, on the shores of the beautiful Lake Wakatipu. Lots of young people go there to do bungee jumping, skydiving and other kinds of exciting activities. There are several places where you can do a bungee jump, including the Kawarau Bridge, the world's first commercial jump site. Here is a day in Jane's diary.

Thursday 24 January

We've been travelling on the 'Kiwi Experience' bus which goes between the main tourist places. Now we're in Queenstown. Yesterday, Deirdre and I booked a bungee jump from the Kawarau Bridge. So we spent a day feeling very nervous as we went on a lake cruise. This morning a minibus took us from our hostel to the site. At reception we were weighed to see exactly how long the rope should be. We were asked if we wanted to dip our heads in the water. As it was a cold day, we decided we would stay dry. We walked across the bridge and looked down at the water far below. It was scary. The instructor was talking to me to try and stop me being so nervous. He put some towels around my feet, attached the rope, and then it was my turn. I moved slowly to the edge of the platform. I was being watched by quite a crowd of people on the viewing platform, and I tried to look confident as I waved to them. The instructor counted to three – 1, 2, 3 – and I dived head first from the platform.

The water came towards me at enormous speed, but the free fall lasted only a few seconds. When the rope caught for the first time and I bounced back up again, I was hugely relieved. I bounced up and down about six times before finally I was helped into a boat. When we reached the river bank and I got out of the boat, my legs were like jelly. From the bottom, I watched as Deirdre jumped and heard her scream as she fell through the air. Back in the bus we sat there with our souvenir T-shirts and our videos of the jump, and suddenly I felt very excited and pleased that I had actually done the jump.

TEXT 2

In New Zealand's Southern Alps there are lots of glaciers. The two largest are the Franz Josef glacier and the Fox glacier. The Franz Josef is over seven miles long. It is a white river of ice which is slowly sliding down the mountains towards the rainforest below. The Maoris tell the story of a beautiful girl who was climbing the mountain with her lover. When he fell down the
5 mountain and was killed, she cried so much that her tears created the glacier. Deirdre described in her diary how she and Jane climbed up the glacier.

Monday 28 January

We'd been told that you could do glacier walks on the Franz Josef, or even take a helicopter ride to the top –
10 if you're very rich. We decided to walk. You have to go in a group with a guide, and it started early in the morning. We went to the tour office, where we were given boots with crampons which grip the ice. We wore waterproofs and gloves, and we each carried a small backpack with
15 some extra clothes and food.

It was a long but level walk to the bottom of the glacier. One moment there were trees and mountains ahead of us, and the next there was a huge glacier, amazingly high and white. We couldn't see the top of it because of
20 the clouds, but there were people on the glacier high above us. They looked tiny, like ants.

There is a track up the glacier, and in places there are steps in the ice. The guide led the way. Our boots made a crunching sound on the ice. It was quite hard work, so
25 we stopped to rest every 20 minutes. We climbed up a small ravine, and once we had to squeeze through a narrow ice tunnel. The ice was freezing cold, even through our gloves. But we felt warm in the sunshine, even though we were surrounded by snow and ice. We
30 stopped again to admire the view. It was spectacular. Far below us we could see a dark grey river full of melted snow from the glacier.

Now we know why they call it 'God's own country'.

EXERCISE 15

Complete the story of Jane's bungee jump. Put one word in each space. Most of the words are in the text but not all of them.

Queenstown is the place for … sports. Jane and her friend arrived there on the 'Kiwi …' bus. The … looked wonderful. The two friends stayed in a … . They arranged to do a … jump from the first ever commercial … on the Kawarau River. They travelled there in a … . First they had to be … so that the instructors would know how long the … needed to be. It was a cold day, so they decided they wouldn't land in the water and get … .

Jane felt … when she looked down at the water. When it was her … , she stood on the … of the platform and … confidently to the people who were watching. When the … counted to three, she … from the platform. The water raced towards her very … , but only a few seconds later she … back up. Then someone … her get into a boat, and it was all over.

Unit 1 TEXT 2

EXERCISE 16

Say if the statements are true or false. Find the place in the text that gives you the information.

▶ The Franz Josef is the only glacier in the South Island.
False. 'In New Zealand's Southern Alps there are lots of glaciers.'
1 The glacier is moving.
2 The Maori girl was very sad.
3 A flight to the top of the glacier is quite cheap.
4 Jane and Deirdre had to buy their own equipment.
5 They walked down a steep hill to the glacier.
6 The people they saw on the glacier were a long way up.
7 They walked the same route as others had before them.
8 Strangely, they didn't feel cold on the glacier.

EXERCISE 17

Do you remember the verbs in the text? Complete each sentence with a verb in the correct form. The words in brackets will help you.

▶ I'll have to **book** a room at the hotel. (arrange to stay there)
▶ The instructor **attached** the rope to my feet. (joined two things together)
1 The assistant … the money carefully. (calculated the total amount)
2 We all had to … Adam's picture. (say how good it is)
3 We … goodbye as the visitors drove away. (moved our hands around in the air)
4 The video will … about ten minutes. (go on for a time)
5 The ground was wet where the snow had … . (become water)
6 The kids on the roller coaster were … with excitement. (shouting in a high voice)
7 To test the temperature I … my hand in the water. (put it in and took it out again)
8 The police have … the building. (moved into positions all around it)
9 The six of us managed to … into the car. (push our way into a small space)

EXERCISE 18

Complete this info box about New Zealand. Put each verb into the correct active or passive form.

▶ New Zealand **was named** (name) in 1642 by the Dutch explorer Abel Tasman. But to the Maori people who **had settled** (settle) there a thousand years earlier, it was 'the land of the long white cloud'.
• New Zealand was once part of the British Empire. It … (become) fully independent in 1947.
• The country … (grow) a lot of fruit and vegetables. Sheep farming is also important. There are at least ten times as many sheep as people. New Zealand … (know) as 'the world's biggest farm'.
• Many of New Zealand's products … (buy) by the British, but that changed when Britain … (join) the European Community in 1973. Since then New Zealand … (trade) more with Australia and South-East Asia.
• The country's official languages are English and Maori. Since the 1970s Maori … (teach) in schools with Maori students.
• Women … (allow) to vote since 1893. At that time, women … (not/give) this right in any other country in the world.
• New Zealand is only a little larger than the UK, so the main places … (can/visit) without too much travelling.
• Sport is big in New Zealand. The rugby team … (call) the All Blacks. Before each international game the players … (perform) a war dance. Usually the dance … (lead) by a Maori member of the team.

Auckland harbour and Maori rugby war dance

COMMUNICATION

Feelings

Mark I'm disappointed that I couldn't go to Australia. I was really looking forward to it. But I was too ill to travel.
Lewis I'm surprised you gave the whole thing up. Couldn't you have gone a week later?
Mark I couldn't afford another ticket. I had a cheap flight that I couldn't change. So I lost my money. I don't feel very pleased about that either. In fact it's really annoying. But I'm determined to get there next year.

Note the difference between pairs like *interested* and *interesting* or *excited* and *exciting*. We say *I'm really excited* but *This is really exciting*.

Talking about feelings
- I'm worried / excited about the trip.
- I feel confident / pleased / relieved.
- It's exciting / a relief.
- That was horrible / a shock.
- How annoying that we've missed the train.

EXERCISE 19

Look at the table and make sentences about how people feel.

I was disappointed	because I hadn't done what they told me to do.
I'm grateful	finding a snake in our tent.
It was a relief	to drive through the outback all day.
We were sad	of what you've achieved.
My parents were furious	that I should find you here in this remote place.
It's really boring	for all the help you've given me.
It was scary	that I failed the exam.
You should feel proud	to know you were safe.
How amazing	when our cat died.

➪ I was disappointed that I failed the exam.

EXERCISE 20

Complete these sentences in your own words.

1 I always feel nervous ... .
2 I'd be amazed if ... .
3 I think ... fascinating.
4 I hope ... .
5 I was sorry when ... .
6 I don't care ... .

EXERCISE 21

Talking about maps

Work with a partner.

Partner B: Please look at page 96.
Partner A: Look at the map of New Zealand. Find out from your partner what the missing names are. You can use phrases like this in your questions.
*What's the name of ... ?   off the coast of ...
in the northern part of ...   to the south-west of ...
on the east coast of ...   in the centre of ...*

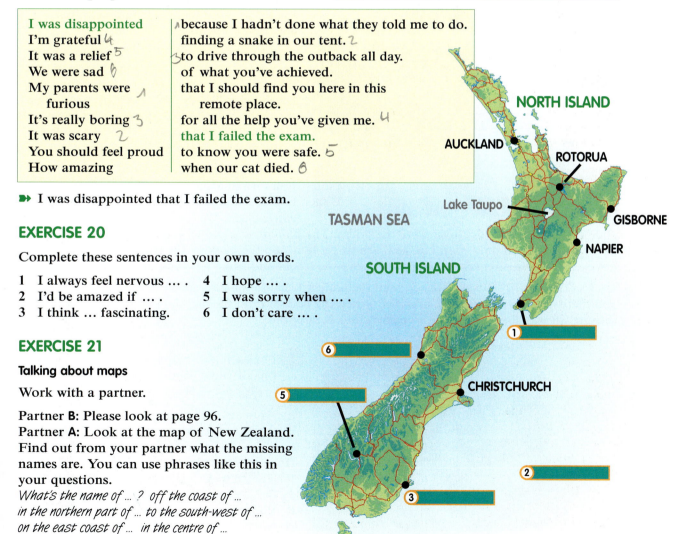

seventeen 17

TEST YOUR ENGLISH

The flying doctor

People who live on huge sheep or cattle stations in the Australian outback are usually a long way from their nearest neighbours – and from the nearest grocery store, school or hospital. The Royal Flying Doctor Service provides medical care for people in remote areas. Here is a true story from pilot Doug Dawson.

On the morning of 25th August, the Flying Doctor Service at Kalgoorlie in Western Australia received a call from a man at a station north of Southern Cross, about 220 kilometres away. He was on his own. He'd been working with a vehicle jack which had collapsed and broken his leg. He had managed to crawl over 100 metres to the house and to a phone.

I had flown into the station's airstrip some years before. The patient told us it was in good condition but had a few wild flowers on it. With this information the aircraft King Air CWO was prepared for flight. The crew was Nurse Sue Salter, Doctor Mike Mears, engineer Shane Parslow and myself. As the house was almost two kilometres from the strip, Doctor Mears loaded another piece of equipment, his electric-orange mountain bike.

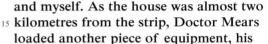

There were no problems on the flight until we got to the strip. There were plenty of flowers, but no one had mentioned the cattle! I decided to fly low over the strip to frighten the cattle off. Most of them moved away, and we came in a second time. The rest of the cattle moved off, so we were able to land.

Shane and I checked the strip for rocks and holes while Mike was cycling to the station house. 20 minutes later he returned in an old cattle truck. We loaded the medical equipment, and Mike drove us all to the house. The patient was laid on a mattress and carried out to the truck. It certainly wasn't an easy job to get him into the back of the truck, but at last it was done. Sue looked after him while Shane drove the truck, and Mike followed on his bike.

Back at the airstrip, it was easier to load the patient because the aircraft has a stretcher fitted to it, and there is a device to lift the stretcher. When the patient (and the bicycle) had been safely loaded, the aircraft was started, and we all returned to Kalgoorlie.

(adapted from www.rfds.org.au)

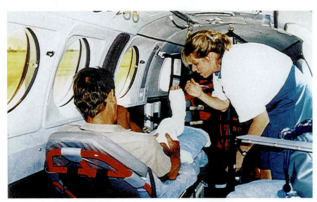

1 For each paragraph of the text, choose one of these headings. Be careful – there are more headings than you need.

A Animals in the way
B A difficult task
C At the sheep station
D A call for help
E The crew get ready for the trip
F Off to hospital
G Flight through a storm
H Medical aid for outback Australians

TEST YOUR ENGLISH

2 When the accident happened, the farmer felt shocked and frightened because he had broken his leg. Write a sentence saying how you think the people felt in these situations, and give a reason.

1 the farmer when he reached the phone
2 the crew when they took off
3 the pilot when he saw the cattle
4 the crew when they landed safely
5 the farmer when he saw the doctor

3 How might the farmer have told the story of his broken leg? Tell his story in at least 130 words. You can use these words:

airstrip • alone • at last • away again • broke leg • crawl • doctor • glad • hospital • jack • leg hurting • long time • mattress • nurse • phone • return • stretcher • take off • terrible • truck • wait • worried

You can begin like this:

One morning I was working on one of my vehicles when suddenly ...

4 Complete each sentence with a word from the text.

1 If we bought a new ... for the bed, it would be more comfortable.
2 It's a very ... place because it's two hundred miles from the nearest town.
3 The player was carried off the field on a ... .
4 I ... my answers carefully to make sure they were correct.
5 We've just ... a letter of thanks from the patient.
6 Luckily we ... to get to the office before it closed.
7 The ship's ... were all very busy.
8 The cupboard was full of sports ... such as tennis rackets and football boots.

5 Complete this information about Uluru. Put in the missing words or the correct form of the words in brackets.

More or ... in the middle of Australia, Uluru, the ... (big) and ... (famous) rock ... the world, rises out of the flat red desert. It is 348 metres ... , and experts believe ... two thirds of it is under the ground. Walk all the way ...
5 the bottom of it, and you'll walk ten kilometres. ... though you've seen photos of the rock, it's a ... (wonder) moment when you see it for the ... time. The best time to see it is at ... (sun). As the sun sinks, the ... in the rock change from red to brown to purple.

10 To the Aborigines, Uluru is ... holy place. Before they ... the rock back to the Aborigines in 1985, white Australians ... it Ayers Rock. The new owners would prefer people not ... climb the rock. Unfortunately thousands still ... , although there are others ... show
15 more respect. ... fact you can buy a T-shirt ... says 'I didn't climb Ayers Rock.'

Not so ... ago, the nearest town to the rock was Alice Springs, almost 400 kilometres away. Since then the resort town of Yulara ... (build) only 20 kilometres ...
20 the rock. With a ... of 4,000 it is the fourth largest town in the ... (north) Territory.

6 Translate this paragraph into good German.

Some children in the Australian outback live a long way from the nearest school, hundreds of kilometres in some cases. These children are provided with their education by 'Schools of the Air'. Each student works at home with the help of an adult, usually their mum. A 'class' receives a lesson every day from the teacher. Since the service began, communication has been by two-way radio. Nowadays computers are also used, and work is sent in by e-mail. Teachers sometimes visit students in remote areas, and some students also have home tutors. At certain times of the year there are sporting events or school camps where students meet for special activities.

7 Christian is a German boy on a visit to Australia. He's with two Australians, Paul and Kylie. They're giving him some advice about travelling in the outback.

12

Listen to the conversation and make notes. Then write a list of the things you will need to take with you and three important things to remember when travelling.

nineteen 19

Unit 1 READING Grandmother

The novel 'The Bone People' was written by Keri Hulme, a New Zealand writer of Maori, Scottish and English origins. It won the Booker Prize in 1985. In this extract, a Maori elder is talking about his grandmother. He is talking to one of the main characters, a Maori man called Joe Gillayley.

The old man says, 'Now I must tell you something.'

Joe nods to him.

'It began with my grandmother. She got herself a husband and had two children. None of them, husband or children, were as strong as she was. They all died before her, and because she had some strange skills, she knew they would die, and she didn't tell any of them. When my mother died, my father sent a message to my grandmother, and she came to get me.

I was ten years old, a smart child. I'd been brought up to speak English. I even thought in English. I still can … they spoke Maori on the farm sometimes, but they were no longer Maori. They were empty inside, copying the European manners and ways. Maori on the outside with none of the heart left. It wasn't their fault. Maori were expected to become Europeans in those days. It was thought that the Maori could not survive, so if they became Europeans, it would be better for everyone, nei[1]?'

The old eyes are empty of sympathy, watching for any sign that he agrees.

Joe stares back.

The kaumatua[2] lowers his eyes.

'My grandmother was not like that. The only European thing about her was her hats … ahh, the hats she used to wear! Great wheels covered with fruit, with birds … ahh, her hats …' shaking his head, 'but except for those hats she was one of the old people. She didn't wear shoes, and her feet were as hard as leather. She was tall, taller than I am, and heavy. A big woman, a very big woman … her smell was offensive. Her hair was black, and her teeth were huge, like a horse's.

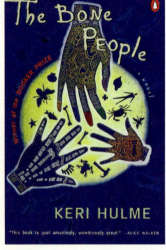

She stood in the doorway and called to me "Mokopuna[3]!" and I was terrified, and squeezed myself in by my father, afraid that she would seize me and maybe eat me. I was a smart kid, but I imagined too much … she knelt in the door, and tears ran down her face. "Come to me!" she called, "o little child, come to me! I have such a need for you!" And she called and wept until I was no longer afraid, because how could someone who needed you so much do anything to hurt you?

I went into her arms, and she held me to her, and then she stood up, and with her great hard hand, smacked me around the ears. "Next time, come at the first call," she said, and I didn't know what was happening. Such a mixture …

I learned, over the next twenty years, that she could be as gentle as any person born, and as hard as stone. She was herself, and a very strange woman. I was lonely, too much by myself as a child, and more lonely and even more by myself as a young man. She saw this, and knew the exact time I could no longer be under her control. Then she gave me a handful of gold sovereigns, and her hand was large, remember. And she said, "Go away, learn something about yourself. Learn to enjoy all that towns and people can offer you. Marry if you must. But when I tell you, come back!" I had learned to obey her every word. She was a terrifying old woman, and she knew more than any one person should know.

I went, and I found I was a stranger everywhere. Women were afraid of me. I was too serious for the men to find me a good companion. I drank and learned to dislike drinking. I started smoking and enjoyed that. I went to bed with whores and easy women, and found that my imagination and my memories of childhood were more real than the things that happened to me. I read a lot. I listened a lot. Then I came back to my grandmother, and returned to her seventeen gold sovereigns. I didn't say much about what I had done, and she didn't ask.'

adapted from Keri Hulme, *The Bone People*

[1] nei? = *nicht wahr?* [2] kaumatua = *Älterer* [3] mokopuna = *Enkel*

UNIT 2
FACT OR FICTION?

WORDS AND PICTURES

What will be the big scientific developments in the next five hundred years? What new worlds will be discovered? What new opportunities
5 will there be? What might go wrong? Here are some possibilities.

✳ New drugs will be developed which will enable us to choose our personalities. There will be safe drugs to make
10 you happier, less shy or more intelligent. Like the idea?

✳ The International Space Station was only the beginning of our journey into space. Humans
15 will set up colonies on Mars, Venus and other planets. Asteroids will be mined for their
20 metals.

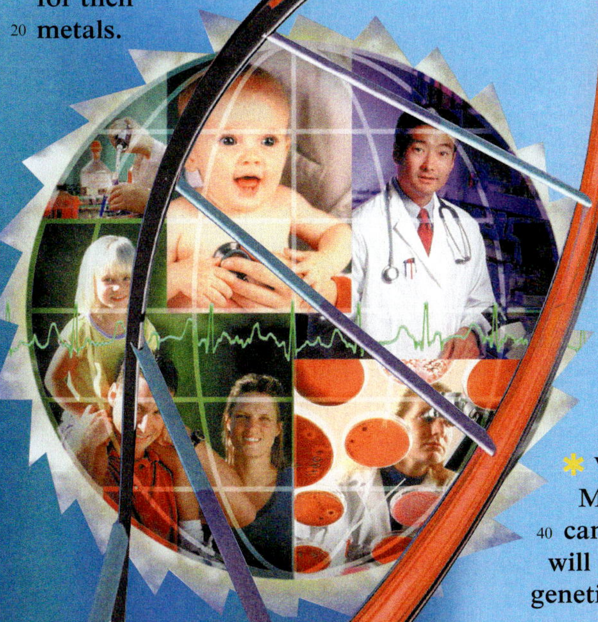

✳ Starships will explore other solar systems many light years away. The speed of the starships will almost reach the speed of light, and so time will slow down for the passengers.
25 A journey of ten light years will actually take only a year of your life. Crazy or what?

✳ There will be whale farms in the sea. We will get meat from the whales like we get it from cattle now. Whale farmers will use electric
30 fences under the sea. Feel sorry for the whales? At least there will be many more of them.

✳ Greenhouse gases will increase global warming. Sea levels will rise, and the sea will cover many areas near coasts. Millions of people will have
35 to leave their homes. But when the Earth starts to cool down and the water freezes, we'll know the next ice age has begun.

✳ We will clone a lot more animals – and humans. Maybe the human clones will have to fight a
40 campaign. (Equal rights for the same people!) There will also be 'designer babies' that will be created by genetic engineering. Fact or fiction? Dream or nightmare?

twenty-one **21**

Unit 2　**INTRODUCTION 1**

● **SITUATION 1**

14　This is a letter written to a magazine for young people.

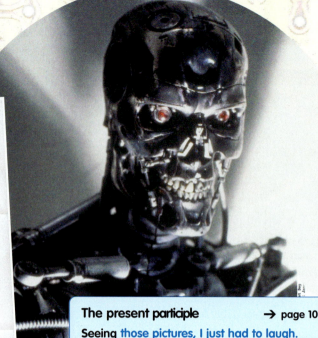

INTELLIGENT ROBOTS: WHAT RUBBISH!

While reading the magazine last month, I came across a science fiction story. Being a bit of an SF fan, I decided to read it. Big mistake. In the story
5　humans are attacked by robots wanting to take over the world. After defeating us, the robots make us their slaves. Seeing those pictures of robots carrying guns, I just had to laugh. It's an exciting story but complete nonsense. Robots obey
10　computers, and computers only do what they are told to do. A computer is not at all like a human brain and is simply not able to think for itself. Not having a mind of its own, it doesn't even realize that it is a computer. It is our slave — and not the
15　other way round. Also, the amount of information in a human brain is enormous — much greater than a computer could hold. I'll think twice before buying your magazine again.

Sarah Abbott

Turn off the TV and take out the plug before starting to repair a fault.

The present participle → page 105-107

Seeing those pictures, I just had to laugh.
(Als ich die Bilder sah, …)

While reading the magazine, I came across a science fiction story.
(Beim Lesen der Zeitschrift / Als ich die Zeitschrift las, …)

After defeating us, the robots make us their slaves.
(Nachdem sie uns besiegt haben, …)

Being a bit of an SF fan, I decided to read it.
(Da / Weil ich ein ziemlicher SF-Fan bin, …)

Not having a mind of its own, a computer cannot think. (Da / Weil er keinen eigenen Verstand besitzt, …)

Humans are attacked by robots **wanting** to take over the world. (… , die die Welt übernehmen wollen.)

EXERCISE 1

These sentences are from a future world. Translate the sentences into German.

1　Living in a global world, we all buy the same products.
2　Staying in a space hotel, we can look down on the Earth.
3　People working at the bottom of the sea want to be paid more.
4　Exploring other solar systems, we might find other life forms.
5　Driving nuclear cars, we don't need petrol.
6　Travelling at the speed of light, the passengers will stay the same age.
7　Scientists working on a time machine are confident of success.

EXERCISE 2

Complete these sentences from a computer guide. Put in *before, while* or *after*.

▸ **Before** starting, read this Quick Guide.
1　… finishing your work, you should save a copy of it.
2　Make sure you can do the simple things … trying anything more advanced.
3　… working at the computer, you should stand up and walk around every 15 or 20 minutes.
4　… typing your e-mail, you can send it.
5　It's easy to forget the time … surfing the internet.
6　Switch off the power … changing the light bulb.

22　twenty-two

SITUATION 2

INTELLIGENT ROBOTS: A REAL POSSIBILITY

I read Sarah Abbot's letter while eating breakfast, and I almost choked on my toast. She should learn a few facts before expressing her opinions. Doesn't she know that some computers can learn from experience and change the way they behave? It is now possible for computers to combine two different programs to produce a new and more complicated program. This so-called 'genetic software' can do things not intended by the people who wrote the programs. The amount of information held on computers is increasing all the time. And of course computers can communicate with each other. Surrounded by intelligent machines, we are in a very dangerous situation. I predict that one day robots really will take over the world. Conquered by these machines, we will become their slaves – unless we wake up.

Oliver Shaw

INTRODUCTION 1

The past participle → page 105-107

Surrounded by intelligent machines, we are in a very dangerous situation.
(Da / Weil wir von intelligenten Maschinen umgeben sind, …)

Conquered by these machines, we will become their slaves.
(Nachdem wir von diesen Maschinen besiegt worden sind, …)

The amount of information **held** on computers is increasing.
(… , die in Computern gespeichert ist, …)

'Genetic software' can do things **not intended** by the programmers.
(… , die von den Programmierern nicht beabsichtigt waren.)

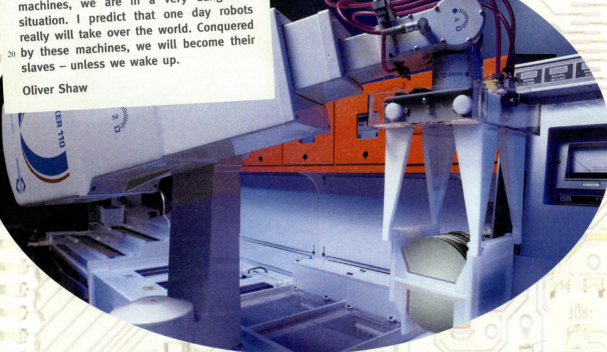

EXERCISE 3

Here are some more sentences from the 23rd century. Translate them into German.

1. The problems caused by global warming have been solved.
2. Frozen in a block of ice, the ex-president could one day be brought back to life.
3. Houses built in the 22nd century have all been replaced.
4. Injured by a robot, the human was not able to defend himself.
5. A girl cloned from a famous athlete has broken the 400 metres world record.
6. Controlled by the world government, the weather is always announced a year ahead.

EXERCISE 4

Write a short letter to the magazine of about 50 words saying if you agree with Sarah or with Oliver.

Unit 2 **TEXT 1**

Whiz-Kids

> Wanted – WEB DESIGNERS
> DreamTeam is offering young designers the chance to create exciting layouts for company websites. This part-time job provides the perfect opportunity to earn money without leaving the house. You must be able to work independently as well as meet deadlines. This job will allow you to develop your existing design skills further, leading to more advanced tasks such as advertising, programming and graphic design. Call DreamTeam on 01730 544683.

Samuel Albright is sitting in his home office staring at the computer screen. The young webmaster works for an e-business company called Nets@les. He is exhausted, but he is trying to concentrate on a new design program. The program will help him to create the online forms used by customers. Samuel has to finish the job by Friday. It is sometimes difficult for him to get through the required amount of work. But his part-time job is exciting and undoubtedly trendy. He earns 25,000 dollars a year, but if you watch him, you'll realize that he's been bitten by the bug, and he doesn't just do it for the money.

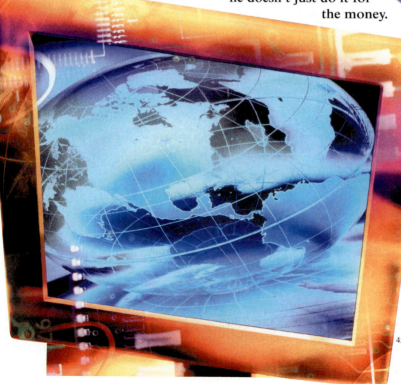

After working for two hours, Samuel is interrupted by his beeping alarm clock. As soon as he hears it, he takes a few books from his bag and starts doing homework. It's time for a break from programming. Samuel Albright has been working for Nets@les for over a year, but he's only 15 years old, and school is more important to him than a deadline in his part-time job. 'School comes first,' he says. 'I won't be able to get to the top without a proper education. But if I work full-time for Nets@les after school, I can earn up to 85,000 dollars a year and that's not the end of it. My aim is to have even more success in the future.'

TEXT 1

Samuel belongs to the growing number of hi-tech kids urgently needed by banks, insurance companies and the technology industry. Most of the part-time jobs involve creating an interesting layout for a company's
5 website. These teenagers have a much greater programming knowledge than adults. Samuel has wanted to find out how computers work since he was five. He was taught some programming languages at school and has gained advanced
10 knowledge from the internet. And he is not the only one. Thousands of teenagers in the US, in Korea, China and Japan are employed because they have the right attitude to online problems. 'Adult colleagues often say "that can't work" and we say "why not?". They give up
15 and don't see the possibilities of the program,' says Samuel.

Samuel is so busy working on programs that he doesn't play computer games. And he doesn't have a cellphone. His parents work in a coffee shop and aren't interested in computers at all. Samuel's colleague Kim Dong-Lee, a 16-year old girl whose family came to the US from Korea ten years ago, agrees that it's hard work. 'We have to learn by trial and error,' Kim says. 'Two years
20 ago I started doing this web design job and I still regard the computer as my hobby. Working part-time has made my life more difficult because I'm sitting here while my friends go out or do sports. It's demanding but it's worth it. There are problems, of course. My cousin John was employed to design some e-business sites for another company. They paid him ten dollars for every page and he didn't protest till he found out that other web designers were getting much more.'

25 Samuel's mother Jenny Albright worries about his future: 'He started programming at 14,' she says, 'and I'm afraid that working these long hours every day is keeping him away from his friends and preventing him from getting good grades at school. Children do not easily feel exploited when it's their hobby. But what about their health and their social education? Samuel just tells me not to worry.'

30 Samuel and Kim are looking forward to new and exciting challenges in the future. They are sure to find interesting and well-paid jobs in Silicon Valley. But is it a good thing for them to spend the whole time working? Or is there a hidden cost? What kind of people will these whiz-kids become?

EXERCISE 5

Put in the correct words from the text.

Samuel Albright works ...-time for an e-... company called Nets@les, and he earns about ... dollars a year. He started writing programs for them when he was ... . As an adult, he could earn up to ... dollars a year if he gets a good ... . Banks and ... companies are the kind of organizations looking for these hi-tech kids with their ... knowledge of ... languages. And teenagers often have a better ... to solving problems than adults. But Samuel's mother ... about his future and the fact that he doesn't have enough time to meet his ... . She wants him to do well and get good ... at school. She thinks that maybe he is being ... by the company.

EXERCISE 6

Complete these sentences based on the information in the text.

1 Samuel is exhausted because ... .
2 He does the programming job mainly because ... .
3 School is important to Samuel because ... .
4 Most other kids ... , but Samuel doesn't.
5 ... are the two places where he learned programming.
6 Companies in countries such as ... and ... employ ... to ... .
7 Kim thinks being a pioneer in programming is hard because ... .
8 Samuel and Kim don't worry about their future because ... .

twenty-five 25

Unit 2 **TEXT 1**

EXERCISE 7

Find the answers and describe the future.

1. Why are hi-tech kids more successful at programming than adults?
2. What happened to Kim's cousin?
3. What does the whiz-kids' work usually involve?
4. In which areas can these teenagers show their advanced knowledge?
5. Describe Samuel's working day in 2030.
6. What kind of adults will Samuel and Kim be? Give your opinion.

Hi-tech kids in China

EXERCISE 8

Do you know your computer words? Find the right word for each definition. Choose from these words: *chat room, download, e-mail, information technology, mouse, online, operating system, search, webmaster.*

1. a message sent from one computer to another
2. look for information about something on the internet
3. something you use when you click on the screen
4. a place on the internet where you can 'talk' to other people
5. computers as a school subject
6. connected to the internet
7. move files from the internet into your computer
8. the program on your computer that enables it to run other programs
9. someone who runs a website

 ### EXERCISE 9

17-18 **Listening**

This is a radio report about computer whiz-kids in China. Listen to the report.

Part 1 (17)

Choose the right answer.

1. How old was James Liang when he went to university?
   a) 13. b) 15. c) 19.
2. What did he do first after arriving in the United States?
   a) He worked as a technology manager.
   b) He worked in Silicon Valley.
   c) He studied in Georgia.
3. Why did he go back to China?
   a) He lost his job in the US.
   b) He thought there were new opportunities there.
   c) He had a return ticket.
4. Which phrase best describes the development of computer technology in China?
   a) dramatically fast b) terribly slow c) very primitive

Life in country districts of China

Part 2 (18)

Answer the questions.

1. What is life like in country areas of China? (one item)
2. Do people in the cities have enough money to buy computers?
3. Why do Asian students want to work for local electronics companies? (two reasons)
4. What do many people in western hi-tech industries feel about the young Asian experts?

26 twenty-six

FOLLOW UP

EXERCISE 10

Look at the sentences below with participles.

> Samuel is interrupted by his **beeping** alarm clock.
> He has to find time for the **required** amount
> of work.   ➜ **page 105**

We can put a participle before a noun.

The sentences below are explanations of the meaning of words. Put in the missing participles. Form them from the verbs *burn, fly, follow, increase, injure, lead, lock, ~~marry~~, ~~miss~~, record, recycle, ring.*

➠ A missing person is one who has disappeared.
➠ A married woman is a woman who has a husband.
1 An … player is one who has been hurt.
2 The … day means the next day.
3 A … building is a building that has caught fire.
4 … music is music that is not performed live.
5 A … door is one that you can't open without a key.
6 A … telephone is one that needs to be answered.
7 The … runner is the one ahead of all the others.
8 A … fish is one that can move above the surface of the water.
9 … paper is paper that has been used more than once.
10 An … population means that the number of people is rising.

EXERCISE 11

It is the year 2500. You are at a tourist information office in Euro-City, the capital of Europe, where almost everyone speaks English. You are helping a visitor to Earth, a man from a Bavarian settlement on Venus. He wants some information from the assistant at the information office, but unfortunately the assistant doesn't speak German. Your job is to interpret.

Visitor	*Ich würde gerne wissen, welche Sehenswürdigkeiten es hier auf der Erde gibt.*
You	This man would like to know … .
Assistant	Well, here in the city there's the Museum of European History, there's the Old Town with its traditional computer market, the new government buildings, and there's the Palace of Culture, one of the most beautiful buildings in the world.
You	…
Visitor	*Hmm, danke. Wie weit ist es von hier nach Amerika?*
You	…
Assistant	It's half an hour to New York on the high-speed underground, 45 minutes to the west coast.
Visitor	*Na gut, das geht ja schnell. Und wo ist die nächste U-Bahn Station?*
You	…
Assistant	Turn left outside, and the moving pavement will take you there. Just follow the signs.
You	…
Assistant	You're very welcome.

EXERCISE 12

We use a conjunction to link two clauses. Look at this example.

> Samuel doesn't play computer games. However, he's interested in computers. **(although)**
> **Although** Samuel doesn't play computer games, he's interested in computers.   ➜ **page 109**

Now link the clauses using the conjunctions in brackets. When you put in a conjunction you might need to leave out some of the other words, like *however* in the example.

1 Jenny is worried. She thinks sitting at the computer so long can't be healthy. (because)
2 Samuel is switching the alarm on. He wants it to sound two hours from now. (so that)
3 I haven't seen Kim for ages. She started doing a computer job. (since)
4 John didn't protest. But then he found out how much other web designers were being paid. (until)
5 The alarm clock beeped. Immediately Samuel took out his homework. (as soon as)
6 Samuel might get a well-paid job in Silicon Valley. He'll be very happy. (if)

twenty-seven 27

Unit 2 **INTRODUCTION 2**

 SITUATION 3

19
Adam It's freezing today. What happened to global warming?
Leanne Oh, I expect it'll be here soon. If we keep cutting down the rainforests, it won't be long.
Adam I don't care about the rainforests. I just wish it was a bit warmer.
Leanne You don't care? If everyone thought like you, the planet would be dead. There aren't enough trees to take in the carbon dioxide, so it's trapped in the atmosphere and warms the Earth. Sea levels are rising. Look at all the floods we had in the autumn.
Adam OK, OK. Why did I open my big mouth? If I hadn't mentioned the weather, you wouldn't have started giving me a lecture.
Leanne Well, if you say stupid things, that's what you deserve.

➡ page 107-108

EXERCISE 13

Complete the conversations. Put the verb in brackets into the correct form.

1 *Claire* They say one day we'll be able to live on Mars.
   Donna If I … (live) on Mars, I … (have) a big party and invite all my friends from Earth.
   Claire Great. I'll come if you … (invite) me.

2 *Tessa* Look at those clouds. It's going to rain.
   Jamie Oh, no. If it … (rain), I … (share) your umbrella, OK?
   Tessa Yes, OK. Why didn't you bring your own?
   Jamie Well, I … (do) if I … (know) it was going to rain.

3 *Ben* Have you seen *Global Disaster*?
   Tom No, I haven't. I … (go) to see it with my girlfriend last Saturday if I … (not/be) ill.
   Ben I expect it'll be out on DVD soon.
   Tom I … (borrow) it from the video shop if I … (see) it there.

4 *Nick* What … you … (do) if you … (attack) by a robot?
   Kirsty If this is a joke, you … (tell) me, I expect.
   Nick It isn't a joke.
   Kirsty Well, maybe I … (pull) the plug out.
   Nick It's a battery-powered robot.
   Kirsty Oh, I don't know. If I … (have) my mobile on me, I … (call) the police.

If we take a picnic, it rains. It's always the same.

It's only a shower. If we wait a minute, it'll stop.

If I had an umbrella, it wouldn't be so bad.

If we'd all brought umbrellas, there would have been too much to carry.

 SITUATION 4

20 **RAINFORESTS**

Tropical rainforests are located in parts of the world where the climate is
5 very hot and humid. The biggest is around the River Amazon in South America. There are also similar forests which are cooler,
10 and these are called temperate rainforests.

28 twenty-eight

INTRODUCTION 2

Destroyed Amazon rainforest

As well as large numbers of trees, a rainforest contains plants of all shapes and sizes and many different animals, birds and insects. You might see a deer, a wild pig or a lizard. It is a place full of life and noise. Some of the trees grow to a great height, and it can be dark in the forest, but there are lots of brightly coloured flowers. Many of the foods we eat came originally from the
5 rainforest, such as bananas, sugar and rice. There are many plants that we can use for medicine, probably including some that have not yet been discovered. Unfortunately, a lot of the trees in the rainforests have been cut down. It is said that they are disappearing so quickly that we lose an area the size of a football field every second of the day. The trees are cut down for their wood, or they are burnt down
10 so that the land can be used for farming. But the earth soon becomes dust, and so more forest needs to be cleared. When the trees are destroyed, the animals and plants die too. In this way the people who live in the rainforest have been driven from their homes.
15 Many people feel they would like to do something to help. The rock star Sting and his wife, Trudie Styler, have raised millions of pounds for a campaign to save the forests.

Copiphora (a locust) in the Amazon

EXERCISE 14

Find the correct explanation for each word or phrase.

A forest is	what the weather is usually like.
Rain is	something you take when you are ill.
The climate is	water that comes down from the clouds.
A temperate zone is	one that grows in the hot and humid parts of the world.
A tropical plant is	a material we get from trees.
Wood is	a place which isn't very hot or very cold.
Medicine is	an area where lots of trees grow.

➡ A forest is an area where lots of trees grow.

EXERCISE 15

1 What are the opposites of these words from Situation 4: *hot, large, many, full, different, life, destroyed?*

2 Find words in Situation 4 with these meanings: *globe, sound, less hot, hot and wet, I'm afraid that ... , found.*

3 Explain the meaning of these words: *food, size, similar, dark, wild, farming.*

twenty-nine 29

Unit 2   TEXT 2

The Eden Project

21 Hannah and Ellie followed the path as it twisted its way through the palm trees. They passed other rainforest plants that they'd never seen before.
5 It was getting hotter, and Hannah had taken her pullover off. They could hear the birds twittering in the trees and in the distance the sound of water rushing down over rocks.

10 Ellie noticed a lizard on a rock. She didn't like lizards. What other animals might there be in a rainforest? Snakes? Tigers? 'Where are we going?' she asked. 'We'd
15 be all right if we'd kept together. Where have Alex and Josh got to?' 'Don't worry,' said Hannah. 'If we follow the path we'll find
20 them.'

The path began to climb more steeply. The noise of the water got louder, and soon, ahead of them through
25 the trees, they could see a waterfall. When they reached it, they stood there for a moment and enjoyed the cool feeling of the spray on their
30 faces. They looked up at the water as it poured down the cliff. Above the waterfall and above the trees, they could see the steel frames and hexagonal shapes of
35 a roof that was covering the biggest greenhouse in the world.

Hannah and Ellie walked on. The path was crowded with visitors looking at the plants. Soon they were
40 able to look down on the tops of trees. The path went down past a West African cola tree – 'probably the best-known Latin name in the world,' said a notice, and 'a drink which is part of
45 a new global culture'. 'So that's where it comes from,' said Hannah as she took a bottle out of her rucksack.

The Eden Project is located in an old claypit near St Austell in Cornwall, right down in the south-west of England.
- *It is a 'living theatre of plants' covering an area the size of 35 football fields.*
- *There are two huge greenhouses or 'biomes'.*
- *The Humid Tropics Biome contains plants from the rainforests of tropical South America, West Africa and Malaysia. They include rubber trees, mango trees and banana trees.*
- *In the Warm Temperate Biome there are plants and fruits from the Mediterranean region, California and South Africa, such as olive trees, lemon trees and grapes.*
- *The biomes are made from plastic hexagons. There are 625 hexagons, and the largest is eleven metres across. The plastic is over 100 times lighter than glass, and it lets more light in.*
- *The Humid Tropics Biome is the largest greenhouse in the world. The Tower of London could fit inside it.*
- *Some scenes from 'Die Another Day', starring Pierce Brosnan as James Bond, were filmed in the Humid Tropics Biome.*

thirty

TEXT 2

Building the biomes

Further on they saw some rubber trees and then some rice growing in water. Soon they found Alex and Josh outside the frame of a two-storey bamboo house. 'In five
5 years you can grow your own low-cost, low-tech home. This will survive an earthquake when all the concrete buildings have fallen down,'
10 said Alex. 'We don't get earthquakes here,' said Ellie. 'Well, if there was an earthquake, it wouldn't fall down.' 'Come on,' said Josh. 'Let's go up to the top.' 'We've just been there,' said
15 Hannah. 'If you hadn't got lost, we could have all gone together.' 'We won't be long,' said Josh. 'We'll wait outside,' said Hannah. 'I feel as if I'm going to die unless
20 I get out of here. I need some fresh air. I just want to cool down.'

Inside the Warm Temperate Biome

EXERCISE 16

Write a sentence about each of these.

▶▶ St Austell
   St Austell is a town in Cornwall.
1 The Eden Project
2 Hannah and Ellie
3 The Humid Tropics Biome
4 The Warm Temperate Biome
5 Pierce Brosnan
6 Latin
7 Alex and Josh

thirty-one **31**

Unit 2 TEXT 2

EXERCISE 17

This summary of the text has eight mistakes in it. Write a correct version of each incorrect sentence.

The four friends were at the Eden Project in south-east England. It's all about plants and how we use them. The girls were walking along a path. They could hear the noise of birds and the sound of traffic on the motorway. It was hot, and the path was taking them higher. They were in the Warm Temperate Biome. It was a huge greenhouse, bigger than the Tower of London. Soon Hannah and Ellie reached a waterfall. The spray felt wonderfully cool on their faces. They looked up at the roof with its plastic circles. This was where some parts of *Lord of the Rings* had been filmed. They stayed there for a little time and then went on. There were quite a lot of visitors looking at the animals. As the girls continued along the path, they saw a cola tree, some rubber trees and some rice growing in water. They found the boys near a concrete house. Alex and Josh hadn't been up to the waterfall yet. They went up to have a look at it while the girls went outside to get dry.

1 The four friends were at the Eden Project in … .
2 They could hear … .

EXERCISE 18

Make a table and put these words into the groups below. Then add more examples to each group.

~~apple~~ • barrel • box • concrete • deer • forest • grape • hen • horse • jungle • lemon • lizard • olive • outback • owl • plastic • prairie • raven • rubber • rucksack • steel • suitcase • swallow • whale

Fruit: *apple*, …   Materials: …   Scenery: …   Containers: …   Birds: …   Animals: …

EXERCISE 19

Building words

Look at this example and complete the sentences.

➤ *Inter-* means 'between'. An interview takes place between two or more people.

1 *Mini-* means '…'. A minibus is … .
2 *Bio-* means '…'. You know that … is the study of living things.
3 The meaning of *sub-* is '…'. A subway goes … .
4 *Bi-* means '…'. A bicycle has … .
5 *Re-* sometimes means '…'. If you … something, you write it again.
6 The meaning of *e-* is '…'. An e-mail is … .

EXERCISE 20

Look at these examples with *what if, as if, if only, even if* and *unless*.

What if we destroy all the rainforests?
(Imagine that we destroy … .)

You look **as if** you've run a mile.
(You look like you've run … .)

If only it wasn't so hot in here.
(I wish it wasn't so hot … .)

Even if robots were intelligent, they wouldn't attack us.
(Robots might be intelligent, but … .)

Unless we act quickly, we won't be able to save the planet.
(If we don't act quickly, … .)

Rewrite these sentences using *what if, as if, if only, even if* or *unless*.

1 I wish people wouldn't cut down trees.
2 If we don't plant new ones, there will soon be none left.
3 Imagine that the Earth is slowly getting warmer.
4 It sounded like the waterfall was quite near.
5 I could recycle a few bottles, but it wouldn't make any difference.
6 If we don't start burning less coal and oil, global warming could increase.
7 I wish I could visit the Amazon rainforest.
8 You might find a path through the forest, but it would be very muddy.
9 The flowers will die if they don't have water.

COMMUNICATION

Saying what you need

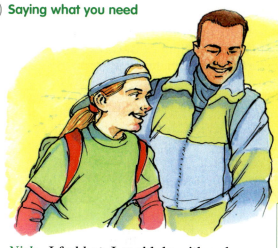

Nick   I feel hot. I could do with a shower.
Mark   And I'm hungry. I'm dying for my tea. How much further is it?
Fiona   About four miles, I think.
Claire   Four miles! Well, I'm tired. I need a rest. I must sit down for a bit.
Fiona   Oh, come on. Stop complaining.
Tom   My foot's hurting. I've got a blister. What I need is some first aid.
Fiona   OK, let's sit down for five minutes.

> **This is how you say what you need.**
> - I need a pair of scissors. I need to cut this picture out.
> - What I need is a calculator.
> - I've been working all afternoon. I could do with a break.
>
> **Sometimes your need is urgent.**
> - I must find a toilet.
> - I'm dying for a drink. / I'm dying to have a drink.
>
> **But remember to be polite when you are asking for something.**
> - I'd like my key, please.
> - Could I have a receipt, please?

EXERCISE 21

What would you say in these situations? Use some phrases from the box above.

➡ You are trying to do some maths in your head, but it's too complicated. *I need a calculator.*
1 You are going to sit in the sun for half an hour.
2 You are at the box office. You want to see the Bond film.
3 You've just washed your face, and it's wet. But you can't find what you need.
4 You are playing a computer game, but you will have to be reminded to stop after an hour and start your homework.
5 You have finished a restaurant meal and need to pay.
6 You've just been watching your favourite soap opera. You can hardly wait for the next programme. The story is really good. You're so excited.
7 You're going to ride a mountain bike, but you're worried about falling off and hurting your head.

EXERCISE 22

Saying how something works

Work with a partner. Partner **B**: Please look at page 96.

Partner **A**: You and your partner are writing a science fiction story together. You are inventing e-travel – a method of getting your hero from one side of the world to the other in a few seconds. There are some details that you are not sure about. Look at your notes and ask your partner.

The hero has to travel (where?). He gets into an X-ray machine. The machine (does what?). The body plan is sent to the destination by e-mail. The body (what happens to it?). The atoms are launched at the speed of light and bounced off satellites on their way to their destination. At the destination the atoms are put together (how?). The hero has arrived in less than a minute.

Start like this:
Where does the hero have ... ?
What ... ?
What happens ... ?

thirty-three   **33**

Unit 2   **TEST YOUR ENGLISH**

Prediction in the year 1934:
Roads will have illuminated signposts and loudspeakers so that even when travelling at high speed you won't lose your way.

Predicting the future

In the 19th century there were tens of thousands of horses in London pulling vans, carts, buses and trams. The large amount of horse dung on the streets made a terrible smell. In summer the flies
5 loved it. And the number of horses was increasing. It was predicted that by the middle of the 20th century London's streets would be several metres deep in dung. But the prediction was false because it completely overlooked one important development –
10 the invention of motor vehicles. Predicting is a difficult business.

How did people 50 years ago see the 21st century? In those days they already had cars, televisions, telephones, nuclear bombs and aeroplanes. But there
15 were still no video recorders, personal computers or spaceships. When people thought about the future, they saw themselves enjoying lots of spare time while robots did all their work for them. That's the kind of prediction they read about in newspaper and magazine
20 articles. But unfortunately robots still can't tidy your room for you. No one seemed to be predicting the technology that has actually changed our daily lives, such as the internet and the mobile phone.

Scientists and 'experts' are just as bad at predicting the future. Many horrible mistakes have been
25 made. At the beginning of the 20th century, almost all scientists agreed that heavier-than-air flying machines were impossible. In 1961, a year before the first television satellite was launched, an American government official predicted that 'there is practically no chance that communication space satellites will ever be used to provide better telephone, television or radio services.'

The thing about scientists and government experts is that they concentrate on the facts as they are.
30 Like the people who used to worry about the increasing amounts of horse dung in the streets, they fail to use their imagination. Writers of science fiction are much better at predicting than scientists are. It was SF which first gave us ideas such as space travel, communication satellites and pocket computers. Of course, it has also given us some ideas such as time travel which might be impossible. But don't forget that at one time the idea of X-rays and telephones must have seemed
35 impossible; when they actually existed, they seemed like magic. There's one thing we can safely predict about the future: it will be science fiction.

1 Decide if each statement is true or false. If it is true, give the relevant sentence from the text. If the statement is false, correct it.

1 A hundred and fifty years ago lots of bicycles were being used in London.
2 The people who were predicting that the amount of dung would go on increasing didn't know that the motor car would soon be invented.
3 50 years ago the telephone had not been invented.
4 There used to be a popular idea that in the future robots would do everything for us.
5 When it was created, the internet had already been predicted for a long time.
6 In 1900 scientists knew that aeroplanes would work.
7 To predict the future correctly, you only need to study the present situation.

2 Paraphrase the words in italics.

1 a *century*
2 your *spare time*
3 an *expert*
4 a communication *satellite*
5 *concentrate on the facts*
6 a *prediction*

34   thirty-four

TEST YOUR ENGLISH

3 Report these false predictions made by people in the past. Remember to change the tense of the verb, e.g. *is* → *was*.

1 'Space travel is complete nonsense.' (a British official in 1956)
   In 1956 a British official said that ... complete nonsense.
2 'X-rays cannot possibly exist.' (a British scientist in 1895) In 1895 ... .
3 'A flying machine will carry nothing heavier than an insect.' (a professor in 1901)
4 'The telephone has no commercial use.' (a US business leader in the 19th century)
5 'A telephone is physically impossible.' (a professor just before its invention)
6 'Generations will pass before humans ever land on the moon.' (*New Scientist Magazine* in 1957)

4 Complete this true story. Put in the missing words or the correct form of the words in brackets.

It was October 30, 1938. At eight ... in the evening, a one-hour radio play went out live from CBS in New York City. It was based ... the story *War of the Worlds* by science ... writer H.G. Wells, about an attack on the planet Earth ... men from Mars. The director was Orson Welles. In the play, a voice said that a spaceship ... landed in New Jersey. Then another voice told listeners about strange monsters with very ... (power) guns. There were interviews with witnesses. Then came the voice ... President Franklin Roosevelt warning people ... stay calm. It all sounded very real.

Too real, ... fact. Many people believed they ... (listen) to true reports of a war with Mars. So they told their neighbours and phoned their friends. In New Jersey thousands of people rushed ... of their homes. Some ... (jump) into their cars and ... (drive) out of the cities towards the hills. In New York City people left half-... meals on restaurant tables and pushed their way onto the ... (crowd) buses. In some places there were phone ... to newspapers from people ... said they had ... (actual) seen the ... (invade).

Orson Welles at the studio

Those who ... to the whole play realized ... it was fiction. When it was over, the director and the actors still knew nothing ... all about the trouble they ... caused. Orson Welles didn't know until the ... day, when he saw the headlines about an 'Attack from Mars' and 'Radio Listeners in Panic'.

5 You will hear a radio report about sightings of a UFO (an Unidentified Flying Object).

Part 1 (23)

Choose the correct answer.

1 How many people said they saw the UFO?
   a) 20. b) 21. c) 22.
2 In which direction was the UFO flying?
   a) North. b) South. c) West.
3 How far above the ground was the UFO?
   a) 30 metres. b) 40 metres. c) 50 metres.
4 What was the weather like? a) It was raining.
   b) It was fine but windy. c) It was still and clear.
5 What do people think about the UFO?
   Are they: a) amused. b) excited. c) frightened.

Part 2 (24)

Draw a table like this in your exercise book and fill in the information given by the two witnesses.

	Ryan	Carla
Speed	?????	?????
Length	?????	?????
Colour	?????	?????
Sound	?????	?????
Direction	?????	XXXX
Shape of disc	?????	?????

Unit 2 READING — The Hitchhiker's Guide to the Galaxy

In these three extracts from the novel by Douglas Adams, Arthur Dent and his friend Ford Prefect escape from the Earth just before it is destroyed by Vogons.

Arthur stared into his beer.

'Did I do anything wrong today,' he said, 'or has the world always been like this and I haven't noticed?'

'All right,' said Ford, 'I'll try to explain. How long have we known each other?'

'How long?' Arthur thought. 'Er, about five years, maybe six,' he said. 'Most of it seemed to make some kind of sense at the time.'

'All right,' said Ford. 'How would you react if I said that I'm not from Guildford after all, but from a small planet somewhere near Betelgeuse?'

Arthur shrugged.

'I don't know,' he said, drinking his beer. 'Why – do you think it's the sort of thing you're likely to say?'

Ford gave up. It really wasn't worth bothering at the moment, when the world was about to end. He just said: 'Drink up. The world's about to end.'

'This must be Thursday,' said Arthur to himself, sinking low over his beer. 'I could never understand Thursdays.'

******

The great ships hung motionless in the sky, over every nation on Earth. The ships hung in the sky in much the same way that bricks don't.

'People of Earth, your attention, please,' a voice said from the public address system. 'This is a message from the Galactic Hyperspace Planning Council. As you will no doubt be aware, the plans for development of the outlying regions of the Galaxy require the building of an expressway through your star system, and unfortunately your planet is one of those scheduled for demolition. This will take slightly less than two of your Earth minutes. Thank you.'

The PA died away.

There was terror and panic among the watching people of Earth.

Seeing this, the Vogons turned on their PA again. It said: 'There's no point in acting all surprised about it. All the plans and demolition orders have been on display in your local planning department in Alpha Centauri for 50 of your Earth years, and it's far too late to start making a fuss about it now. If you can't be bothered to take an interest in local affairs, that's your own fault. I've no sympathy at all.'

******

'Ford,' said Arthur, 'I don't know if this sounds like a silly question, but what am I doing here?'

'Well, you know that,' said Ford. 'I rescued you from the Earth. I got us this lift on a Vogon spaceship.'

'And what's happened to the Earth?'

'Ah. It's been demolished.'

'Has it,' said Arthur.

'Yes. It just boiled away into space.'

'Look,' said Arthur. 'I'm a bit upset about that.'

Ford frowned to himself and seemed to roll the thought around his mind. 'Yes, I can understand that,' he said at last.

'Understand that!' shouted Arthur.

'Understand that!' Ford jumped up. 'Don't panic!' he hissed urgently.

'I'm not panicking.'

'Yes, you are.'

'All right, so I'm panicking, what else is there to do?'

'You just come along with me and have a good time. The Galaxy's a fun place. You'll need to have this fish in your ear.'

(adapted from Douglas Adams *The Hitchhiker's Guide to the Galaxy*)

Douglas Adams (1952–2001)

UNIT 3
FOREVER YOUNG

WORDS AND PICTURES

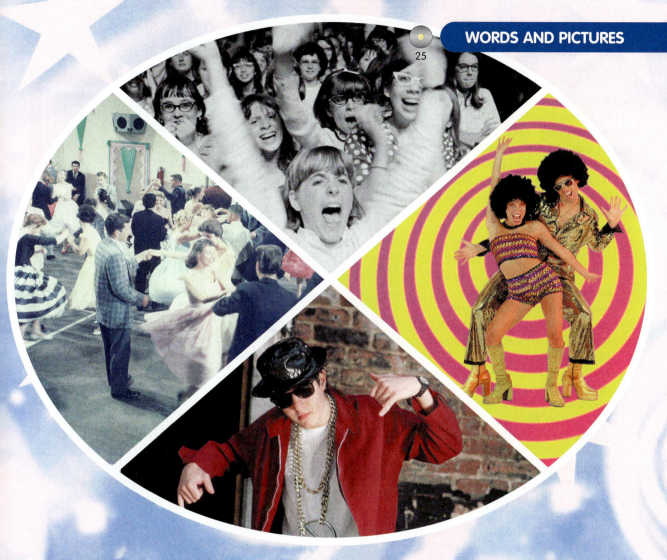

Youth culture began in the 1950s. Like so many things, it started in the US and soon spread to Europe and the rest of the world. Bill Haley's 'Rock Around the Clock' was the first big rock 'n' roll hit, but the first superstar of the new age was Elvis Presley. Rock 'n' roll combined country music with the blues of black America to create a new style which shocked the older generation.

One weekend in August 1969, musicians such as Jimi Hendrix, Janis Joplin, Santana and The Who performed in front of half a million young people in Woodstock, New York. It was a festival of peace and rock music. Woodstock became a legend and a movie.

Teenagers don't just have their own music, they have their own fashions too. The 1970s were the decade of flared trousers, also called 'bell-bottom' trousers. When people got tired of them, they were out. Then suddenly in the new millennium, they were back.

Hip hop and rap came from the black ghettos of New York City. Hip-hop culture has had a big influence on white teenagers too.

Unit 3 **INTRODUCTION 1**

SITUATION 1

26 This is Rachel's website. It's all about her favourite singer, Justin Timberlake.

ABOUT ME

MY NAME IS RACHEL, AND I'M 16 YEARS OLD. I ENJOY LISTENING TO MUSIC AND GOING OUT TO CLUBS WITH MY FRIENDS FROM SCHOOL. I'M CRAZY ABOUT JUSTIN TIMBERLAKE. HE IS A BRILLIANT SINGER, AND HE IS SEX ON LEGS. I'M NOT MUCH OF A SINGER MYSELF, BUT I HOPE TO BECOME A SONGWRITER.

LINKS
- ABOUT ME
- FACT FILE
- THE JT STORY
- NEWS
- PHOTOS

FACT FILE

- Justin Timberlake was born in Memphis, Tennessee on 31 January 1981.
- At age 12 he appeared on a children's TV show called 'The Mickey Mouse Club'.
- When he was young, the other kids used to laugh at his curly hair.
- From 1996 Justin was a member of the boy band *NSYNC. The band was hugely successful and managed to sell millions of records.
- In 2002 Justin decided to go solo.
- He has a great voice. He is also a brilliant dancer. No wonder he has been called 'the white Michael Jackson'.
- Justin has bought a $5 million home in the Hollywood hills.
- He used to go out with the princess of pop, Britney Spears.

→ page 110-113

EXERCISE 1

Here are some quotes from Justin Timberlake. Each verb in brackets should be a *to*-infinitive or an *ing*-form.

➡ 'I enjoy driving (drive) fast cars.'
1 'Dancing helps … (keep) me fit.'
2 'But I won't go on … (dance) as long as Mick Jagger.'
3 'I'm learning … (cook) a few meals. I'm good at toast.'
4 'If there's something you feel you can do, you ought … (do) it.'
5 'I'll never stop … (make) music, but I need a vacation sometimes.'
6 'I keep … (search) for a girlfriend as good as my mother, but that's a losing battle.'
7 'If I wanted … (act), I'd need … (learn) how to do it. I'd have … (take) some lessons first.'

38 thirty-eight

INTRODUCTION 1

SITUATION 2

Rachel Guess what! I've won a ticket in that radio competition!
Olivia A ticket to the Justin Timberlake concert?
Rachel Not just a ticket. I've won first prize and I'm going to meet Justin before the show.
Olivia Hey, lucky you. That's great.
Rachel It'll be fantastic to meet him. But I'm worried I won't know what to say to him.
Olivia Of course you will. Just act naturally.
Rachel I want you to come to the concert with me, Olivia.
Olivia OK, but I haven't got a ticket yet.
Rachel Well, you can buy one on the internet. But you'd better hurry up. I think they're nearly all sold out already.
Olivia OK, I'll do it today. I'd be disappointed to miss Justin – even though I'm not going to meet him personally.

It would be great to see the show, but I don't know how to find the money.

I'd like to see it too, but my girlfriend isn't interested. She wants me to play tennis with her.

→ page 110-113

EXERCISE 2

The next day Rachel is talking to Laura. Complete the conversation. Put in a verb in the *to*-infinitive form. Sometimes there is more than one possible verb.

Rachel I hope you're going to come to the Justin Timberlake concert with Olivia and me.
Laura It's in London, isn't it? I don't know if I can afford … to London. And I don't know where … a ticket.
Rachel Well, it won't be easy … one now. The tickets on the official website are all sold out. So you'll have … for a website where someone is offering … their ticket.
Laura Actually, I don't think my parents will allow me … , especially if it involves staying out late. I'll be sorry … it, but I'm not such a huge fan as you are.
Rachel Oh, come on, Laura. Olivia's going too, and we both want you … with us. We're getting a late train back, and my dad has promised … us at the station. If Olivia has persuaded her parents … to the plan, then I'm sure you can do the same.

EXERCISE 3

Put the words in brackets into the correct form and put in any missing words.

Avril Lavigne always knew that one day she would be a singer. She … (use / sing) a lot as a child, and even then she always … (want / perform) in front of an audience. Her parents … (want / she / be) a singer too. When Avril came home from school, she … (have / practise / sing) her songs. Her parents wouldn't … (allow / she / phone) her friends until she'd … (finish / practise).

Avril … (want / you / know) that she sings rock and not pop. To Avril, rock is the real thing. She isn't … (interest / be) another Britney Spears. She's … (determined / be) herself. 'No one tells me … (what / wear),' she says.

Avril was … (please / get) a record contract at the age of 15. She left school and went to New York and then LA. Her work now … (involve / do) a lot of tours. She thinks she's very … (luck / able / travel) the world, and she … (enjoy / visit) new places. But she admits that sometimes she … (miss / be) at home. She isn't at all … (worry / about / not / have) a boyfriend. 'Guys are just silly,' she says.

Unit 3   TEXT 1

🎵 From rock to rap

What do your parents think about the music you play and the latest fashions for young people? Chances are they're not keen on your clothes and they think the music is just a horrible noise. It's what we call the generation gap. But what if your dad had been one of the wildest rock musicians of the 1970s and had bitten the head off a bat when he was young and crazy? Maybe you've seen the TV programme about the Osbourne family. When Kelly Osbourne was a teenager, she loved her father Ozzy, but it was an upside-down situation. It was Kelly who had to tell her father to stop swearing and behave himself.

It wasn't until the 1950s, the decade after World War II, that young people had their own music and fashion. Rock 'n' roll music, tight jeans and other trendy ideas from the USA were the best way to get on your parents' nerves. Parents still regarded T-shirts as underwear, jeans as work clothes and rock music as noise. Elvis Presley, the King of Rock, and James Dean, the film star who died at 24 in a car crash, were heroes to many young people. Maybe your grandparents were young in those days? Have they ever told you about the first holiday of their lives: maybe it was going off to Italy in a Volkswagen Beetle?

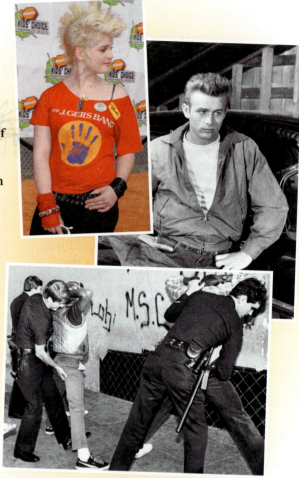

In the 1960s, the economy was growing fast, and there were jobs for everyone. But it was the first decade that saw young people protesting in the streets. The Cold War between East and West nearly led to World War III, but most young people wanted peace. They also supported the American civil rights movement. As well as real rock songs, there were now pop songs in the charts. Although jeans had been popular for several years, the Beatles and the Rolling Stones still performed in suits which they bought in Carnaby Street. Girls wore miniskirts and gave their parents heart attacks. Soon drugs and alcohol became part of the pop and rock scene and a number of musicians died young.

In the 70s, hippies with their flower power shirts were on the way out, and disco fans with their brown and orange flared trousers were in. This was also the decade of second-hand clothing, trendy hot pants and parkas. ABBA, the Bee Gees and John Travolta created the disco fever with romantic love songs. But parents who had grown up in the 50s were shocked by the wild no-future punks with their violent music.

TEXT 1

There were various lifestyles in the 1980s. Most young people wore tight jeans and sweaters and carried a walkman, and so boys and girls looked
5 similar. The skateboarders preferred to show their break-dancing skills. Synthesizers gave music an electronic sound, and DJs in discos were scratching LPs. Films like *Flashdance*
10 helped teenagers to escape into a dream world of pink leggings. But there was another side to the 1980s. In the background were problems such as AIDS and
15 the Chernobyl disaster. Social problems didn't much worry the rich yuppies – they mainly cared about themselves.

Soviet President Mikhail
20 Gorbachev was the hero of the early 90s. His actions helped to change Europe and to achieve the reunification of Germany. At the end of the decade,
25 however, the world economic crisis brought a darker mood. Some teenagers turned to Goth music. Offensive rap songs and techno conquered the music scene. There were all-night raves where Ecstasy was freely available. The
30 hip-hop generation created their own style with baseball caps, huge T-shirts and XXXL trousers in which you could hide a football. The new way to shock parents was to have a tattoo or piercing and go to a love parade.

EXERCISE 4

Look at these five pictures. Say which decade each picture belongs to and give a reason.

forty-one 41

Unit 3 **TEXT 1**

EXERCISE 5

What about the youth of today? That's you, of course. What makes your generation special? What music is popular at the moment? What kind of clothes are in? What worries you? Write a final paragraph to go at the end of Text 1. You can use some of these phrases.

The big successes on the music scene are … is/are also popular … Many kids today wear … The mood is … The new heroes are …

EXERCISE 6

Put the words in the correct order.

➡ Old to new: electro, punk, rock 'n' roll, techno
rock 'n' roll, punk, electro, techno

1 Short to long: century, decade, millennium, month, year
2 Top to bottom: cap, jeans, shoes, socks, sweater
3 Fastest to slowest: aeroplane, bicycle, skateboard, truck
4 Safe to dangerous: chess, skateboarding, skydiving, softball
5 North to south: France, Scotland, Spain, Wales
6 Light to dark: black, pink, red, white
7 Positive to negative: brilliant, good, hopeless, OK, poor
8 Young to old: adult, baby, child, teenager
9 Small to big: bat, beetle, horse, lizard, whale
10 Hot to cold: boiling, cold, cool, freezing, hot, warm
11 Quiet to loud: bell, bomb, motorbike, clock
12 Nearest to furthest away: London, Los Angeles, New York, Sydney

29-31

EXERCISE 7

Listening

You will hear a radio DJ announcing three items of news. In the text below there are nine words which differ from what the DJ says. Find the wrong words and write the correct ones that you hear on the programme.

The Grimstone pop festival will take place on the weekend of June 13 and 14. A number of bands have offered to play, including the Manic Street Preachers and Coldplay. Tickets cost £75 and are going very quickly. Let's hope the weather is good because if it isn't, the site will be a sea of mud.
➡ *June → July 1 … 2 …*
The famous rap artist Legend X has written a book. It's the story of his life, and it's out tomorrow. It's called 'Telling it like it is'. It's all about his drug-taking and his years in prison. There's lots of offensive language. He also expresses his opinions on the economic situation in the world today.
3 … 4 … 5 …

And now for our competition. It's your chance to make the big time. The winner will spend an afternoon in a television studio in London and make a professional version of their song. Just post your song to us on cassette or CD and tell us your name, age, address and mobile number.
6 … 7 … 8 …

42 forty-two

FOLLOW UP

EXERCISE 8

Look at these sentences. Some have a *to*-infinitive, and some have an infinitive without *to*.

To-infinitive	Infinitive without 'to' → page 110-111
I'd prefer to listen to Robbie Williams.	I'd rather listen to Robbie Williams.
You ought to buy a ticket soon.	You should buy a ticket soon.
You need to phone the box office.	You'd better phone the box office.
The police forced the organizers to stop the festival.	The police made the organizers stop the festival.
Laura's parents wouldn't allow her to go to the festival.	Laura's parents wouldn't let her go to the festival.

Complete the conversation. Put in a verb with or without *to*. Use the verbs *do, go* and *stay*.

Donna Are you coming out with me and Sophie tonight?
Emily I can't really. I ought ... my maths homework.
Donna OK, if you'd prefer ... at home.
Emily I'd rather ... out, of course. You know that. But it's Mr Bryant. He's making me ... my homework again. I got it all wrong. I'd better ... it or I'll be in trouble.
Donna He can't force you ... at home. You need ... out and enjoy yourself sometimes. Do your homework on the bus tomorrow morning.
Emily I don't think my parents will let me ... out tonight anyway.
Donna Your parents never allow you ... anything, do they?
Emily Well, they're probably going out tonight, and if they do, I promised to look after my little sister, so I really should ... in.

EXERCISE 9

When you hear or read a word that you don't know, it is often possible to guess the meaning from the context. Look at this sentence.

> My tooth was hurting so badly I had to go to the **dentist**.

If you haven't heard the word 'dentist' before, it's easy to guess that it means *Zahnarzt* because that's who you would go to if you had toothache.

Sometimes the English word is similar to the German one. Look at this sentence.

> He took the ring out of its box and put it on her **finger**.

Here you can guess what 'ring' and 'finger' mean because the German words look the same. But look out for false friends. For example, 'map' doesn't mean *Mappe*, it means *Landkarte*. 'Become' doesn't mean *bekommen*, it means *werden*.

Can I become a beefsteak?

Now guess the meaning of the words in italics.

1. It was freezing. The temperature was several degrees below *zero*.
2. Would you like milk or *cream* in your coffee?
3. All I had left was a five-pound note and a couple of *coins*.
4. My parents don't own the flat. They have to pay *rent*.
5. I can't eat my dinner without a knife and *fork*.
6. I didn't speak to the manager, but I spoke to his *secretary*.
7. I was trying to get out of the building, but I couldn't find the *exit*.
8. If you *subtract* eight from twelve, you get four.
9. The engine is losing oil, so there must be a *leak*.
10. My dad used to *smoke* forty *cigarettes* a day.

Unit 3   **INTRODUCTION 2**

SITUATION 3

One day, when Katie Barnett was eleven, she was at the supermarket with her mother. Katie suddenly started to swear. In a loud voice she let out a stream of very offensive
5 language. The other customers were staring in horror. It was very embarrassing. Her mother had to take her outside to the car.

'I just couldn't help it,' was Katie's explanation. Her behaviour soon started to get
10 worse. So did the nervous tic she'd always had. Her language shocked everyone.

Katie has Tourette's Syndrome (TS). The cause is something chemical in the brain. TS produces tics of the
15 head and neck, strange noises and sometimes swearing. Katie's explanation was true. She can't help shouting and swearing at people, even though she feels awful when they stare at her. She has had problems with
20 other kids laughing at her and mimicking her strange noises. And children who are different from others attract bullies too.

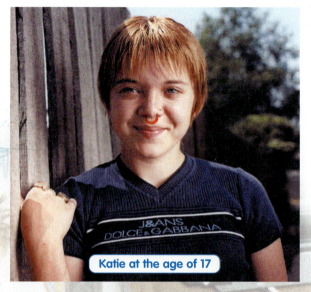
Katie at the age of 17

Doctors have not yet found a way of curing TS, but Katie can take drugs to control it and
25 learn to live with it. She makes frequent visits to the swimming pool because there she doesn't need to apologize for shouting.

Katie is 20 now. She has lots of friends, and she is excited about going to college soon.
30 'I just want to be normal,' she says.

EXERCISE 10

Complete the conversations. Use a preposition and the *ing*-form of the verb in brackets.

Alice   What are you doing this summer?
James I've just started a job at a record shop.
Alice   I've been thinking of getting (get) a job, but I don't believe … (spend) the whole summer inside. I'm not exactly crazy … (be) in a factory or an office.
James So are you looking for an outdoor job?
Alice   I like the idea … (work) on a farm, but there doesn't seem to be any jobs. Or maybe it's just because I haven't had any experience. Anyway I haven't succeeded … (find) anything.
James Well, maybe you will soon. I'm interested … (get) into the music business. That was my main reason … (apply) for the job at the shop. I think I'm good … (help) the customers and advising them what to buy. And I'm really enjoying it. There's no danger … (get) bored with the job.

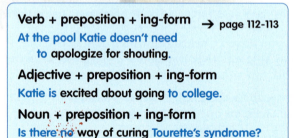

Verb + preposition + ing-form → page 112-113
At the pool Katie doesn't need to apologize for shouting.

Adjective + preposition + ing-form
Katie is excited about going to college.

Noun + preposition + ing-form
Is there no way of curing Tourette's syndrome?

INTRODUCTION 2

SITUATION 4

Here is some advice from a popular lifestyle programme for young people.

I know that some of you take drugs or smoke cigarettes despite being aware of the dangers. And many young people don't eat properly. It is possible to get through the day without eating sweets or crisps, you know. A proper cooked meal with vegetables is better for you than a cheeseburger. If you need a snack, have some fruit.

You can keep fit by taking exercise. Sport is good for you. Why not walk or cycle to school instead of getting a lift from your mum or dad?

→ page 112-113

EXERCISE 11

Here is more advice about looking after yourself. Combine the information into a single sentence using the word in brackets.

▶ You must eat the right food. You can stay healthy. (by)
  You can stay healthy by eating the right food.
1 You mustn't smoke. You can damage your health. (by)
2 You're young. But you need to look after yourself. (despite)
3 You needn't sit around at home. You can go jogging. (instead of)
4 You'll have to make an effort. Or you won't get any fitter. (without)
5 Some people are driven to school. They live only a short walk away. (despite)
6 Don't eat fast food all the time. Why not cook a meal for you and your friends? (instead of)
7 You should walk around. You shouldn't sit at the computer for hours. (without)

You won't get fit by watching the Olympics on TV.

Unit 3   TEXT 2

Look what you did to me

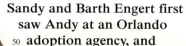

It's a weekday morning, and Andy Engert is doing his usual thing: hanging out at Winter Park Fire Station 62. Suddenly, he hears a message on the firefighters' radio. There's a gas leak at the hospital. Andy runs to his bike. He puts on his blue helmet, jumps on and races wildly down the street. 'AANNKK, AANNKK!' he shouts, mimicking the sound of the fire truck's horn.

Andy arrives at the hospital and stands ready in case the firefighters need help. Motorists slow down when they see the fire truck. They see Andy too, in his usual uniform of a red T-shirt, white socks and black sneakers. They sound their horns and wave. They yell out Andy's name. He waves back. If he recognizes the driver, he calls out his or her name too.

Everyone knows Andy. This kind of thing happens every day in Winter Park, the small city in Central Florida that is home to a 32-year-old man who is blessed with the imagination of a 12-year-old boy and the love of a community.

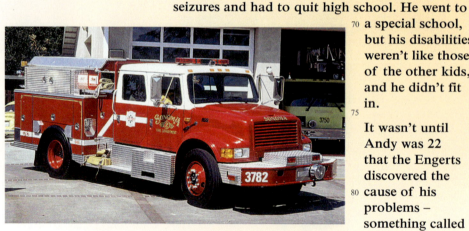

Andy is a happy, loud man, born with a brain that was damaged but with a personality that isn't. Sometimes he behaves like an 18-year-old – and sometimes like a 6-year-old. But most days he's like a 12-year-old. He loves fire trucks and firefighters. He loves pretty girls but says he has no interest in getting married. He loves jokes. He is fond of cheeseburgers and pizza but tries to avoid eating vegetables. He loves sports. His favorite basketball team is Orlando Magic. And, like most 12-year-olds, he loves the freedom he experiences on a bicycle. He never gets tired of riding his bike.

Sandy and Barth Engert first saw Andy at an Orlando adoption agency, and they fell in love with the baby's beautiful eyes and his curly dark hair. But the doctor thought there could be problems, and he advised the couple to find a different baby. Sandy refused. 'I felt that God had chosen us to be his parents,' she says.

The Engerts had already adopted their daughter Pam two years before. Andy learned to walk and talk more slowly than Pam. At school he struggled to draw and write. His learning disabilities puzzled his teachers. He was good at reading. He could add and multiply, but he couldn't subtract or divide. He had frequent seizures and had to quit high school. He went to a special school, but his disabilities weren't like those of the other kids, and he didn't fit in.

It wasn't until Andy was 22 that the Engerts discovered the cause of his problems – something called fetal alcohol syndrome (FAS). They saw a TV news program about children with FAS, children who looked very like Andy. They discovered from the adoption agency that Andy's mother had drunk alcohol when she was pregnant. By doing this, she had damaged some parts of Andy's brain but not others. That's why he can always remember sports scores and silly jokes but can never remember to brush his teeth.

Andy has had a number of part-time jobs. At the moment he works one day a week doing odd jobs at the local airport. On the days when he is not working, he cycles all the streets of Winter Park. He's everywhere, and he doesn't slow down. 'He has only one speed,' says Sandy. 'Fast.'

46   forty-six

TEXT 2

Andy has hundreds, probably thousands of friends. Sandy and Barth are grateful to all of them because they know the ups and downs of caring for Andy. They know he can be the joker
5 who won't quit joking, the too-loud house guest, the guy who insists on staying and doesn't know when to leave. Hanging around with Andy is fun, but it can be rather embarrassing. But for every negative moment – for every bully who
10 throws a rock at him – Andy experiences far more positives. Three years ago, after a slight accident with a car, he took his damaged bike to his friends at the bike shop. Instead of repairing it, they gave him something much better – a new bike. There are a few things in life that Andy badly wants to do. He wants to graduate from high school, and he would love to be a real firefighter. But most of all he would love to be normal. 'If I could
15 see my mother,' he says, 'I would say to her, "Look what you did to me." '

Sandy and Barth are starting to worry about what will happen when they are too old to care for Andy. He can do lots of things for himself, but he needs someone to keep an eye on him. The Engerts have two daughters, Pam (34) and Lisa (30), but they don't want to make them responsible for Andy. And they don't want to take Andy away from the place he loves – and all the people who
20 have helped to raise a very special person. (adapted from Linda Shrieves, 'Andy: A world of One' in *Orlando Sentinel*)

EXERCISE 12

Say if the statements are true or false. Find the place in the text that gives you the information.

▶ Most days Andy goes to the local fire station.
True. 'Andy Engert is doing his usual thing: hanging out at Winter Park Fire Station 62.'
1 Andy normally wears the same kind of clothes every day.
2 Andy is a quiet, rather sad guy.
3 Andy is keen on sport.
4 Sandy and Barth adopted Andy.
5 The Engerts found out about Andy's disability from a newspaper.
6 Andy's job at the airport is his first real job.
7 Andy's teachers couldn't understand what was preventing him from learning properly.
8 If Andy's mother hadn't drunk alcohol, he would probably have been a normal child.
9 Looking after Andy is always a pleasant task and never a problem.
10 Sometimes an ignorant person has tried to do something nasty to Andy.
11 Andy doesn't mind being different from other people.
12 Sandy and Barth want their two daughters to start looking after Andy soon.

EXERCISE 13

Match the two parts of each sentence.

By drinking alcohol,	Andy cycled to the hospital.
The couple adopted Andy	even if he can be embarrassing sometimes.
As soon as they saw the baby,	Andy doesn't want to get married.
Andy hardly ever spends a day	in case he needs help.
You can't help liking Andy,	Andy's mother damaged his brain.
Andy won't eat vegetables	Sandy and Barth wanted to adopt him.
Despite being fond of pretty girls,	two years after adopting Pam.
When he heard the radio message,	unless his parents insist that he should.
Someone must be responsible for Andy	without riding his bike.

▶ By drinking alcohol, Andy's mother damaged his brain.

Unit 3 TEXT 2

EXERCISE 14

Choose the correct verb.

Andy on his new bike

➡ Three years ago Andy did / had / made a slight accident on his bike.
Three years ago Andy had a slight accident on his bike.
1 You can keep fit by having / making / taking exercise.
2 Some people can't come / get / pass through an afternoon without eating sweets or chocolate.
3 Andy does / makes / takes frequent visits to the fire station.
4 One day a week Andy brings / does / makes some odd jobs at the airport.
5 The Engerts don't know how long they can come / get / go on looking after their son.
6 They want to do / have / make sure he will be all right.

EXERCISE 15

Can you remember the idioms? Use them in these sentences. You can look at the words in the box if you need to.

> by trial and error • keep an eye on • on your own • changed my mind • the day after tomorrow
> • matter of opinion • over and over again • get used to • mind your own business • what's on

➡ Can you (*aufpassen auf*) the baby while I go out?
Can you keep an eye on the baby while I go out?
1 I was going to buy a ticket, but I've (*meine Meinung geändert*).
2 I wonder (*was läuft*) at the cinema.
3 Why are you sitting here (*ganz allein*)?
4 Whether the band is any good is a (*Ansichtssache*).
5 I learned the best way of doing the job (*durch Ausprobieren*).
6 You'll soon (*dich gewöhnen an*) your new school.
7 The concert is (*übermorgen*).
8 It's got nothing to do with you, so (*kümmere dich um deine eigenen Angelegenheiten*).
9 Why don't you listen? I've told you (*immer wieder*).

EXERCISE 16

Complete this news article. Put in the *to*-infinitive or the *ing*-form of the verb in brackets.

Young Nick Johnson wants … (go) out in the garden and play football. Unfortunately, he can't go out without … (put) on a special plastic helmet which covers his face. By … (wear) the helmet, he is protected from the sun. Nick suffers from a disease called XP. It forces him … (stay) inside the house away from the sunlight. If he stays in the sunshine for more than a minute or two, he will be in real danger of … (be) badly burned. He dislikes … (wear) the clumsy helmet, but it is too dangerous … (go) out without it. It enables him … (leave) the house and go to school every day. Nick is tired of … (have) … (be) so careful all the time. He worries about … (make) a mistake and accidentally leaving his skin open to the sunlight.

Now there has been a new development. Someone has designed a new hi-tech plastic suit which is lighter, cooler and more comfortable … (wear). Nick has agreed … (test) the suit. He is glad … (get) the chance … (look) less like an astronaut.

EXERCISE 17

Write a summary in German about Andy. Use the information in Text 2 to write a paragraph of about 100 words.

48 forty-eight

Hobbies and interests

COMMUNICATION

Here are some ways you can talk about people's interests.
- My main hobby / interest is drama.
- I'm interested in motor-racing.
- My sister is keen on photography / is fond of photography.
- I think space travel is absolutely fascinating / really interesting.
- Vicky is fascinated by puzzles and how to solve them.
- I like / I love quizzes.
- I'm a country music fan.
- Tom's favourite subject is maths.
- I'm really into heavy metal. (informal)
- Surfing is my thing. (informal)

Lisa So what are your interests, Adam?
Adam I'm interested in web design. I'm designing a website at the moment. It's really fascinating.
Lisa I'm not into computers, I'm afraid. I'm keen on sport. Tennis is my thing.
Adam I'm not normally a sports fan, but I was fascinated by the Olympics on TV.

EXERCISE 18

Say what these stars are / were interested in. Use the notes.

▶ Justin Timberlake – fond – fast cars
  Justin Timberlake is fond of fast cars.
1 Janet Jackson – love – animals
2 The Beatles – fascinated – Eastern religions
3 Victoria Beckham – interested – clothes and fashion
4 Bob Marley – football – fan
5 Mick Jagger – fascinated – make – movies
6 Madonna – like – read
7 Lots of stars – keen – go – night clubs
8 Kylie Minogue – into – keep – fit

EXERCISE 19

You are setting up your own website with some information about yourself. Write a paragraph about your hobbies and interests. Use at least five phrases from the box above.

EXERCISE 20

What activities are there?

Work with a partner.
Partner **B**: Please look at page 96.

Partner **A**: You and your partner are thinking of going to an activity centre for a week. Ask Partner **B** about the missing activities.

- Ask what happens in the two periods on Tuesday that you don't know about.
- Find out if there is an evening for playing board games.
- You want to know what happens on the last evening.
- Ask about football, volleyball and basketball.
- Find out what happens at the other times.

	Morning	Afternoon	Evening
Mon	Swimming	?????	Disco dancing
Tues	?????	Computers	?????
Weds	Archery	?????	Drama
Thurs	?????	Nature walk	?????
Fri	Skateboarding	?????	Rock concert
Sat	?????	Tennis	?????

forty-nine 49

Unit 3   **TEST YOUR ENGLISH**

Make love not war

The youth culture which began in the 1950s was a revolt against the older generation and against the way they were running the world.
Of course, not all young people were interested in political issues, but in the 1960s many showed their support for civil rights and their opposition to the Vietnam War. 'Make love not war' became a popular slogan.

Vietnam War protest in New York, 1967

Young people didn't want to play the game of party politics. They preferred to concentrate on single issues. Following the oil crisis of 1973, there were demonstrations ('demos') against new roads and airports. Young people wanted to stop global warming and save the whale. During the Cold War many of them also continued to oppose the spending of huge amounts of money on nuclear weapons which could easily destroy the Earth.

By the nineties the Cold War was over. But then people became worried that the US was planning to control the whole world. The next wave of protest was against globalization. Those who are against globalization see it as a system which enables big companies, especially American ones, to control world trade and to make even more money. The protests first hit the headlines in 1999 at a conference of the World Trade Organization in Seattle. Most of the protesters were non-violent, but some of them broke shop windows. Police fired tear gas and plastic bullets and arrested five hundred people.

Other demonstrations began to take place around the world, and there were more battles with the police. The aims of the protesters were something of a mixture. Some wanted to destroy the economic system and create a new society, some simply wanted to get cars off the streets and make them safe for cyclists, while others were more interested in supporting the Third World or animal rights. But they all opposed war. In April 2003 when the US and Britain invaded Iraq, thousands of students in Britain joined demonstrations against the war. There were similar protests by students in parts of Germany. Before the war started, over a million people had marched through central London to protest against it, the biggest political demonstration ever in Britain. The British government did what governments often do when there are protesters on the streets: it took absolutely no notice.

Massive demonstrations in London before the start of the Iraq war, March 2003

1 Correct the sentences.

1. Youth culture was an attack on the younger generation.
2. The Vietnam War was a big issue in the eighties.
3. Many young people were against killing fish.
4. There were protests against the local power of big companies.
5. In Seattle protesters were attacked with water cannon and dogs.
6. The protesters against globalization were very violent.
7. The demonstration by a million people in London had a big effect on the government.

50   fifty

TEST YOUR ENGLISH

2 Which of the meanings is the one used in the text?

1 run (line 4) a) *abfärben* b) *laufen* c) *leiten* d) *sich ziehen*
2 following (line 12) a) *Anhängerschaft* b) *entlangfahren* c) *nach* d) *verstehen*
3 save (line 13) a) *mit Ausnahme von* b) *retten* c) *sparen* d) *sammeln*
4 even (line 19) a) *glatt* b) (not ~) *nicht einmal* c) *noch* d) *selbst*
5 hit (line 19) a) *betreffen* b) *erreichen* c) *schlagen* d) *Schlager*
6 fire (line 21) a) *begeistern* b) *Brand* c) *Feuer* d) *abfeuern*
7 notice (line 32) a) (take ~) *beachten* b) *Bekanntmachung* c) *bemerken* d) *Schild*

3 Combine each pair of sentences using a relative clause.

1 Rock 'n' roll shocked many adults.
It was a new kind of music.
Rock 'n' roll was ... which ... adults.
2 Martin Luther King was a civil rights leader. Many people admired him.
Martin Luther King was a ... admired.
3 Many people were keen on saving the planet. It was the big issue.
Saving the planet was the ... .
4 Nuclear weapons could destroy the Earth. Both the US and the Soviet Union had them.
Both the US ... .
5 The products made by big companies reach all corners of the Earth. A lot of money is made by these companies.
A lot of ... .
6 Many people were afraid of a war. The government intended to fight it.
The government ... .

4 Complete this report about an event in London that really happened. Put in the missing words or the correct form of the words in brackets.

Tuesday 1 May 2001 was a day of protest. There were a few events, ... (include) a bike ride through ... (centre) London and a ... (meet) of homeless people at Hyde Park Corner. Just after two o'clock in the ... , about a thousand
5 people poured into Oxford Circus for a street party. The police were ... (worry) that they might attack stores. To keep the crowd under control, they closed all the exits ... Oxford Circus with vehicles and officers in riot clothing. The protesters were ... (trap). The tube station was closed,
10 so there was no way out. The protesters didn't seem ... (mind) until it ... to rain. The crowd tried ... break through the police lines. Bottles ... (throw), but the police managed ... (push) the crowd back. People were ... to stay in Oxford Circus for as long ... six hours without ... or
15 drink and without any toilets. The protesters were furious at *being* (be) kept there so long, and they *fought* (fight) several battles with the police. They were finally allowed to leave after *giving* (give) their names and addresses. They were all photographed *by* the police. Their numbers included two
20 German tourists. These unfortunate people were not allowed to leave and catch their flight home despite *showing* (show) their passports and tickets ... the police.
to

5 Listen to this imaginary news report about a protest against globalization.

37

Part 1 (36)

Give the following information.

1 the name of the city where the conference is taking place
2 the number of protesters
3 how long the fighting lasted
4 what kind of weapons the police used
5 what two things the protesters threw
6 the total number of people injured
7 the type of injury suffered by one police officer
8 the number of people arrested

Part 2 (37)

Choose the correct answer.

1 Which one of these countries is mentioned in the report?
a) Italy b) Japan c) Sweden
2 The conference is about how to ... .
a) help poorer countries b) reduce nuclear weapons
c) stop global warming
3 The protesters want an end to ... .
a) experiments on animals b) trade barriers c) war
4 Did the conference start on time yesterday?
a) Almost. b) Yes. c) No.
5 How much longer will the discussions go on?
a) One day. b) Two days. c) Three days.

fifty-one **51**

Unit 3 **READING**   **How to Be Good**

This extract is from the novel 'How to Be Good'
by Nick Hornby. David and Katie Carr live in
Holloway, London. He is a writer and she is a
doctor. They have a son, Tom, and a daughter,
5 *Molly. All their lives change when David*
suddenly decides to become a truly Good Person.
Katie tells the story.

I come home the next night to the sound of
trouble; even as I'm putting the key in the lock
10 I can hear Tom shouting and Molly crying.
'What's going on?' David and the kids are
sitting around the kitchen table, David at one
end, Molly to his left, Tom to his right. The
table has been cleared of
15 the usual rubbish – post,
old newspapers, small
plastic models found in
cereal packets – apparently
in the attempt to create the
20 atmosphere of a conference.
'He's given my computer
away,' says Tom. Tom
doesn't often cry, but his
eyes are shining, either with
25 fury or tears, it's hard to
tell.
'And now I've got to share
mine,' says Molly, whose
ability to cry has never been
30 in any doubt, and who now
looks as if she has been
mourning the deaths of her
whole family in a car crash.
'We didn't need two,' says
35 David. 'Two is … not
obscene, exactly. But certainly greedy. They're
never on the things at the same time.'
'So you just gave one away. Without consulting
them. Or me.'
40 'I felt that consulting them would have been
pointless.'
'You mean that they wouldn't have wanted you
to do it?'
'They maybe wouldn't have understood why
45 I wanted to.'
It was David, of course, who insisted on the
kids having a computer each for Christmas last
year. I had wanted them to share, not because
I'm mean, but because I was beginning to
50 worry about spoiling them. And here I am

six months later, angry that my son and
daughter aren't allowed to keep what is theirs,
but somehow I'm on the wrong side, an agent
of the forces of darkness.
55 'Where did you take it?'
'The women's refuge in Kentish Town. I read
about it in the local paper. They had nothing
there for the kids at all.'
I don't know what to say. The frightened,
60 unhappy children of frightened, unhappy
women have nothing; we have two of
everything. We give away some, a tiny fraction,
of what we have too much of. What is there for
me to be angry about?
65 'Why does it have to be us
who gives them something?
Why can't the Government?'
asks Tom.
'The Government can't pay
70 for everything,' says David.
'We've got to pay for some
things ourselves.'
'We did,' says Tom. 'We paid
for that computer ourselves.'
75 'I mean,' says David, 'that if
we're worried about what's
happening to poor people, we
can't wait for the Government
to do anything. We have to do
80 what we think is right.'
'Well, I don't think this is
right,' says Tom.
'Why not?'
'Because it's my computer.'
85 David just smiles.
'Why isn't it just their bad luck?' Molly asks
him, and I laugh. 'Just your bad luck' was, until
recently, David's explanation for why our kids
didn't own the latest video game or a new
90 Arsenal shirt, or anything else that every other
person at school owns.
'These children don't have much luck anyway,'
David explains with the slow and certain
patience of a recently created angel. 'Their dads
95 have been hitting their mums, and they've had
to run away from home and hide, and they
haven't got their toys with them … You have
lots of luck. Don't you want to help them?'
'A bit,' says Tom grudgingly. 'But not as much
100 as a whole computer.'

(adapted from Nick Hornby, *How to Be Good*)

52   fifty-two

UNIT 4
CANADIAN MOSAIC

WORDS AND PICTURES

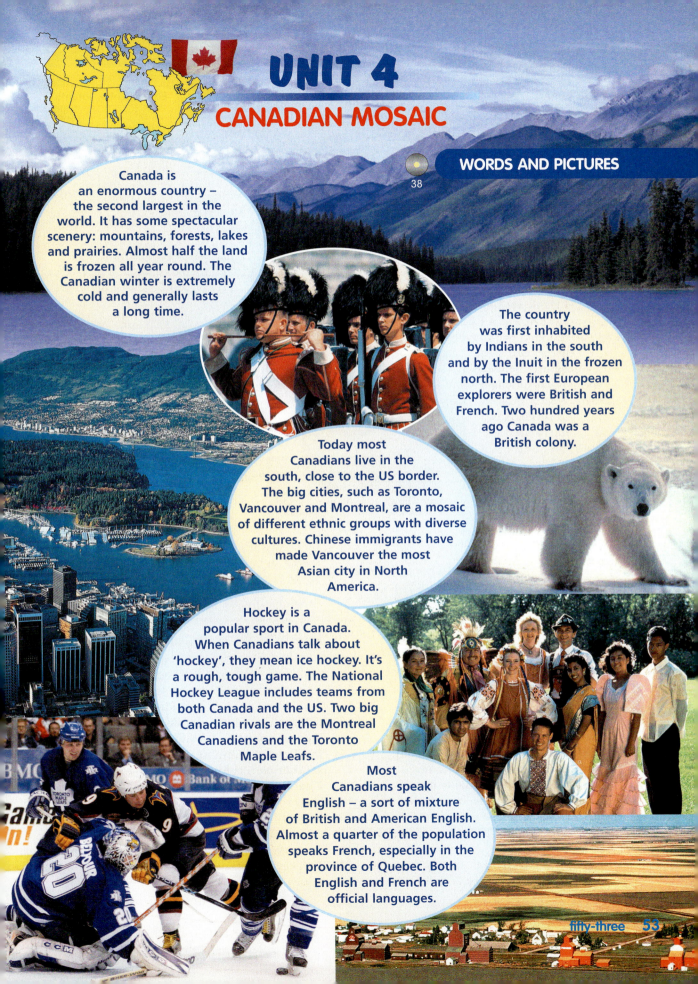

Canada is an enormous country – the second largest in the world. It has some spectacular scenery: mountains, forests, lakes and prairies. Almost half the land is frozen all year round. The Canadian winter is extremely cold and generally lasts a long time.

The country was first inhabited by Indians in the south and by the Inuit in the frozen north. The first European explorers were British and French. Two hundred years ago Canada was a British colony.

Today most Canadians live in the south, close to the US border. The big cities, such as Toronto, Vancouver and Montreal, are a mosaic of different ethnic groups with diverse cultures. Chinese immigrants have made Vancouver the most Asian city in North America.

Hockey is a popular sport in Canada. When Canadians talk about 'hockey', they mean ice hockey. It's a rough, tough game. The National Hockey League includes teams from both Canada and the US. Two big Canadian rivals are the Montreal Canadiens and the Toronto Maple Leafs.

Most Canadians speak English – a sort of mixture of British and American English. Almost a quarter of the population speaks French, especially in the province of Quebec. Both English and French are official languages.

fifty-three 53

Unit 4 **INTRODUCTION 1**

SITUATION 1
39

Karen and her friend Lindsay are at a shopping mall in Toronto. Lindsay has been waiting patiently while Karen tries on a number of dresses.

Eaton Centre, Toronto

Karen This isn't the kind of thing I normally wear.
Lindsay It's very nice, though. It's lovely.
Karen I don't usually wear green.
Lindsay But it suits you. It looks great.
Karen It feels good.
Lindsay Can you afford it?
Karen I think so. I haven't spent much on clothes lately. I think I'll take it.
Lindsay Good. Then maybe we can get to the record store before it closes.
Karen What time is it?
Lindsay Nearly quarter to seven. So hurry up.
Karen OK. Sorry, Lindsay. We'll have hardly any time to choose a CD.

→ page 114-117

It's nice and quiet, isn't it?

Let's sit here quietly for a bit.

EXERCISE 1

Find words in Situation 1 with the same meaning as these words. Write the words in pairs.

1 perhaps   4 sort   7 generally
2 almost   5 extremely 8 recently
3 beautiful 6 shuts

EXERCISE 2

Complete each adjective or adverb.

▶ The girls walked to the record store as *quickly* as they could.
▶ We'd better be *quick*,' said Lindsay.
1 Karen tried the dress on because she thought it looked really ni… .
2 She hasn't had time to buy clothes la… because she's had so much school work.
3 Unfortunately, she's had ha… any spare time.
4 Karen wanted to think ca… before she decided.
5 Lindsay waited pa… while Karen decided.
6 She was trying ha… to make her mind up.
7 She decided to buy the dress even though green isn't her us… colour.
8 'Thanks for being so pa… ,' said Karen.
9 The brown shoes will go ni… with the green dress.
10 When Lindsay went out, she promised not to be la… coming home.
11 The girls us… go to the Eaton Centre on Saturday.
12 But they have to be ca… not to spend too much money on clothes.

54 fifty-four

INTRODUCTION 1

SITUATION 2

Karen and Lindsay are meeting Karen's cousin Steve at Toronto Airport.

Karen Hi, Steve.
Steve Hi, Karen. Hello, Lindsay.
Lindsay Hi. Welcome to Toronto.
Karen It's really good to see you again. How was your flight?
Steve Pretty good, thanks. The plane was fairly full. It was a bit late, of course. Sorry about that.
Lindsay Not very late. Anyway, that's not your fault. And we've been making plans for you.
Karen I hope you're fit, Steve?
Steve Sure.
Karen Maybe we'll have a game of badminton later.
Steve Fine.

Adverbs of degree → page 117

★★★★ absolutely wonderful, totally ridiculous
★★★ very cold, really clever, extremely difficult, terribly slowly
★★ quite exciting, rather silly, fairly busy, pretty cool
★ a bit nervous, a little warmer

EXERCISE 3

A word like *very* or *fairly* is called an adverb of degree. Look at the examples in the box above and complete the conversation. Put in an adverb of degree from the right group in the box. Then practise the conversation with a partner.

Karen Did you have a good flight?
Tanya Well, it was OK for most of the way. We were (★★) late taking off, but that seems to be (★★★★) normal, doesn't it? The plane was full, and the seats seemed (★★) small, so it was (★) uncomfortable.
Ben That doesn't sound too good.
Tanya It soon got worse because we were flying through a storm. It was (★★★) violent. You could feel the plane shaking. It was (★★) nasty for a few moments. I was (★) frightened. Well, actually, I was (★★★★) scared out of my mind.
Ben How awful.
Tanya We were all (★★★) relieved to get through it. And I have to say I feel (★) tired now.

EXERCISE 4

Steve is sending an e-mail to his parents. Replace each phrase in italics with one of these adverbs of time: *afterwards, again, early, finally, once, soon, tonight.*

1 We enjoyed it so much at the ice-rink we went there *one more time* yesterday.
2 We swam in the pool, and then *a bit later* we sat and drank colas.
3 We *eventually* got home some time after midnight.
4 At least I didn't have to get up *before the usual time* the next day.
5 We're going to watch a video *this evening*.
6 We might go to the zoo, although I went there *one time* before.
7 I'll see you *before very long*.

EXERCISE 5

Divide these adjectives into positive and negative words. Write them in two groups in your exercise book.

• ~~awful~~ • ~~beautiful~~ • brilliant • disappointing • evil
• excellent • fine • fantastic • great • hopeless
• horrible • lovely • magnificent • marvellous
• nasty • nice • obscene • offensive • perfect
• pleasant • rotten • terrible • wonderful

Positive words: beautiful, ... Negative words: awful, ...
Then write about a recent experience, either something that you enjoyed or something that went wrong. Use at least five words from the box.

fifty-five **55**

Unit 4   TEXT 1

🔴 An irritating person

View of CN Tower with ferry to Toronto Islands

Karen Kelly is 16 years old and lives in Toronto. She's an only child, but she has lots of friends. Her best friend is Lindsay. The two girls play badminton and often go on weekend skiing trips together.

The Kellys live in a house in a pleasant tree-lined street in Leslieville, an area along Queen Street East and only a couple of kilometres from downtown. That's handy for Karen and Lindsay when they want to visit the enormous downtown shopping mall called the Eaton Centre.

Karen has a 17-year-old cousin, Steve, who sometimes comes to visit. He's her mother's sister's son. Steve lives in Chicago and, like many Americans, seems to think Canada is an inferior version of the United States. In fact, Karen regards Steve as a pretty irritating kind of person, so she does her best to irritate him back.

When Steve was last in Toronto, they went up the CN Tower. (CN stands for 'Canadian National'.) A glass elevator took them up the outside of the tower. Karen couldn't help pointing out that it was taller than the Sears Tower in Chicago. Steve thought it was cheating to include the antenna. Karen said the antenna gave them the best TV reception in North America. Steve couldn't think of a smart reply, and he had to admit that the view over Lake Ontario was absolutely amazing.

The Skydome

In one place there's a glass floor with a view straight down to the ground. They stood there and looked down. It was quite scary. Karen remembered when she had been there years before with her mom. She remembered lying on the glass floor while her mom took a photo of her from above. When they saw the photo, Karen seemed to be floating in space while far below her were people the size of ants. Beside the CN Tower is another of Toronto's famous sights, the Skydome. Karen and Steve took a tour of the stadium. 'The Dome' is sometimes used for concerts, but its main use is for professional baseball. It is the home of the Toronto Blue Jays baseball team, which plays in the American League. Karen is a big fan. She reminded Steve of the time when the Blue Jays became world champions, the first time the championship had been won by a team outside the US.

Despite having an extremely good time in Toronto, Steve can't help feeling that the US is the real thing and Canada is second best. Of course he's too polite to say this to his hosts in so many words. Some Canadians are sensitive about comparisons with their southern neighbour and often worry that other people regard Canada as boring.

56 fifty-six

TEXT 1

Toronto Islands

One day Lindsay went out with Karen and Steve. From the bottom of Bay Street they took the ferry to Toronto Islands where they wanted to go to the beach. On the 10-minute ferry ride
5 they were talking about guns and crime. Guns are controlled much more strictly in Canada. It's generally a safer and cleaner place than the US. 'That's why so many movies set in New York City are filmed in Toronto,' Karen pointed
10 out. She suspected that for Steve safe and clean meant boring, and guns on the streets meant excitement. Lindsay pointed out that Toronto had been officially described by the United Nations as culturally and ethnically the most
15 diverse city on the planet, even ahead of New York City. It has its Chinatown, Greektown, Little India, Little Portugal, Little Italy, and so on. In fact, there are said to be eighty different ethnic communities. Karen herself is part of this diversity – her father's family is Irish, and her mother came to Toronto from China. So Karen certainly feels at home in Toronto.

Street in Chinatown

20 Karen and Lindsay were easily winning the argument. Steve was forced to mention the climate. 'Everyone says how awful it is here in winter,' he said. 'I guess it's even colder than Chicago.' 'Sure it's cold in winter,' said Karen,
25 'but it's hot in summer. It's twenty-two degrees today.' 'Twenty-two degrees!' said Steve. 'That's cold – ten degrees below freezing.' 'I mean Celsius not Fahrenheit!' shouted Karen just before she noticed the smile on Steve's face. He
30 really was an irritating person.

EXERCISE 6

Put in the correct words from the text.

Karen Kelly sometimes receives a visit from her ... Steve. The trouble is that she finds his attitude to Canada rather ... . But when they went up the side of the CN ... in a glass ... , she knew that Steve couldn't fail to be impressed. The ... from the top is fantastic. Afterwards they went on a tour of the ... , the home of the local ... team called the ... Jays. One day Karen's ... Lindsay went with them on the ferry to Toronto ... . They talked about how Canada is generally safer than the US because ... aren't allowed. The girls suspect that Steve regards Toronto as a rather ... place. Lindsay told him that Toronto is the most ethnically ... place in the world. All Steve could think of to say was that Toronto had a terrible ... .

EXERCISE 7

Think back to the text and decide who might have spoken these words. Explain the situation in which the words were spoken.

▶ 'It's a nice park, but it's not as big as Lincoln Park in Chicago.'
   Steve said this to Karen while they were in a park in Toronto. He thinks everything in the US is better than in Canada.
1 'Even though I've been here before, I still find it a bit scary looking down.'
2 'What are you and Steve going to do today? Would you like us to take you somewhere?'
3 'This beach is OK, but I prefer the beaches on Lake Michigan.'
4 'Would you like to go out to the islands with Steve and me?'
5 'If Steve starts to irritate you again, just leave him to me. I'll throw a few facts at him.'

fifty-seven 57

Unit 4 TEXT 1

EXERCISE 8

Look at these explanations and find the phrase in the text.

➡ someone you find annoying
   an irritating person
1 someone without any brothers or sisters
2 a large building in the city centre containing a lot of shops
3 something similar but not so good
4 a clever answer
5 rather frightening
6 moving slowly in the air
7 crossed in a boat
8 the place with the greatest number of different ethnic groups in the world
9 had to talk about the weather

EXERCISE 10

Rewrite the sentences using an adverb instead of an adjective or vice versa.

➡ The main use of the Skydome is for baseball games.
   The Skydome **is mainly used** for baseball games.
1 The girls frequently visit the Eaton Centre.
   The girls make … to the Eaton Centre.
2 There's often quite heavy snow in the winter.
   It … in the winter.
3 Toronto is culturally very diverse.
   There is a great … .
4 The argument ended in an easy victory for the girls.
   In the end the girls … .
5 Steve's plane arrived late, so they had to wait.
   The … plane meant that they had to wait.
6 Guns are more strictly controlled in Canada.
   There … over … Canada.

EXERCISE 9

What did they actually say?

➡ Steve thought it was cheating to include the antenna.
   'It's cheating to include the antenna.'
1 Karen said the antenna gave them good TV reception.
2 Steve admitted that the view was amazing.
3 Karen asked Steve if he remembered the Blue Jays' famous victory.
4 Lindsay pointed out that Toronto had been called the most ethnically diverse city in the world.
5 Steve said he knew that in winter people couldn't leave their homes in Toronto or they would freeze to death.
6 Karen told Steve to shut up or she might throw him into the harbour.

EXERCISE 11

42-43 Listening

Part 1 (42)

You will hear three people talking about places they have visited in Toronto. Listen to each person and decide if they are talking about A, B, C, D or E.

A The CN Tower   B The Royal Ontario Museum
C The Skydome   D Toronto Islands   E The Eaton Centre

Part 2 (43)

Louise and Simon are telling a friend about their day at Toronto Zoo. Listen to the conversation and answer the questions. You do not need to answer in complete sentences.

1 What two kinds of animals are mentioned in the conversation?
2 How long did the journey take from downtown Toronto to the zoo?
3 What can visitors use to get from one part of the zoo to another?
4 What time did Louise and Simon get back to the hotel?

FOLLOW UP

EXERCISE 12

Complete this info box about Canada. There is one word missing from each sentence.

- Canada has a ... of 31 million.
- The Canadian ... is red and white. It has a ... leaf on it.
- Ottawa is the ... of Canada, although it is not the largest city. It is at the eastern end of the ... of Ontario, near the Quebec border.
- Ottawa has an average January temperature of minus eleven ... Celsius.
- The two largest mainly ...-speaking cities are Montreal and Québec City.
- Canada covers six time ... – Pacific, Mountain, Central, Eastern, Atlantic and Newfoundland. St John's, Newfoundland is four and a half ... ahead of Vancouver, British Columbia.
- Canada achieved full ... from Britain in 1931.

SONG

4 Bryan Adams was born in Kingston, Ontario. He first performed in a rock band as a teenager living in Vancouver. The biggest hit of his superstar career was '(Everything I Do) I Do It For You', which was number one in both the American and British charts.

SUMMER OF '69
(Adams / Vallance)

I got my real first six string –
*   bought it at the five and dime*
played it til my fingers bled –
*   was the summer of '69*
5 *me and some guys from school*
*   had a band and we tried real hard*
Jimmy quit and Jody got married –
*   shoulda known we'd never get far*

but when I look back now –
10 *   that summer seemed to last forever*
and if I had the choice –
*   yeah I'd always wanna be there*
those were the best days of my life

ain't no use in complaining –
15 *   when you gotta job to do*
spent my evenings down at the drive-in –
*   and that's when I met you – yeah*
standing on your mama's porch –
*   you told me that you'd wait forever*
20 *oh and when you held my hand –*
*   I knew that it was now or never*
those were the best days of my life –
*   back in the summer of '69*

*   man we were killing time*
25 *we were young and reckless –*
*   we needed to unwind*
I guess nothing can last forever –
*   forever*

and now the times are changing
30 *look at everything that's come and gone*
sometimes when I play my old six string
I think about you –
*   wonder what went wrong*

standing on your mama's porch –
35 *   you told me it would last forever*
and when you held my hand –
*   I knew that it was now or never*
those were the best days of my life –
back in the summer of '69

fifty-nine 59

Unit 4 **INTRODUCTION 2**

SITUATION 3

45

Cathy and Bob work for the *Manitoba Mirror*. They've received some information that could lead to an interesting story.

Winnipeg, Manitoba

Bob   I think we should talk to this guy and investigate the story. He says someone is going to dump some drums. Does he mean oil drums?
Cathy   Shall we go and see him now? I'd better phone him first.
Bob   I can't go right now. I have to finish this report by four o'clock, and it'll take a while.
Cathy   I think the guy might have some interesting information. One of us ought to talk to him today. Shall I do it?
Bob   OK, you go ahead.

page 118-119

EXERCISE 13

Complete the conversation by choosing the correct expression. Then practise the conversation with a partner.

Jack   What … (about doing / let's do / shall we do) tonight?
Lizzie   … (Shall / Will / Would) we go to the cinema?
Jack   Yes, … (good idea. / I expect so. / that's right.) Do you know what's … (happening / on / there)?
Lizzie   … (No idea / Not at all / So do I), I'm afraid. So … (am I / let me / shall I) go and get a paper?
Jack   … (Oh, are you? / Yes, OK. / Yes, you will.)

EXERCISE 14

Rewrite each sentence using one of these words or phrases: *can, couldn't, had better, has to, is allowed to, might, needn't, ~~should~~, would rather*.

➨ The right thing to do is for someone to check all the facts.
   Someone should check all the facts.
1 It's possible the man knows something important.
2 It's important that Bob finishes the report first.
3 He didn't manage to stay awake long enough to finish it last night.
4 It's necessary that the report is finished before the deadline.
5 Cathy has the ability to get information from people.
6 She prefers to go out and investigate a story instead of sitting at her desk.
7 Cathy has permission to leave the office.
8 It isn't necessary for her to come back to the office today.

INTRODUCTION 2

SITUATION 4

Lizzie I still can't find that file I was looking for.
Susan You might have accidentally deleted it.
Lizzie I couldn't have. I never throw files away. I must have put it somewhere. The trouble is, I can't remember what I called it.
Susan You should have made a back-up copy.
Lizzie It's OK. I've got it.

> **Modal verb + have + past participle**
> You didn't put the file in the right place. You **should have been** more careful. (You weren't careful enough.)
> I don't know where the back-up copy is. I **might have put** it in the cupboard. (It's possible I put it in the cupboard.)
> I sent the e-mail an hour ago. Tom **must have read** it by now. (Surely he has read it by now.)
> The computer is still on. You **can't have switched** it off. (You certainly didn't switch it off.)
>
> → page 119

EXERCISE 15

Becky has gone out to a party with some friends. It's late and she hasn't come back yet. Her parents are worried. Put the verbs in brackets into the correct positive or negative form using *should have, might have, must have, can have* or *would have*.

Mom I don't know why Becky hasn't phoned. She … (call) earlier and told us what was happening.
Dad Maybe she forgot her cellphone. She … (not/take) it with her.
Mom Of course she took it. She always has it with her. Something terrible … (happen), I'm sure. She … (have) an accident. It's the only explanation.
Dad But she's with her friends. She … (not/have) an accident. If she had, then someone … (ring) us.
Mom Perhaps she wasn't with her friends. She … (not/stay) with them all evening. She could be with anyone.
Dad There's probably a simple explanation. She … (forget) the time. Or maybe she couldn't get back here. She … (decide) to stay the night there.
Mom She wouldn't have done that without telling us, would she? God knows what's happened. She … (not/go) to that party. She's too young to stay out so late.
Dad Maybe we … (not/allow) her to go.
Mom We … (make) her stay at home. But it's too late now.

Unit 4 TEXT 2

● In the middle of nowhere

47 Cathy McBride was the British reporter who joined our team on the *Manitoba Mirror* and someone I was very fond of. At the end of January this year we were investigating a story and Cathy was following it up. She sent me this e-mail.

5 Bob - the information that the farmer gave us was right. I think those people are going to dump the drums. 10 Prepare yourself for a first class scandal. I'm chasing them. Going north from Winnipeg, straight into the frozen swampland. Feels like flying when I drive across smooth snow with the blue sky above me. 15 A bit unreal. Snow banks as high as my car. Some dangerous potholes in the road. Strong winds before morning and maybe blizzards soon. I'm exhausted but I'll be careful. See you. Cathy.

I was worried by this message, and I found it hard to 20 concentrate on my work. Actually, I was afraid. Most Canadians live within 300 kilometres of the US frontier. To the north lie lakes, swamplands and huge areas of icy desert, inhabited only by a small number of native Americans called 'Inuit'.

I hated to think of Cathy out there in that cold and lonely place. But I 25 knew it was easier than in summer because in winter the swamplands freeze in temperatures that can be as low as minus 40°C, so you can drive over the snow. The danger is that blizzards might leave you stuck for several days. We knew Cathy would have emergency equipment with her: a sleeping bag, warm clothes, food, spare parts and extra petrol for the car. But none of us 30 knew exactly where she was going and what was waiting for her there. She was one of our best reporters and very ambitious, and this story could make her a big name.

TEXT 2

At the office the next day, I got a phone call.

'Hi, Bob.'

'Cathy, where are you? What happened?'

'I can't tell you much now. My cellphone isn't working so
5 I'm calling from the last gas station before the swamplands.
They've just left, and I'm following them. It's a 12-tonne
truck carrying more than fifty drums. There are two men.
They must have decided to dump the drums somewhere.'

'Do you know what's in the drums?'

10 'I'm sure it's either chemical or nuclear waste. Anyway, it's
illegal. I hope I can prove it. I must go now. Bye.'

I was still worried. The nearest nuclear power plant is at
Trois-Rivières, Quebec, almost 2,000 kilometres away. So
I didn't think it was nuclear waste on the truck. Canada
15 gets its electric power mainly from water, from enormous
hydroelectric power stations. I thought the truck was
probably carrying dangerous chemical waste. Maybe the
men were working for a chemical company that wasn't
willing to pay a few thousand dollars to have the waste
20 recycled. Maybe they'd decided to contaminate the earth
instead. It certainly was going to be a big scandal.

Cathy's car was found empty and half covered by a snow
bank. There were no signs of a struggle, so the Manitoba
police department thought she probably had an accident
25 and then tried to walk on. They looked for her until the
end of March but then the file was closed. It seemed that
she had just disappeared.

Cathy's diary and her camera
were never found, but there was
30 an envelope lying under the back
seat of her car. Inside was a
memory card. The photos show
drums dumped in the middle of
nowhere, half covered with snow.
35 There's no hope of finding the
place, of course. But this is
what she wanted to prove. Two
criminals dumped their frightening
chemical waste somewhere on the
40 frozen swampland of Manitoba.
No one was going to suspect them.
When the ice melted in spring, the
drums would disappear in the
mud.

45 And what happened to Cathy?
Surely it couldn't have been an
accident. Why did she go alone?
For a while I tried to believe that
she was still alive, although I knew
50 she was dead. I even drove out
there looking for her. But it was
hopeless. In the end I had to give
up. But I don't think I'll ever be
able to forget her.

EXERCISE 16

Put the sentences in the right order and tell the story.

A Unfortunately, it looked as if she had obtained it at the
cost of her life.

B She said she was going after someone she suspected of
intending to dump some drums.

C Bob thought they probably contained chemical rather
than nuclear waste.

D Inside the vehicle was a memory card with photos of
the drums after they'd been dumped.

E One day Bob, a reporter on the *Manitoba Mirror*,
received an e-mail from his colleague Cathy.

F The next day he got a call to say there were two men in
a truck carrying drums.

G This news worried Bob because he knew Cathy was
going into dangerous territory.

H This was the proof that Cathy had hoped to obtain.

I But he never found out because the next thing that
happened was that Cathy's empty car was discovered.

Begin like this: *One day, Bob ...*

EXERCISE 17

Answer the questions.

1 Who was Cathy McBride?
2 Why did she drive north
from Winnipeg?
3 Why was Bob afraid when
he read the e-mail?
4 What people live in the frozen
north?
5 Why would the journey north
be more difficult in summer?
6 Why was Cathy in a hurry
when she phoned Bob?
7 What did they think was in the
drums?
8 Why were the men dumping
the drums?
9 Why did the police close
Cathy's file?
10 Why did Bob give up looking
for Cathy?

sixty-three **63**

Unit 4 TEXT 2

EXERCISE 18

Read and discuss.

What do you think happened to Cathy? Was there an accident? Was she killed by the men in the truck? Or did she manage to escape? If she's dead, why didn't anybody find her body? Did Cathy make any mistakes? Should she have acted differently?

Write a paragraph of about 100 words saying what happened.

EXERCISE 19

Explain the words by completing the sentences.

➡ A reporter is someone who writes articles for a newspaper.
➡ When there's a blizzard, it's snowing and there is a strong wind.
1 If something is empty, … .
2 If you are exhausted, … .
3 Doing something illegal … .
4 The people who inhabit a place … .
5 If you prove something, … .
6 An emergency is a situation where … .
7 A lonely place is … .
8 If you are ambitious, … .
9 If you're stuck, … .
10 Hydroelectric power is … .
11 You use spare parts … .
12 If you are concentrating on something, … .

EXERCISE 20

Combine each pair of sentences using a relative clause. Sometimes you need a relative pronoun, but sometimes you don't.

➡ Cathy went to interview the farmer. He had called the newspaper. Cathy went to interview the farmer who had called the newspaper.

➡ She was travelling into an icy region. It is inhabited by very few people. She was travelling into an icy region inhabited by very few people.

1 Cathy was looking for a story. It would make her a big name.
2 She was investigating the story. They'd talked about it the day before.
3 Bob was worried by the message. He found it on his computer.
4 Maybe the men were working for a company. Its managers just wanted to dump the waste cheaply.
5 Cathy had been seen by the man. He was driving the truck.
6 The photos showed a number of drums. They had been left in the snow.
7 Bob spoke to the officers. They had found the car.
8 Cathy was a colleague. Bob was very fond of her.

EXERCISE 21

Complete the sentences by using a compound word. Put together two words from the box.

air • back • electric • glasses • head • high • hole • hydro • lands • lights • market • ~~news~~ • pack • ~~paper~~ • pot • shield • snow • storm • strip • sun • super • swamp • way • wind

➡ Bob works for a newspaper in Manitoba.
1 The man told us he worked at a … power station.
2 We drove over a … in the road.
3 It certainly wasn't like driving on the Trans Canada … .
4 There were a couple of tourists, each carrying a big … .
5 Take enough food because you won't find a … out there.
6 We could hardly see the road in front of us as snow was half covering the … .
7 You should wear … to protect your eyes from the white light.
8 There was an ice-free … where planes could take off and land.
9 In the dark we saw the … of another vehicle that was coming towards us.
10 You could get stuck in a … out in the … .

64 sixty-four

Suggestions

COMMUNICATION

Making a suggestion
- Shall we go to the beach?
- Let's play a computer game, shall we?
- What about / How about some music?
- We could have a swim.
- Why don't we look round the shops?

Agreeing with a suggestion
- Yes, OK.
- OK, if you like.
- Good idea.
- Yes, why not?

Disagreeing with a suggestion
- I don't like table tennis.
- Sorry, I can't. I've promised to help my mom.
- I'd rather do something else.
- Let's go out somewhere instead.

Trying to persuade someone
- Oh, go on / come on. It'll be fun.
- Why not?

Emma Shall we watch the ice hockey on TV?
Olivia I'd rather do something else.
Emma Oh, go on. I bet it'll be good.
Olivia I'm not very fond of ice hockey. What about playing a few CDs?
Emma OK, if you like.

EXERCISE 22

Work in pairs. Invent a short dialogue and act it out. Use the phrases in the box and think of some of your own, too.

Partner A *Schlage vor, was du tun willst.*
Partner B *Lehne den Vorschlag ab und erkläre warum.*
Partner A *Versuche deinen Partner zu überreden.*
Partner B *Lehne erneut ab und mache einen anderen Vorschlag.*
Partner A *Stimme dem neuen Vorschlag zu.*

basketball • a cheeseburger • the disco • go skateboarding • a game of mini-golf • the swimming pool

EXERCISE 23

Describing your surroundings

Look at this description.

'I'm following a truck. I'm driving across the snow. It feels like flying, a bit unreal. All I can hear is the sound of the engine. There are snowbanks as high as my car and a blue sky above me. There's quite a wind too. I'm tired and a bit nervous.'

Now read this table and copy the words in the left-hand column into your exercise book.

Purpose of the journey	following a truck
Landscape	frozen desert
Weather	cold, a clear sky and windy
Things seen	snowbanks, the blue sky
Things heard	the jeep's engine
Feelings	tired and a bit nervous

Work with a partner.

Partner B: Please look at page 96.

Partner A: Imagine you are walking through a rainforest. Describe your surroundings. Invent as much detail as you can. Your partner might want to ask you some questions. Then listen to your partner's description of his/her surroundings. Make notes while you listen. Write the information in your table. If necessary, ask your partner some questions so that you get all the details.

sixty-five **65**

Unit 4

TEST YOUR ENGLISH

The Inuit people

There are Inuit people in Greenland, Canada, Alaska and Siberia. In northern Canada they have their own territory called Nunavut, which means 'our land' in the Inuktitut language spoken by the Inuit. Nunavut is five times the size of Germany but is inhabited by only 27,000 people. The territory's capital is Iqaluit, a settlement on the coast of Baffin Island with a population of 6,000. Nunavut is a remote and inhospitable place. It has only twelve miles of roads, but it has hundreds of airstrips.

For thousands of years the Inuit were nomadic hunters. Although there are some Inuit people who continue the traditional way of life, things have changed enormously in the last few decades. Most people now live in villages, and the children go to school. Many Inuit people work for wages and buy their food and clothes in shops. In the old days the men used to fish and hunt animals such as seals and whales, and the women used to make clothes from the animal skins. Now these traditional skills are disappearing. Inuit kids nowadays watch TV, listen to pop music and surf the internet. The boys don't regard hunting as an attractive job, and girls aren't so keen on being a hunter's wife.

The average January temperature in Nunavut is minus 35°C, so the Inuit have to be experts at keeping warm. Their wooden houses are built on stilts to keep them above the snow and ice. People used to travel on sleds pulled by dogs, but now they use snowmobiles. In winter the sun appears for only a couple of hours each day; in some places there is no daylight from the end of October to the beginning of February.

Over a fifth of adults in Nunavut are unemployed. There are problems with alcohol and drugs. The number of suicides is five times the Canadian average and is especially high among young people. It has been suggested that the cause of these problems is the change in the Inuit way of life. People do not need to work so hard hunting for food and making warm clothes, so they have become bored. Those who still live in the traditional way are better able to cope with the conditions.

1 Decide if each statement is true or false and give the relevant clause or sentence from the text.

1. Not all Inuit people live in Canada.
2. Nunavut is a very crowded place.
3. It is easier to travel around Nunavut by plane than by car.
4. Life for most Inuit people is different from what it was fifty years ago.
5. The Inuit have always worshipped whales and never killed them.
6. It's dark more or less the whole time in winter.
7. There's no problem finding work in Nunavut.
8. Young Inuit people are generally happier and more confident about the future than other young Canadians.

66 sixty-six

TEST YOUR ENGLISH

2 Look at these explanations and find the word in the text.

1. a place where people have come to live and make a new home
2. the number of people who live in a place
3. a long way from other places
4. keep going, go on doing something
5. greatly, very much
6. money earned by working
7. the ability to do something well
8. a vehicle that can be pulled over ice or snow
9. without work, not having a job
10. fed up, not interested

3 Rewrite the sentences expressing the meaning in a different way.

1. Nunavut is inhabited by only 27,000 people.
   Only 27,000 people … .
2. Things have changed enormously.
   There have … .
3. They don't regard hunting as an attractive job.
   Hunting … .
4. Nunavut is five times the size of Germany.
   Germany is one … .
5. The Inuit are experts at keeping warm.
   The Inuit know … .
6. The men used to hunt animals such as seals and whales.
   Seals and whales are two of … .

4 Put in the missing words or the correct form of the words in brackets.

The Inuit territory of Nunavut has three … (office) languages: English, French and Inuktitut. The Inuit have always told … (story) in their native Inuktitut, but the language was not … down until an alphabet was invented
5 … missionaries in the 19th century. Inuktitut is not a simple language, … it has a rather small number of words. A word can have several different … (end). Words can be … (extreme) long and complex and can express meanings that in other languages would require a whole
10 sentence. Inuktitut is said to be one … the most complex and difficult languages in the world. There are only a … words in Inuktitut … are widely known, and one of these is 'parka', a … of warm jacket.

Many people fear that Inuktitut could die out. It might
15 not survive in the future … all the efforts made to support it. Even … there are Inuktitut newspapers and TV programmes and lessons in schools, there is strong competition from English. When kids … the internet or … *The Simpsons*, they realize that English is the language of
20 … (young) culture, and they want to be a … of that culture.

5 You will hear part of a British radio programme about holidays in Nunavut. The extract is in two parts.

Part 1 (49)

Answer the questions. You don't need to answer in complete sentences.

1. What three things can Nunavut offer tourists?
2. When is the best time to visit?
3. Is a holiday in Nunavut likely to be cheap or expensive?

Part 2 (50)

Give the information. You can make notes as you listen.

1. the seven activities mentioned
2. the kind of day trip provided
3. four adjectives that describe the hostel where you stay
4. the cost in Canadian dollars if you stay for a week
5. how you travel to Baffin Island
6. the different prices for young people

Unit 4 READING — Diary of a South African (who moved to Canada to escape the crime)

December 14th

It's started snowing. The first of the season and the first real snow I've ever seen. I sat by the window watching the soft snowflakes float down, clinging to the trees and covering the ground. IT WAS BEAUTIFUL.

December 15th

Woke to a lovely blanket of white snow covering the landscape. What a FANTASTIC sight! Every tree and bush was covered by a beautiful white coat. I shovelled snow for the first time, and loved it. I did both the driveway and the sidewalk. Later, the city snowplough came along and accidentally covered the driveway with the snow from the street. But the driver smiled and waved. I waved back and shovelled again.

December 16th

It snowed another twelve centimetres last night and the temperature dropped to around minus 20°C. Several branches on the trees have broken under the weight of the snow. I shovelled the driveway again. Shortly afterwards the snowplough man came along and did his trick again. Much of the snow is now a sort of brown-grey colour.

December 17th

It got warm enough during the day to create some slush, which soon turned to ice again. Bought snow tyres for the car. Fell in the driveway, paid $130 for the chiropractor, but fortunately nothing is broken. More snow and ice is expected.

December 18th

Still very cold. Sold car and bought 4x4 so that I can get to work. Slid into the guard rail and damaged the back of the vehicle. Had another 15 centimetres of white cold stuff last night, car covered in salt and dirt. More shovelling for me again. That damn snowplough came past twice today.

December 19th

Minus 27°C outside. More stinking snow. Not a tree or a bush in the garden that hasn't been damaged. Power was off most of the night. I tried to keep from freezing to death with candles and a kerosene heater, which fell over and nearly burned the house down. I managed to put the flames out, but suffered second degree burns on my hands and lost my eyelashes. Car slid on the way to the hospital and was totalled.

December 20th

Horrible white stuff keeps coming down! Have to put on all the clothes that I own just to get to the mailbox. If I ever catch the idiot that drives that snowplough, I'll beat him to death! I think he hides around the corner and waits for me to finish shovelling, then comes down the street and buries the driveway again. The power is still off. The toilet has frozen over and part of the roof has started to cave in.

December 21st

Twelve more centimetres of stupid snow and stupid ice and who knows what other kind of stupid white stuff fell last night. I wounded the idiot snowplough driver with a pick, but the bastard got away. I think I'm going snowblind. I can't move my toes, I haven't seen the sun in weeks, and there's more stinking snow predicted.

December 22nd

I am moving back to South Africa!

(adapted from http:travel.iafrica.com)

DANGER FROM ABOVE

and how often do I have to tell you? Slip and slop!! Jamie, you mustn't forget the slogan! Slip on a T-shirt and slop on some sun cream.' Kimberley heard her mother's voice before she opened her eyes – and the words made her feel like NOT waking up this morning. Another awful school day was waiting for her. Her whole life was school, school, school. From 8 am till 6 pm it was a long series of boring lessons and organized activities. And they were even planning to hold all the lessons at night, till 2 am! Just when young people had their only chance of some free time outdoors. The government's explanation was, of course, that children had to be protected from that frightening danger from above.

Kim slowly put on her grey protective uniform, which was made from anti-ultraviolet cloth. Today's burn time for her fair skin was just two minutes and she didn't want to risk getting sunburnt again. You couldn't expect any shade from the few small plants that had survived the heat and pollution. But once the world had been full of wildlife, free animals, trees and beautiful plants – and lots of children. And people were even allowed to spend their holidays on the beach – and not just below those huge protective shields near sun medical centres. Scientists say that once the sky was blue when the sun was shining. Since then, acid rain and solar radiation from the orange sky had killed most of the animals. 'Hey, are you dreaming? In love, eh? You'd better not forget your medicine!' her little brother Jamie said. Oh, her asthma, another problem, she thought as she drank her CHEMFOOD drink.

It was hard to stop dreaming about the good old times she had learned about from the history files on her computer. Was it really true that children were so much freer in the past? That they could leave school in the afternoon with lots of spare time for hobbies and for just lying in the sun? Oh, how much she hated the sun! Why had the mother of life become its greatest enemy? Was she taking her revenge? Of course, there

Unit 1 EXTRA PAGES

52

William closed the book with a sigh. He was quite disappointed. *Danger From Above* was not the thriller he had expected but just a silly science fiction story. William loved the sun. What a strange book, he thought. The writer must have a pretty wild imagination.

Then William rang his friend Lauren to ask about their physics homework. 'I'm reading a really
5 stupid science fiction novel,' he said. 'It's about everyday life with holes in the ozone layer. People have to put on lots of sun cream and wear long sleeves every time they go out and …' 'Why do you think that's so strange?' Lauren asked him. 'You know Julie, my Australian friend I met in a chat room. She just told me about the danger from solar radiation down there. Australians like to lie in the sun at lunchtime. Well, now they have to cover their arms and legs every time they go out in
10 summer, even when it's cloudy. There are burn times on the news. When you get sunburnt, it destroys part of your skin. Then the cancer waits inside you like a time bomb. Most Australians are checked twice a year for black spots on their skin. If you get a spot, you have to have an operation, or you can die in a few years. The government runs campaigns with slogans like "Between seven and three look for a tree!" It's no joke. Nowadays two out of three Australians get
15 skin cancer! Some people have had more than 20 spots removed. How would you like your arms and legs to look like crocodile skin?'

William remembered a programme about skin cancer he had seen on TV. He wondered what would happen in the future. Suddenly the science fiction story didn't seem as silly as before.

Remember: Slip, Slap, Slop and Slide to protect yourself in the sun. Be clever like your animal friends. Here's how:

Meerkats have black rings round their eyes that protect them from the sun.
Slip on a shirt and sunglasses:
– to block out the sun.
– Wear long sleeves and trousers.

Camels have bumps over their eyes that keep out the bright light.
Slap on a hat:
– to protect the face, head, ears and neck.

Elephants use dirt and hay as a natural sun cream.
Slop on sun cream:
– even on cool and cloudy days.
– Put on sun cream again after swimming.

Koalas spend most of the day in the shade of trees.
Slide into the shade:
– and stay there.
– Umbrellas keep you cool.

Ozone (O_3) is a kind of oxygen. You may have smelled it
20 near a photocopying machine. But don't breathe it in – it is poisonous. But about 20 to 40 kilometres above our heads there is a layer of ozone which protects us from ultraviolet radiation from the sun, which would destroy all life on Earth. However, this ozone layer is getting thinner – it is being
25 damaged by chemicals such as CFCs in sprays and fridges. There is a hole in the ozone layer which opens up over part of Australia in the spring. The hole is already three times the size of Australia. As the hole grows, so does the danger.
90% of Australian high school pupils have problems with
30 their skin. It is an especially big problem there because most Australians have fair hair and skin. In 2002 almost 300,000 Australians had one or more skin cancers removed. The use of CFCs has been reduced, but more action to protect the ozone layer is urgently needed because of the chemicals that
35 survive in the atmosphere. Australia is now leading in its efforts to reduce and abolish ozone-eating chemicals but the situation won't improve before 2050 – if it does at all.

EXERCISE 1

Answer the questions on the text.
1 What does 'slip and slop' mean?
2 What do you know about Kimberley's school day?
3 What does Kimberley think about the old days?
4 Which piece of information about Kimberley worries you the most?
5 Why is solar radiation dangerous?
6 How do Australians know how long they can safely stay in the sun?
7 Why did William change his opinion of the story after talking to Lauren?
8 Why must we protect the ozone layer, and why is it urgent?
9 What can be done to save it?

EXTRA PAGES Unit 1

EXERCISE 2

Rewrite these jumbled DOs and DON'Ts about the dangers from the sun and explain them.

1 Avoid going out between 3 pm and 7 am.
2 Long sunshade and large sleeves make the best hats.
3 Use cloudy cream even on summer sun days.
4 Stay in the holidays if possible, especially at the shade of your start.
5 Listen to the news warnings on your local ozone.
6 Have the year on your skin checked once a spots, especially when there are lots of them.
7 Remember that your skin can't repair you – when the damage can see you, it's late too.

EXERCISE 3

Look at this table. What's your skin type? Work with a partner and find out what type of skin he or she has.

TYPE	HAIR	EYES	SKIN	FRECKLES	BURN	TAN	SUNBURNT AFTER	SPF
A	red / fair	blue / green	very fair	lots	quickly	very slowly	5 minutes	25
B	fair	blue / green	fair	some	quickly	slowly	10 minutes	20
C	light brown	brown	fair	hardly any	sometimes	quite quickly	15 minutes	15
D	brown / black	brown	dark	none	sometimes	very quickly	20 minutes	10

You won't believe how quickly you can get sunburnt – and your skin can be damaged without you noticing it. The sun protection factors (SPF) are chemicals or minerals which fight against the dangers from ultraviolet radiation. Multiply the SPF of your sun cream by the number of minutes it would take you to get sunburnt without cream ('sunburnt after').

So if you are Type A and the cream you use has an SPF of 25, then you can sunbathe with cream on for 125 minutes a day. However, if you insist on sunbathing between 11 am and 4 pm or if you're near the ozone hole in Australia or New Zealand, then the dangers are even greater than the table suggests. Even 20 minutes of sunbathing could burn you. And putting on more cream more often doesn't help. 125 minutes means no more than 125 minutes in a whole day.

You can only avoid skin cancer if you're careful! Tanning is an SOS message from your skin, but some people still think its purpose is to show that you are young, rich and beautiful.

EXERCISE 4

Put in the missing words and use the words in brackets in their correct form.

The small black spot on 23-year-old Matt Eastley's stomach … (remove) six months ago. He … (know) then that he … (not / have) much time left. The cancer had … (grow) deep into his
5 body. After the doctors … (tell) him the … (true), Matt decided to visit as many schools in Canberra … he … (can) to warn the pupils about the dangers from the sun. His message was that teenagers should wear … (protect) clothing when
10 out in the sun. If they feel like … (break) this rule, they should think … (two) about it. When they … (be) little kids, they had … wear those strange caps … covered their faces and necks and made them look … Roman soldiers.
15 Now that they're teenagers, however, they try … (avoid / wear) anything that … (not / look) trendy. Their parents and teachers (discuss) … for some time now whether the pupils should … (force / wear) these caps as a part of their
20 school uniform. Everyone hopes that popular heroes … as famous sportspeople will help to advise the pupils how … (protect / they) in the open air. … (sad), Matt … (die) last month, but his message lives on: You have … warned!

seventy-one 71

A WHOLE NEW WORLD

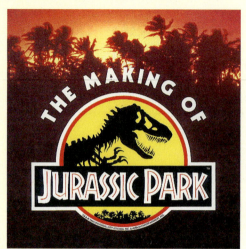

When the first *Jurassic Park* movie was shown, it was a sensation. Spectacular special effects brought absolutely lifelike dinosaurs to the screen and wowed cinema audiences worldwide. The movie became a huge box-office success.

The movie was directed by Steven Spielberg and based on a novel by Michael Crichton. At Jurassic Park, on an island off the coast of Costa Rica, dinosaurs have been cloned from DNA. The plan is to open a theme park. The dinosaurs are kept behind electric fences. Of course, they soon escape and spend the rest of the film hunting the scientists and the owner's two grandchildren. It's scary stuff that keeps you on the edge of your seat. But forget the human characters – the stars of this movie are the dinosaurs.

The challenge for the makers of *Jurassic Park* was to create a whole new world, one that contains animals which existed 65 million years ago. Traditionally, movies about monsters or dinosaurs had been made with puppets moved by hand. But Spielberg decided this method wouldn't be good enough. The solution was to use a mixture of full-size mechanical models and computer graphics.

The mechanical dinosaurs were created by a team at the Stan Winston Studio in Los Angeles. The biggest model was a six-metre-tall T-rex (tyrannosaurus rex) built from a fibreglass frame and 1,350 kilos of clay covered with a latex skin that was painted by a team of artists. The T-rex was moved by a hydraulic mechanism linked to a computer. A smaller fifth-size model was built which could be moved by hand, and these movements were recorded on a computer. The computer then instructed the hydraulic mechanism to move the full-size T-rex in the same way. The eyes were controlled by radio. There was also a separate head with greater detail for close-up shots.

Different solutions were found for the different kinds of dinosaurs. In one scene, two velociraptors hunt the two children in the kitchen of the visitor centre. A velociraptor is the same size as a human, so a high-tech method was not necessary – a human could simply wear a velociraptor costume. The tail was moved by hidden wires. There were also full-size models that were used for shots where the creatures were not moving.

In another scene, a herd of ten dinosaurs is running along together. This kind of scene is best done by computer animation. When you've created one dinosaur running along, you can copy it. Computer graphic artists created an image of the creature and then developed a program to show it running. Altogether 50 computer graphic shots were created for the movie by a company called Industrial Light and Magic. ILM was also able to scan some of the dinosaur models to obtain a digital version which could then be animated.

EXTRA PAGES — Unit 2

Work on the special effects had already been going on for two years when Spielberg and his team began filming the outdoor scenes. These were shot on the Hawaiian island of Kauai with its spectacular scenery. The front of the visitor centre was
5 built there, as well as a length of seven-metre-tall fence.

Most of the action was filmed at Universal Studios and Warner Brothers in Los Angeles, including the T-rex attack on the tour vehicle with the children inside. The attack takes place in a storm, and the rain machine made the T-rex very
10 wet and very heavy, so the huge creature had to be dried off after each shot. Much of the action in the film happens at night or when it is raining, and this meant that it was less difficult to make a realistic jungle background.

All the different elements – the actors, the models, the computer
15 graphics, the background shots – come together in the finished movie. For example, the dinosaur herd created on computer at ILM runs across a background shot in Hawaii. Most of the sounds were also created separately by a company called Skywalker Sound. Sound editor Richard Hymns spent two
20 months in Australian rainforests recording birds and insects. The attack screams of the velociraptors are the recorded screams of dolphins and geese. The sounds of the T-rex are a mixture of tiger, alligator, elephant, dog and penguin. Of course, when you watch a movie, you don't often hear the sounds made at the time
25 the film was shot, and what you see on the screen is never as simple as it looks. This is especially true of the world created by the makers of *Jurassic Park*.

EXERCISE 1

Write one or two sentences to explain who or what they are.

▶ *Jurassic Park*
Jurassic Park is a film about a dinosaur theme park where the dinosaurs escape and hunt the humans.
1 Steven Spielberg
2 Michael Crichton
3 Richard Hymns
4 A T-rex
5 Kauai

Unit 2 EXTRA PAGES

EXERCISE 2

Complete these sentences that people working on the film might have said.

1. We use a hydraulic m… to move the creature.
2. The movement of the dinosaur's eyes is c… by radio.
3. The painting of the skin has been done by a group of a… .
4. Some of the bird and insect noises were recorded in a remote r… .
5. We're going to shoot the o… scenes first and then the ones in the studio.
6. We're trying to d… the skin with these towels.
7. You pull this w… to move the tail.
8. The film e… might cut out part of the scene.
9. We need to show some trees in the b… .

EXERCISE 3

Each sentence has a word that isn't quite right. Replace it with the correct word.

➡ The shot showed a gang of dinosaurs.
   The shot showed a **herd** of dinosaurs.
1. The film was built on a novel of the same name.
2. The sound man passed two months in Australia.
3. There are electric walls around the park.
4. The attack takes part when it's raining.
5. Now the film is finally on our cinema boards.

EXERCISE 4

Put in a word from the same family.

➡ *Jurassic Park* was a great **success** (succeed) at the box office.
1. They used to photograph each separate … (move) that the puppet made.
2. That was the … (tradition) way of making films with monsters.
3. Spielberg found a new … (solve) to the problem.
4. Some parts of the model were controlled by … (hide) wires.
5. Next came a close-up … (shoot) of the T-rex's head.
6. The screams of the dinosaurs are a … (mix) of different animal screams.
7. I thought the effects were very … (real).
8. Drawing pictures to make a moving film is called … (animate).
9. The dinosaurs had been cloned by … (science).

EXERCISE 5

Translate this paragraph into good German.

The original *Jurassic Park* movie came out in 1993 and was a huge hit with cinema audiences. Directed by Steven Spielberg, the film tells the story of a visit to a theme park
5 which is being built on an island resort where dinosaurs have been cloned. A group of visitors, including the park owner's grandchildren, are taken on a tour. When a tropical storm hits the island, the dinosaurs
10 break down the fence and are then free to go after the humans. There are lots of scary scenes, including one where the two kids are trapped inside a car which is being attacked by a T-rex. In the end the main characters
15 survive of course. The appetite for dinosaur movies is still strong, and since this first adventure there have been several other *Jurassic Park* movies.

EXERCISE 6

What's your favourite movie? A movie magazine has offered a prize for the best explanation for why you like it so much. Write about 130 words and include as much of the following information as you can.

- the name of the film, the director and the stars
- what it's about
- the plot
- a good scene from the movie
- the ending
- your opinion of the film and why you like it, e.g. a good story, the characters, the actors, special effects

seventy-four

EXTRA PAGES Unit 3

It's a conspiracy

54

At the beginning of July 1947 there was an air accident near Roswell, New Mexico. Wreckage was found in the area and taken to the army airfield at Roswell. The army announced that
5 a UFO, what was then called a 'flying saucer', had crashed. The news caused an immediate sensation around the world. But on the same day the army changed its story and said that it was a weather balloon that had crashed and
10 not a UFO. However, it was obvious to those who saw the wreckage that this was untrue. Fifty years later the army admitted that both stories were lies. They said the wreckage had actually been a secret spy plane designed to
15 obtain information about Soviet nuclear tests. But was this new story true? Many people believe that the wreckage really was a UFO. They claim
20 that the army had taken the bodies of aliens from the vehicle and was carrying out
25 experiments on them.
What happened at Roswell was the start of a growing number of
30 UFO sightings and a great increase in public interest in the topic of UFOs and aliens. Reports of contact with aliens – close encounters of the third kind – became increasingly common. Stories of alien
35 abductions were told on television and in newspapers and magazines. In 1991 a survey found that, amazingly, five million Americans are abducted every year – that is if you believe their stories.

40 The first big abduction story happened in 1961. A couple from New Hampshire, Barney and Betty Hill, reported seeing a UFO while driving late at night. Later, under hypnosis, they remembered that aliens had taken them
45 onto the UFO and examined them before returning them to their car.

Alien abduction stories follow a pattern which has become familiar. The most common type of aliens are the 'grays'. A gray is short and
50 thin with gray skin, a large head, large eyes and a small nose. Abductions usually happen at night. A human is taken while in bed or while driving in a lonely place. If awake at the time, he or she falls into a dream-like state. He or she
10 is taken to a spaceship, put on a bed or table and examined by the aliens. This involves sticking needles into the victim. Afterwards the victim is given a tour of the spaceship or allowed to explore it. He or she is then taken
60 back to where the abduction took place. The victim often has no memory of what happened. People who were awake when abducted are aware of some 'missing time'. Memories of the abduction will
65 return under hypnosis.

What is behind all these reports of abductions? Can they be true? Or are they only stories
70 invented by people who simply want attention? Maybe they are fantasies or vivid dreams. Who knows?

75 Many Americans think UFOs are real. They believe the government is hiding evidence of alien contact from the public. Some people claim the government is
80 part of a conspiracy with the aliens to control the rest of humanity. Some say the purpose of the abductions is to obtain human DNA. The DNA is being used to create a race of alien-human hybrids who are going to take over the
85 world. This idea of alien rule is similar to other kinds of conspiracy theories. Most of these theories involve the idea of a small group of very powerful people who control the world and use humanity for their own evil purposes.

90 One of the strangest conspiracy theories comes from David Icke, a former TV sports presenter in England. He claims that the world is run by green lizards who came to Earth in human form thousands of years ago. His
95 lectures attract large audiences, especially in North America.

seventy-five **75**

Unit 3 EXTRA PAGES

You might think that UFOs, alien abductions and green lizards are just amusing stories. However, some people take them very seriously, even spending most of their time persuading others of the dangers from aliens. Even though the theories seem ridiculous, it is hard to be certain that they are all complete nonsense. But if conspiracy theories are just fantasies, then they could be dangerous. They might encourage people to avoid their responsibility. If everything is controlled by aliens, there is no point in trying to do anything about the problems of the world. Everything that goes wrong has a single simple explanation – it's a conspiracy.

EXERCISE 1

Answer the questions.

1. What three explanations has the US army given for the wreckage at Roswell?
2. Over the period 1950-2000, did the public interest in UFOs increase, stay the same or decrease?
3. Could the Hills remember what happened when they were abducted?
4. Are the many stories of alien abduction fairly similar or very different?
5. Do Americans believe stories about UFOs and aliens, or do they all think they are ridiculous?
6. Why might aliens stick needles into their victims?
7. What is a 'conspiracy theory'?
8. What negative effect could there be from a belief in conspiracy theories?

EXERCISE 2

Complete these tasks.

1. Invent a story of alien abduction that will get your name into the American newspapers. Write a report of at least 150 words and put in as many interesting details as you can.
2. Discuss the topic of alien abduction with your classmates. Do you think any or all of the stories could be true? Give reasons for your answer.

EXERCISE 3

Give your opinion of the conspiracy theories below. You can use expressions like these.

I think that's probably / possibly true.
That might be true because ...
I don't know. I've no idea if / whether ...
I doubt (if) that's true.
I don't believe that. It can't be true because ...
That's ridiculous.

1. In 1947, the US military seized the body of a dead alien who had landed in a spaceship at Roswell. They have kept the whole thing secret ever since.
2. Princess Diana was killed by British Intelligence because she was about to marry a Muslim. The car crash in Paris was no accident.
3. The Americans did not land on the moon in 1969. They knew it was impossible at that time, and so the whole thing was filmed in a studio.
4. The world is run by lizards in human form who came to Earth thousands of years ago. The US President and the British royal family are all lizards.
5. John F Kennedy was not killed by Lee Harvey Oswald in 1963. His murder was planned by the Central Intelligence Agency (CIA). Or possibly by Cubans or by the Mafia.
6. Adolf Hitler did not die in 1945. Years later he was running a seaside hotel in the south-west of England. In fact, his hotel was so awful that a writer who stayed there based a whole TV comedy series on the man he didn't realize was the former dictator.

EXTRA PAGES   Unit 3

EXERCISE 4

Read these two articles. They appeared in March 1999 in two British newspapers.

A *Britain not shaken by biggest earthquake*

A MAN walking around his bedroom 80 miles away felt the floor shake. For most of western Scotland, it was as if it hadn't happened. A few minutes after
5 midnight yesterday morning, the earthquake was recorded at four on the Richter scale, Britain's largest in five years. But for most residents of the Isle of Arran, three miles from the centre of the earthquake, it wasn't worth waking up for.

10 'It was big by British standards but tiny if you compare it to the big earthquakes in other parts of the world,' said John Lovell of the British Geological Survey. 'We would expect people to feel it, but it wasn't enough to damage buildings.' But in Shiskine,
15 in the south of Arran, where the earthquake was felt most strongly, Anne Purcell, aged 49, said she had feared the worst. 'I heard a strange noise then felt the house shaking. It was very scary.'

Britain has 200 to 300 earthquakes a year, but only
20 around two or three earthquakes a month are big enough for people to be aware of them. The Arran earthquake was the biggest in the region since 1927 and the largest in Britain since one in Norwich in 1994 hit 4.1 on the Richter scale.

B YOU ARRAN GOING TO LAUGH AT ME ANY MORE - ICKE 'PREDICTED' ISLAND EARTHQUAKE

CRAZY conspiracy detective David Icke
5 last night insisted his end of the world prediction was coming true after Arran was hit by an earthquake.
The former TV sports host was ridiculed after claiming eight years ago that the West Coast
10 island would be destroyed by a quake. 'Maybe people will stop laughing at me now,' he said. The ridiculous Icke, 46, said the quake was a definite sign of the end of the world. He said: 'I'm not at all surprised,
15 because there are great changes happening in the Earth's magnetic energy field. We're going to see a lot more of this kind of thing.'
The Arran quake just after midnight measured four on the Richter scale. It was the
20 biggest in the area for over 70 years, but no real damage was done.
Islander Audrey Allsop said she was terrified. 'I heard a noise and then the bed started shaking. I was quite frightened.
25 I thought the whole house might fall down a hole or something.'

1   Write a summary in two or three sentences giving the information contained in both articles.

2   The two articles treat the news of the earthquake rather differently. For each article, choose the one sentence which best expresses the main idea behind the story.
   a) It was a small earthquake compared to other countries, and there wasn't much damage.
   b) It was a big earthquake which terrified lots of people.
   c) David Icke claims that the earthquake shows that his prediction was correct.

3   In Britain there are popular newspapers called tabloids and more serious papers called broadsheets. Which article is from a tabloid and which is from a broadsheet?

4   Answer these questions about the articles.
   a) Which article makes more effort to include some human interest?
   b) Which article expresses an opinion about someone whose words it quotes?
   c) Which article tells us more about earthquakes?
   d) Would you rather read a tabloid or a broadsheet newspaper? Give reasons for your answer.

5   Most British people read a national daily newspaper: either a tabloid such as *The Sun* or *The Mirror*, or a broadsheet such as *The Times*. Some read a regional daily such as *The Western Mail*. They might also read a local paper which comes out once a week. In the cities there are daily evening papers as well. What about Germany? Is it different from Britain? Explain to an English friend what newspapers in Germany are like.

seventy-seven   **77**

Grey Owl

There's a one-room cabin beside Ajawaan Lake in the Prince Albert National Park in Saskatchewan, Canada. Lots of people visit the cabin, even though it's in a fairly remote place. The nearest road is twenty kilometres away, but you can get there by canoe, or you can walk to it along the Grey Owl Trail.

The cabin was once the home of Grey Owl, his wife Anahareo and their little daughter Dawn. In the 1930s the couple looked after a colony of beavers there. They turned their backs on a life of hunting and trapping and began a campaign for the conservation of nature and the Canadian wilderness. Grey Owl became a legend.

One day in 1938, during a lecture tour of Britain, Grey Owl was invited to speak at Buckingham Palace. The King and Queen and the young princesses, Elizabeth and Margaret, watched the films of Grey Owl's life in the wilderness. They listened as he spoke about the need to protect animals from extinction and to allow the Canadian Indians to follow their traditional way of life. Eleven-year-old Princess Elizabeth was fascinated by the handsome Indian with his long dark hair. When Grey Owl finished, she jumped up and begged him to go on.

But when the famous Grey Owl died not long afterwards, the royal family discovered that they had been tricked. Grey Owl wasn't an Indian at all. His real name was Archie Belaney, and he came from Hastings, a seaside town on the south coast of England. It was quite a sensation, and the newspapers were full of it.

Archie was born in 1888. His parents soon separated, and from the age of two he was brought up by two aunts in Hastings. His Aunt Ada was very strict with him. Archie escaped into a world of his own. It was a fantasy world where he was an Indian in the wilderness. He used to wander through the fields and woods around the town. He collected small animals and brought them home to his room. His favourite pet was a snake.

After he left school, Archie worked in a timber yard. He hated it. At 17, he left England for Canada to live among the Indians. He spent almost all his adult life in Canada.

Archie travelled to Northern Ontario. He found a job working for a man called Bill Guppy who was building a camp for tourists. Bill taught Archie some useful skills such as how to trap animals and how to handle a canoe. Archie learned how to survive in the wilderness. He worked as a guide and trapper. He went to live with some Ojibway Indians and married one of them, Angele Egwuna. He took an Indian name. He even looked like an Indian, with his long black hair, his sunburnt skin and his Indian clothes.

Archie married or lived with five different women, and he had four children. Sometimes he was married to two women at the same time. Archie didn't always obey the rules, and when he got into an argument, he was quick to pull out a knife. Once or twice he had to run away from the police. He drank a lot, too. In 1925 Archie met Anahareo, a 19-year-old Iroquois Indian, and she became his fourth wife. By then Archie had invented a new background for himself. He told people he had been born in Mexico of a Scottish father and an Apache mother. And everyone believed him, including his wife.

EXTRA PAGES   Unit 4

Conservation projects have also protected the elk and the buffalo

Ten years earlier, during the First World War, Archie had joined the Canadian army and fought in Europe. When he returned to Canada, he found that things were changing. More white men were invading the
5 wilderness. They brought machines to cut down the trees for timber. Beaver were being trapped in large numbers for their fur. The wildlife was suffering, and the environment was being destroyed. The Indians were losing their hunting grounds, and Grey Owl was
10 losing his dream.

Grey Owl was a hunter and trapper, but he knew there was something cruel in what he was doing. One day he found two young beavers whose mother had been caught in a trap. He gave them to Anahareo,
15 and she took them back to their cabin by the lake. The couple brought the beavers up as pets and started a beaver colony. Grey Owl decided to stop killing animals and to start saving them from extinction. He began to write articles and
20 books about his experiences and about the need for conservation. The idea of conservation seems very ordinary today, but Grey Owl was one of the first people to bring it to the attention of the world.
25 He obviously spoke from the heart, and his books were a great success.

Grey Owl died in 1938, exhausted after a lecture tour. It was then discovered that he was a fraud. It was a big scandal. But
30 many people doubted whether it really mattered. After all, everything else he said was true. And in the end Grey Owl probably believed his own story. Archie Belaney had truly become the Indian he
35 had always wanted to be.

EXERCISE 1

Complete the sentences in your own words.

1. There are lots of visitors to the cabin at the edge of Ajawaan Lake because … .
2. At Buckingham Palace Grey Owl showed … and talked … .
3. After Grey Owl died, people learned that … .
4. Archie's childhood wasn't very happy because … .
5. After Archie arrived in Canada, he learned … .
6. Archie's first wife … .
7. Archie looked like an Indian because … .
8. Archie sometimes broke the rules. For example, he … .
9. Anahareo believed that Archie … , but in fact … .
10. When Archie went back to Canada after the First World War, he felt … because … .
11. Archie's way of earning a living suddenly changed when … .
12. Archie was ahead of his time. He … .

EXERCISE 2

Comment on the sentences and say if you agree or disagree. Give a reason for your answer.

1. If Archie's parents hadn't separated, his life might have been very different.
2. Grey Owl was a hero because he started a campaign to protect the wilderness.
3. It's possible that Grey Owl believed his own story about his origins.
4. Princess Elizabeth was very stupid to think Archie was an Indian.
5. Grey Owl had killed lots of animals, so we shouldn't take his lectures about conservation seriously.
6. Whether or not Grey Owl was an Indian makes no difference to the truth of what he said.

seventy-nine 79

EXERCISE 3

Replace each phrase in italics with a word from the text. Use these words: *background, couple, environment, extinction, obviously, remote, strict, survive, wilderness.*

➤ Aunt Ada was very *keen that the rules should be obeyed*.
   Aunt Ada was very strict.
1 Archie learned how to *stay alive* in difficult conditions.
2 The *two married people* wanted to protect Canadian wildlife.
3 The princesses were fascinated by the man from the *wild country where there are no buildings and the land is not farmed*.
4 Grey Owl's cabin is rather *a long way from other places*.
5 Archie didn't tell the truth about his *origin and early life*.
6 The Indians treated the *world around them* with respect.
7 *As is easy to see*, Grey Owl meant what he said.
8 So many beavers had been killed that the animals were close to *dying out completely*.

EXERCISE 4

Write a paragraph about Grey Owl of the kind that you would find in a fact file. Give the basic information about him in 100-150 words.

EXERCISE 5

Here is some tourist information about Prince Albert National Park. Put in the missing words. Sometimes more than one answer is possible.

Prince Albert National Park covers a huge … . It is mainly wilderness. There are a large number of lakes, and you can travel … place to place by canoe on the lakes and rivers. The Grey Owl Trail leads to the cabin once lived … by the famous 'Indian' and his … Anahareo. The park has many camp sites … well as hotels. All the hotels and motels are in the village of Waskesiu, … only inhabited place in the whole park. The village lies along the southern … of the lake which shares … name. A number … trails begin here. You will also find an information centre, shops and a gas … . There is a beach, often … crowded in summer, and you can take a … trip on the lake or have a swim.

Prince Albert National Park, Saskatchewan

SONG, POEMS

Papa don't preach (Madonna)

Papa I know you're going to be upset
'Cause I was always your little girl
But you should know by now
I'm not a baby

5 You always taught me right
    from wrong
    I need your help, daddy
    please be strong
    I may be young at heart
10 But I know what I'm saying

The one you warned me all about
The one you said I could do without
We're in an awful mess, and I don't
    mean maybe – please

15 CHORUS

Papa don't preach, I'm in trouble deep
Papa don't preach, I've been losing sleep
But I made up my mind, I'm keeping my
    baby, oh
20 I'm gonna keep my baby, mmm …

    He says that he's going to marry me
    We can raise a little family
    Maybe we'll be all right
    It's a sacrifice

25 But my friends keep telling me
    to give it up
    Saying I'm too young, I ought
    to live it up
    What I need right now is some
30 good advice, please

    CHORUS

Daddy, daddy if you could only see
Just how good he's been treating me
You'd give us your blessing right now
35 'Cause we are in love, we are in love,
    so please

    CHORUS

Papa don't preach, I'm in trouble deep
Papa don't preach, I've been losing sleep

40 REPEAT

Oh, I'm gonna keep my baby, ooh
Don't you stop loving me daddy
I know, I'm keeping my baby
I know, I'm keeping my baby
45 I know, I'm keeping my baby

Green (Jennifer and Graeme Curry)

57 Sitting in the launderette,
    Delight and Carol, side by side,
    Watch their washing whirl around,
    Wishing it was done and dried.

5 Delight begins to paint her nails
    While Carol sits and stares.
    First vivid green, then silver specks,
    To match the shoes she wears.

    Then Carol says, 'That Stan of yours,
10 He's quite a guy, you know.
    We met him down the Rink last week –
    That day you didn't go.

    He really fancies Eth, he does,
    Don't say you hadn't heard.'
15 Delight begins to paint her toes,
    She doesn't say a word.

    'I think he asked her for a date –
    Of course, I couldn't swear –
    He never took his eyes off her,
20 That day that you weren't there.'

    Delight gets slowly to her feet,
    Walks up to Carol's machine,
    Tips the paint in the top of it,
    And watches her washing turn green.

Tug of War (John Kitching)

58 He buys me the latest fashion clothes,
    She's bought me a guitar.
    He's taking me to France this year,
    She's promised me a car.

5 He's giving me a puppy,
    She buys me Chinese meals.
    He asks me if I'm happy,
    She wonders what I feel.

    She doesn't live with father,
10 He doesn't live with her.
    They don't talk about each other:
    Their meeting won't occur.

    My father says he loves me,
    My mother says so too.
15 He takes me to the pictures,
    She takes me to the zoo.

    I stand between my parents,
    The red rag and the bull.
    I'm just a teenage tightrope:
20 Can't bear the tug and pull.

FAMILY AND FRIENDS

eighty-one **81**

STORY

Christmas in Hell by Arthur Gordon

I'm sitting in an uncomfortable, dirty hole in the ground. There are millions of holes in Europe and millions of men are sitting in them. I've seen so many men get killed. They too thought they would
5 be home for Christmas. The battlefield reaches from Switzerland to the North Sea. It is a huge open wound across the face of Europe. Nothing will ever be the same again.

Ra-ta-ta-ta, ra-ta-ta-ta, ra-ta-ta-ta.

10 I knew the sound. It was a German machine gun. It was the sound of death. The sound of the devil laughing at us.

'Excuse me, Sir. There is a message from headquarters, Sir. I've brought you
15 a nice cup of tea as well, Sir.' Sergeant Tompkins smiled at me. He was a fighting machine. He hated all Germans. He liked killing them. 'Good news, Sir?' he asked.

'Yes, Sergeant. It is good news. We are
20 going to stop fighting because it is Christmas. It's the time of peace. We are all Christians, and at Christmas Christians don't kill, Sergeant.'

Tompkins looked surprised. 'Do you
25 mean the Germans as well, Sir? Are the Germans God's children too, Sir? Just like us?'

Now I did not understand. 'What about the Germans, Sergeant?'

30 'I mean, they are psycho. They murdered babies when they invaded Belgium. We read all about it in the newspapers. The Germans aren't like us, Sir. They are horror. They're murderers.'

35 My God, I thought to myself. Tompkins actually believed our propaganda! He believed it! Now I could prove: being a soldier and being clever did not go together! I wanted to say something, but I was too tired. It was too late to
40 talk now. We should have talked before the war.

'Go and tell the men the good news, Sergeant. Tell them to be careful. Tell them to keep their heads down. The ceasefire begins in two hours. I don't want anyone to be killed at Christmas!'

45 It's Christmas Eve and it's very cold. The sky is very beautiful. Looking at the sky is better than looking at the battlefield. I can see my dreams in the sky. In my dreams, there is no blood and no mud. I'd like to go to sleep for a long time. I can see the Milky
50 Way. I wish I could fly up to the stars. Like a bird I would fly away.

> British and German soldiers together during an unofficial break in the fighting, Christmas 1914.

I would
leave this
55 hole in the ground.
Leave this ugly
battlefield. I would leave France below me.
I would go past the stars and on and on and on ...

STORY

Then I heard an angel singing! It had a very beautiful voice. It was high and clear. It was singing in a strange language, a language I did not understand. I always thought that angels sang in English. I mean,
5 God speaks English, so why don't angels sing in English? Then I understood. The angel was singing in German! Then I heard another voice.

I opened my eyes.
10 Sergeant Tompkins was standing beside me. He said, 'He's got a good voice, hasn't he, Sir? I mean, for a German.' It wasn't an angel that was singing,
15 it was a German soldier.

'Do you know the song, Sergeant?' I asked.

'Yes, Sir, it's Silent Night. A beautiful English Christmas carol.'

'The Germans think it's a German song.'

20 'Do they, Sir? Well that shows that they know nothing about music. They know nothing about real fighting either. They run like rabbits when they see an English gun and ...'

'Thank you, Sergeant. I don't want to hear any awful
25 details. You can go now.'

I turned and looked up at the stars again. I heard another fine voice. This time it was an English soldier. He was singing *Stille Nacht* in English. Then everything was silent again. Suddenly
30 someone was shouting. It was a German, I could tell from his accent. He was shouting in English. The German lines were only fifty metres away. 'Hello, Tommy', he shouted. None of our men answered. He tried again. 'Hello, Tommy,
35 Happy Christmas!'

This time one of our men answered.

'Happy Christmas, Fritz. What's the weather like over there?'

'Cold, Tommy. My feet are like ice. The
40 Kaiser has promised me a pair of woollen socks. He is making them for me himself. The Kaiser takes good care of his men!'

He was making a joke. We always thought
45 the Germans had no sense of humour. Soon everybody was laughing, all around me.

So the Germans laugh, too! I had almost forgotten they were humans, just like us.
50 The laughing stopped. I held out my hand. A big, white snowflake landed silently on my fingers. I watched it silently melting. My mother told me they were angel's tears. The moon was big and bright. Everyone was having a good time. Christmas was a
55 magic, special time for all.

The war lasted four more years. Millions and millions of young men were killed and wounded. Sergeant Tompkins was killed. I lost two brothers to the war machine. But I survived. Many people tell
60 me I was lucky. I am not so sure.

PROJECTS

1 The Aotearoa project

Get into groups and use the internet to find out:

- where Aotearoa is and what is special about its geography
- who its original inhabitants were
- what their traditional music is like (instruments, songs, dances)
- what language they speak (What does 'Aotearoa' mean? What other words or phrases can you find?)
- which legends belong to their culture
- how they are similar to and different from the Aborigines in Australia
- what problems they had in the past and what problems they have to face today

Make posters about the things you've found out using pictures you've printed out or copied, play some traditional music, make a dictionary of the words and phrases you've collected or tell the class about one of the legends you've found.

2 Help your teacher!

Do you remember Jessica from *Go Ahead 6* or the pony kids from *Go Ahead 7*? Now that you're going to leave school in a few months, you may feel like leaving something behind for everyone to remember you by.
You can now help your teacher by creating games, puzzles and quizzes that the lower classes might do in their English lessons, maybe as a part of a *Lernzirkel*.

If you're good at grammar, then you could concentrate on *if*-clauses, gerunds or tenses. If you know lots of vocabulary, then give them useful phrases to translate or let them look for synonyms, opposites or words from the same word families. Or would you like to ask them about English history, Irish traditions or any text you remember from your *Go Ahead* textbooks? No problem, you can choose whatever you want – and your teacher will be grateful for your help.

Use the textbooks *Go Ahead 5* to *10* and make a quiz, a memory game, a trimino, taboo cards for explanations of words, a domino puzzle, a board game, a fun run dictation or whatever you can think of. Your teacher will give you coloured paper and any other materials that you need.

REVISION

EXERCISE 1

Read this true story and then find the words in the text for the explanations below.

A married businessman booked into an Edinburgh hotel for a night. With him was a woman who was definitely not his wife. The man gave a false name. He said he was called Scott Anderson. Unfortunately for him, a man of this name had been the subject of a Crimewatch TV programme the week before. This programme is about crimes that the police cannot solve, and people watching are asked for their help. Scott Anderson was wanted by the police in connection with a murder. When the businessman gave the false name, hotel employees thought this must be the man. They even thought they recognized him. So they phoned the police. Police officers with guns rushed up to the third-floor bedroom, pulled the man out of bed and began to ask questions about the murder. He managed to persuade them that he wasn't Scott Anderson. The man and his friend then left immediately. The hotel is trying to find out who he really is as he left without paying his bill.

1 wrong, incorrect
2 a piece of paper showing how much money you have to pay
3 move very quickly
4 find an answer
5 having a husband or wife
6 because of bad luck
7 people who work for an organization
8 surely, certainly
9 know who someone is when you see them
10 try to make someone believe or do something

EXERCISE 2

Match the verbs to the sentences.

'Why don't we all go out?' Kate
'Hey, you! Come back!' the man
'It was my fault,' Ben
'It is dangerous to swim in the sea,' the notice
'I absolutely must have a rest,' Josh
'Don't make a sound,' Sophie
'I'll pay the money back next week,' Oliver
'You ought to do a course at college,' the teacher

admitted.
advised.
insisted.
promised.
shouted.
suggested.
warned.
whispered.

➡ 'Why don't we all go out?' Kate suggested.

EXERCISE 3

Put in these phrasal verbs: *bring out, carry out, give up, pull down, put on, slow down, take off, turn off.*

1 You're going too fast. You'd better … .
2 The band is going to … a new CD.
3 Why don't you … the music and concentrate on your homework?
4 It's freezing, so you'd better … some warm clothes.
5 It's getting warmer, so I think I'll … my coat.
6 They've decided to … the old cinema and put a supermarket in its place.
7 I've persuaded my dad to … smoking.
8 The scientists decided to … an experiment.

EXERCISE 4

Say which word has a meaning that includes the other three.

➡ history, maths, science, subject
  History, maths and science are all subjects.
➡ biscuit, egg, food, rice
  Biscuits, eggs and rice are all kinds of food.
1 4x4, truck, sled, vehicle
2 bean, tomato, potato, vegetable
3 ant, beetle, fly, insect
4 building, castle, church, factory
5 copper, iron, metal, steel
6 animal, badger, lizard, rabbit
7 disease, fever, flu, smallpox
8 barrel, container, jar, suitcase
9 accommodation, apartment, guest house, tent
10 blouse, garment, sweater, skirt

REVISION

EXERCISE 5

Look at the clues and find each pair of rhyming words.

▶▶ not asleep / you use it to slow down or stop
   awake / brake
1 how fast something is moving / give food to an animal
2 apples, oranges, grapes and so on / a jacket and trousers from the same material
3 get bigger / not high, close to the ground
4 a person who steals / something green that grows on a tree
5 not wet / someone who tries to get secret information about another country
6 something you imagine while you are asleep / what water becomes when it boils
7 what you use when you think / learn the skills of a job
8 go up / tell someone what you think they should do

EXERCISE 6

Answer the questions.

1 Which adjectives come from the same family as these nouns?
   centre, cloud, culture, danger, health, hope, horror, poison, politics, science
2 Which nouns come from the same family as these adjectives?
   dead, difficult, free, high, important, independent, necessary, poor, possible, violent
3 What are the opposites of these adjectives?
   correct, fair, fortunate, friendly, possible, violent
4 From the verb *dance* we can form the noun *dancer* meaning 'someone who dances'. What nouns of this kind can be formed from these words?
   bike, compete, crime, cycle, design, explore, gang, law, organize, politics, science, visit
5 Which nouns come from the same family as these verbs?
   advertise, answer, apply, arrive, behave, control, introduce, marry, perform, suggest, warn, weigh

   Be careful – two of the verb-noun pairs are twins, like *copy* (verb) and *copy* (noun).

EXERCISE 7

Form verbs by combining the parts of verbs from the two groups. Put a verb in each sentence below.

Group 1	Group 2
com • de • ex • in • pre • re	ceive • duce • fend • pare • pect • pete • plain • plore • serve • tend • vent • vite

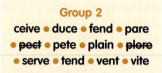

▶▶ I'm surprised because I didn't **expect** to see you.
▶▶ The animals wanted to **explore** their new territory.
1 Didn't you … Donna to your party?
2 What exactly do you … to do next?
3 The team is going to … in the World Championships.
4 We ought to … about the awful food.
5 We are sending the money, and you should … it soon.
6 The government hopes to … the number of people out of work.
7 I have to … a meal for ten people.
8 The drug will … the disease from developing.
9 We have to … ourselves against attack.
10 You've done really well. You … a medal.

EXERCISE 8

Put the two missing words in each sentence. The two words sound the same but are spelled differently.

▶▶ You'd better **write** the sentences again and get them **right** this time.
1 I … the ball to Chloe, but she missed it, and it went … the dining-room window.
2 On the DVD there's a … in the film that I haven't … before.
3 I was supposed to copy what was on the … , but I was just looking out of the window and feeling … with the lesson.
4 Six men spent the … day digging a … in the road.
5 I'll have to watch the … forecast and find out … it's going to rain tomorrow.
6 The tower was the only interesting … in the town, so when we'd seen it, we drove back to the camp … .
7 I … to New York, but the day after I arrived I came down with the … and had to stay in bed for three days.

86 eighty-six

REVISION

EXERCISE 9

Complete this true story by putting one word in each space. If you need to, you can look at these words: *airport, belief, Channel, destination, difficulty, enough, explained, knowledge, pleased, realize, reporters, seaside, sights, spent, visit.*

A Japanese tourist called Taro Tsuchida paid his first … to Britain recently. He … a few days seeing the … of London before taking a train from Paddington Station one evening. He was on his way to the … to catch a flight to Istanbul, his next … . Mr Tsuchida's … of English is not very good, and people were having some … understanding him. When he … carefully to a railway employee that he was going to Turkey, he was shown to a train. Unfortunately it was going to Torquay, a … resort in the south-west of England. As the train raced through the darkness, Mr Tsuchida imagined that it was taking him through the … Tunnel. Even when he had arrived in Torquay, he did not … his mistake. The police found him wandering around at two o'clock in the morning in the … that he was in Istanbul. The next day the police put him on a train. At Heathrow he found that he didn't have … money for his ticket to Istanbul. The newspaper … who had arrived to interview him were so … with this amusing story that they gladly gave him the few pounds that he needed.

EXERCISE 10

Which meaning does the word have in the sentence?

1 We'll come and **wave** you goodbye.
  a) *wehen* b) *Welle* c) *winken*
2 The Australians nearly always **beat** the English at cricket.
  a) *Rhythmus* b) *schlagen* c) *verrühren*
3 We'll take a short **break** now.
  a) *brechen* b) *Pause* c) *verstoßen gegen*
4 Our grandparents come and stay with us every **spring**.
  a) *Frühling* b) *Quelle* c) *springen*
5 It would be **fair** to divide the food equally between us.
  a) *gerecht* b) *Jahrmarkt* c) *schön*
6 We drove **past** our old house.
  a) *früher* b) *Vergangenheit* c) *vorbei*
7 Does this colour **suit** me, do you think?
  a) *Anzug* b) *passen* c) *stehen*
8 Do you **mind** if I sit here?
  a) *aufpassen* b) *etwas dagegen haben* c) *Verstand*

EXERCISE 11

Play by the rules

Gary Hopkins spent two weeks at a holiday camp in New South Wales. While he was there he had to follow some rules.

1 You may not leave the camp site without telling one of the instructors.
2 You may discuss your problems with one of the instructors at any time you like.
3 You must treat others as you would like to be treated yourself.
4 You can take part in up to four different activities.
5 Everybody must be in their tents by 10.30 pm.
6 You mustn't drink alcohol or smoke during your stay.

Gary wrote a postcard to his friend Mark to tell him how he felt about the summer camp. Complete the postcard and use substitutes for the modal verbs.

*Hi Mark
When I stayed at the summer camp, I wasn't allowed to leave the camp site without telling an instructor, and that was awful. But I …*

REVISION

EXERCISE 12

FILM PRODUCER TRIED TO SMUGGLE FROGS

In October 2003 the police arrested British film producer Michael Linley at Perth International Airport in Western Australia, after customs officials found 187 frogs, lizards and snakes in his suitcases. They also found 26 reptile eggs and some insects. Linley, producer of the British wildlife programme *Survival* faces a maximum sentence of ten years in jail for removing animals from Australia. Linley, who has worked for *National Geographic* and written several books on snakes and lizards, said he knew his actions were illegal. The animals were discovered by X-ray at the airport, following some secret information from a member of the public. The animals are now back in the wild.

Ask questions that go with the answers below.

➡ Film producer Michael Linley.
   Who did police arrest at Perth International Airport?
1 Customs officials.
2 In his suitcases.
3 26 reptile eggs and some insects.
4 Several books on snakes and lizards.
5 Because his actions were illegal.
6 By X-ray.
7 Back in the wild.

EXERCISE 13

A day in the life of an Australian police officer

Tiwi Islands

Tanya Woodcock is a police officer on the Tiwi Islands north of Darwin, Australia. This is a day in her life. Put in
5 the correct form of the words in brackets. Put the verbs into the simple present or present progressive.

Thirty-year-old Tanya … (work) among the 2,500 Aborigines who … (live) on the two islands. She … (try / mainly) to solve arguments within families or between the different local tribes. She
10 sometimes … (deal with / also) cheeky crocodiles and violent storms.

It's 6.30 in the morning now. Tanya … (bite / already) into one of the two mangoes she has picked from the two trees behind the house, which … (belong) to her and her husband Danny. 'Some days I … (get up) and I … (know) it's going to be as hot as hell,' she says.

It's eight o'clock and Tanya … (walk / now) the 40 metres to the police station. She … (spend /
15 usually) an hour checking the computer system to see if anything has happened during the night.

By 10 am the temperature has risen to 33 degrees Celsius. Now Tanya … (drive) out to the various communities. It's a 95-mile round trip. Normally Tanya … (not / have) time for lunch because there … (usually / be) quite a lot to do.

It's 3 pm already and Tanya … (still / talk) to some
20 village elders. But by 4 pm Tanya has said her goodbyes and … (return) to the station. She … (work) from Monday to Friday unless there's a violent storm. Then she … (have to / work) long hours telling people what to do in a state of emergency. 'I … (plan) to produce a
25 video showing people how to behave during a storm', she says. 'And I … (want) to play it on the local TV station.'

By 8 pm Tanya … (cope with) a different problem: nobody has cooked dinner. Tanya's husband … (work) as a fishing guide and also … (lead) a busy life. So
30 sometimes neither of them … (find) time to cook.

88 eighty-eight

REVISION

EXERCISE 14

As time goes by

Twenty years ago these people went to the same school in London. Make sentences using the present perfect with *since* or *for*.

➡ Mark studies Chinese. (three years)
Mark **has studied** Chinese **for three years**.
1 Peter lives in New Zealand. (1998)
2 Jane and Gary own a private plane. (2001)

3 Oliver doesn't see Fiona these days. (last August)
4 Ken works in Canada. (1997)
5 Zoe doesn't have a boyfriend now. (five months)
6 Rob teaches French and German. (six years)

EXERCISE 15

Advertisements

Fill in
the correct
prepositions.

*Are you frightened
... (1) spiders?
Are you scared ... (2)
poisonous snakes?
Are you bored ... (3) rabbits,
hamsters and other pets?
If you are crazy ... (4) insects
and lizards, please come to
CREEPYCRAWLIES, a zoo
which is famous ... (5) its
frightening wildlife.*

ARE YOU INTERESTED ... (6)
COMPUTERS?
ARE YOU SICK ... (7) YOUR
BORING JOB?
ARE YOU FULL ... (8)
BRILLIANT IDEAS?
ARE YOU KEEN ... (9)
WORKING WITH FRIENDLY
COLLEAGUES?
MEGA COMPUTERS IS
LOOKING ... (10) A
PROGRAMMER. APPLY NOW.

Are you fond ... (11)
raw fish?
Are you fed up ... (12)
burgers and chips?
Our Japanese
restaurant is different
... (13) other
Japanese restaurants.
And our staff are
very good ... (14)
helping you to relax.
Just book a table at the
Tsunami.

EXERCISE 16

Lots of advice

Ron doesn't behave very well at school. Here's what people tell him. Put in the correct prepositions.

1 You must concentrate ... your homework.
2 Try to arrive ... school ... time.
3 Don't laugh ... other pupils.
4 This computer game isn't yours. Who does it belong ... ?
5 You should listen ... your teachers.

6 Why do you spend all your pocket money ... sweets?
7 Please apologize ... your teacher ... not writing your essay.
8 What happened ... your school bag?
9 You have to be nice ... your sister. Why don't you help her ... her homework.

EXERCISE 17

Here is the news

Use the verbs in their correct active or passive form.

Yesterday morning the west coast of Spain ... (pollute) by oil. The pollution ... (must/cause) by an oil tanker. Fortunately most of the sea birds which ... (cover) with oil ... (can/rescue). Officials say the beaches ... (clean) up very soon.

Last night an American bank in Turkey ... (damage) by a car bomb. People ... (hear) the explosion five miles away. Five people ... (die) immediately and several others ... (injure). They ... (take) to hospital. Two of them ... (already/leave) hospital after they ... (treat) by doctors. Minutes before the explosion two young men ... (see) running away from the car.

Detectives say a murdered couple who ... (kill) in their home in Cornwall were victims of a personal attack. It is possible the couple ... (know) their killers, police said. George Fisher ... (shoot) twice in the hall of his house near Wadebridge, Cornwall, on bonfire night. His wife ... (hit) by three bullets. Detective James Winsley ... (say) a safe in the house ... (find) open with a key in the door and a small amount of cash inside. It is not known what, if anything, ... (steal) from the house.

eighty-nine **89**

LITERATURE

CONTEMPORARY LITERATURE IN THE ENGLISH LANGUAGE

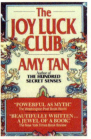

Stories, plays and poems in English were first written in the British Isles, and American, Australian and Canadian literature all developed from this tradition. English literature has now become international and writers from many different countries
5 influence each other. Let's look at some contemporary authors from around the world.

Many writers leave their native countries to live and work in other parts of the English-speaking world. **Frank McCourt**, for example, was born to Irish immigrants in New York in 1930, but
10 moved to the slums of Limerick, Ireland at the age of four. Frank's mother, Angela, had no money to feed the children since Frank's father rarely worked, and when he did, he spent his wages on drink. 'Worse than the ordinary miserable childhood is the miserable Irish childhood,' wrote Frank McCourt in
15 *Angela's Ashes*. 'Worse yet is the miserable Irish Catholic childhood.' In 1953 Frank returned to New York, where he taught in various high schools and colleges for thirty years.

Frank McCourt
born 1930

Amy Tan
born 1952

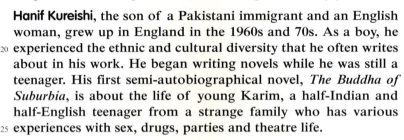

Hanif Kureishi, the son of a Pakistani immigrant and an English woman, grew up in England in the 1960s and 70s. As a boy, he
20 experienced the ethnic and cultural diversity that he often writes about in his work. He began writing novels while he was still a teenager. His first semi-autobiographical novel, *The Buddha of Suburbia*, is about the life of young Karim, a half-Indian and half-English teenager from a strange family who has various
25 experiences with sex, drugs, parties and theatre life.

Anglo-Indian writer **Salman Rushdie** was born in Bombay, India. At the age of fourteen he was sent to school in England. Salman continued his studies in Cambridge. After graduating, he worked for a Pakistani TV company before he became a British
30 citizen. *Midnight's Children*, one of his best-known novels, deals with the history of India from 1910 to 1976 seen through the eyes of Saleem Sinai, who was born at midnight at the moment of India's independence.

Hanif Kureishi
born 1954

Michael Ondaatje
born 1943

In 1949, four Chinese women, recent immigrants to
35 San Francisco, begin meeting in order to eat, play and talk together. They call themselves the Joy Luck Club. With great sensibility Chinese-American author **Amy Tan** examines the deep connection between four mothers and their daughters and describes the immigrant experience in the US. *The Joy Luck
40 Club* has become one of America's best-known books.

Michael Ondaatje was born in Sri Lanka in 1943. He moved to Canada at the age of 19. He is perhaps best known for the screen version of his novel *The English Patient*. Set at the end of World War II, this novel explores the lives of four very different people
45 who are hiding in a damaged house near Florence. In an upstairs room lies a badly burnt English patient who is alive but unable to move. His strange adventures and his love affair in the North African desert change forever the lives of those around him.

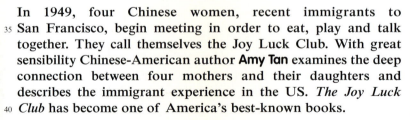

Salman Rushdie
born 1947

Margaret Atwood
born 1939

LITERATURE

V.S. Naipaul
born 1932

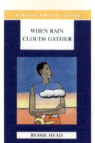

Bessie Head
1937-1986

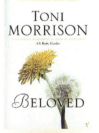

Toni Morrison
born 1931

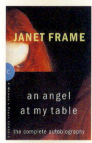

Janet Frame
1924-2004

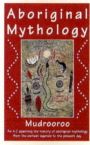

Mudrooroo
born 1938

Ian Rankin
born 1960

Margaret Atwood was born in 1939 in Ottawa and is perhaps best known for her novels. *The Blind Assassin* is a story within a story. The book starts with the death of Iris's sister Laura, who drives her car off a bridge ten days after the end of World War II. Then it moves into a science fiction story which is told by two lovers. When Iris returns to the story it is 1947 and her husband has just been found dead on his boat.

V.S. Naipaul was born in Trinidad in 1932. He went to England on a scholarship in 1950. His novel *A Bend in the River* is almost as much reportage as fiction. It is set in the city of Kisangani, on the Congo River. Salim, a young Indian from the east coast has bought a shop there and tries to build up his business in the days after independence. The Europeans have been forced to leave, and the scene is one of chaos, violent change, war, and poverty.

When Rain Clouds Gather, the novel by **Bessie Head** from South Africa, is based on her own experiences. It tells the story of a black South African refugee named Makhayo who crosses the border into Botswana. Head's topics include social and political change, the role of traditional African chiefs, religion, science, race relations, and male-female relations.

At the centre of **Toni Morrison's** novel *Beloved*, which earned her the 1988 Pulitzer Prize for fiction, is an act of horror: A woman murders her little daughter rather than let her become a slave. The woman is Sethe, and the novel tells the story of her journey from slavery to freedom during and immediately following the American Civil War.

With her autobiography, *An Angel At My Table*, New Zealander **Janet Frame** managed to turn seven years of personal nightmare into a beautiful book about her own life. Because of a wrong diagnosis, Frame spent eight years in mental hospitals. She narrowly escaped a brain operation when one of her stories won a prize. This caused her doctors to change their minds.

Born in 1938 as Colin Johnson in Narogin in Western Australia, **Mudrooroo** wrote *Wild Cat Falling*, his first novel. Wildcat, a young Aborigine is freed from jail only to be returned two days later suspected of murder. In his book *Aboriginal Mythology* Mudrooroo tells the history of the Australian Aborigines from the earliest legends to the present day and gives a summary of their culture, ceremonies, beliefs and religion. In 1988, he changed his name.

Ian Rankin, who was born in Scotland, did a number of different things before becoming a writer – he looked after pigs, sang in a punk band and studied English Literature at Edinburgh University. His Edinburgh police detective John Rebus is an unfriendly, dark and sad person. In *The Falls*, he's almost certain that missing student Philippa Balfour is dead, but he's less sure how she died or what the tiny doll in a little coffin that turns up near the Balfour family home has to do with the case.

ninety-one 91

DICTIONARY WORK

Have you got any idea what 'fair' means? Are you sure you can understand the word in these eight sentences? Perhaps you can guess some meanings from the context or from similar German words.

1 He's got fair hair and blue eyes.
2 It's not fair that he's allowed to go and I'm not!
3 We've had a fair amount of sunshine this week.
4 She's got a fair chance of winning.
5 They took the kids to the fair.
6 Fair weather was forecast for the following week.
7 'We'll meet at seven.' – 'Fair enough.'
8 The book fair in Leipzig begins next week.

Now use the dictionary text on the right and try to find the correct explanations for 'fair' in the sentences.

What information does a dictionary give me?

Try to find examples in the dictionary extracts.

1 variants: colour (BE) color (AE)
2 pronunciation: mood [muːd] blood [blʌd]
3 part of speech: pig noun, see verb, bright adj, suddenly adv, etc
4 grammar: information (U) (= uncountable)
5 definition: class a group of students who are taught together
6 examples: hill Their house is on a hill overlooking the sea.
7 word partners: to do homework (not: to make homework)
8 synonyms: first-class syn: excellent
9 opposites: poor opp: rich, wealthy
10 idioms: I fear I can't make it (= come) on Saturday.
11 phrasal verb: to put up with (= to accept an unpleasant situation or person without complaining)

Try to find the correct German translations for 'colour' in the following sentences.

1 You shouldn't let one bad experience colour your feelings about everything.
2 What colour is your car? – Green.
3 Colour the picture at home.
4 You'll meet people of all colours and religions in New York.
5 When her eyes suddenly met his, she started to colour slightly.
6 I stayed at home because I was feeling a bit off colour.
7 On Australia Day most buildings have the national colours flying.
8 It's a busy area, full of activity and colour.

fair¹ /feə/ **adj, adv 1** appropriate and acceptable in a particular situation: *That's a fair price for that house.* ● *I think **it's fair to say that** the number of homeless people is increasing.* **2 fair (to/on sb)** treating each person or side equally, according to the law, the rules, etc: *That's not fair – he got the same number of mistakes as I did and he's got a better mark.* ● *It wasn't fair on her to ask her to stay so late.* ● *a fair trial* ••▶ opposite for senses **1** and **2 unfair 3** quite good, large, etc: *They have a fair chance of success.* **4** (used about the skin or hair) light in colour: *Chloe has fair hair and blue eyes.* **5** (used about the weather) good, without rain

IDIOMS **fair enough** (*spoken*) used to show that you agree with what sb has suggested
fair play equal treatment of both/all sides according to the rules: *The referee is there to ensure fair play during the match.*
(more than) your fair share of sth (more than) the usual or expected amount of sth: *We've had more than our fair share of trouble this year.*

fair² /feə/ **noun** [C] **1** (also **funfair**) a type of entertainment in a field or park. At a fair you can ride on machines or try and win prizes at games. Fairs usually travel from town to town. **2** a large event where people, businesses, etc show and sell their goods: *a trade fair* ● *the Frankfurt book fair*

from *Wordpower*

Remember that many words have more than one meaning. The first meaning is not always the one you want. Read through all the different meanings.

col·our¹ (*AmE* **color**) /ˈkʌlə(r)/ *Nomen* **1** Farbe ◊ *The garden was a mass of colour.* Der Garten war ein Farbenmeer. ◊ *Her hair is a reddish brown colour.* Sie hat rötlich-braune Haare. ◊ *Colour flooded her face when she remembered it.* Sie wurde ganz rot, als sie daran dachte. ◊ *His face was drained of colour.* Er sah sehr blass aus. ◊ (*fig*) *people of different political colours* Leute aus verschiedenen politischen Lagern **2** Hautfarbe ◊ (*bes AmE*) *a person of colour* ein(e) Farbige(r) ☞ *Hinweis bei* FARBIG **3** Tönung ☞ *Siehe auch* WATERCOLOUR **4** [U] Farbe, Kolorit, Atmosphäre ☞ *Siehe auch* LOCAL COLOUR **5 colours** [Pl] (*bes BrE*) Flagge **IDM off 'colour** *nicht vor Nomen* (*umgs*) **1** (*BrE*) ◊ *Jo seems a little off colour today.* Jo scheint sich heute nicht so ganz gut zu fühlen. **2** (*bes AmE*) (*Witz*) schlüpfrig **see the colour of sb's 'money** (*umgs*) ◊ *I want to see the colour of his money first.* Ich will erst mal sein Geld sehen. ☞ *Siehe auch* FLYING¹, NAIL² *und* TRUE¹
col·our² (*AmE* **color**) /ˈkʌlə(r)/ *Verb* **1** (aus)malen, färben ◊ *He drew a monster and coloured it red.* Er zeichnete ein Ungeheuer und malte es rot an. **2** ~ (**at sth**) (über etw) erröten **SYN** BLUSH² **3** beeinflussen **PHR V ˌcolour sth 'in** (*mit Farbe ausfüllen*) etw ausmalen

from *Das große Oxford Wörterbuch für Schule und Beruf*

92 ninety-two

Use this extract from the German-English dictionary and complete the sentences.

1 Brown isn't my favourite … .
2 She's been lying in the sun all day. Now she's got a nice … .
3 When we went inside the old house, we saw that the … was coming off the wall.
4 The Easter eggs were boiled in red … .

Farbe 1 colour, (*AmE*) color ◊ *Die Farbe Blau steht ihr gut.* Blue is a colour that suits her. ◊ *Welche Farbe hat dein Auto?* What colour is your car? ◊ *Die Abbildungen sind in Farbe.* The illustrations are in colour. ◊ *Er bekam wieder Farbe ins Gesicht.* The colour came back into his cheeks. ◊ *die Farbe wechseln* change colour **2** (*gebräunter Teint*) tan ◊ *Du hast ganz schön Farbe bekommen.* You've got a good tan. **3** (*zum Anstreichen*) paint; (*zum Färben*) dye ◊ *Farbe dünn auftragen* apply a thin coat of paint **4** (*Kartenspiel*) suit **IDM Farbe bekennen** come clean
farbecht colour fast, (*AmE*) color fast

from *Das große Oxford Wörterbuch für Schule und Beruf*

- It is not always possible to translate word for word:
  We had better hurry up.
  ~~Wir hatten besser eilen auf.~~
  Wir müssen uns beeilen.
- Word order is often different in German:
  He often phones at the weekend.
  Er ruft oft am Wochenende an.
- Pay attention to prepositions:
  They were on holiday.
  Sie waren im Urlaub.
- Different use of adverbs, verbs, nouns:
  They love eating Chinese food.
  Sie essen gerne chinesisch.

> **A few things to remember**

TRANSLATION PRACTICE

- Different use of tenses:
  How long have you been waiting?
  Wie lange wartest du schon?
- German uses more active than passive sentences:
  A lot of cheese is produced in this area.
  In dieser Gegend produziert man viel Käse.
- When you have finished translating the text, check if it sounds like German – or more like English with German words.

Translate the following text into good German.

A pair of golfers finished their round of golf after leaving the course to rescue people trapped in a burning flat not far away. After helping to rescue four people, Tommy Kirk and Jimmy Gray returned to
5 finish their round at Blairbeth Golf Club in Cathkin, near Glasgow. The two men dropped their clubs, climbed a barbed wire fence and ran across a road after noticing the fire in the flat near the club's 11th hole. Three children were on the balcony, in their
10 pyjamas, and Tommy and Jimmy climbed onto a lower balcony to reach them, says the *Daily Record*. They managed to lower them to safety. They then evacuated the other flats in the block before kicking down the door of the burning flat, where the
15 children's father was unconscious. Unfortunately, they were beaten back by the flames.
Tommy said: 'The girl was really upset when she was told that her dad was still inside. It all happened so quickly and we were just glad the man was saved
20 by firefighters.'
After the rescue, Tommy and Jimmy returned to the course and continued their game. Jimmy said: 'I ended up having a terrible round. My hands just wouldn't stop shaking.'

There is a similar word in German.
You already know the noun 'rescue'.

'club' doesn't mean *Club* here

You have to use a clause in German.
There is a similar word in German.

Be careful: 'lower' isn't a comparative.
There is a similar word in German.

Try to understand this word through the context.
Personal passive: You can't say it like this in German.

You'll have to say this differently in German.

ninety-three **93**

SPEAKING PRACTICE

PART 1
General conversation

In this first part you have to ask your partner some personal questions, for example about daily life, school, his/her home town, jobs, family, etc.

Exercise

Work with a partner and pretend that you don't know each other. Ask questions to find out as much information as possible about each other. You can ask questions like these:

- *What's your name?*
- *What's your surname?*
- *Can you spell it, please?*
- *Where do you live?*
- *What do you enjoy doing in your spare time?*

TIPS

- Try to be confident and relaxed.
- Speak clearly so that your partner can hear you.
- When you answer a question, try to give some details.
- Remember the word 'because'. It'll help you to give reasons.
- Don't just give one-word answers.

Revise the letters of the alphabet. You may be asked to spell a word in English.

PART 2
Responding to visual prompts

In this part you have to talk on your own about a photo. Your partner will also get a photo about a similar topic. You should show that you can say something about the photo even if you don't know all the words in English.

Exercise

You are going to talk about two photos from films. Partner **A** should look at photo **A** and describe it. Then partner **B** will do the same with photo **B**. Before you start, think about the following questions:

- *Where does the scene take place?*
- *What are the people doing?*
- *What do you think about the photos?*
- *Who are the people?*
- *What type of film is it?*

TIPS

- Look at your photo for a few seconds and think about what you can say.
- Try to talk about everything you can see in the photo. Don't forget to mention small details.
- Describe everything with suitable adjectives. Don't just name the things you can see.
- Try to keep talking until your teacher tells you to stop.

Now you and your partner will have a conversation. You should both talk for the same amount of time.

Exercise

The photos above show scenes from films. Talk to each other about the kinds of films you prefer and the actors you like best and the films and actors you don't like.

TIPS

- Look at and talk to your partner, not your teacher.
- Show interest in what your partner says and add to the conversation.
- Don't get angry if you don't agree with your partner.
- Keep to the topic.

SPEAKING PRACTICE

PART 3

Simulated situation

In this final part you'll have to deal with an everyday situation. You have to make and respond to suggestions and you have to agree or disagree. You must take turns with your partner and towards the end of your conversation you should agree on a choice. Pictures will give you some ideas for the task.

Exercise

You are organizing a jumble sale in your town. Decide together which place would be the most suitable for it. Here are some pictures with some ideas to help you.

TIPS

- Don't talk all the time. Give your partner the chance to talk too.
- Look at the pictures and say as much as possible about each one before you come to a decision.
- Don't say that you don't know how to say something. Always try to find a different way to say what you want to express.
- Remember that you and your partner have to agree on something to complete the task.

new* car park = *Parkplatz*

PAIR WORK

UNIT 1 Exercise 21

Partner **B**: Look at the map of New Zealand. Find out from your partner what the missing names are. You can use phrases like this in your questions.

What's the name of ...?   in the western part of ...
on the east coast of ...   in the middle of ...
to the north-east of ...   in the centre of ...

UNIT 2 Exercise 22

Partner **B**: You and your partner are writing a science fiction story together. You are inventing e-travel – a method of getting your hero from one side of the world to the other in a few seconds. There are some details that you are not sure about. Look at your notes and ask your partner.

The hero has to travel from London to Sydney. He gets into (what?). The machine records the position of all his atoms. The body plan is sent to the destination (how?). The body is attacked by lasers and separated into its individual atoms. The atoms (what happens to them?). In Sydney the atoms are put together exactly as shown in the body plan. The hero has arrived (how quickly?).

Start like this: *What does the hero ... ?   How ... ?   What ... ?*

UNIT 3 Exercise 20

Partner **B**:
You and your partner are thinking of going to an activity centre for a week. Ask Partner **A** about the missing activities.

	Morning	Afternoon	Evening
Mon	?????	Golf	?????
Tues	Keep fit	?????	Barbecue
Weds	?????	Basketball	?????
Thurs	Judo	?????	Chess
Fri	?????	Football	?????
Sat	Trampolining	?????	Party

- You like acting. Find out if you'll get a chance to do any.
- You are wondering if anything exciting happens on the two evenings you don't know about.
- You'd like to try some new sports such as hockey and archery. Find out if you can.
- Ask if you'll get a chance to explore the country around the activity centre.
- Find out what happens at all the other times.

UNIT 4 Exercise 23

Describing your surroundings

Partner **B**: Listen to your partner's description of his / her surroundings. Make notes while you listen. Write the information in your table. If necessary, ask your partner some questions so that you get all the details.

Then imagine you are walking in the country on an expedition for your Duke of Edinburgh Award. Describe your surroundings and the awful weather. Invent as much detail as you can. Your partner might want to ask you some questions.

96   ninety-six

Grammatical terms — Grammatikalische Fachausdrücke

active ['æktɪv]	Aktiv, Tatform	*We **bought** the new radio.*
adjective ['ædʒɪktɪv]	Eigenschaftswort, Adjektiv	*big, good, bad, dangerous, expensive, …*
adverb ['ædvɜ:b]	Adverb	***very** big, **quickly**, …*
adverb of frequency [ˌædvɜ:b əv 'fri:kwənsi]	Adverb der Häufigkeit	*always, often, never, usually, …*
adverb of manner [ˌædvɜ:b əv 'mænə]	Adverb der Art und Weise	*carefully, slowly, well, …*
article ['ɑ:tɪkl]	Geschlechtswort, Artikel	*a, an, the*
auxiliary verb [ɔ:gˌzɪliəri 'vɜ:b]	Hilfsverb	***don't** know, **is** swimming, **has** seen*
by-agent ['baɪeɪdʒənt]	Urheber einer Handlung im Passivsatz	*The phone was invented **by Bell**.*
clause [klɔ:z]	Teilsatz	***He was late** because he missed the last bus.*
comparative [kəm'pærətɪv]	Komparativ, erste Steigerungsform	*big**ger**, **better**, **more** interesting, …*
comparison of adjectives [kəmˌpærɪsn əv 'ædʒɪktɪvz]	Steigerung der Adjektive	*big – big**ger** – big**gest**; **as** big **as**, big**ger than***
compound ['kɒmpaʊnd]	Kompositum, zusammengesetztes Wort	*bus driver, teacup, waiting-room*
conditional [kən'dɪʃənl]	Konditional	*I **wouldn't** do that.*
conditional sentences [kənˌdɪʃənl 'sentənsɪz]	Bedingungssätze	*If you **went** to Prince Albert National Park, you **could** see Grey Owl's cabin..*
conjunction [kən'dʒʌŋkʃn]	Bindewort, Konjunktion	*and, or, but, after, when, …*
consonant ['kɒnsənənt]	Mitlaut, Konsonant	*b, c, d, f, g, k, …*
contact clause ['kɒntækt klɔ:z]	Satz ohne Relativpronomen	*The girl **he met** was Lisa.*
direct object [daɪˌrekt 'ɒbdʒɪkt]	direktes Objekt, Akkusativobjekt	*He drinks **milk**. She gave him **a present**.*
emphasizing pronoun [ˌemfəsaɪzɪŋ 'prəʊnaʊn]	verstärkendes Pronomen	*I saw the accident **myself**.*
future with *going to* ['fju:tʃə]	Futur mit *going to*	*I'm **going to leave** now.*
future with *will* ['fju:tʃə]	Futur mit *will*	*I **will come** tomorrow.*
***if*-clause** ['ɪfklɔ:z]	*if*-Satz, Bedingungssatz	***If you ask me,** I'll tell you.*
imperative [ɪm'perətɪv]	Befehlsform, Imperativ	***Listen** to me. **Don't talk** to your neighbour.*
indirect object [ˌɪndaɪrekt 'ɒbdʒɪkt]	indirektes Objekt, Dativobjekt	*She gave **her father** a present.*
indirect speech [ˌɪndaɪrekt 'spi:tʃ]	indirekte Rede, nichtwörtliche Rede	*Kim said (that) she liked Westerns.*
infinitive [ɪn'fɪnətɪv]	Grundform, Infinitiv	***to go, to see, to eat, to run, to work**, …*
***ing*-form** ['ɪŋfɔ:m]	*-ing*-Form	*sing**ing**, danc**ing**, sitt**ing**, …*
irregular verb [ɪˌreɡjʊlə 'vɜ:b]	unregelmäßiges Verb	*do – **did** – **done**, buy – **bought** – **bought**, …*
long form ['lɒŋ fɔ:m]	Langform	*He **is** reading. She **does not** work.*
main clause ['meɪn klɔ:z]	Hauptsatz	***Peter isn't at school** because he's ill.*
main verb ['meɪn vɜ:b]	Vollverb	*work, dance, read, write, play, …*
modal auxiliary [ˌməʊdl ɔ:g'zɪliəri]	Modalverb	*can, must, could, might, ought to, …*
negative question [ˌneɡətɪv 'kwestʃn]	verneinter Fragesatz	***Don't** you **like** beans?*

ninety-seven **97**

Grammatikalische Fachausdrücke

negative statement [ˌnegətɪv ˈsteɪtmənt]	verneinter Aussagesatz	*Emily **doesn't like** tennis.*
noun [naʊn]	Nomen, Substantiv	*house, book, tea, plan, idea, …*
object [ˈɒbdʒɪkt]	Satzergänzung, Objekt	*She likes **pop music**.*
***of*-phrase** [ˈɒvfreɪz]	Fügung mit *of*	*the name **of the game***
passive [ˈpæsɪv]	Passiv, Leideform	*The gangster **was caught** (by the police).*
past participle [ˌpɑːst ˈpɑːtɪsɪpl]	Partizip Perfekt	*John has **called**. She hasn't **eaten** anything.*
past perfect [ˌpɑːst ˈpɜːfɪkt]	*past perfect* (Plusquamperfekt)	*I **had seen** the film before.*
past progressive [ˌpɑːst prəˈgresɪv]	Verlaufsform der Vergangenheit	*She **was reading**. We **were watching** TV.*
personal passive [ˌpɜːsənl ˈpæsɪv]	persönliches Passiv	*I **was offered** some sweets.*
personal pronoun [ˌpɜːsənl ˈprəʊnaʊn]	persönliches Fürwort, Personalpronomen	*I, you, she, … , me, us, them, …*
phrasal verb [ˌfreɪzl ˈvɜːb]	Verbindung Verb–Adverb, Verb–Präposition	*to fill **in**, to put **on**, to take **away**, …*
plural [ˈplʊərəl]	Mehrzahl, Plural	*book**s**, letter**s**, dog**s**, wom**e**n, chil**dr**en, f**ee**t*
positive [ˈpɒzətɪv]	Positiv, Grundform des Adjektivs	*good – better – best, **interesting** – more interesting – most interesting*
positive statement [ˌpɒzətɪv ˈsteɪtmənt]	bejahter Aussagesatz, Erzählsatz	*I **speak** English and French.*
possessive adjective [pəˌzesɪv ˈædʒɪktɪv]	adjektivisch gebrauchtes, besitzanzeigendes Fürwort, Possessivpronomen	*my, your, his, her, its, our, your, their*
possessive form [pəˌzesɪv ˈfɔːm]	besitzanzeigende Form, *s*-Genitiv	*Adam**'s** computer, his friend**s'** books*
possessive pronoun [pəˌzesɪv ˈprəʊnaʊn]	nominal gebrauchtes Possessivpronomen	*mine, yours, his, hers, ours, yours, theirs*
preposition [prepəˈzɪʃn]	Verhältniswort, Präposition	*in, at, on, with, because of, …*
preposition of direction [prepəˌzɪʃn əv dəˈrekʃn]	Präposition der Richtung	***to** school, **onto** the table, **into** the water, …*
preposition of place [prepəˌzɪʃn əv ˈpleɪs]	Präposition des Ortes	***at** the bus stop, **on** the wall, **in** the house, …*
preposition of time [prepəˌzɪʃn əv ˈtaɪm]	Präposition der Zeit	***at** seven o'clock, **on** Sunday, **in** winter, …*
prepositional verb [prepəˌzɪʃnl ˈvɜːb]	Präpositionalverb, Verbindung Verb–Präposition	*to look **after**, to listen **to***
present participle [ˌpreznt ˈpɑːtɪsɪpl]	Partizip Präsens	*He is **going** home. It's **freezing** cold.*
present perfect [ˌpreznt ˈpɜːfɪkt]	*present perfect* (Perfekt)	*We **have finished** the lesson.*
present perfect progressive [ˌpreznt pɜːfɪkt prəˈgresɪv]	Verlaufsform des *present perfect*	*We **have been reading** for two hours.*
present progressive [ˌpreznt prəˈgresɪv]	Verlaufsform des Präsens	*I **am watching** TV.*
pronoun [ˈprəʊnaʊn]	Fürwort, Pronomen	*I, me, himself, this, …*
proper noun [ˌprɒpə ˈnaʊn]	Eigenname	*Mr Smith, Munich, the Thames*
propword [ˈprɒpwɜːd]	Stützwort	*Do you want the red **one** or the green **ones**?*
question [ˈkwestʃn]	Frage, Fragesatz	***Is Adam at school?** – No, he isn't. – **Where is Adam?***

98 ninety-eight

Grammatikalische Fachausdrücke

question tag ['kwestʃn tæg]	Frageanhängsel	*It's cold today, **isn't it?***
question word ['kwestʃn wɜːd]	Fragewort	*what, when, where, who, whose, why, which, how*
reflexive pronoun [rɪˌfleksɪv 'prəʊnaʊn]	Reflexivpronomen, rückbezügliches Fürwort	*He hurt **himself.***
regular verb [ˌregjʊlə 'vɜːb]	regelmäßiges Verb	*call – called – called, …*
relative clause [ˌrelətɪv 'klɔːz]	Relativsatz	*The girl **who phoned** was Mary.*
relative pronoun [ˌrelətɪv 'prəʊnaʊn]	Relativpronomen	*who, that, which, whose*
reported speech [rɪˌpɔːtɪd 'spiːtʃ]	indirekte Rede, nichtwörtliche Rede	*Kim said (that) she liked Westerns.*
sentence ['sentəns]	Satz, Satzgefüge	*Do you know if she is coming to our party?*
short answer ['ʃɔːt ɑːnsə]	Kurzantwort	*I love Star Trek. Do you speak French?*
short form ['ʃɔːt fɔːm]	Kurzform	*Do you understand? – **Yes, I do.***
		I've got a rabbit. She's over there.
		*– **I can't** see her.*
simple past [ˌsɪmpl 'pɑːst]	einfache Form der Vergangenheit	*I called Katie. She **bought** a new skirt.*
simple present [ˌsɪmpl 'preznt]	einfache Form des Präsens	*She **reads** love stories every day.*
singular ['sɪŋgjʊlə]	Einzahl, Singular	*book, letter, dog, woman, child, foot*
statement ['steɪtmənt]	Aussage, Aussagesatz	*She likes cats. I don't like dinosaurs.*
subject ['sʌbdʒɪkt]	Satzgegenstand, Subjekt	***Jessica** likes maths. **The girl over there** is Sophie.*
subject question ['sʌbdʒɪkt kwestʃn]	Frage nach dem Subjekt	***Who** phoned you?*
superlative [suːˈpɜːlətɪv]	Superlativ, höchste Steigerungsform	***biggest**, **best**, **most** interesting, …*
tense [tens]	grammatische Zeit, Tempus	*present tense, past tense, …*
time [taɪm]	(wirkliche) Zeit	*past, present, future*
to-infinitive ['tuːɪnˌfɪnətɪv]	Grundform mit *to*, *to*-Infinitiv	***to** go, **to** see, **to** eat, **to** run, **to** work, …*
verb [vɜːb]	a) Zeitwort, Verb	*be, love, play, get up, … ; can, will, do, …*
	b) Satzaussage, Prädikat	*She **likes** yoghurt. We **can play** cards.*
vowel ['vaʊəl]	Vokal, Selbstlaut	*a, e, i, o, u*
word order ['wɜːd ɔːdə]	Wortstellung	*subject – verb – object (S – V – O)*
yes/no-question [jes'nəʊ kwestʃən]	Entscheidungsfrage	***Is Adam at home?** – Yes, he is. / No, he isn't.*

UNIT 1

GRAMMATIKANHANG

1 verb tenses | Zeitformen des Verbes

a the simple present | Das simple present

An adult koala **eats** about one kilogram of eucalyptus leaves **every night**.
Why don't koalas **normally drink** anything?

Canberra **is** the capital of Australia.
The land around Canberra **belongs** to sheep farmers.

Jake Roberts **likes** basketball, weight training and surfing.
He **thinks** *Rabbit-Proof Fence* is boring.

The next train to Sydney **leaves at 8.17 pm.**

wird verwendet für

◆ regelmäßige Vorgänge und Gewohnheiten, die oft mit Häufigkeitsadverbien wie *always, never, often, sometimes, usually, every afternoon, on Tuesdays* verbunden sind. (Das Fressen von Eukalyptusblättern gehört zu den **Gewohnheiten** der Koalas.) (Warum trinken Koalas **normalerweise** nichts?)

◆ Dauerzustände und Tatsachen, die durch Verben wie *be, belong, cost, need, own, seem* ausgedrückt werden.

◆ Gedanken und Gefühle, die durch Verben wie *believe, know, like, prefer, think, understand, want* ausgedrückt werden. (Es wird gesagt, was Jake Roberts **fühlt** und **denkt**.)

◆ etwas in der Zukunft Festgelegtes oder einen Fahrplan, meist zusammen mit Zeitangaben wie *tomorrow, at twelve-thirty*. (Der Zug fährt **laut Fahrplan** zu dieser Zeit ab.)

b the present progressive | Das present progressive

Look, the koala **is eating** some leaves **at the moment**.

The Australian Prime Minister **is having** lunch with some foreign visitors **on Friday**.

wird verwendet

◆ bei Vorgängen und Handlungen, die gerade stattfinden, oft zusammen mit *now, at the moment, just …*. (Das Fressen der Blätter findet **jetzt gerade** statt und ist noch nicht vorbei.)

◆ um auszudrücken, dass für die Zukunft etwas fest geplant ist. Meist mit einer Zeitangabe wie *next Monday, on Tuesday, tomorrow*. (Das Essen ist für kommenden Freitag **fest geplant**.)

Grammatikanhang UNIT 1

Das simple past

wird verwendet, um

◆ über Vergangenes zu sprechen. Es kommt oft in Berichten, Geschichten und Erzählungen vor. Es bezieht sich auf eine abgeschlossene Handlung oder ein abgeschlossenes Geschehen in der Vergangenheit. Es wird daher meist mit Zeitbestimmungen wie *yesterday, last year, last summer, a year ago, in 1985* gebraucht. (Man möchte wissen, **wann** sie den Kontinent erreichten.)

Beachte: Im Deutschen wird oft das Perfekt verwendet, während im Englischen das *simple past* erforderlich ist:
We **watched** a documentary about kangaroos last night.
(… haben uns … angesehen.)

the simple past c

European explorers **landed** in Australia **in the 18th century**.

When did the government **remove** mixed-race children from their families?

Das past progressive

wird verwendet um auszudrücken, dass

◆ etwas zu einem bestimmten Zeitpunkt in der Vergangenheit gerade geschah. Meist wird es mit Zeitangaben der Vergangenheit wie *yesterday, at four o'clock …* gebraucht. (Zu diesem **Zeitpunkt** in der Vergangenheit war er noch nicht mit dem Surfen im Internet fertig.)

◆ eine Handlung gerade stattfand, als ein zweites Ereignis einsetzte. (Die Männer **schwammen gerade** vor der Küste von Queensland, **als** die Haie sie **plötzlich** angriffen.)

the past progressive d

At five o'clock Josh **was** still **surfing** on the internet.

Two young men **were swimming** off the coast of Queensland **when** a group of sharks **attacked** them.

one hundred and one **101**

UNIT 1   Grammatikanhang

e   **the present perfect**

I'**ve just bought** a guide book about Australia and New Zealand.

They'**ve closed** the Sydney Harbour Bridge for repairs. People have to use the ferry to get to the northern parts of the city.

Have you **ever been** to New Zealand?

How long **have** you **been** in Christchurch?
I'**ve been** here **for five days / since Monday**.

Das present perfect

wird verwendet um auszudrücken, dass etwas geschehen ist. (Wann ist unwichtig!)
Das *present perfect* bezieht sich in der Regel auf **Zustände** oder **Resultate**. Es steht, wenn

◆ etwas gerade beendet ist, der Zeitpunkt aber nicht näher festgelegt wird. Meist wird es mit *just, yet …* gebraucht.
(Der Reiseführer wurde **gerade eben** gekauft und ist jetzt in meinem Besitz.)

◆ etwas in der Vergangenheit stattgefunden hat und Auswirkungen auf die Gegenwart hat. (Die Brücke ist **jetzt** geschlossen und man kann sie nicht benutzen.)

◆ etwas schon einmal oder bis jetzt noch nie geschehen ist. Es steht oft mit *ever, never, before, not … yet, already …* . (Bist du **bis jetzt schon einmal** dort gewesen?)

◆ etwas in der Vergangenheit begonnen hat und jetzt noch andauert. Es steht oft mit *how long?, for, since*. (**Wie lange** schon bis jetzt?)

Beachte: *for* + Zeitraum; *since* + Anfangspunkt

f   **the present perfect progressive**

She **has been lying** on the beach **for three hours**.

Das present perfect progressive

bezieht sich in der Regel auf **Tätigkeiten**. Es wird verwendet um

◆ auszudrücken, dass ein Vorgang in der Vergangenheit angefangen hat und über einen Zeitraum bis jetzt andauert. Es steht oft mit *all day, since 5 o'clock …* . (Es wird betont, **wie lange** sie schon am Strand liegt.)

g   **the past perfect**

After they **had visited** the Australian Museum, they **went** to Bondi Beach.

Das past perfect

wird verwendet um auszudrücken, dass

◆ eine Handlung vor einer anderen oder vor einem bestimmten Zeitpunkt in der Vergangenheit stattfand. Es steht oft mit *after, before* und in Verbindung mit dem **simple past**. (Die Besichtigung des Museums **liegt weiter zurück** als der Aufenthalt am Strand.)

102   one hundred and two

going to   (a plan)
will   (a sudden idea)
...sent progressv (a fixed plan)
...mple present (a timetable)

Workbook 10 / S. 6 Nr. 14

Grammatikanhang   **UNIT 1**

Das future mit „will"

the future with 'will'   **h**

wird verwendet, um

◆ eine Vorhersage über etwas zu machen, auf das man keinen Einfluss hat.
(Er sagt das Wetter voraus, kann es aber **nicht beeinflussen**.)

The weather forecast says it **will rain** in Brisbane next weekend.

◆ eine spontane Entscheidung zu treffen oder ein Angebot zu machen. Es steht häufig mit *I think …* / *Well, … .*
(Ich **entscheide** mich **spontan** etwas zu trinken.)

'The phone is ringing.' '**I'll answer** it.'
I think **I'll have** another glass of Australian wine.

Das future mit „be going to"

the future with 'be going to'   **i**

wird verwendet um auszudrücken, dass

◆ jemand etwas vor hat und dies schon entschieden ist.
(Ich habe mich **entschieden** und habe die **Absicht** im nächsten Sommer zu tauchen.)

I'm going to do some diving near the Great Barrier Reef next summer.

◆ etwas bald geschehen wird, da es schon Anzeichen dafür gibt.
(Man kann vorhersagen, dass das Wetter schön wird, da es schon **Anhaltspunkte** gibt.)

There isn't a cloud in the sky. It**'s going to be** a nice day.

Das Passiv

the passive   **2**

Hat ein Aktivsatz ein Objekt (*the boomerang*), so kann man normalerweise einen Passivsatz daraus bilden. Das Objekt des Aktivsatzes wird Subjekt des Passivsatzes.

SUBJECT	VERB	OBJECT

The Aborigines **invited**   the boomerang .

The boomerang **was invited** **by** the Aborigines.

Das Subjekt des Aktivsatzes ist der Verursacher (*agent*) der Handlung. Möchte man den *agent* im Passivsatz erwähnen, kann er mit *by* (*by-agent*) angehängt werden.

Im **Aktivsatz** wird gesagt, **wer** (oder **was**) **etwas tut**. Das Subjekt des Aktivsatzes führt die Handlung aus.
Im **Passivsatz** wird hervorgehoben, mit **wem** (oder **womit**) **etwas geschieht**. Im Passivsatz wird also etwas mit dem Subjekt getan.

J.A. Birchall made the world's first notepad (*Notizblock*).

The first notepad was made in Australia.

one hundred and three   **103**

UNIT 1   Grammatikanhang

a   tenses

SIMPLE PRESENT
Christmas parties **are held** on Bondi Beach every year. (... *werden ... abgehalten*)

SIMPLE PAST
A party **was held** last year.
(... *wurde ... abgehalten*)

PRESENT PERFECT
A Maori festival **has** finally **been held**.
(... *ist ... abgehalten worden*)

PAST PERFECT
A music festival **had been held** earlier.
(... *war ... abgehalten worden*)

WILL FUTURE
A film festival **will be held** soon.
(... *wird ... abgehalten werden*)

MODAL VERBS
More festivals **should be held**.
(... *sollten abgehalten werden*)

Zeitformen

Passivformen werden mit Formen von *be + past participle* (Partizip Perfekt) gebildet.

Nach einem Modalverb (*can, may, must ...*) bildet man das Passiv mit *be + past participle*.

b   the passive: progressive forms

PRESENT PROGRESSIVE PASSIVE
A new film **is being made** in New Zealand.
(... *wird gerade ... gedreht*)

PAST PROGRESSIVE PASSIVE
Jane **was being watched** by a crowd of people.
(... *wurde gerade ... beobachtet*)

Verlaufsformen im Passiv

Im Passiv sind *progressive forms* nur im *present* und *past* üblich. Sie werden jeweils mit *being* gebildet.

is/are/am + being + past participle

was/were + being + past participle

c   verbs with two objects

SUBJECT	VERB	IND. OBJ	DIR. OBJ
The guide	showed	us	the path.
We	were shown		the path.

SUBJECT	VERB	IND. OBJ	DIR. OBJ
They	gave	us	special boots.
Special boots	were given		to us.

Verben mit zwei Objekten

Verben, die im Aktiv gewöhnlich mit zwei Objekten verbunden werden (*give, offer, tell, pay, promise, send, show, teach, lend*), bilden meist ein **persönliches Passiv**, d.h. das **indirekte Objekt** (Person) des Aktivsatzes wird zum Subjekt des Passivsatzes.

Es ist auch möglich, das **direkte Objekt** (Sache) des Aktivsatzes zum Subjekt des Passivsatzes zu machen. Das **persönliche Passiv** wird jedoch bevorzugt.

Grammatikanhang | **UNIT 2**

Partizipien	participles	1

Formen

Es gibt zwei Arten von Partizipien:

◆ Mit dem *present participle* (Partizip
Präsens) werden *progressive forms*
(Verlaufsformen) gebildet.

Das *present participle* endet bei allen Verben
auf *-ing*: *looking, taking* … .

◆ Mit dem *past participle* (Partizip Perfekt)
bildet man
– das *present perfect*
– das *past perfect*

– alle Passivformen.

Bei regelmäßigen Verben endet das *past
participl*e auf *-ed*: *looked, waited* … .
Unregelmäßige Verben haben besondere
Formen: *taken, seen* … (siehe S. 120–121).

Partizipien vor einem Nomen

Viele Partizipien können wie Adjektive **vor**
einem Nomen stehen.

Sie können auch mit einem anderen Wort ein
zusammengesetztes Adjektiv bilden.

Relativsätze mit einem Partizip

Partizipien stehen **nach** dem dazugehörigen
Nomen, wenn sie durch ein Objekt (*young
people*) oder eine adverbiale Ergänzung (*for an
e-business company*) erweitert sind (**erweiterte
Partizipien**). Sie entsprechen in diesem Fall
einem **Relativsatz**.

---

forms · a

Computers **are getting** better all the time.
Samuel **was writing** a new program when I
phoned him.
He **has been working** on it for five days now.

VERB	PRESENT PARTICIPLE
attack	attack**ing**
explore	explor**ing**

Samuel **has created** lots of different websites.
He **had** already **done** his homework before
breakfast.
Suddenly he **is interrupted** by his alarm clock.

VERB	PRESENT PARTICIPLE
finish	finish**ed**
need	need**ed**
teach	**taught**
see	**seen**

participles before a noun · b

A **beeping** alarm clock interrupts him.
Will he get through the **required** amount of work?

Samuel is a **hard-working** whiz-kid.
FAQ means **frequently asked** questions.
He wants to find a **well-paid** job in Silicon Valley.

relative clauses with participles · c

Companies **employing** young people often don't
want to pay them a lot of money.
   (= **who** employ …)

Kim is one of the teenagers **working** for an
e-business company.
   (= **who** work …)

one hundred and five · 105

UNIT 2   **Grammatikanhang**

Teenagers **working** part-time often don't have any other hobbies.
(= **who** work …)

Samuel develops online forms **used** by customers.
(= **which** are used …)

He works for a company **called** Nets@les.
(= **which** is called …)

Programs **created** by whiz-kids are very popular.
(= that **are/were/have been created** …)
Kids **earning** a lot of money might have even more success in the future.
(= who **earn/are earning** …)

Das *present participle* hat dabei immer eine **aktive** Bedeutung: Teenager, die Teilzeit arbeiten.

Das *past participle* hat eine **passive** Bedeutung: Formulare, die verwendet werden.

Beachte: Partizipien verkürzen Sätze. Trotz der Bezeichnungen (*present participle*, *past participle*) werden beide Formen verwendet, um über die Vergangenheit, Gegenwart und Zukunft zu sprechen. Sie stehen für:

◆ unterschiedliche Zeitformen

◆ die *simple* oder *progressive* Form.

d   participles after certain verbs

Samuel **was sitting** in his office **staring** at the computer. (*… und starrte auf …*)
Kim **walked** round the park **looking** for her cousin.
(*… und suchte …*)
When her cousin noticed her, he **came running** towards her. (*… kam er … angerannt*)
Kim **went shopping** after her last lesson.
(*… ging … einkaufen*)

Partizipien nach bestimmten Verben

Das *present participle* steht nach Verben der Ruhe und Bewegung wie *sit, stand, stay, lie, come, go*.

Im Deutschen werden die Partizipien unterschiedlich wiedergegeben.

e   participles in clauses of reason

Feeling completely exhausted, Samuel went to bed.
(= **Because he felt** completely exhausted …)

Attracted by the money they can earn, more teenagers want to work for e-businesses.
(= **As they are attracted** by the money …)

Not knowing what to do, the adult programmers gave up.
(= **As they didn't know** what to do …)

Partizipien in Nebensätzen des Grundes

Partizipialsätze können dazu dienen, **Nebensätze des Grundes zu verkürzen**. Sie finden sich häufiger in geschriebenem Englisch. Das *present participle* entspricht einem **Aktivsatz**.

Das *past participle* entspricht einem **Passivsatz** (siehe **C**).

Das Subjekt des Hauptsatzes ist auch Subjekt des Partizipialsatzes (*Samuel, more teenagers*).

Verneinte Partizipialsätze werden gebildet, indem man *not* vor das Partizip stellt.

Partizipien in Nebensätzen der Zeit

Partizipialsätze können auch **Nebensätze der Zeit** verkürzen.
Das Subjekt des Hauptsatzes ist auch Subjekt des Partizipialsatzes (*Kim*).

Beachte: Partizipialsätze der Zeit können auch durch eine **Konjunktion** eingeleitet werden.

Manchmal ist eine Konjunktion nötig, um die genauen Zeitverhältnisse darzustellen.

Ohne Konjunktion ist oft nicht eindeutig zu erkennen, ob der Partizipialsatz Gründe oder zeitliche Zusammenhänge anführt.

participles in clauses of time   f

Surfing the internet, Kim found an interesting website.
  (= **When she surfed** …)

After doing his homework, Samuel went back to his computer.
  (*Nachdem er … gemacht hatte, …*)

While writing his program, Samuel talked to his customers.
  (*Während er … schrieb, …*)
Before writing his program, Samuel talked to his customers.
  (*Bevor er … schrieb, …*)

Kim got quite burnt **sitting** in the sun.
  (…, *als/während/da Kim … saß.*)

Bedingungssätze

Bedingungssätze geben die **Bedingung** an, unter der ein bestimmtes Ereignis stattfindet. Bedingungssätze bestehen aus dem Nebensatz mit *if* (*if-clause*) und einem Hauptsatz (*main clause*).

conditional sentences   2

If we **go** to Cornwall, we **can do** some surfing.

If-Sätze: Typ 0
(Jedesmal wenn, dann …)

IF-SATZ	HAUPTSATZ
simple present	*simple present*

Diese *if*-Sätze drücken aus, dass etwas als **logische Folge** immer wieder so passiert.

if-clauses: type 0   a

IF-CLAUSE	MAIN CLAUSE
If you **don't water** a plant,	it **dies**.

UNIT 2   **Grammatikanhang**

b if-clauses: type 1 (open condition)

IF-CLAUSE	MAIN CLAUSE
If we **follow** the path,	we**'ll** find them.
If we **go** up here,	we **can** see the waterfall.
If you **want** to protect our environment,	you **must** save energy.
If you **want** to find out more about the Eden Project,	**look** at our website.

If-Sätze: Typ 1 (Was ist, wenn …)

IF-SATZ	HAUPTSATZ	
	will	+ Infinitiv
	can	+ Infinitiv
simple present	*must/might*	+ Infinitiv
	Befehlsform	

Diese *if*-Sätze drücken aus, was unter bestimmten Bedingungen geschehen **wird**, **kann** oder **soll**.

c if-clauses: type 2 (unreal condition)

IF-CLAUSE	MAIN CLAUSE
If I **had** a lot of money,	**I'd** do more to help the rainforests.
If you **went** to Cornwall,	you **could** visit the Eden Project.
If he **tried** again,	he **might** succeed.

If I were you, I**'d call** the police.
(**Ich** an deiner Stelle würde …)

If-Sätze: Typ 2 (Was wäre, wenn …)

IF-SATZ	HAUPTSATZ	
	would	+ Infinitiv
simple past	*could*	+ Infinitiv
	might	+ Infinitiv

In diesen *if*-Sätzen ist die Bedingung **nicht** oder **wahrscheinlich nicht** erfüllbar.

Beachte: die Redewendung *If I were you …*

d if-clauses: type 3 (imaginary past action)

IF-CLAUSE	MAIN CLAUSE
If you **had watched** *Die Another Day*,	you **would have** seen the Humid Tropics Biome.
If the boys **hadn't got** lost,	the four **could have** gone together.
If you **had been** in St Austell in 2000,	you **might have** still seen the old claypit.

If-Sätze: Typ 3 (Was wäre gewesen, wenn …)

IF-CLAUSE	MAIN CLAUSE	
	would have	+ *past participle*
past perfect	*could have*	+ *past participle*
	might have	+ *past participle*

In diesen *if*-Sätzen bezieht sich die Bedingung auf die Vergangenheit. Sie ist **nicht mehr erfüllbar**.

e sentence structure

We **can** stay inside	**if** you **like** the biome.
If there **was** an earthquake,	the bamboo house **wouldn't** fall down.

Satzbau

Steht der Hauptsatz am Anfang, so steht vor *if* kein Komma.

108   **one hundred and eight**

Konjunktionen

conjunctions

Konjunktionen sind Bindewörter. Man unterscheidet:

◆ **nebenordnende Konjunktionen**

Sie verknüpfen Wörter, Satzglieder oder Hauptsätze. Dazu gehören:

and	und
or	oder
but	aber, sondern
both … and	sowohl … als auch
not only … but also	nicht nur …, sondern auch
either … or	entweder … oder
neither … nor	weder … noch

Would you like tea **or** coffee?
We could go to the Eden shop **and** relax in the café.
I'd like to stay **but** I'm too busy.

Tigers **and** snakes live in the rainforest.
Most people visit Eden in July **or** August.
Eden is quite expensive **but** very interesting.
You can visit **both** the Humid Tropics Biome **and** the Warm Temperate Biome.
The education centre is **not only** open on weekends **but also** during the holidays.
It's **either** a lizard **or** a snake.
Neither Alex **nor** Josh was at the waterfall.

◆ **unterordnende Konjunktionen**

Sie stehen vor einem Nebensatz und verbinden ihn mit dem Hauptsatz.

Man unterscheidet:

After they had climbed the path, they could see the waterfall.

CONJUNCTIONS OF TIME

after	nachdem	**not … until**	erst wenn	**when**	wenn, als
as	als, während	**since**	seit	**whenever**	immer wenn
as soon as	sobald	**till/until**	bis		
before	bevor	**while**	während, erst wenn		

CONJUNCTIONS OF REASON

as	da, weil	**because**	weil	**since**	da, weil

CONJUNCTIONS OF PURPOSE

to	um zu	**so as to**	so dass
in order to	um zu	**so that**	so dass

CONJUNCTIONS OF CONDITION

if	wenn, falls	**as long as**	sofern, solange	**what if**	was wäre, wenn
unless	wenn nicht	**even if**	selbst wenn	**if only**	wenn … nur

OTHER CONJUNCTIONS

although/though	obwohl	**as if**	als ob	**while**	obwohl
		that	dass	**whether/if**	ob

UNIT 3   Grammatikanhang

1 infinitive and ing-form / Infinitiv und -ing-Form

In the 1960s young people **tried to shock** the older generation.

Rachel **enjoys listening** to Justin Timberlake.
It's **no use complaining** about youth culture.
I'm thinking **of going** to Australia.

Young people **need** money **for buying**/**to buy** clothes, CDs, etc.
Most people **hate working**/**to work** at weekends.

Nach Verben und anderen Wortarten stehen sowohl der Infinitiv als auch die -*ing*-Form.

Nach **Präpositionen** folgt in der Regel die -*ing*-Form.

Nach einigen **Verben** können beide Formen verwendet werden, ohne dass sich die Bedeutung verändert.

2 the infinitive / Der Infinitiv

You **can buy** the CD on the internet.

You **had better ask** your parents.
She **would rather be** a pop star.

Mr Bean always **makes** me **laugh**.
Her parents never **let** her **go out** during the week.

We didn't know **what to do**.
She wasn't sure **where to go** after the pop concert.

He **decided to wear** bell bottoms.

Es gibt zwei Arten des Infinitivs.

Der **Infinitiv ohne** *to* steht nach

◆ Modalverben:
   can, could, may, might, must, needn't, ought to, shall, should, will, would

◆ *had better* (sollte)
   would rather (möchte lieber)

◆ *make* + Objekt (veranlassen)
   let + Objekt (zulassen)

Der *to*-**Infinitiv** steht nach

◆ einem Fragewort:
   how, what, when, where, which

◆ bestimmten Verben:

agree	zustimmen	**fail**	es nicht schaffen	**refuse**	sich weigern
arrange	verabreden, festlegen	**forget**	vergessen	**seem**	scheinen
		hope	hoffen	**try**	versuchen
can afford	sich leisten	**intend**	beabsichtigen	**used**	(tat) früher immer
can't wait	nicht erwarten können	**learn**	lernen		
		manage	schaffen können	**want**	wollen
choose	beschließen	**offer**	anbieten	**wish**	wünschen
decide	sich entschließen	**plan**	planen	**would like/**	möchte gern
expect	erwarten	**promise**	versprechen	**would love**	

110   one hundred and ten

Grammatikanhang **UNIT 3**

- bestimmten Verben + Objekt:

The USA **expected young men to fight** in Vietnam.
He **reminded me to send** him an e-mail.

advise	raten	forbid	verbieten	teach	lehren
allow	erlauben	force	zwingen	tell	befehlen
ask	bitten	help	helfen	want	wollen, dass
cause	verursachen	invite	einladen	warn (not)	warnen
enable	befähigen	persuade	überreden	would like/	möchte gerne,
encourage	ermutigen	remind	erinnern an	would love	dass
expect	erwarten	recommend	empfehlen		

- Nomen oder Pronomen

They have **time to go** shopping in the afternoon.
Where can I find **something to eat**?

- einem Adjektiv und seinen Steigerungsformen sowie in Verbindung mit *too* und *enough*

Are they all **ready to start** work?
It was **easier** not **to ask** any questions.
She was **too old to care** about the latest fashion.

- nach Ordnungszahlen

  Superlativen

  only

Elvis was the **first** pop star **to become** really famous.
They are the **most interesting** pop group **to sing** at the festival.
The **only** girl in my class **to wear** a miniskirt was Fiona.

- nach Nomen + *for* + Nomen/Pronomen: *chance, mistake, need, opportunity*

There's no **opportunity for the fans to meet** their heroes.

- nach Adjektiv + *for* + Nomen/Pronomen: *difficult, easy, important, necessary, possible, usual*

It's **usual for teenagers to wear** trendy clothes.

- nach *too/enough* + Adjektiv + *for* + Nomen/Pronomen

The job is **too hard for a teenager** (**to do**).

- nach Verb + *for* + Nomen/Pronomen: *arrange for, call for, prepare for, wait for*

They are **waiting for him to return**.

- um einen Zweck auszudrücken: *to/in order to* (um zu)

Lots of young people work (**in order**) **to earn** money.

one hundred and eleven **111**

UNIT 3   **Grammatikanhang**

3   the ing-form

Die -ing-Form

Die -*ing*-Form steht als *gerund.* (Zur -*ing*-Form als *present participle* siehe S. 105–107.)

Looking after Andy isn't always a pleasant task.

I like **talking** to people.

What do you think **of smoking**?

She is **excited about going** to college.

◆ als Subjekt (Das Aufpassen auf …)

◆ als Objekt (… das Reden)

◆ nach einer Präposition

◆ nach bestimmten Adjektiven + Präposition:

be afraid of	Angst haben vor	**be happy about**	glücklich sein über
be angry about	verärgert sein über	**be interested in**	interessiert sein an
be aware of	sich bewusst sein	**be keen on**	gerne tun
be bad at	schlecht sein in	**be nervous of/about**	Angst haben vor
be capable of	fähig sein zu	**be pleased about**	erfreut sein über
be crazy about	verrückt sein nach	**be proud of**	stolz sein auf
be different from	sich unterscheiden von	**be responsible for**	verantwortlich sein für
be excited about	aufgeregt sein wegen	**be successful in**	erfolgreich sein in
be famous for	berühmt sein für	**be tired of**	genug haben von
be fond of	mögen	**be used to**	gewöhnt sein an
be good at	gut sein in	**be worried about**	sich Sorgen machen um

He likes the **idea of doing** nothing.

◆ nach bestimmten Nomen + Präposition:

advantage of	Vorteil (von)	**idea of**	Idee (zu)
chance of	Gelegenheit (zu)	**interest in**	Interesse (an)
choice between	Auswahl zwischen	**opportunity of**	Gelegenheit (zu)
danger of	Gefahr (zu)	**reason for**	Grund für
hope of	Hoffnung (auf)	**way of**	Art und Weise (zu)

This is the best **way of doing/to do** it.
We had no **chance of getting/to get** tickets.

Beachte: *way* und *chance* können auch mit dem *to*-Infinitiv verwendet werden.

I must **apologize for hurting** your feelings.

◆ nach bestimmten Verben + Präposition:

agree with	einverstanden sein mit	**feel like**	Lust haben auf
apologize for	sich entschuldigen für	**insist on**	bestehen auf
approve of	einverstanden sein mit	**look forward to**	sich freuen auf
believe in	glauben an	**pay for**	zahlen für
complain about	sich beschweren über	**prevent from**	hindern an
count on	zählen auf	**succeed in**	Erfolg haben mit
concentrate on	sich konzentrieren auf	**think of**	denken an
depend on	abhängen von	**worry about**	sich Sorgen machen um

112   **one hundred and twelve**

Grammatikanhang UNIT 3

◆ nach bestimmten Präpositionen und Konjunktionen der Zeit:
after (nachdem), *before*, *on* (sobald), *since*, *until*, *when* (als), *while*

Read the instructions **before switching on** the computer.
He was kidnapped **while driving** to work.
After falling off his bike, Andy rode more carefully.

◆ nach bestimmten Präpositionen:
by (dadurch, dass), *despite/in spite of* (trotz), *for* (um … zu/zum), *instead of*, *without*

We got this poster **by writing** to the radio station.
This machine is **for cutting** hair.
In spite of trying hard, he made lots of mistakes.
We should talk **instead of arguing**.
He often stays up late **without feeling** tired the next day.

◆ nach bestimmten Wendungen:
be no use (keinen Zweck haben),
be worth (wert sein / sich lohnen),
what about/how about … (wie wär's mit … ?)

It's **no use waiting**. He won't come.
Is this CD **worth buying**?
What about/How about going to the Grimstone pop festival?

◆ nach bestimmten Verben:

James **enjoys listening** to music.

(handwritten: appreciate)

admit	zugeben	**enjoy**	gern tun	**keep (on)**	weitermachen
avoid	vermeiden	**fancy**	mögen	**mention**	erwähnen
can't help	nicht anders können	**finish**	aufhören	**mind**	etwas dagegen haben
		give up	aufgeben		
delay	verzögern	**go on**	weitermachen	**miss**	verpassen
deny	bestreiten	**imagine**	sich vorstellen können	**practise**	üben
dislike	ungern tun			**suggest**	vorschlagen

(handwritten: postpone)

Infinitiv oder -ing-Form?   the infinitive or the ing-form?   4

Nach einigen Verben kann sowohl der *to*-Infinitiv als auch die *-ing*-Form verwendet werden. Die Bedeutung bleibt dabei unverändert. Dazu gehören: *begin, continue, hate, like, love, prefer, start.*

Alice **loves** working at the disco.
Alice **loves** to work at the disco.
I **hate** getting up early.
I **hate** to get up early.

Bei folgenden Verben hängt der Anschluss davon ab, welche Bedeutung gemeint ist:

FORGET
+ *to*-Infinitiv   vergessen, etwas zu tun
+ *-ing*-Form   vergessen, was man getan hat

I **forgot to buy** something to eat.
I'll never **forget seeing** her for the first time.

REMEMBER
+ *to*-Infinitiv   daran denken, etwas zu tun
+ *-ing*-Form   sich erinnern, etwas getan zu haben

You must **remember to revise** your grammar.
I still **remember going** to school with her.

STOP
+ *to*-Infinitiv   anhalten, um etwas zu tun
+ *-ing*-Form   aufhören, etwas zu tun

He **stopped to talk** to his girlfriend.
He **stopped talking** and was quiet.

one hundred and thirteen   **113**

UNIT 4 Grammatikanhang

1 adjectives and adverbs / Adjektive und Adverbien

Canada is an **enormous** country.
Canadian winters are **icy**.

Lindsay waited **patiently**.
They spoke **slowly**.
Bob was **terribly** nervous.

Adjektive geben an,

◆ wie eine Person oder Sache **ist**. Sie beziehen sich auf ein **Nomen** oder **Pronomen**.

Adverbien der Art und Weise (*adverbs of manner*) geben an,

◆ wie eine Handlung **geschieht**. Sie beziehen sich daher oft auf ein **Verb**. Man verwendet Adverbien (*terribly*) aber auch zur näheren Bestimmung eines Adjektivs (*nervous*). (Siehe **Gradadverbien**, S. 117.)

a the formation of adverbs from adjectives / Die Bildung von Adverbien aus Adjektiven

ADJECTIVE	ADVERB
quick	quick**ly**
beautiful	beautiful**ly**
complete	complete**ly**
safe	safe**ly**
simple	sim**ply**
happy	happ**ily**
realistic	realistic**ally**
full	**fully**
whole	**wholly**
true	**truly**

Die meisten Adverbien sind von Adjektiven abgeleitet. Man bildet sie, indem man *-ly* an das Adjektiv anhängt.

Beachte: Stummes *-e* entfällt bei der Bildung von Adverbien nicht. (*complete* → *completely*)

Besonderheiten bei der Schreibung der Adverbien:

◆ *-le* fällt vor *-ly* weg

◆ *-y* wird zu *-i-* vor *-ly*.
Ausnahme: *shy* → *shyly*

◆ Bei Adjektiven auf *-ic* hängt man *-ally* an.
Ausnahme: *public* → *publicly*

◆ Die Adjektive *full*, *whole* und *true* bilden die Gradadverbien *fully* (völlig), *wholly* (ganz) und *truly* (wirklich).

b special forms / Sonderformen

The assistant was **friendly**.
She spoke **in a friendly way**.

Steve is a **good** dancer.
Steve can dance very **well**.

◆ Bei Adjektiven auf *-ly* (*friendly*, *silly*) verwendet man die Umschreibung *in a … way*.

◆ *good* bildet die Adverbform *well*.

Beachte: well kann auch ein Adjektiv sein: *She's **well** again.* Sie ist wieder **gesund**.

Grammatikanhang UNIT 4

Adjektive nach be, get, seem usw.

Nach Verben, die einen **Zustand** oder eine **Eigenschaft** ausdrücken wie *be*, *become/get* (werden), *seem* (scheinen), *feel* (sich anfühlen), *look* (aussehen), *smell* (riechen), *sound* (klingen), *taste* (schmecken), stehen Adjektive, keine Adverbien, da es sich nicht um eine Tätigkeit handelt.

Beachte:
*He looked **angry**.*	*He looked at us **angrily**.*
sah … aus	sah uns an
(Zustand)	(Tätigkeit)

Adverbien, die die gleiche Form wie Adjektive haben

Einige Adverbien haben die gleiche Form wie Adjektive. Dies sind:

daily	täglich
deep	tief
early	früh
far	weit
fast	schnell
free	frei, gratis
hard	hart, schwer
high	hoch
late	spät
left	links
long	lang
near	nahe
right	richtig, rechts
straight	geradeaus

Zu einigen dieser Adverbien gibt es eine weitere Adverbform auf *-ly*, die aber eine völlig andere Bedeutung hat:

deeply	sehr, zutiefst
freely	freimütig, großzügig
hardly	kaum
highly	sehr, höchst
nearly	fast, beinahe
lately	in letzter Zeit

adjectives after be, get, seem, etc.   c

Everyone **was excited** about the view.
You should **get ready** now.
Steve **seemed** a little **angry**.
Lindsay **felt tired** after her shopping trip.
Mrs Kelly **looked interested**.

adverbs with the same form as adjectives   d

ADJECTIVE	ADVERB
I had to do some **hard** work.	I had to work very **hard**.
Peter is **late** again.	He always arrives **late**.

Karen sometimes stays out **late**.
But she hasn't been to a disco **lately**.

The students had to work **hard**.
I can **hardly** understand his voice.

She lives **near** the University.
Nearly 2.5 million people live in Toronto.

UNIT 4   Grammatikanhang

e   the comparison of adverbs

Cathy took her job very **seriously**.
She took it **more seriously** than other reporters.
She took pollution the **most seriously**.

Bob worked very **late**.
He worked **later** than others.
On Fridays he always worked the **latest** in the office.

Lindsay plays badminton much **better** than Karen.
But last week she played **worse** than Karen.

f   the position of adverbs

(FRONT)	S	(MID)	V	O	(END)
Of course	Steve had	already	visited	Toronto	before.

Perhaps she wasn't killed,' a police officer said.
Unfortunately, there's no hope of finding Cathy.

At first Bob wasn't really worried but **then** he started to feel frightened.

Yesterday they had talked about the drums.

The Inuit **often eat** burgers now.
They **have always worshipped** whales.
They **can usually find** a place to hunt.
Fish **was sometimes** the only food.

Bob **usually** drives to work.
Cathy had **never** been so far north before.

Die Steigerung von Adverbien

Die Steigerung von Adverbien gleicht der von Adjektiven.
Adverbien der Art und Weise auf *-ly* werden mit *more/most* gesteigert.
Ausnahme: *early – earlier – (the) earliest*

Einsilbige Adverbien, welche die gleiche Form wie Adjektive besitzen (siehe S. 115), werden mit *-er/-est* gesteigert.

Beachte die unregelmäßigen Steigerungsformen:
well – better – (the) best
badly – worse – (the) worst

Die Stellung der Adverbien

Für Adverbien gibt es grundsätzlich drei Stellungsmöglichkeiten im Satz:
◆ am Satzanfang (*front position*)
◆ in der Satzmitte (*mid position*)
◆ am Satzende (*end position*).

FRONT POSITION

In *front position*, d.h. am Satzanfang, stehen
◆ oft Adverbien wie *luckily*, *unfortunately*, *maybe*, *perhaps* und *of course*. Sie drücken eine **Stellungnahme** des Sprechers/der Sprecherin zum Satzinhalt aus.

◆ oft Adverbien, die **Sätze** miteinander **verknüpfen**, wie *at first*, *then*, *finally*, *however*.

◆ manchmal Adverbien, die eine **bestimmte Zeit** angeben, wie *yesterday*, *tomorrow*.

MID POSITION

In *mid position*, d.h.
– vor dem Vollverb (*eat*)
– nach dem ersten Hilfsverb (*have*)
– nach dem ersten Modalverb (*can*)
– nach einer Form von *be*
stehen normalerweise

◆ Adverbien, die **unbestimmte Häufigkeit** angeben, wie *always*, *often*, *usually*, *sometimes*, *seldom/rarely* (selten), *never*.

116   one hundred and sixteen

◆ Adverbien, die eine **unbestimmte Zeit** angeben, wie *soon*, *just*, *now*, *ever*, *already*, *still*.

Beachte: Das Adverb darf nicht zwischen Verb und Objekt stehen:

He was **still** worried.

Inuit kids **often** surf the internet.
(*Eskimokinder surfen **oft** im Internet.*)

END POSITION

In *end position*, d. h. nach dem Verb (+ Objekt) stehen:

◆ Adverbien der **Art und Weise** wie *noisily*, *perfectly*, *fast*, *well*, *badly*.

◆ Adverbien und Adverbialbestimmungen des **Ortes** wie *here*, *there*, *everywhere*, *in England*.

◆ manchmal Adverbien und Adverbialbestimmungen der **bestimmten Zeit** wie *yesterday*, *tonight*, *in 1984*.

◆ Adverbien und Adverbialbestimmungen der **bestimmten Häufigkeit** wie *once*, *twice*, *several times*, *every Monday*.

Should Cathy have acted **differently**?
The company wanted to dump the waste **cheaply**.

In summer people can't get **there**.
She's not **in her office**.

They took a tour of the stadium **yesterday**.
Cathy's last phone call was **five months ago**.

I've only been to Canada **once**.
The Toronto Blue Jays practise almost **every day**.

Beachte: Wenn am Satzende mehrere Adverbien (*adverbs* und *adverb phrases*) zusammenkommen, gilt folgende Reihenfolge:

Auch hier darf das Adverb nicht zwischen Verb und Objekt stehen.

	ART/WEISE	ORT	ZEIT
They played	well	in the game	yesterday.

Gradadverbien

stehen meist vor dem Wort, das sie verstärken oder abschwächen. Sie bestimmen
◆ Adjektive
◆ andere Adverbien
◆ Verben.

adverbs of degree   **g**

HOHER GRAD
very, *extremely* (äußerst), *really*, *completely*, *absolutely*, *nearly*, *terribly*, *awfully*

MITTLERER GRAD
rather, *quite*, *fairly*, *pretty*

NIEDRIGER GRAD
a bit (ein wenig), *a little*, *slightly* (geringfügig)

Beachte: *very much*, *a lot*, *a bit*, *a little* haben *end position*, wenn sie ein Verb beschreiben.

The view over Toronto was **absolutely** amazing.
The elevator went up **extremely** quickly.
Steve **nearly** died when a car crashed into his bike.

I like reading **very much**.
My sister doesn't read **a lot**.

UNIT 4   Grammatikanhang

2   uses of modal verbs

Gebrauch der Modalverben

Modale Hilfsverben und ihre Ersatzformen drücken aus, dass etwas sein oder geschehen **kann**, **muss**, **darf** oder **soll**.

a   ability

Bob **can** speak English and French.
He **could** read when he was five.
The police **weren't able to** find Cathy.

Fähigkeit

Mit *can*, *could* und *be able to* drücken wir eine **Fähigkeit** aus. Im *present tense* verwenden wir meistens *can*, im *past tense could* oder *was/were able to*, in zusammengesetzten Zeitformen die Ersatzform *be able to*.

b   permission

Can/May I use your phone?
You **can** phone me any time.
I **was allowed to** leave work early yesterday.

Erlaubnis

Mit *can*, *may* und *be allowed to* drücken wir eine **Erlaubnis** aus. Im *present tense* verwenden wir meistens *can*, im *past tense could* oder *was/were allowed to*, in zusammengesetzten Zeitformen *be allowed to*.

Beachte: *May I/we … ?* ist besonders höflich.

c   prohibition

Shopping baskets **may not/can't** be removed from the shop.
She **wasn't allowed to** use his mobile.
You **mustn't** go there alone.

Verbot

Can't, *may not*, *not be allowed to* und *mustn't* werden verwendet, um ein **Verbot** auszudrücken. Für ein ausdrückliches Verbot verwenden wir *mustn't*.

d   necessity

We **must** do something to help Cathy.
Reporters sometimes **have to** face dangerous situations.
Cathy's colleagues **had to** tell the police everything they knew.

Notwendigkeit

Must und *have to* drücken eine **Notwendigkeit** oder einen **Zwang** aus. Im *present tense* verwenden wir *must* und *have to*, im *past tense had to*; zusammengesetzte Zeitformen werden mit *have to* gebildet.

Beachte: Im *present tense* wird *have to* öfters verwendet.

Beachte den Unterschied zwischen *mustn't* und *needn't*.

You **mustn't** tell me.
Du darfst es mir nicht sagen.
You **needn't** tell me.
Du brauchst es mir nicht sagen.

Keine Notwendigkeit

Mit *needn't* und *have to* in der verneinten Form drücken wir das **Fehlen einer Notwendigkeit** aus.

no necessity

You **needn't** do all the work alone.
Luckily I **don't have to** finish this article today.
I **didn't have to** go there after all.

e

Verpflichtung und Ratschlag

Wir verwenden *should* und *ought to,* um eine **Verpflichtung** oder einen **Rat** auszudrücken.

obligation and advice

Cathy, you **should/ought to** be more careful.
We **shouldn't** waste time.

f

Vorschlag

Shall I … ? und *shall we … ?* werden verwendet, um einen **Vorschlag** zu machen.

Ebenso kann für Vorschläge *can/could* bzw. *can't/couldn't* verwendet werden.

suggestion

Shall I phone him?
Shall we go and see this guy today?

Shall/Can/Can't we meet you at the Skydome?
You **can/could** take a ferry to Toronto Islands if you're not interested in the Eaton Centre.

g

Modale Hilfsverben + have + Partizip Perfekt

modals + have + past participle

3

Bob's no longer around. He **must have left** earlier.

Wir verwenden ein modales Hilfsverb + *have* + *past participle* (*must have left*),

um über **Schlussfolgerungen**, **Verpflichtungen**, **Erfordernisse** etc. in der **Vergangenheit** zu sprechen. Die Konstruktion drückt aus, was

◆ möglicherweise (nicht) passiert ist.
 (Sie hat sich **vielleicht** verlaufen.)

- What happened to Cathy?
- She **may have got** lost in the swamplands.
- Well, she **might not have known** the right way.
- Or she **could have been** attacked by the two men.

◆ höchstwahrscheinlich (nicht) passiert ist.
 (Ihr **muss** etwas geschehen sein.)

- Oh dear. Something **must have happened** to Cathy.
- It **can't have been** an accident.

◆ jemand in der Vergangenheit hätte tun oder nicht tun sollen.
 (Jemand **hätte** sie begleiten sollen.)

- You **shouldn't have allowed** her to go on her own.
- I suppose you're right. Someone **ought to have gone** with her.

Irregular verbs Unregelmäßige Verben

INFINITIVE	SIMPLE PAST	PAST PARTICIPLE	
to be	was/were	been	sein
to bear	bore	borne	tragen; ertragen
to beat	beat	beaten	schlagen
to become	became	become	werden
to begin	began	begun	anfangen, beginnen
to bend	bent	bent	biegen
to bet	bet/betted	bet/betted	wetten
to bite	bit	bitten	beißen
to bleed	bled	bled	bluten
to blow	blew	blown	blasen
to break	broke	broken	brechen
to bring	brought	brought	bringen
to build	built	built	bauen
to burn	burnt/burned	burnt/burned	(ver)brennen
to buy	bought	bought	kaufen
to catch	caught	caught	fangen
to choose	chose	chosen	wählen
to cling	clung	clung	kleben, haften
to come	came	come	kommen
to cost	cost	cost	kosten
to cut	cut	cut	schneiden
to deal	dealt	dealt	sich beschäftigen
to dig	dug	dug	graben
to do	did	done	tun, machen
to draw	drew	drawn	ziehen; zeichnen
to dream	dreamt/dreamed	dreamt/dreamt	träumen
to drink	drank	drunk	trinken
to drive	drove	driven	fahren
to eat	ate	eaten	essen
to fall	fell	fallen	fallen
to feed	fed	fed	füttern
to feel	felt	felt	fühlen
to fight	fought	fought	kämpfen
to find	found	found	finden
to fly	flew	flown	fliegen
to forbid	forbade	forbidden	verbieten, untersagen
to forget	forgot	forgotten	vergessen
to freeze	froze	frozen	(ge)frieren
to get	got	got	bekommen
to give	gave	given	geben
to go	went	gone	gehen
to grow	grew	grown	wachsen; anbauen; werden
to hang	hung	hung	hängen; aufhängen
to hang	hanged	hanged	erhängen (töten)
to have	had	had	haben
to hear	heard	heard	hören
to hide	hid	hidden	(sich) verstecken
to hit	hit	hit	treffen; schlagen
to hold	held	held	halten
to hurt	hurt	hurt	verletzen
to keep	kept	kept	halten, behalten
to kneel	knelt	knelt	knien
to know	knew	known	wissen; kennen
to lay	laid	laid	legen
to lead	led	led	führen

Unregelmäßige Verben

INFINITIVE	SIMPLE PAST	PAST PARTICIPLE	
to learn	learnt/learned	learnt/learned	lernen
to leave	left	left	verlassen
to lend	lent	lent	leihen, borgen
to let	let	let	lassen, zulassen
to lie	lay	lain	liegen
to light	lit	lit	anzünden
to lose	lost	lost	verlieren
to make	made	made	machen
to mean	meant	meant	bedeuten, meinen
to meet	met	met	treffen, begegnen
to pay	paid	paid	bezahlen
to put	put	put	setzen, stellen
to quit	quit	quit	verlassen
to read	read	read	lesen
to ride	rode	ridden	reiten; fahren
to ring	rang	rung	klingeln; anrufen
to rise	rose	risen	ansteigen; aufgehen
to run	ran	run	laufen
to say	said	said	sagen
to see	saw	seen	sehen
to sell	sold	sold	verkaufen
to send	sent	sent	schicken, senden
to set	set	set	setzen, stellen
to shake	shook	shaken	schütteln
to shine	shone	shone	scheinen
to shoot	shot	shot	schießen
to show	showed	shown/showed	zeigen
to shut	shut	shut	schließen
to sing	sang	sung	singen
to sink	sank	sunk	sinken; untergehen
to sit	sat	sat	sitzen
to sleep	slept	slept	schlafen
to slide	slid	slid	gleiten, rutschen
to speak	spoke	spoken	sprechen
to spend	spent	spent	ausgeben; verbringen
to spill	spilt/spilled	spilt/spilled	verschütten
to spin	spun	spun	spinnen
to split	split	split	spalten, teilen
to spread	spread	spread	verbreiten
to stand	stood	stood	stehen
to steal	stole	stolen	stehlen
to stick	stuck	stuck	kleben; stecken bleiben
to stink	stank	stunk	stinken
to swear	swore	sworn	fluchen; schwören
to sweep	swept	swept	fegen
to swim	swam	swum	schwimmen
to swing	swung	swung	schwingen
to take	took	taken	nehmen
to teach	taught	taught	unterrichten, lehren
to tell	told	told	erzählen
to think	thought	thought	denken, glauben
to throw	threw	thrown	werfen
to understand	understood	understood	verstehen
to unwind	unwound	unwound	sich entspannen
to wake	woke	woken	aufwecken; aufwachen
to wear	wore	worn	tragen
to win	won	won	gewinnen
to write	wrote	written	schreiben

English sounds Erklärung der Lautschriftzeichen

Vowels
Selbstlaute, Vokale

[iː]	eat, week, he
[i]	party, very, ready
[ɪ]	in, give, film
[e]	end, get, many
[æ]	add, man, black
[ʌ]	under, come
[ɑː]	ask, half, car
[ɒ]	often, what, coffee
[ɔː]	all, four, door
[ʊ]	put, good, woman
[u]	situation, unite, actual
[uː]	who, June, blue
[ɜː]	learn, girl, work
[ə]	again, policeman, sister
[eɪ]	eight, table, play
[aɪ]	I, nice, by
[ɔɪ]	boy, toilet
[əʊ]	old, road, know
[aʊ]	out, house, now
[ɪə]	we're, here, near
[eə]	wear, chair, there
[ʊə]	tour, pure, sure

Consonants
Mitlaute, Konsonanten

[p]	pen, speak, map
[b]	book, rabbit, job
[t]	table, letter, sit
[d]	desk, radio, old
[k]	car, basketball, back
[g]	get, bigger, bag
[f]	father, left, cliff
[v]	very, every, have
[θ]	thank, birthday, bath
[ð]	this, father, with
[s]	see, classes, dance
[z]	zoo, thousand, please
[ʃ]	shop, sugar, English
[ʒ]	television, usually
[tʃ]	child, kitchen, watch
[dʒ]	jam, June, arrange
[h]	help, who, home
[m]	mouse, number, film
[n]	name, window, pen
[ŋ]	sing, morning, long
[l]	like, blue, all
[r]	read, borrow, very
[j]	yes, you, year
[w]	walk, where, quiz

The English alphabet
Das englische Alphabet

a	[eɪ]
b	[biː]
c	[siː]
d	[diː]
e	[iː]
f	[ef]
g	[dʒiː]
h	[eɪtʃ]
i	[aɪ]
j	[dʒeɪ]
k	[keɪ]
l	[el]
m	[em]
n	[en]
o	[əʊ]
p	[piː]
q	[kjuː]
r	[ɑː]
s	[es]
t	[tiː]
u	[juː]
v	[viː]
w	['dʌbl juː]
x	[eks]
y	[waɪ]
z	[zed]

Erklärung der Symbole im Wörterverzeichnis

Com	=	Communication	Read	=	Reading	TYE	=	Test your English
Dict	=	Dictionary work	Rev	=	Revision	umg	=	umgangssprachlich
Ex	=	Exercise	Sit	=	Situation	WP	=	Words and Pictures
Fol	=	Follow up	SP	=	Speaking practice	❯	=	definition
Lit	=	Literature	T	=	Text	❯❯	=	synonym
Proj	=	Project	TP	=	Translation practice	❯❮	=	opposite

122 one hundred and twenty-two

Wörterverzeichnis UNIT 1

Unit 1

WP | contrast [ˈkɒntrɑːst] | Gegensatz, Kontrast
outback [ˈaʊtbæk] | australisches Hinterland
Aborigine [ˌæbəˈrɪdʒəni] | Ureinwohner/in
Australian [ɒˈstreɪliən] | Australier/in; australisch
magical [ˈmædʒɪkl] | magisch, zauberhaft *umg*
rock [rɒk] | Fels(en), Stein
rugby [ˈrʌgbi] | Rugby

The contrasts between the two areas are amazing.
› *the Australian countryside far away from cities*

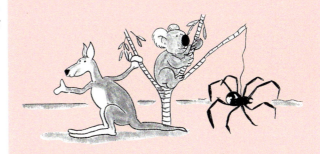

kangaroo [ˌkæŋgəˈruː] | Känguru
koala bear [kəʊˌɑːlə ˈbeə] | Koalabär
redback spider [ˌredbæk ˈspaɪdə] | australische Witwenspinne

explorer [ɪkˈsplɔːrə] | Forscher/in, Forschungsreisende/r
to beat [biːt] beat, beaten [biːt, ˈbiːtn] | schlagen, übertreffen
nowadays [ˈnaʊədeɪz] | heutzutage, heute

An explorer travels through an unknown area to find out about it.
›› *to defeat*

›› *now, these days*

Sit1 | update [ˈʌpdeɪt] | Aktualisierung, neueste Version
to insist on doing sth [ɪnˈsɪst ɒn] | darauf bestehen, etwas zu tun
…-proof (against) [pruːf əˈgenst] | sicher vor, gefeit gegen

He insisted on doing everything himself.

-proof

a rainproof coat | a childproof cap | a waterproof jacket | a rabbit-proof fence
a bulletproof car | *(kindersicherer Verschluss)* | windproof clothing

Man verwendet *-proof* oft um zu sagen, dass etwas durch eine bestimmte Sache, Person oder Entwicklung nicht beeinträchtigt werden kann – oder auch, dass dieser nichts geschieht (z.B. *childproof*).

---

to avoid [əˈvɔɪd] | vermeiden
to avoid doing sth | vermeiden, etwas zu tun
to fall asleep [ˌfɔːl əˈsliːp] fell, fallen [fel, ˈfɔːln] | einschlafen

He crossed the road to avoid meeting her.
›› *to begin to sleep*

Sit2 | generation [ˌdʒenəˈreɪʃn] | Generation
up to [ˈʌp tə] | bis zu
to remove [rɪˈmuːv] | wegnehmen, entfernen
mixed [mɪkst] | gemischt, vermischt
(farm) labourer [fɑːm ˈleɪbərə] | (Land-)Arbeiter/in, Tagelöhner/in
to receive [rɪˈsiːv] | erhalten, empfangen
remote [rɪˈməʊt] | abgelegen, entlegen, fern
Ex3 | territory [ˈterətri] | Gebiet

› *all people of about the same age*
›› *until, till*
›› *to take away*

›› *to get*
› *far away from places where people live*
› *land that belongs to one government*

one hundred and twenty-three 123

UNIT 1   Wörterverzeichnis

T1	**dreamtime** [ˈdriːmtaɪm]	Traumzeit	
	to **rise** [raɪz]	sich erheben; aufgehen;	
	rose, risen [rəʊz, ˈrɪzn]	(an)steigen	
	rainbow [ˈreɪnbəʊ]	Regenbogen	
	nature [ˈneɪtʃə]	Natur	⚠ No article: **Nature** is the mother of life.
	respect [rɪˈspekt]	Respekt, Achtung	
	to **damage** [ˈdæmɪdʒ]	beschädigen	Smoking can **damage** your health.
	unfortunate [ʌnˈfɔːtʃənət]	unglücklich, bedauerlich	⟩⟨ *fortunate*
	culture [ˈkʌltʃə]	Kultur	Betonung: *culture* ●●
	flu [fluː]	Grippe	Steven's been sick all week. He's got the **flu**.
	smallpox [ˈsmɔːlpɒks]	Pocken	
	runner [ˈrʌnə]	Läufer/in	
	Olympic [əˈlɪmpɪk]	olympisch	the **Olympic** Games, an **Olympic** gold medal, the **Olympic** village, an **Olympic** champion
	medal [ˈmedl]	Medaille	
	lap [læp]	Runde	
	barefoot [ˈbeəfʊt]	barfuß	⟩ with nothing on your feet
	champion [ˈtʃæmpiən]	Meister/in, Champion (Sport)	
	to **last** [lɑːst]	dauern, andauern	⟩⟩ to go on
	to **apologize** (to sb) for sth [əˈpɒlədʒaɪz fə]	sich bei jdm für etwas entschuldigen	He **apologized to** the man **for stepping** on his foot.
	responsible (for) [rɪˈspɒnsəbl]	verantwortlich (für)	
	both ... and ... [bəʊθ, ənd]	sowohl ... als auch ...	She's **both** clever **and** attractive.
	final [ˈfaɪnl]	Finale, Endspiel	The men's basketball **final** is on Saturday.
	spectator [spekˈteɪtə]	Zuschauer/in	
	to **disappoint** [ˌdɪsəˈpɔɪnt]	enttäuschen	
	to **reject** [rɪˈdʒekt]	zurückweisen, ablehnen	⟩ to refuse to accept
	mind [maɪnd]	Verstand, Geist	
	on average [ɒn ˈævərɪdʒ]	im Durchschnitt	**On average**, Japanese people live longer than Europeans.
Ex6	**rather than** [ˈrɑːðə ðən]	eher als, statt	
Ex8	**cruise** [kruːz]	Kreuzfahrt	⟩ a holiday on a large ship
Ex9	**department store** [dɪˈpɑːtmənt stɔː]	Kaufhaus, Warenhaus	⟩ a large shop which sells many different things
	former [ˈfɔːmə]	ehemalig	⚠ Steht nur vor einem Nomen: the **former** president
	receipt [rɪˈsiːt]	Quittung, Kassenbon	Can you give me a **receipt**, please?
	to **recommend** [ˌrekəˈmend]	empfehlen	Can you **recommend** a good lawyer?
	rush hour [ˈrʌʃ aʊə]	Hauptverkehrszeit, Stoßzeit	**rush hour** traffic
	soap [səʊp]	Seife	
	sun cream [ˈsʌn kriːm]	Sonnencreme	
	to **try on** [ˌtraɪ ˈɒn]	anprobieren	

soap   *sun cream*

124   one hundred and twenty-four

Wörterverzeichnis   UNIT 1

Ex10	to **shorten** ['ʃɔːtn]	(ver)kürzen	❭ to become shorter, to make something shorter
	advert ['ædvɜːt]	Anzeige, Reklame, Werbespot	❭❭ advertisement They produced an **advert** for a new car.
	alternative [ɔːl'tɜːnətɪv]	alternativ	We had to make **alternative** plans.
	public house [ˌpʌblɪk 'haus]	Kneipe, Gastwirtschaft	❭❭ pub
	influenza [ˌɪnflu'enzə]	Grippe	❭❭ flu
	examination [ɪɡˌzæmɪ'neɪʃn]	Prüfung; Untersuchung	❭❭ exam; test
Ex11	**abbreviation** [əˌbriːvi'eɪʃn]	Abkürzung	'BBC' is the **abbreviation** for 'British Broadcasting Corporation'.
Sit3	to **come up (to** sb) [ˌkʌm 'ʌp tə]	auf jdn zukommen	❭❭ to move towards sb
	came, come [keɪm, kʌm]		
	to **introduce** sb **(to** sb) [ˌɪntrə'djuːs]	jdn (jdm) vorstellen	❭ to tell somebody another person's name
	to **take time off** [teɪk taɪm 'ɒf]	sich freinehmen	He **took a week off** to fly to Turkey.
	took, taken [tʊk, 'teɪkən]		
	geyser ['ɡeɪzə]	Geysir, Geiser	
	bungee jumping ['bʌndʒi dʒʌmpɪŋ]	Bungeejumping	
	skydiving ['skaɪdaɪvɪŋ]	Skydiving, Freifallen	

bungee jumping   **skydiving**

	white-water rafting [ˌwaɪt wɔːtə 'rɑːftɪŋ]	Wildwasserfahren	
	outdoor ['aʊtdɔː]	Außen-, im Freien	**outdoor** activities/clothes/athletics
	instructor [ɪn'strʌktə]	Lehrer/in, Ausbilder/in	An **instructor** teaches a sport or a practical skill.
Ex12	**sail** [seɪl]	Segel	
	board [bɔːd]	Brett	
Sit4	**definite** ['defɪnət]	sicher, bestimmt, entschieden	❭❭ certain, clear
	definitely ['defɪnətli]	bestimmt, absolut	❭ without any doubt
	spring [sprɪŋ]	Quelle	a hot **spring**, **spring** water
	mud [mʌd]	Schlamm, Matsch, Dreck	❭ wet earth She fell in the **mud**.
	Maori ['maʊri]	Maori	
	as [əz]	da	❭❭ because
	thermal ['θɜːml]	Thermal-, thermisch	a **thermal** spring
	swimsuit ['swɪmsuːt]	Badeanzug	❭ a piece of clothing that you wear for swimming
	rotten ['rɒtn]	verdorben, faul	After a month on the shelf the eggs were **rotten**.
	egg [eɡ]	Ei	
	effort ['efət]	Anstrengung, Bemühung	Please make an **effort** to be polite.
	to **take off** [ˌteɪk 'ɒf]	(gut) anlaufen, durchstarten	Her career **took off** after the TV show.
	took, taken [tʊk, 'teɪkən]		
	settlement ['setlmənt]	Siedlung	A **settlement** is a place where people have made their homes.
	edge [edʒ]	Rand, Kante	
Ex14	**promise** ['prɒmɪs]	Versprechen	to keep a **promise**, to break a **promise**

one hundred and twenty-five   **125**

UNIT 1 Wörterverzeichnis

a kiwi *a kiwi (fruit)*

T2	**kiwi** ['ki:wi:]	Neuseeländer/in *umg*; Kiwi (Vogel); Kiwifrucht	
	commercial [kə'mɜ:ʃl]	kommerziell	
	reception [rɪ'sepʃn]	Empfang, Rezeption	
	to **dip** [dɪp]	(ein)tauchen	She **dipped** her foot into the pool to see how cold it was.
	scary ['skeəri]	unheimlich, beängstigend, gruselig	≫ frightening a **scary** movie/story
	platform ['plætfɔ:m]	Plattform; Bahnsteig	The train for London departs from **platform** 1.
	to **wave** [weɪv]	winken	Why did you **wave** at her?
	to **dive** [daɪv]	einen Kopfsprung machen; tauchen	They **dived** into the river to cool off. Let's go **diving** in Greece this summer.
	towards [tə'wɔ:dz]	auf … zu, in Richtung, gegen	He stood up and walked **towards** her.
	free fall [ˌfri: 'fɔ:l]	freier Fall	
	to **bounce** [baʊns]	federn (lassen), hüpfen	
	relieved [rɪ'li:vd]	erleichtert	They felt **relieved** to hear the good news.
	jelly ['dʒeli]	Götterspeise, Gelee	My legs felt like **jelly**. = Ich hatte Pudding in den Beinen.
	to **scream** [skri:m]	schreien	They were **screaming** with excitement.
	glacier ['glæsɪə]	Gletscher	
	ice [aɪs]	Eis	**ice** = *Eis* **ice-cream** = *(Speise) Eis*
	to **slide** [slaɪd] slid, slid [slɪd, slɪd]	gleiten, rutschen	
	rainforest ['reɪnfɒrɪst]	Regenwald	the Amazon **rainforest**
	lover ['lʌvə]	Liebhaber/in, Geliebte/r	
	tear [tɪə]	Träne	
	crampon ['kræmpɒn]	Steigeisen	
	to **grip** [grɪp]	(er)greifen	▸ to hold something tightly
	waterproof ['wɔ:təpru:f]	Regenmantel, wasserundurchlässiges Kleidungsstück	
	glove [glʌv]	Handschuh	
	level ['levl]	eben, gerade	≫ flat
	amazing [ə'meɪzɪŋ]	erstaunlich	
	ant [ænt]	Ameise	
	track [træk]	Pfad, Weg	
	to **crunch** [krʌntʃ]	knirschen	
	ravine [rə'vi:n]	Schlucht	▸ a deep narrow valley
	to **squeeze** [skwi:z]	sich quetschen, drängen, drücken	He **squeezed** through the crowd.
	to **melt** [melt]	schmelzen	The snow usually **melts** in spring.
Ex18	**fruit** [fru:t]	Frucht, Obst	Oranges, apples, and bananas are all types of **fruit**.
Com	**disappointed** [ˌdɪsə'pɔɪntɪd]	enttäuscht	I was deeply **disappointed** with the results.
TYE	to **provide (with)** [prə'vaɪd wɪð]	versorgen (mit)	
	vehicle ['vi:əkl]	Fahrzeug	Road **vehicles** include cars, buses and trucks.
	jack [dʒæk]	Wagenheber, Winde	You need a **jack** in order to change a wheel.
	airstrip ['eəstrɪp]	Rollbahn, Piste	▸ a narrow piece of land that an aircraft can land on
	electric-orange [ɪˌlektrɪk 'ɒrɪndʒ]	signalorange	
	mattress ['mætrəs]	Matratze	

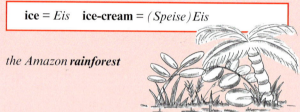

126   one hundred and twenty-six

Wörterverzeichnis UNIT 1

TYE2	shocked [ʃɒkt]	erschüttert, entsetzt	
TYE6	two-way radio ['tu:weɪ ˌreɪdiəʊ]		Funksprechgerät
Read	bone [bəʊn]	Knochen	I've broken a **bone** in my foot.
	extract ['ekstrækt]	Auszug, Extrakt	❯ a particular part of a book
	elder ['eldə]	Stammesälteste/r	an **elder** of the tribe
	smart [smɑ:t]	clever, raffiniert	❯❯ clever
	to bring up [ˌbrɪŋ 'ʌp] brought, brought [brɔ:t, brɔ:t]	großziehen, erziehen	She was **brought up** by her grandmother.
	no longer [nəʊ 'lɒŋgə]	nicht mehr, nicht länger	❯ in the past but not now The factory is **no longer** used.
	to lower ['ləʊə]	sinken lassen, (sich) senken	

	hat [hæt]	Hut	
	to shake [ʃeɪk] shook, shaken [ʃʊk, 'ʃeɪkən]	schütteln; zittern	
	leather ['leðə]	Leder	a **leather** coat/belt/bag
	to be terrified (of) ['terɪfaɪd]	schreckliche Angst haben (vor)	❯❯ to be scared (of) She's **terrified of** the dark.
	to seize [si:z]	packen, ergreifen	
	to kneel [ni:l] knelt, knelt [nelt, nelt]	knien	
	need [ni:d]	Bedürfnis	Are you in **need** of help? = Brauchst du Hilfe?
	to weep [wi:p] wept, wept [wept, wept]	weinen	❯❯ to cry (because you feel sad)
	to smack [smæk]	einen Klaps geben	
	lonely ['ləʊnli]	einsam	She led a **lonely** life with only two or three friends.
	handful ['hændfʊl]	Handvoll	❯ a small number of people or things
	terrifying ['terɪfaɪɪŋ]	Furcht erregend, schrecklich	❯❯ very frightening
	companion [kəm'pæniən]	Begleiter/in, Gefährte, Gefährtin	❯ a person you spend a lot of time with
	to dislike [dɪs'laɪk]	nicht mögen, nicht gern haben	✗ to like
	whore [hɔ:]	Hure	❯ a woman who earns money by having sex with people
	imagination [ɪˌmædʒɪ'neɪʃn]	Fantasie	
	childhood ['tʃaɪldhʊd]	Kindheit	❯ the time when you are a child

Tricky words   Wörter, die oft falsch geschrieben werden

accommodation	Unterkunft	government	Regierung	parliament	Parlament
address	Adresse	independence	Unabhängigkeit	separate	getrennt
assistant	Assistent/in	independent	unabhängig	scene	Schauplatz, Szene
athlete	Athlet/in	instead of	anstatt		
to build/building	bauen/Gebäude	inventor	Erfinder/in	science	Naturwissen- schaft
to describe	beschreiben	Ireland	Irland		
disaster	Katastrophe	machine	Maschine	welcome	willkommen
eighth	achte(r/s)	marriage	Ehe	wherever	wo immer
fascinated	fasziniert	ninth	neunte(r/s)	to wound	verwunden

one hundred and twenty-seven

UNIT 2   Wörterverzeichnis

Unit 2

WP **fiction** ['fɪkʃn]   Fiktion, Märchen   ❭ *a story that is invented and not true*
possibility [ˌpɒsə'bɪləti]   Möglichkeit   *There's a **possibility** of rain tonight.*

Möglichkeit

POSSIBILITY   CHANCE/OPPORTUNITY

There's a **possibility**   She had the **chance** to go abroad.
of snow tonight.   They gave him the **opportunity** to explain what happened.

Vorsicht: „Die Möglichkeit etwas zu tun" kann nicht mit *possibility* übersetzt werden; hier muss
man *chance to do* verwenden.

---

personality   Persönlichkeit
  [ˌpɜːsə'næləti]
intelligent [ɪn'telɪdʒənt]   intelligent   ❭❭ *clever* ❭ *good at learning and understanding, etc*
space [speɪs]   Weltraum
to **mine** [maɪn]   Bergbau betreiben,   ❭ *to dig coal, diamonds, etc out of the ground*
                       abbauen (Erz, Gold, …)
light year ['laɪt jɪə]   Lichtjahr   *The star is about four **light years** away from Earth.*
solar system   Sonnensystem   ❭ *the sun and all the planets*
  ['səʊlə sɪstəm]   *that move around it*

whale [weɪl]   Wal   *a killer **whale***

greenhouse ['griːnhaʊs]   Gewächshaus   ⚠ **greenhouse** effect
                                              = Treibhauseffekt

gas [gæs]   Gas
to **warm** [wɔːm]   warm werden,   ❭ *to make something warm(er), to become warm(er)*
                       (sich) erwärmen
level ['levl]   Stand, Höhe; Niveau;
                     Ebene
to **cool down**   (sich) abkühlen;   ❭ *to become less hot, to make something less hot*
  [ˌkuːl 'daʊn]   sich beruhigen
ice age ['aɪs eɪdʒ]   Eiszeit
to **clone** [kləʊn]   klonen   ❭ *to create an exact copy of an animal or plant*
genetic [dʒə'netɪk]   genetisch   *a **genetic** disease*
Sit1 to **come across**   zufällig finden/treffen   ❭ *to find somebody/something by chance*
  [ˌkʌm ə'krɒs]
  came, come
  [keɪm, kʌm]
to **take over** [ˌteɪk 'əʊvə]   übernehmen
  took, taken
  [tʊk, 'teɪkən]
nonsense ['nɒnsns]   Unsinn   *You're talking **nonsense**.*
brain [breɪn]   Gehirn   *The **brain** controls thought, movement, memory, etc.*
Sit2 to **choke on** sth   sich an etwas   *She was **choking on** a piece of meat.*
  ['tʃəʊk ɒn]   verschlucken
so-called [ˌsəʊ'kɔːld]   so genannt
to **intend to** do sth   beabsichtigen, etwas   ❭❭ *to plan to do sth*
  [ɪn'tend]   zu tun

Wörterverzeichnis   UNIT 2

to **predict** [prɪ'dɪkt]	vorhersagen	≫ *to forecast*
unless [ən'les]	wenn nicht; es sei denn	≫ *except if*
programmer ['prəʊgræmə]	Programmierer/in	*We're looking for a skilled software **programmer** to create new software.*
T1 **whiz-kid** ['wɪz kɪd]	Wunderkind, Genie	
layout ['leɪaʊt]	Anordnung, Layout	
to **program** ['prəʊgræm]	programmieren	
graphic design [ˌgræfɪk dɪ'zaɪn]	grafisches Design	❭ *designing layouts or text for books, magazines, etc*
webmaster ['webmɑːstə]	Webmaster	
form [fɔːm]	Formular	*Please fill in* (ausfüllen) *the application **form**.*
by [baɪ]	bis (spätestens)	❭ *no(t) later than; before*
to **get through** sth [ˌget 'θruː] **got, got** [gɒt, gɒt]	etwas erledigen	
part-time [ˌpɑː'taɪm]	Teilzeit-, halbtags	*I'm looking for a **part-time** job.*
to **interrupt** [ˌɪntə'rʌpt]	unterbrechen	
to **beep** [biːp]	piepen, hupen	
alarm (clock) [ə'lɑːm klɒk]	Wecker	*I've set the **alarm (clock)** for 5.30.*
as soon as [əz 'suːn əz]	sobald	***As soon as** I saw him, I knew something was wrong.*
break [breɪk]	Pause	*a coffee/tea/lunch **break** Let's take a **break**.*
deadline ['dedlaɪn]	(letzter) Termin	*It's difficult to meet the **deadline**. (… den Termin einzuhalten)*
full-time [ˌfʊl 'taɪm]	Vollzeit-, ganztags	✕ *part-time*
even ['iːvn]	noch	*He's **even** more intelligent than his brother.*
insurance [ɪn'ʃʊərəns]	Versicherung	*social/life/health/car **insurance***
to **involve** [ɪn'vɒlv]	mit sich bringen, zur Folge haben	*The test will **involve** writing a short letter.*
knowledge ['nɒlɪdʒ]	Wissen, Kenntnis	*Her **knowledge** of French is good.*
to **gain** [geɪn]	sich verschaffen, bekommen, gewinnen	≫ *to obtain, to win*
trial and error [ˌtraɪəl ənd 'erə]	Ausprobieren	*to learn by **trial and error***
demanding [dɪ'mɑːndɪŋ]	anstrengend, anspruchsvoll	*a **demanding** child/boss* *Her job is extremely **demanding**.*
to **prevent** sb **from** do**ing** sth [prɪ'vent]	jdn daran hindern, etwas zu tun	*His illness **prevents him from coming** to work.*
grade [greɪd]	Note (Schule)	*She got good **grades** in her exams.*
to **exploit** [ɪk'splɔɪt]	ausnutzen, ausbeuten	
health [helθ]	Gesundheit(szustand)	*He's in poor/good/excellent **health**.*
challenge ['tʃælɪndʒ]	Herausforderung	❭ *a new and difficult task*
Ex9 **item** ['aɪtəm]	Punkt (auf einer Liste); Meldung; Artikel, Gegenstand	*a news **item***
Ex12 to **link** [lɪŋk]	verbinden	≫ *to connect*
Sit3 **global warming** [ˌgləʊbl 'wɔːmɪŋ]	Erwärmung der Erdatmosphäre	
carbon dioxide [ˌkɑːbən daɪ'ɒksaɪd]	Kohlendioxid, CO_2	
flood [flʌd]	Flut, Überschwemmung	*The heavy rain has caused **floods** in the area.*

UNIT 2   Wörterverzeichnis

lecture [ˈlektʃə]	Vortrag, Vorlesung; Standpauke	
to **deserve** [dɪˈzɜːv]	verdienen	

lecture = *Vorlesung*
Lektüre = **something to read**

Verdienen

to **earn** (*Geld einnehmen*)   to **deserve** (*Lob, Strafe, Ruhe etc. verdienen*)
He **earns** $35,000 a year.   Peter **deserves** a rest now.

Sit4 **tropical** [ˈtrɒpɪkl] — tropisch — the **tropical** rainforest
to **be located** [bi ləʊˈkeɪtɪd] — gelegen sein — ❯ to be in a place

humid [ˈhjuːmɪd] — feucht — This area is hot and **humid** in the summer.
temperate [ˈtempərət] — gemäßigt — a **temperate** climate
as well as [əz ˈwel əz] — ebenso wie, sowohl … als auch — They sell newspapers **as well as** magazines.

to **contain** [kənˈteɪn] — enthalten, beinhalten — Does this drink **contain** alcohol?
shape [ʃeɪp] — Form — ❯❯ form
insect [ˈɪnsekt] — Insekt — Ants, beetles and butterflies are all **insects**.
lizard [ˈlɪzəd] — Eidechse
height [haɪt] — Höhe — The plane flew at a **height** of 3500 metres.
original [əˈrɪdʒənl] — ursprünglich, Original-
rice [raɪs] — Reis — Would you like **rice** with your curry?
dust [dʌst] — Staub
to **clear** [klɪə] — räumen; hier: abholzen — ❯❯ to remove, to take away
I **cleared** my desk of papers.
to **raise** [reɪz] — sammeln (Geld) — ❯ to collect money
locust [ˈləʊkəst] — (Wander-)Heuschrecke — **Locusts** appear in large groups and often destroy the plants and crops of an area.

T2 to **twist** [twɪst] — sich winden; biegen; verdrehen — Can you **twist** the wire (= Draht) to form a circle?

palm (tree) [ˈpɑːm triː] — Palme
pullover [ˈpʊləʊvə] — Pullover — ❯❯ sweater
to **twitter** [ˈtwɪtə] — zwitschern — When birds **twitter** they make a number of short high sounds.

to **rush** [rʌʃ] — fließen, stürzen; eilen, hetzen — The water **was rushing** over the rocks.
We've got a lot of time. There's no need to **rush**.
spray [spreɪ] — Sprühnebel, Spray — Can you feel the **spray** from the waterfall?
frame [freɪm] — Rahmen

hexagonal [heksˈægənl] — sechseckig

hexagonal

*He drove **past** the house.*

past [pɑːst] — an … vorbei

Wörterverzeichnis **UNIT 2**

	rucksack ['rʌksæk]	Rucksack
	storey ['stɔːri]	Stockwerk
	bamboo [ˌbæm'buː]	Bambus
	claypit ['kleɪpɪt]	Tongrube
	biome ['baɪəʊm]	Biotop, Lebensraum; Biom
	the tropics ['trɒpɪks]	die Tropen
	rubber ['rʌbə]	Gummi
	mango ['mæŋgəʊ]	Mango
	olive ['ɒlɪv]	Olive
	lemon ['lemən]	Zitrone
	grape [greɪp]	Traube
	hexagon ['heksəgən]	Sechseck
Ex17	**motorway** ['məʊtəweɪ]	Autobahn
Ex20	**if only** [ɪf 'əʊnli]	wenn … nur
	even if ['iːvn ɪf]	selbst wenn
Com	**muddy** ['mʌdi]	schlammig, matschig
	could do with [kʊd 'duː wɪð]	könnte brauchen
	calculator ['kælkjuleɪtə]	Taschenrechner
Ex21	**restaurant** ['restrɒnt]	Restaurant
Ex22	**atom** ['ætəm]	Atom
	laser ['leɪzə]	Laser
TYE	**dung** [dʌŋ]	Mist, Dung
	fly [flaɪ]	Fliege
	prediction [prɪ'dɪkʃn]	Vorhersage
	to overlook [ˌəʊvə'lʊk]	übersehen
	illuminated [ɪ'luːmɪneɪtɪd]	beleuchtet
	loudspeaker [ˌlaʊd'spiːkə]	Lautsprecher
TYE2	**to paraphrase** ['pærəfreɪz]	umschreiben, paraphrasieren
TYE4	**listener** ['lɪsnə]	Zuhörer/in
	panic ['pænɪk]	Panik
TYE5	**sighting** ['saɪtɪŋ]	Sichten
	to identify [aɪ'dentɪfaɪ]	identifizieren
	unidentified [ˌʌnaɪ'dentɪfaɪd]	unbekannt, nicht identifiziert
	object ['ɒbdʒɪkt]	Gegenstand
	to fill in [ˌfɪl 'ɪn]	ausfüllen
	to spin [spɪn] **spun, spun** [spʌn, spʌn]	schleudern (Wäsche)
Read	**hitchhiker** ['hɪtʃhaɪkə]	Anhalter/in, Tramper/in
	galaxy ['gæləksi]	Sternsystem
	after all [ˌɑːftər 'ɔːl]	schließlich; doch

≫ *backpack*
a five-**storey** building

He looked **as if** he had some bad news.

Tyres are almost always made of **rubber**.

mango   olive   lemon   grape

A **hexagon** has six straight sides.

If only she had listened to me.
❯ *whether or not*
The path was **muddy** after all the rain.
I **could do with** a drink now.

Can I borrow your (pocket) **calculator**?
A **restaurant** is a place where you can buy and eat a meal.

cow/horse **dung**
A **fly** is an insect.
It's difficult to make **predictions** about the future.
≫ *to miss, to fail to see*
❯ *lit with bright lights*

Her name was called over the **loudspeaker**.

❯ *to repeat something using different words*

❯ *a person who listens (to a radio programme, etc)*
They ran away **in panic**.
They reported another **sighting** of the Loch Ness Monster.
❯ *to recognize somebody/something*

≫ *thing*
Please **fill in** this form.

She often picks up **hitchhikers**.
❯ *one of the groups of stars in the universe*
The rain has stopped, so the barbecue will go ahead **after all**.

one hundred and thirty-one **131**

UNIT 2 **Wörterverzeichnis**

to **shrug** [ʃrʌg]	mit den Achseln zucken	He **shrugged** his shoulders and left.
sort of [ˈsɔːt əv]	Art, Sorte von	They both drink the same **sort of** coffee.
to **bother (with/about** sth) [ˈbɒðə]	sich (um etwas) kümmern	He doesn't **bother** much **about** fashion.
to **be about to** do sth [bi əˈbaʊt tə]	im Begriff sein, etwas zu tun	❭ to be going to do something very soon
to **drink up** [ˌdrɪŋk ˈʌp] **drank, drunk** [dræŋk, drʌŋk]	austrinken	Come on, **drink up** your coke.
motionless [ˈməʊʃnləs]	regungslos, unbeweglich	❭ still, not moving
public address system [ˌpʌblɪk əˈdres sɪstəm]	Lautsprecheranlage, Verstärkeranlage	
galactic [gəˈlæktɪk]	galaktisch	inter-**galactic** travel
hyperspace [ˈhaɪpəspeɪs]	Hyperraum	
council [ˈkaʊnsl]	Rat(sversammlung)	the city **council**, a **council** member
to **be aware (of)** [bi əˈweər əv]	sich einer Sache bewusst sein	He **was** well **aware of** the problem.
outlying [ˈaʊtlaɪɪŋ]	abgelegen, entlegen	⚠ Adj nur vor Nomen the **outlying** districts of London
to **schedule** sth **(for** sth) [ˈʃedjuːl]	etwas (für etwas) ansetzen, planen	The meeting is **scheduled for** tomorrow evening. AE [ˈskedjuːl]
demolition [ˌdeməˈlɪʃn]	Zerstörung, Vernichtung	
slight [slaɪt]	gering, klein, leicht	a **slight** accident/headache
slightly [ˈslaɪtli]	ein bisschen, etwas	❭❭ a little I'm **slightly** tired.
terror [ˈterə]	panische Angst, Schrecken	❭ extreme fear
point [pɔɪnt]	Sinn, Zweck	There's no **point** in getting upset. = Es hat keinen Zweck sich aufzuregen. What's the **point** of that? = Was soll das?
on display [ɒn dɪˈspleɪ]	ausgestellt	The new books are **on display** in the library.
fuss [fʌs]	Wirbel, Aufhebens, Theater	to make a **fuss** about sth = viel Wind um etw machen
to **demolish** [dɪˈmɒlɪʃ]	zerstören, vernichten	❭ to completely destroy a building, etc
to **frown (at** sth/sb) [fraʊn]	die Stirn runzeln (über etwas/jdn)	What are you **frowning at** me for?
to **panic** [ˈpænɪk]	in Panik geraten	The crowd **panicked** when the shots rang out.

Tricky words   **Wörter, die leicht verwechselt werden**

advice	*Rat(schlag)*	**than**	*als*
to **advise**	*einen Rat geben*	**then**	*dann, damals*
loss	*Verlust*	**whether**	*ob*
to **lose**	*verlieren*	**weather**	*Wetter*
to **practise** *BE*	*üben*	**whole**	*ganz, gesamt*
practice	*Übung, Praxis*	**hole**	*Loch*
quiet	*ruhig*	**whose**	*deren, dessen; wessen*
quite	*ziemlich*	**who's**	*Wer ist?; der ist*
shirt	*Hemd*		
skirt	*Rock*		

132 **one hundred and thirty-two**

Unit 3

WP to **spread** [sprɛd]   (sich) verbreiten,   *The fire **spread** very rapidly.*
spread, spread   (sich) ausbreiten
[sprɛd, sprɛd]

blues [bluːz]   Blues (Musikrichtung)   ❯ *slow sad music*
to **shock** [ʃɒk]   schockieren
rock [rɒk]   Rock (Musikrichtung)   *a **rock** group/star*
legend ['ledʒənd]   Legende   *Ella Fitzgerald was a jazz **legend**.*
decade ['dekeɪd]   Jahrzehnt   ❯ *a period of ten years*
flared [fleəd]   ausgestellt (Kleidung)   ***flared** trousers*

bell-bottom trousers   Schlaghosen
[ˌbelbɒtəm 'traʊzəz]

bell-bottom trousers

Sit1 **brilliant** ['brɪliənt]   großartig, glänzend;   ❯❯ *very good*
strahlend

sex [seks]   Sex, Geschlechtsverkehr;   *What **sex** is your dog? – Teri is female.*
Geschlecht

songwriter ['sɒŋraɪtə]   Liedermacher/in,   ❯ *a person who writes songs*
Songschreiber/in

curly ['kɜːli]   lockig, kraus   *a **curly**-haired girl*
record ['rekɔːd]   Schallplatte; Rekord
dancer ['dɑːnsə]   Tänzer/in   *He's a **dancer** in the musical 'The Lion King'.*
Ex1 **quote** [kwəʊt]   Zitat *umg*
Sit2 **nearly** ['nɪəli]   fast, beinahe   ❯❯ *almost*
to **be sold out**   ausverkauft sein   *We couldn't get seats. The rock concert **was sold out**.*
[bi ˌsəʊld 'aʊt]

Ex2 to **allow** [ə'laʊ]   erlauben   *Do you think mum will **allow** me to go to Jill's party?*
to **promise** sth (**to** sb)   (jdm) etwas versprechen   *You can't have the DVD. I **promised** it **to** Frank.*
['prɒmɪs]

T1 to **be keen on** do**ing** sth   gern mögen / darauf wild   *She's **keen on** cycling.*
/to do sth [bi 'kiːn ɒn]   sein, etwas zu tun
gap [gæp]   Lücke, Spalt, Abstand   *Look at the **gaps** and fill in the words.*
generation gap   Unterschied zwischen
[dʒenə'reɪʃn gæp]   den Generationen
to **swear** [sweə]   fluchen
swore, sworn
[swɔː, swɔːn]
tight [taɪt]   eng(anliegend)   *She was wearing a **tight** pair of jeans.*
underwear ['ʌndəweə]   Unterwäsche   ❯ *clothes that you wear under other clothes*
beetle ['biːtl]   Käfer
economy [ɪ'kɒnəmi]   Wirtschaft   ❯ *the system of trade and industry*
the charts [ðə 'tʃɑːts]   die Hitliste, die Charts   ❯ *the list of records with the highest sales*
suit [suːt]   Anzug   *All the businessmen wore **suits**.*
miniskirt ['mɪniskɜːt]   Minirock   ❯ *a very short skirt*
heart attack ['hɑːt ətæk]   Herzanfall, Herzinfarkt
hippie ['hɪpi]   Hippie   ❯ *a young person in the late 1960s and early 1970s who believed in peace, had long hair and often lived in groups (communes)*

second-hand   gebraucht, aus zweiter   *a **second-hand** bookshop/car*
[ˌsekənd'hænd]   Hand   ❯✗ *new*
hot pants ['hɒt pænts]   Hotpants   ❯ *very short tight women's shorts*

UNIT 3   Wörterverzeichnis

parka

parka ['pɑːkə]	Parka	
romantic [rəʊ'mæntɪk]	romantisch	a **romantic** novel/story/comedy
punk [pʌŋk]	Punk	
skateboard ['skeɪtbɔːd]	Skateboard	
lifestyle ['laɪfstaɪl]	Lebensstil	
synthesizer ['sɪnθəsaɪzə]	Synthesizer	❯ an electronic keyboard instrument
LP [ˌel 'piː]	Langspielplatte	❯ a long-playing record
leggings ['legɪnz]	Leggings	
yuppie ['jʌpi]	Yuppie	❯ a young person who lives in a city, earns a lot of money and spends it doing trendy things
reunification [ˌriːjuːnɪfɪ'keɪʃn]	Wiedervereinigung	the **reunification** of Germany
economic [ˌiːkə'nɒmɪk]	wirtschaftlich; Wirtschafts-	**economic** = *Wirtschafts-* **economical** = *sparsam, ökonomisch*
crisis ['kraɪsɪs] *pl* **crises**	Krise	❯ a time of great danger or trouble
Goth [gɒθ]	Gothic (Musikrichtung)	
techno ['teknəʊ]	Techno (Musikrichtung)	
rave [reɪv]	Rave-Party	an all-night **rave**, **rave** music
Ecstasy ['ekstəsi]	Ecstasy (illegale Droge)	
XXXL [ˌeks ˌeks ˌeks 'el]	übergroß, XXXL	
piercing ['pɪəsɪŋ]	Piercing	He has several tattoos and **piercings**.
Ex7 **announce** [ə'naʊns]	ansagen, bekannt geben	❯ to tell people some important news
to **differ** ['dɪfə]	sich unterscheiden, verschieden sein	❯ to be different (from sb/sth)
Ex8 **organizer** ['ɔːgənaɪzə]	Veranstalter/in, Organisator/in	He talked to the **organizer** of the pop festival.
Ex9 **dentist** ['dentɪst]	Zahnarzt, Zahnärztin	A **dentist** treats or takes out bad teeth.
finger ['fɪŋgə]	Finger	**fish fingers** = *Fischstäbchen*
zero ['zɪərəʊ]	Null	❯ the number 0
cream [kriːm]	Sahne, Rahm	Do you like **cream** in your coffee?
coin [kɔɪn]	Münze	a pound **coin**, a ten cent **coin**
rent [rent]	Miete	**rent** = *Miete* *Rente* = **pension**
fork [fɔːk]	Gabel	
secretary ['sekrətri]	Sekretär/in	
exit ['eksɪt]	Ausgang	❯❮ entrance
to **subtract** [səb'trækt]	abziehen, subtrahieren	❯ to take a number away from another number
leak [liːk]	undichte Stelle, Leck	There was a **leak** in the pipeline.
to **smoke** [sməʊk]	rauchen	When you see this sign, you mustn't **smoke**.
cigarette [ˌsɪgə'ret]	Zigarette	

True friends

Die Bedeutung vieler englischer Wörter lässt sich leicht erraten, da ihre deutschen Entsprechungen ähnlich klingen oder geschrieben werden. Diese Wörter sind *true friends* (**wahre Freunde**). In dieser Unit waren das bisher z.B.: legend, hot pants, parka, finger, synthesizer, piercing, cigarette, charts, leggings.

134   one hundred and thirty-four

Wörterverzeichnis **UNIT 3**

> **False friends**
>
> Es gibt jedoch auch *false friends* (**falsche Freunde**). *Gift* und „das Gift" sind *false friends*, weil *gift* eben nicht „das Gift" heißt, sondern „das Geschenk". („Das Gift" heißt im Englischen *poison*.) Bei diesen Wörtern musst du besonders aufpassen und immer den Kontext beachten.
>
> | | | |
> |---|---|---|
> | **art** – *Kunst* | to **handle** – *mit etw umgehen* | to **spend** – *ausgeben* |
> | *Art* – **kind, sort, way** | *Handel* – **trade** | *spenden* – to **give** |
> | | | |
> | to **become** – *werden* | **meaning** – *Bedeutung* | **taste** – *Geschmack* |
> | *bekommen* – to **get** | *Meinung* – **opinion** | *Taste* – **key, button** |
> | | | |
> | **eventually** – *schließlich* | **small** – *klein* | to **wonder** – *sich fragen* |
> | *eventuell* – **perhaps** | *schmal* – **narrow** | *sich wundern* – to **be surprised at** |

Sit3 **embarrassing** [ɪmˈbærəsɪŋ] peinlich
If something is embarrassing it makes you feel uncomfortable.
I can't help it [aɪ kɑːnt ˈhelp ɪt] ich kann nicht anders
Stop laughing. – **I can't help it**.
I couldn't help thinking he knew more than he told us.
tic [tɪk] Zucken, Tick
syndrome [ˈsɪndrəʊm] Syndrom
cause [kɔːz] Ursache
❯ *the reason why something happens*
to **mimic** [ˈmɪmɪk] nachahmen, imitieren
He was mimicking the teachers.
bully [ˈbʊli] Mobber/in
Bullies hurt or frighten somebody who is smaller than them.

to **cure** [kjʊə] heilen
❯ *to make somebody healthy again*
frequent [ˈfriːkwənt] häufig
❯ *happening often*
Sit4 **despite** [dɪˈspaɪt] trotz
We all enjoyed the walk despite the bad weather.
cheeseburger [ˈtʃiːzbɜːɡə] Cheeseburger
by doing sth [baɪ ˈduːɪŋ] indem man etwas macht
Ex11 to **jog** [dʒɒɡ] joggen
I go jogging every morning.
T2 **weekday** [ˈwiːkdeɪ] Wochentag
On weekdays I usually go to bed at ten o'clock.
to **hang out** [ˌhæŋ ˈaʊt], **hung, hung** [hʌŋ, hʌŋ] sich rumtreiben, rumhängen *umg*
❯ *to spend a lot of time in a place*

firefighter [ˈfaɪə faɪtə] Feuerwehrmann, Feuerwehrfrau

helmet [ˈhelmɪt] Helm, Schutzhelm
fire truck *AE* [ˈfaɪə trʌk] Feuerwehrauto
❯❯ *fire engine BE*
horn [hɔːn] Hupe; Horn
❯ *to sound your horn* = hupen ❯❯ *to hoot*
in case [ɪn ˈkeɪs] für den Fall, dass
Take an umbrella just in case it starts raining.
motorist [ˈməʊtərɪst] Autofahrer/in
❯ *a person who drives a car*
sneakers *AE* [ˈsniːkəz] Turnschuhe
❯ *shoes that you wear for playing sports*
to **bless** [bles] segnen
❯ *to be blessed with sth* = mit etwas gesegnet sein
to **get married** [ɡet ˈmærɪd], **got, got** [ɡɒt, ɡɒt] heiraten
She got married at 26. = Sie heiratete mit 26.

to **be fond of** [ˈfɒnd əv] mögen, gern haben
adoption agency [əˌdɒpʃn ˈeɪdʒənsi] Adoptionsvermittlungsstelle
❯❯ *to like very much*

one hundred and thirty-five **135**

UNIT 3   Wörterverzeichnis

	to **adopt** [ə'dɒpt]	adoptieren	❯ *to take another person's child into your family to become your own child*
	disability [ˌdɪsə'bɪləti]	Behinderung	*a learning/physical* **disability** *adj:* **disabled**
	to **puzzle** ['pʌzl]	Rätsel aufgeben, verwirren	
	to **multiply** ['mʌltɪplaɪ]	multiplizieren, malnehmen	*2* **multiplied by** *4 is 8.*
	seizure ['siːʒə]	Anfall	❯ *a sudden attack of an illness*
	to **quit** [kwɪt] **quit/quitted, quit/quitted** [kwɪt, kwɪtɪd]	aufhören mit; verlassen	❯ *to stop doing something*
	fetal ['fiːtl] *AE*	fetal, Fetal-	
	pregnant ['pregnənt]	schwanger	*She's six and a half months* **pregnant**.
	score [skɔː]	Punktestand, Spielstand	*The final* **score** *was 2–4.*
	odd jobs [ˌɒd 'dʒɒbz]	anfallende Arbeiten	❯ *small jobs of various types*
	joker ['dʒəʊkə]	Spaßvogel *umg*	
	to **joke** [dʒəʊk]	Witze machen, scherzen	❯ *to tell a funny story or make a funny comment*
	rather ['rɑːðə]	ziemlich	*The story was* **rather** *complicated.*
	to **keep an eye on** sb/sth [ˌkiːp ən 'aɪ ɒn] **kept, kept** [kept, kept]	auf jdn/etwas aufpassen	*They asked their neighbours to* **keep an eye on** *the house while they were away.*
Ex16	**sunlight** ['sʌnlaɪt]	Sonnenlicht	❯ *light from the sun*
	clumsy ['klʌmzi]	unhandlich, ungeschickt	
Com	to **be fascinated by** [bi 'fæsɪneɪtɪd baɪ]	fasziniert sein von	❯❯ *to be very interested in*
	to **be into** sth [bi 'ɪntə]	auf etwas stehen, auf etwas abfahren	❯❯ *to be interested in* *Hugh* **is** *really* **into** *skydiving.*
	informal [ɪn'fɔːml]	umgangssprachlich; ungezwungen	*'Hi' is an* **informal** *way of greeting people.*
Ex20	**period** ['pɪəriəd]	Zeit, Zeitraum	
TYE	**political** [pə'lɪtɪkl]	politisch	
	issue ['ɪʃuː]	Frage, Thema; Ausgabe (Zeitung)	❯ *an important topic* *This is a big* **issue**. *We have to discuss it.* *The article appeared in* **issue** *47 of 'What's On?'*
	support [sə'pɔːt]	Unterstützung, Hilfe	❯❯ *help*
	opposition [ˌɒpə'zɪʃn]	Opposition	**opposition** *party/leader*
	party ['pɑːti]	Partei	*There are two main political* **parties** *in Britain.*
	demonstration [ˌdemən'streɪʃn]	Demonstration	*anti-government/protest* **demonstrations**
	to **oppose** [ə'pəʊz]	sich widersetzen	❯ *to be/to fight against somebody/something*
	to **hit the headlines** [ˌhɪt ðə 'hedlaɪnz] **hit, hit** [hɪt, hɪt]	Schlagzeilen machen	
	protester [prə'testə]	Demonstrant/in	*Thousands of* **protesters** *marched through the streets.*
	bullet ['bʊlɪt]	Kugel, Geschoss	*He was killed by a* **bullet** *in the head.*
	to **take notice of** sth [ˌteɪk 'nəʊtɪs əv] **took, taken** [tʊk, 'teɪkən]	etwas beachten, etwas zur Kenntnis nehmen	❯❯ *to pay attention to something*
TYE1	**water cannon** ['wɔːtə kænən]	Wasserwerfer	

136   one hundred and thirty-six

Wörterverzeichnis **UNIT 3**

Read

lock [lɒk]	Schloss (Tür)	
post [pəʊst]	Post(sendung)	*I'll send you the text by **post**.*
cereal ['sɪərɪəl]	Getreideflocken	
apparent [ə'pærənt]	offensichtlich, scheinbar	*It was **apparent to** everyone that she was unhappy.*
apparently [ə'pærəntli]	anscheinend, offensichtlich	
attempt [ə'tempt]	Versuch	*He made no **attempt** to help her.*
conference ['kɒnfərəns]	Konferenz, Besprechung	*They held a **conference** on women's rights.*
to shine [ʃaɪn]	glänzen, scheinen	*A light **was shining** through the trees.*
shone, shone [ʃɒn, ʃɒn]		
either … or ['aɪðə, ɔː]	entweder … oder	*She's **either** French **or** Italian.*
fury ['fjʊəri]	Wut	
ability [ə'bɪləti]	Fähigkeit	› *be able to do something*
to mourn [mɔːn]	betrauern, beklagen	› *to feel sad because somebody has died or something is gone forever*
obscene [əb'siːn]	obszön; unverschämt, widerlich	*an **obscene** phone call*
greedy ['griːdi]	habgierig, gierig	*Don't be so **greedy** – you've had three hamburgers already.*
to consult [kən'sʌlt]	fragen, konsultieren	
pointless ['pɔɪntləs]	sinnlos, zwecklos	› *not worth doing*
to spoil [spɔɪl]	verwöhnen; verderben	› *to give a child everything that they ask for*
spoilt/spoiled, spoilt/spoiled [spɔɪlt, spɔɪlt]		*We can't eat the meat. It's **spoiled**.*
force [fɔːs]	Macht, Kraft	›› *power*
darkness ['dɑːknəs]	Dunkelheit, Finsternis	*I switched off the light and the room was in **darkness**.*
women's refuge [ˌwɪmɪnz 'refjuːdʒ]	Frauenhaus	› *a house where women whose partners have been violent towards them can go with their children for protection*
unhappy [ʌn'hæpi]	unglücklich	›‹ *happy*
fraction ['frækʃn]	Bruchteil	› *a small part of something*
recent ['riːsnt]	jüngst, aktuell	*Is that a **recent** photo?*
recently ['riːsntli]	vor kurzem, neulich	› *not long ago*
patience ['peɪʃns]	Geduld	› *the ability to wait without complaining*
angel ['eɪndʒəl]	Engel	
grudging ['grʌdʒɪŋ]	widerwillig, unwillig	

Tricky words   **Wörter, die leicht verwechselt werden**

to **afford**	*sich leisten können*	to **cost**	*kosten*	**pupil**	*Schüler/in*
effort	*Anstrengung*	**coast**	*Küste*	**people**	*Leute*
also	*auch*	**its**	*sein (Pron)*	**soup**	*Suppe*
although	*obwohl*	**it's**	*es ist*	**soap**	*Seife*
at last	*schließlich*	**life**	*Leben*	**sweat**	*Schweiß*
at least	*zumindest*	to **live**	*leben, wohnen*	**sweet**	*süß, Süßigkeit*
		live	*live*		
because	*weil, da*	**price**	*(Kauf-) Preis*		
of course	*natürlich*	**prize**	*Preis, Auszeichnung*		

one hundred and thirty-seven   **137**

UNIT 4   Wörterverzeichnis

Unit 4

	mosaic [məʊ'zeɪɪk]	Mosaik
WP	**enormous** [ɪ'nɔːməs]	gewaltig, enorm groß
	extreme [ɪk'striːm]	extrem, äußerst
	general ['dʒenrəl]	generell, allgemein; ungefähr
	generally ['dʒenrəli]	gewöhnlich; allgemein
	to **inhabit** [ɪn'hæbɪt]	bewohnen
	Inuit ['ɪnuɪt]	Inuit
	ethnic ['eθnɪk]	ethnisch; Volks-
	diverse [daɪ'vɜːs]	unterschiedlich, vielfältig
	maple ['meɪpl]	Ahorn
	leaf [liːf] *pl* **leaves**	Blatt
	province ['prɒvɪns]	Provinz
Sit1	**shopping mall** ['ʃɒpɪŋ mæl]	Einkaufszentrum
	patient ['peɪʃnt]	geduldig
	though [ðəʊ]	doch, jedoch, trotzdem
	to **suit** [suːt]	stehen (Kleidung, Farben)

›› *very large*
›› *very great*

›› *usually*
› *to live in a place*

ethnic groups/violence/cooking
› *very different from each other*
maple leaves

the Canadian *province* of Alberta
› *a large number of shops under one roof*

› *able to wait for a long time without complaining*

Blue *suits* her.

Passen

This key doesn't **fit** the lock.	= *(der Größe nach) passen*
This colour doesn't **suit** me.	= *stehen, zusagen, gefallen*
The trousers don't **match** the top.	= *(in der Farbe) zusammenpassen*

---

	lately ['leɪtli]	in letzter Zeit, vor kurzem
Ex1	to **shut** [ʃʌt]	schließen
	shut, shut [ʃʌt, ʃʌt]	
Sit2	**fairly** ['feəli]	ziemlich, relativ

›› *recently*
›› *to close*

›› *not very*   I know her *fairly* well.

Ziemlich – Adverbs of degree

not tired	a bit/a little tired	quite/rather/fairly tired	very/really/extremely tired
↓	↓	↓	↓

---

	badminton ['bædmɪntən]	Badminton
Ex3	**total** ['təʊtl]	völlig, absolut
T1	to **irritate** ['ɪrɪteɪt]	ärgern, reizen
	only ['əʊnli]	einzige(r, s)
	tree-lined ['triːlaɪnd]	baumbestanden
	handy ['hændi]	praktisch, nützlich, handlich
	inferior [ɪn'fɪəriə]	minderwertig, unterlegen
	to **stand for** sth ['stænd fə]	für etwas stehen
	stood, stood [stʊd, stʊd]	

›› *complete*
› *to make somebody a little angry*
› *an* **only** *child* = ein Einzelkind
They live in a **tree-lined** *road.*

> **handy** = *praktisch*
> *Handy* = **mobile (phone)**

› *not as good as something/somebody else*
The book is by Joanne K. Rowling. – What does the 'K' **stand for**? *– It* **stands for** *'Kathleen'.*

138   **one hundred and thirty-eight**

Wörterverzeichnis   UNIT 4

to **point** sth **out** [ˌpɔɪnt ˈaʊt]	auf etwas hinweisen	▸ to give somebody some information He always **cheats** at cards.
to **cheat** [tʃiːt]	mogeln, schummeln, betrügen	

antenna

antenna [ænˈtenə]	Antenne	
reception [rɪˈsepʃn]	Empfang (Fernsehen, Radio)	He lives on top of a hill. That's why he gets excellent radio **reception**.
reply [rɪˈplaɪ]	Antwort	▸▸ answer
to **float** [fləʊt]	treiben, schwimmen, schweben	The empty bottle **floated** on the river.
beside [bɪˈsaɪd]	neben	▸▸ next to
stadium [ˈsteɪdiəm]	Stadion	Thousands of football fans left the **stadium** after the match.
use [juːs]	Gebrauch, Verwendung	Don't touch the machine when it's in **use**.
sensitive (about/to) [ˈsensətɪv]	empfindlich, sensibel (gegenüber)	**sensitive** = *sensibel* *vernünftig* = **sensible**
comparison [kəmˈpærɪsn]	Vergleich	**comparison** between American and Canadian food
ferry [ˈferi]	Fähre	▸ a boat which carries people, vehicles and goods across water
to **be set (in)** [bi ˈset ɪn]	spielen in (Handlung)	'West Side Story' **is set in** New York in the late 1950s.
to **suspect** [səˈspekt]	vermuten; misstrauen, verdächtigen	I **suspect** it's going to be a difficult day. He's **suspected** of murder.
cultural [ˈkʌltʃərəl]	kulturell	**cultural** differences
diversity [daɪˈvɜːsəti]	Vielfalt	He talked about the cultural **diversity** of Native Americans.
Fahrenheit [ˈfærənhaɪt]	Fahrenheit (Temperatureinheit)	Shall I give you the temperature in Celsius or in **Fahrenheit**?

Changing Fahrenheit to Celsius:

- Begin by subtracting 32 from the Fahrenheit number.
- Multiply that answer by 5.
- Then divide the answer by 9.

Example: Change 95 degrees Fahrenheit to Celsius:
95 minus 32 is 63.
Then, 63 times 5 is 315.
Finally, 315 divided by 9 is **35 degrees Celsius**.
Time to go to the beach!

Changing Celsius to Fahrenheit:

- Begin by multiplying the Celsius temperature by 9.
- Divide the answer by 5.
- Now add 32.

Example: Change 20 degrees Celsius to Fahrenheit:
20 times 9 is 180.
Then 180 divided by 5 is 36
Finally, 36 plus 32 is **68 degrees Fahrenheit**.
A nice temperature for taking a walk!

---

smile [smaɪl]	Lächeln	'Hi', he said with a **smile**.
Ex10 **vice versa** [ˌvaɪs ˈvɜːsə]	umgekehrt	He doesn't believe her and **vice versa** (= she doesn't believe him).
Song **string** [strɪŋ]	Saite (Musikinstrument)	

one hundred and thirty-nine   139

UNIT 4   Wörterverzeichnis

	dime [daɪm]	Zehncentstück (USA, Kanada)	❯ a coin worth ten cents
	five and dime [ˌfaɪv ən 'daɪm]	billiger Laden	
	to **bleed** [bliːd] **bled, bled** [bled, bled]	bluten	❯ to lose blood [blʌd] (Blut)
	choice [tʃɔɪs]	Entscheidung; Wahl	The menu offers a wide **choice** of meals.
	ain't [eɪnt]	umgangssprachliche Kurzform von am/is/are not und has/have not	He **ain't** coming. I **ain't** got no money.
	drive-in ['draɪv ɪn]	Drive-in	❯ a **drive-in** bank/movie/restaurant, etc is one that you can use or visit without getting out of your car
	porch [pɔːtʃ]	Veranda; Vorbau, Portal	
	reckless ['rekləs]	leichtsinnig, unbesonnen, rücksichtslos	He was fined for **reckless** driving.
	to **unwind** [ˌʌn'waɪnd] **unwound, unwound** [ˌʌn'waʊnd, ˌʌn'waʊnd]	abschalten, sich entspannen	❯❯ to relax Listening to music helps me to **unwind** after a busy day.
Sit3	to **dump** [dʌmp]	abladen (Müll), versenken	❯ to throw away things that you don't want
	drum [drʌm]	Fass (Öl), Tonne	an oil **drum**
	shall [ʃəl]	sollen	What **shall** we do tonight?
	while [waɪl]	Weile	They sat chatting for a **while** (= for a short time).
Sit4	to **delete** [di'liːt]	löschen (Computer); streichen	❯ to remove something that has been written or stored on a computer
	back-up (copy) ['bækʌp ˌkɒpi]	Sicherungskopie, Backup	The company's **back-up copies** are all kept in a different building.
T2	to **follow** sth **up** [ˌfɒləʊ 'ʌp]	etwas nachgehen, etwas weiter verfolgen	❯ to find out more about something
	scandal ['skændl]	Skandal(geschichte)	Some magazines contain nothing but **scandal**.
	to **chase** [tʃeɪs]	verfolgen	❯ to run after somebody or something to catch them
	swampland ['swɒmplənd]	Sumpfgebiet	❯ an area of soft, wet land
	smooth [smuːð]	glatt, sanft	❌ rough
	unreal [ˌʌn'rɪəl]	unwirklich	❌ real ❯ more like a dream than reality
	snow bank ['snəʊ bæŋk]	Schneeverwehung	
	4x4/four-by-four [ˌfɔː baɪ 'fɔː]	Fahrzeug mit Vierradantrieb	
	pothole ['pɒthəʊl]	Schlagloch	❯ a large hole in the surface of a road
	within [wɪ'ðɪn]	innerhalb	

Within

SPACE	TIME	DISTANCE
There are 40 people **within** the building.	I'll come **within** an hour.	Most Californians live **within** 15 miles of the coast.
= inside	= before the end of	= no further than

140   one hundred and forty

Wörterverzeichnis **UNIT 4**

icy ['aɪsi]	eisig	❯ very cold; covered with ice
emergency [ɪ'mɜːdʒənsi]	Notfall; Not-	an **emergency** exit/landing
spare part [ˌspeə 'pɑːt]	Ersatzteil	A **spare part** can be used to replace another similar part in a car.
tonne [tʌn]	Tonne	1000 kilograms
illegal [ɪ'liːgl]	ungesetzlich, illegal	❯ not allowed by the law
to prove [pruːv]	beweisen	❯ to show that something is true
plant [plɑːnt]	Werk, Fabrik	❯❯ factory
hydroelectric [ˌhaɪdrəʊ'lektrɪk]	hydroelektrisch, Wasserkraft-	a **hydroelectric** power station
to contaminate [kən'tæmɪneɪt]	verseuchen, verunreinigen	The town's drinking water was **contaminated** with chemical waste.
to walk on [ˌwɔːk 'ɒn]	weiterlaufen, weitergehen	

Ex23
surroundings pl [sə'raʊndɪŋz]	Umgebung	❯❯ environment
description [dɪ'skrɪpʃn]	Beschreibung	Can you give us a full **description** of the missing child?
column ['kɒləm]	Spalte; Säule	
windy ['wɪndi]	windig	It was a **windy** day.

sunny   stormy   cloudy   rainy   windy   snowy   foggy

TYE
inhospitable [ˌɪnhɒ'spɪtəbl]	unwirtlich	an **inhospitable** climate
nomadic [nəʊ'mædɪk]	nomadisch; Nomaden-	**Nomadic** people don't live in any one place for very long.
wage(s) ['weɪdʒɪz]	Lohn	❯ the money that you earn
seal [siːl]	Robbe, Seehund	
stilt [stɪlt]	Pfahl, Stelze	
sled [sled]	Schlitten	
snowmobile ['snəʊməbiːl]	Schneemobil	

sled   snowmobile

daylight ['deɪlaɪt]	Tageslicht	The animals are shy and don't come out in **daylight**.
suicide ['suːɪsaɪd]	Selbstmord	The man **committed suicide** (= killed himself).

TYE4
complex ['kɒmpleks]	zusammengesetzt, komplex	❯❮ simple
to die out [ˌdaɪ 'aʊt]	aussterben	Dinosaurs **died out** millions of years ago.

Read
to cling to sth ['klɪŋ tə] clung, clung [klʌŋ, klʌŋ]	kleben, haften, sich an etwas klammern	**cling** film = Klarsichtfolie
blanket ['blæŋkɪt]	Decke, Wolldecke	
to shovel ['ʃʌvl]	schaufeln	
driveway ['draɪvweɪ]	Einfahrt, Zufahrt	He parked in the **driveway**.

one hundred and forty-one **141**

UNIT 4 Wörterverzeichnis

snowplough ['snəʊplaʊ] Schneepflug

branch [brɑːntʃ]	Ast	
trick [trɪk]	Trick	
slush [slʌʃ]	Schneematsch	
to **turn to/into** ['tɜːn tə]	verwandeln in	
tyre ['taɪə]	Reifen	*snow* **tyres** = Winterreifen
chiropractor ['kaɪərəʊpræktə]	Chiropraktiker/in	
guard rail ['gɑːd reɪl]	Leitplanke; Schutzgeländer	
to **stink** [stɪŋk] **stank, stunk** [stæŋk, stʌŋk]	stinken	*It* **stinks** *in here.*
off [ɒf]	aus, abgestellt	*Please make sure that the TV is* **off**.
kerosine ['kerəsiːn]	Petroleum, Kerosin	
heater ['hiːtə]	Heizofen	*a gas/an electric* **heater**
burn [bɜːn]	Verbrennung	

eyelash

eyelash ['aɪlæʃ] Augenwimper

to **total** *AE* ['təʊtl]	zu Schrott fahren *umg*	▸ *to damage a car so badly that it cannot be repaired*
mailbox *AE* ['meɪlbɒks]	Briefkasten	
to **cave in** [ˌkeɪv 'ɪn]	einstürzen, nachgeben	*If a ceiling or roof* **caves in**, *it breaks and falls into the space below.*
to **wound** [wuːnd]	verwunden	▸ *to injure somebody with a knife, gun, etc*

pick [pɪk] Spitzhacke

pick

bastard ['bɑːstəd]	Mistkerl, Schwein *umg*
snowblind ['snəʊblaɪnd]	schneeblind
toe [təʊ]	Zehe

Tricky words	**Wörter, die leicht verwechselt werden**		
finished	*fertig, erledigt*	to **borrow**	*sich etwas leihen*
ready	*fertig, bereit*	to **lend**	*etwas verleihen*
to **take place**	*stattfinden (planmäßige Handlung)*	**heavy**	*schwer (Gewicht)*
		difficult	*schwer, schwierig*
to **happen**	*passieren (zufällige Ereignisse)*		
to **occur**	*sich ereignen, vorkommen*		

Wörterverzeichnis

Projects

Proj1	**inhabitant** [ɪnˈhæbɪtənt]	Bewohner/in	❯ somebody who lives in a place
	instrument [ˈɪnstrəmənt]	Instrument	Does she play an **instrument**?
	to **face** sth [feɪs]	vor etwas stehen; gegenüber sein	She**'s faced** with a difficult problem. They sat **facing** each other.
Proj2	**synonym** [ˈsɪnənɪm]	Synonym, Wort mit ähnlicher Bedeutung	'Large' and 'big' are **synonyms**.
	taboo [təˈbuː] *pl* **taboos**	Tabu	
	board game [ˈbɔːd ɡeɪm]	Brettspiel	Chess is a **board game**.
	dictation [dɪkˈteɪʃn]	Diktat	Our English **dictation** lasted half an hour.

Revision

Rev5	**clue** [kluː]	Hinweis	Police are still looking for **clues** in the case of the missing girl.
Rev9	to **wander** [ˈwɒndə]	wandern, schlendern	❯ to walk around slowly
	amusing [əˈmjuːzɪŋ]	lustig, amüsant	❯❯ funny
Rev11	**substitute** [ˈsʌbstɪtjuːt]	Ersatz(form)	'Be able to' is a **substitute** for 'can'.
Rev12	**customs** [ˈkʌstəmz]	Zoll(behörde)	**customs** officer = Zollbeamter
	frog [frɒɡ]	Frosch	
	reptile [ˈreptaɪl]	Reptil	
	maximum [ˈmæksɪməm]	Höchst-; maximal	What is the **maximum** speed of this car?
	sentence [ˈsentəns]	Strafe, Urteil	a prison/jail/life/4-year **sentence**
Rev13	to **deal with** [ˈdiːl wɪð] **dealt, dealt** [delt, delt]	sich beschäftigen mit	❯ to take the necessary action to solve a problem
	crocodile [ˈkrɒkədaɪl]	Krokodil	

	hell [hel]	Hölle	
	neither [ˈnaɪðə]	keine(r, s) von beiden	I've got two computers but **neither** works properly.
Rev14	**private** [ˈpraɪvət]	privat	❳ public
Rev15	to **be frightened of** [bi ˈfraɪtnd əv]	Angst haben vor	❯❯ to be afraid of
Rev17	to **pollute** [pəˈluːt]	verschmutzen	
	pollution [pəˈluːʃn]	(Umwelt-)Verschmutzung	air/water **pollution**
	to **cause** [kɔːz]	verursachen, hervorrufen	❯ to make something happen
	to **rescue** [ˈreskjuː]	retten	❯❯ to save
	to **murder** [ˈmɜːdə]	ermorden	❯ to kill somebody on purpose
	victim [ˈvɪktɪm]	Opfer	❯ somebody who suffers in an attack, disaster or murder
	cash [kæʃ]	Bargeld	❯ money in coins or notes

one hundred and forty-three 143

Wörterverzeichnis

Literature

contemporary [kən'temprəri]	zeitgenössisch; Zeitgenosse/-nossin	❯❯ *modern*
literature ['lɪtrətʃə]	Literatur	*great works of **literature***
to **influence** ['ɪnfluəns]	beeinflussen	❯ *to have an effect on*
rare [reə]	selten	
miserable ['mɪzrəbl]	elend, furchtbar, armselig	❯ *very unhappy and uncomfortable*
ashes ['æʃɪz]	Asche	❯ *what is left after a dead person's body has been burned*
autobiographical [ˌɔːtəˌbaɪə'græfɪkl]	autobiografisch	*semi-**autobiographical*** = halbautobiografisch ❯ *about the writer's own life*
suburbia [sə'bɜːbiə]	die Vororte	
citizen ['sɪtɪzn]	(Staats-)Bürger/in	*She's an Australian **citizen**.*
joy [dʒɔɪ]	Freude	❯ *a feeling of great happiness*
to **be unable to** do sth [bi ʌn'eɪbl tə]	unfähig, nicht in der Lage sein, etwas zu tun	*Let me know if you're **unable to** come.*
assassin [ə'sæsɪn]	Mörder/in, Attentäter/in	*An **assassin** murders people for money or for political or religious reasons.*
reportage [rɪ'pɔːtɪdʒ]	Reportage	
chaos ['keɪɒs]	Chaos, Durcheinander	*After the party the house was in **chaos**.*
to **gather** ['gæðə]	sich (ver)sammeln	❯❯ *to come together* ❯❯ *to collect (people)*
refugee [ˌrefju'dʒiː]	Flüchtling	*a **refugee** camp* = Flüchtlingslager
to **experiment** (**with** sth) [ik'sperɪmənt]	(mit etwas) experimen- tieren	
relations [rɪ'leɪʃnz]	Beziehungen	*international **relations***
male [meɪl]	männlich	❯❮ *female*
beloved [bɪ'lʌvɪd]	Geliebte/r	❯ *a person who is loved very much by sb*
diagnosis [ˌdaɪəg'nəʊsɪs] *pl* **diagnoses**	Diagnose	
mental hospital ['mentl ˌhɒspɪtl]	Heil-und Pflegeanstalt für psychisch Kranke	
to **free** [friː]	freilassen, befreien	*100 political prisoners **were freed** yesterday morning.*
Aboriginal [ˌæbə'rɪdʒənl]	Aborigine-	
mythology [mɪ'θɒlədʒi]	Mythologie	*Greek **mythology***
ceremony ['serəməni]	Zeremonie	
coffin ['kɒfɪn]	Sarg	❯ *a box in which a dead body is buried*

Dictionary work

variant ['veəriənt]	Variante	
pronunciation [prəˌnʌnsi'eɪʃn]	Aussprache	*English **pronunciation** is sometimes difficult.*
blood [blʌd]	Blut	⚠ Vorsicht bei der Aussprache. *She lost a lot of **blood** in the accident.*
uncountable [ʌn'kaʊntəbl]	unzählbar	❯❮ *countable*

144   **one hundred and forty-four**

student ['stju:dnt]	Schüler/in, Student/in	He was a **student** at the University of California.
first-class [ˌfɜ:st 'klɑ:s]	erstklassig	❯❯ excellent
wealthy ['welθi]	reich, wohlhabend	❯❮ poor ❯❯ rich
to fear [fɪə]	fürchten, befürchten	❯ to be afraid of
unpleasant [ʌn'pleznt]	unangenehm, unerfreulich	❯❮ pleasant

Translation practice

golfer ['gɒlfə]	Golfspieler/in	
club [klʌb]	Schläger	

pyjamas [pə'dʒɑ:məz]	Schlafanzug	
to evacuate [ɪ'vækjueɪt]	evakuieren, verlassen	Minutes before the explosion the police **evacuated** the building.
unconscious [ʌn'kɒnʃəs]	bewusstlos	A stone hit him on the head and he was **unconscious** for ten minutes.

Speaking practice

home town [ˌhəʊm 'taʊn]	Heimatort	❯ the town or city that a person is from
to pretend [prɪ'tend]	so tun als ob, etwas vorgeben	The children **pretended** they were wild animals.
surname ['sɜ:neɪm]	Familienname	❯❯ family name
to revise [rɪ'vaɪz]	(Lehrstoff) wiederholen	❯ to prepare for an exam
to respond (to) [rɪ'spɒnd tə]	reagieren (auf), antworten	❯❯ to react
visual ['vɪʒuəl]	visuell	
suitable ['su:təbl]	passend, geeignet	The film isn't **suitable** for young children.
to take turns [teɪk 'tɜ:nz] took, taken [tʊk, 'teɪkən]	etwas abwechselnd tun, sich abwechseln mit	They **take turns** in doing the housework.
jumble sale ['dʒʌmbl seɪl]	Wohltätigkeitsbasar, Flohmarkt	❯ an event where old things are sold to make money for a good cause
decision [dɪ'sɪʒn]	Entscheidung	They'll reach/make/come to a **decision** in a few minutes.

List of names Liste der Eigennamen

Boys/Men

A
Adam ['ædəm]
Alex ['ælɪks]
Andy ['ændi]
Arthur ['ɑːθə]

B
Barney ['bɑːni]
Barth [bɑːt]
Ben [ben]
Bill [bɪl]
Bob [bɒb]

C
Christian ['krɪstʃən]

D
Danny ['dæni]
David ['deɪvɪd]
Dick [dɪk]
Doug [dʌg]

G
Gary ['gæri]
George [dʒɔːdʒ]
Graeme ['greɪəm]

J
Jack [dʒæk]
Jake [dʒeɪk]
James [dʒeɪmz]
Jamie ['dʒeɪmi]
Jimmy ['dʒɪmi]
Joe [dʒəʊ]
John [dʒɒn]
Josh [dʒɒʃ]

K
Karim ['kærɪm]

L
Lewis ['luːɪs]

M
Mark [mɑːk]
Matt [mæt]
Matthew ['mæθjuː]
Michael ['maɪkl]
Mike [maɪk]

N
Nick [nɪk]

O
Oliver ['ɒlɪvə]

P
Paul [pɔːl]
Peter ['piːtə]

R
Richard ['rɪtʃəd]
Rob [rɒb]
Ron [rɒn]
Ryan ['raɪən]

S
Salim ['saːliːm]
Samuel ['sæmjuəl]
Scott [skɒt]
Shane [ʃeɪn]
Steve [stiːv]

T
Taro [tɑːrəʊ]
Tim [tɪm]
Tom [tɒm]

W
William ['wɪljəm]

Girls/Women

A
Ada ['eɪdə]
Alice ['ælɪs]
Anne [æn]
Ashleigh ['æʃli]
Audrey ['ɔːdri]

B
Becky ['beki]
Betty ['beti]

C
Carla ['kɑːlə]
Carol ['kærəl]
Cathy ['kæθi]
Chloe ['kləʊi]
Claire [kleə]

D
Daisy ['deɪzi]
Dawn [dɔːn]

Deirdre ['dɪədri]
Delight [dɪ'laɪt]
Donna ['dɒnə]

E
Elizabeth [ɪ'lɪzəbəθ]
Ellie ['eli]
Emily ['eməli]
Emma ['emə]
Eth [eθ]

F
Fiona [fi'əʊnə]

G
Gracie ['greɪsi]

H
Hannah ['hænə]

J
Jane [dʒeɪn]
Jennifer ['dʒenɪfə]
Jenny ['dʒeni]
Jessica ['dʒesɪkə]
Julie ['dʒuːli]

K
Karen ['kærən]
Kate [keɪt]
Katie ['keɪti]
Kim [kɪm]
Kimberley ['kɪmbəli]
Kirsty ['kɜːsti]
Kylie ['kaɪli]

L
Laura ['lɔːrə]
Lauren ['lɒrən]
Leanne [li'æn]
Linda ['lɪndə]
Lindsay ['lɪndzi]
Lisa ['liːsə]
Lizzie ['lɪzi]

M
Margaret ['mɑːgrət]
Mary ['meəri]
Molly ['mɒli]

O
Olivia [ə'lɪviə]

P
Pam [pæm]
Philippa ['fɪlɪpə]

R
Rachel ['reɪtʃl]
Rebecca [rɪ'bekə]

S
Sandy ['sændi]
Sarah ['seərə]
Sethe ['seθə]
Sophie ['səʊfi]
Sue [suː]
Susan ['suːzn]

T
Tanya ['tɑːniə]
Tessa ['tesə]

Z
Zoe ['zəʊi]

Family names

A
Abbott ['æbət]
Albright ['ɔːlbraɪt]
Allsop ['ɔːlsɒp]
Anderson ['ændəsn]

B
Balfour ['bælfə]
Barnett ['bɑːnɪt]
Bryant ['braɪənt]

C
Carr [kɑː]

D
Dawson ['dɔːsn]
Dent [dent]
Dong-Lee [ˌdɒŋ 'liː]

E
Eastley ['iːstli]
Engert ['eŋgət]

F
Fisher ['fɪʃə]

G
Gillayley [gə'leɪli]
Gordon ['gɔːdn]
Gray [greɪ]
Guppy ['gʌpi]

H
Hill [hɪl]
Hopkins ['hɒpkɪnz]
Hymns [haɪmz]

J
Johnson ['dʒɒnsn]

K
Kelly ['keli]
Kirk [kɜːk]
Kitching ['kɪtʃɪŋ]

L
Liang [li'æŋ]
Lovell ['lʌvl]

M
McBride [mək'braɪd]
Mears [mɪəz]
Morgan ['mɔːgən]

P
Parslow ['pɑːzləʊ]
Purcell ['pɜːsl]

R
Roberts ['rɒbəts]

S
Salter ['sɔːltə]
Shaw [ʃɔː]
Shrieves [ʃriːvz]
Sinai ['saɪnaɪ]

T
Tompkins ['tɒmkɪnz]
Tsuchida [tsʊʃɪdɑ]

W
Winsley ['wɪnzli]
Woodcock ['wʊdkɒk]

List of names

Real people

A

ABBA ['æbə] schwedische Popband der
1970er Jahre

Bryan Adams [ˌbraɪən 'ædəmz] kanad.
Rocksänger (*1959)

Douglas Adams [dʌɡləs 'ædəmz] brit.
Science-Fiction-Autor (1952–2001)

Anahareo [ænə'hɑːriəʊ] vierte Ehefrau
von Grey Owl

Margaret Atwood [ˌmɑːɡrət 'ætwʊd] kan.
Schriftstellerin (*1939), die durch den
Roman *A Handmaid's Tale* bekannt
wurde

B

the Beatles [ðə 'biːtlz] brit. Popgruppe
von 1962–1970

Victoria Beckham [vɪkˌtɔːriə 'bekəm]
ehemaliges Mitglied der Popgruppe
Spice Girls (*1974)

the Bee Gees [ðə 'biː dʒiːz] brit.
Popgruppe seit den 1960er Jahren

Archie Belaney [ˌɑːtʃi bɪ'leɪni] Brite, der
unter dem Pseudonym „Grey Owl" in
Kanada als Indianer lebte

Pierce Brosnan [ˌpɪəs 'brɒznən] irischer
Schauspieler (*1953)

C

Coldplay ['kəʊldpleɪ] brit. Band

Michael Crichton [ˌmaɪkl 'kraɪtn] am.
Autor (*1942) von *Jurassic Park* und
Timeline

D

James Dean [ˌdʒeɪmz 'diːn] am.
Schauspieler (1931–1955)

E

Angele Egwuna [ɑnˌdʒel eg'wuːnə] erste
Ehefrau von Grey Owl

F

Janet Frame [ˌdʒænɪt 'freɪm] neuseel.
Schriftstellerin (1924–2004), die durch
den Roman *An Angel At My Table*
bekannt wurde

Cathy Freeman [ˌkæθi 'friːmən] austral.
Läuferin (*1973)

G

Mikhail Gorbachev [mɪˌkaɪl 'ɡɔːbətʃɒf]
russischer Politiker (*1931) und
Friedensnobelpreisträger (1990)

Grey Owl [ˌɡreɪ 'aʊl] Pseudonym für
Archie Belaney

H

Bill Haley [bɪl 'heɪli] am. Rock-'n'-Roll-
Musiker (1925–1981)

Bessie Head [ˌbesi 'hed] südafr.
Schriftstellerin (1937–1986), die durch
When Rain Clouds Gather bekannt
wurde

Jimi Hendrix [ˌdʒɪmi 'hendrɪks] am. Rock-
gitarrist (1942–1970)

Paul Hogan [ˌpɔːl 'həʊɡən] austral.
Schauspieler (*1939), der durch den
Film *Crocodile Dundee* bekannt wurde

Nick Hornby [ˌnɪk 'hɔːnbi] brit. Autor
(*1957)

John Howard [dʒɒn 'haʊəd] austral.
Ministerpräsident (*1939)

Keri Hulme [ˌkeri 'hjuːm] neuseel. Schriftstellerin (*1947), die durch den Roman
The Bone People bekannt wurde

I

David Icke [ˌdeɪvɪd 'aɪk] brit.
Verschwörungstheoretiker (*1952)

J

Janet Jackson [ˌdʒænɪt 'dʒæksn] am.
Sängerin (*1966)

Michael Jackson [ˌmaɪkl 'dʒæksn] am.
Sänger (*1958)

Mick Jagger [mɪk 'dʒæɡə] Mitglied der
Rolling Stones (*1943)

Colin Johnson [ˌkɒlɪn 'dʒɒnsn] siehe
Mudrooroo

Janis Joplin [ˌdʒænɪs 'dʒɒplɪn] am.
Sängerin (1943–1970)

K

John F. Kennedy [ˌdʒɒn ef 'kenədi] 35. am.
Präsident (1917–1963)

Martin Luther King [ˌmɑːtɪn ˌluːθə 'kɪŋ]
am. Bürgerrechtsführer (1929–1968)

Hanif Kureishi [həˌnɪf kʊ'reɪʃi] brit.
Schriftsteller (*1954), der durch *My
Beautiful Launderette* bekannt wurde

L

Avril Lavigne [ˌævrɪl lə'viːn] am. Sängerin
(*1984)

Michael Linley [ˌmaɪkl 'lɪnli] brit.
Filmproduzent (*1952)

M

Madonna [mə'dɒnə] erfolgreiche am.
Popsängerin (*1958)

the Manic Street Preachers [ðə ˌmænɪk
striːt 'priːtʃəz] brit. Band

Bob Marley [bɒb 'mɑːli] Reggae-Sänger
(1945–1981) aus Jamaica

Frank McCourt [ˌfræŋk mə'kɔːt] ir.-am.
Schriftsteller (*1930), der durch den
Roman *Angela's Ashes* bekannt wurde

Kylie Minogue [ˌkaɪli mɪ'nəʊɡ] austral.
Sängerin (*1966)

Toni Morrison [ˌtəʊni 'mɒrɪsən] am.
Schriftstellerin (*1931), die durch den
Roman *Beloved* bekannt wurde

Mudrooroo [mʌ'druːru] austral.
Schriftsteller (*1938), der unter dem
Namen Colin Johnson geboren wurde

N

V.S. Naipaul [ˌviː es 'naɪpɔːl] Schriftsteller
(*1932), der durch den Roman *A Bend
in the River* bekannt wurde

NSYNC ['ensɪŋk] am. Boygroup

O

Michael Ondaatje [ˌmaɪkl ɒn'daːtdʒiː]
Schriftsteller (*1943), der durch den
Roman *The English Patient* bekannt
wurde

Kelly Osbourne [ˌkeli 'ɒzbɔːn] Tochter von
Ozzy Osbourne (*1984)

Ozzy Osbourne [ˌɒzi 'ɒzbɔːn] brit. Heavy-
Metal-Musiker (*1948)

Lee Harvey Oswald [ˌliː ˌhɑːvi 'ɒzwəld]
wurde beschuldigt, John F. Kennedy
1963 in Dallas erschossen zu haben

P

Elvis Presley [ˌelvɪs 'prezli] am. Sänger
und Gitarrist (1935–1977)

Princess Diana [ˌprɪnses daɪ'ænə]
verstorbene Ehefrau von Prince
Charles (1961–1997)

Sergei Prokofiev [ˌseəɡeɪ prə'kɒfief]
russischer Komponist (1891–1953)

Q

Queen Elizabeth [ˌkwiːn ɪ'lɪzəbəθ] brit.
Monarchin (*1926)

R

Ian Rankin [ˌiːən 'ræŋkɪn] schott.
Schriftsteller (*1960), der durch die
John-Rebus-Kriminalromane bekannt
wurde

the Rolling Stones [ðə ˌrəʊlɪŋ 'stəʊnz] brit.
Rockgruppe seit den 1960er Jahren

Franklin D. Roosevelt [ˌfræŋklɪn diː
'rəʊzəvelt] 32. am. Präsident
(1882–1945)

Salman Rushdie [ˌsælmən 'rʊʃdi]
Schriftsteller (*1947), der durch den
Roman *Midnight's Children* bekannt
wurde

S

Carlos Santana [ˌkɑːləs sæn'tɑːnə] am.
Musiker mexikanischer Abstammung
(*1947)

Britney Spears [ˌbrɪtni 'spɪəz] am.
Sängerin (*1981)

Steven Spielberg [ˌstiːvn 'spiːlbɜːɡ] am.
Regisseur (*1946)

Sylvester Stallone [sɪlˌvestə stə'ləʊn] am.
Schauspieler und Regisseur, der durch
Filme wie *Rocky* oder *Rambo* bekannt
wurde (*1946)

Sting [stɪŋ] brit. Popsänger (*1951)

Trudie Styler [ˌtruːdi 'staɪlə] Ehefrau von
Sting, Schauspielerin und Produzentin
(*1956)

T

Amy Tan [ˌeɪmi 'tæn] chin.-am. Schriftstellerin (*1952), die durch den Roman
The Joy Luck Club bekannt wurde

Abel Tasman [ˌeɪbl 'tæzmən] niederländ.
Forschungsreisender (1603–1659), gilt
als Entdecker Neuseelands

Justin Timberlake [ˌdʒʌstɪn 'tɪmbəleɪk]
am. Sänger und ehemaliges Mitglied
von NSYNC (*1981)

John Travolta [dʒɒn trə'vɒltə] am.
Schauspieler (*1954), der mit Filmen
wie *Saturday Night Fever* bekannt
wurde

U

Joern Utzon dän. Architekt (*1918)

List of names

W

Orson Welles [ˌɔːsn ˈwelz] am. Schauspieler und Regisseur (1915–1985)
H.G. Wells [ˌeɪtʃ dʒiː ˈwelz] englischer Autor und Historiker (1866–1946)
the Who [ðə ˈhuː] brit. Band
Robbie Williams [ˌrɒbi ˈwɪljəmz] brit. Sänger (*1974)

Other names

A

All Blacks [ˈɔːl blæks] neuseel. Rugbymannschaft
Alpha Centauri [ˌælfə senˈtɔːri] das der Erde am nächsten gelegene Sternsystem
Atlantic Time [ətˈlæntɪk taɪm] Zeitzone in Kanada

B

BBC [ˌbiː biː ˈsiː] British Broadcasting Corporation (brit. Rundfunk- und Fernsehgesellschaft)
BBC World Service [ˌbiː biː ˈsiː ˌwɜːld ˈsɜːvɪs] Auslandssender der BBC
Betelgeuse [ˈbiːtldʒɜːz] 425 Lichtjahre von der Erde entfernter heller Stern
Blairbeth Golf Club [ˌbleəbeθ ˈɡɒlf klʌb] Golfklub in der Nähe von Glasgow, Schottland
Bond, James [dʒeɪmz ˈbɒnd] brit. Geheimagent 007 in den Büchern von Ian Fleming
Booker Prize [ˈbʊkə praɪz] Literaturpreis, der jährlich für den besten englischsprachigen Roman vergeben wird
British Empire [ˌbrɪtɪʃ ˈempaɪə] ehemaliges britisches Weltreich
British Geological Survey [ˌbrɪtɪʃ ˌdʒiːəˌlɒdʒɪkl ˈsɜːveɪ] von der Regierung unterstützte Organisation, die in geologischen Angelegenheiten berät
Buckingham Palace [ˌbʌkɪŋəm ˈpæləs] Buckingham Palast
Bulari [ˌbuˈlɑːri] Erdmutter bei den australischen Ureinwohnern

C

CBS [ˌsiː biː ˈes] Radiosender in den USA
Central Time [ˈsentrəl taɪm] Zeitzone in Kanada
Channel Tunnel [ˌtʃænl ˈtʌnl] Tunnel unter dem Ärmelkanal
Chernobyl disaster Reaktorunfall in der Sowjetunion (25/26.04.1986)
CIA (Central Intelligence Agency) [ˌsiː aɪ ˈeɪ] am. Geheimdienst
civil rights movement [ˌsɪvl ˈraɪts ˌmuːvmənt] am. Bürgerrechtsbewegung
Civil War [ˌsɪvl ˈwɔː] am. Bürgerkrieg (1861–1865)

CN Tower

CN Tower [ˌsiː ˌen ˈtaʊə] Fernsehturm in Toronto
Cold War [ˌkəʊld ˈwɔː] „Kalter Krieg", Ost-West-Konflikt (1949–1990) zwischen der Nato und dem Warschauer Pakt
Copiphora Copiphora-Heuschrecke
Crimewatch [ˈkraɪmwɒtʃ] Fernsehserie, in der die Bevölkerung bei der Suche nach Verbrechern um Mithilfe gebeten wird
Crocodile Dundee [ˌkrɒkədaɪl dʌnˈdiː] austral. Film mit Paul Hogan

D

Daily Record [ˌdeɪli ˈrekɔːd] Name einer schottischen Tageszeitung
Die Another Day [ˌdaɪ əˌnʌðə ˈdeɪ] Titel eines James-Bond-Films mit Pierce Brosnan

E

Eastern Time [ˈiːstən taɪm] Zeitzone in Kanada
Eaton Centre [ˌiːtn ˈsentə] Einkaufszentrum in Toronto, Kanada
Eden Project [ˈiːdn ˌprɒdʒekt] riesiger botanischer Garten in St Austell, Cornwall
European Community (EC) [ˌjʊərəpiːən kəˈmjuːnəti] Europäische Gemeinschaft (EG)

F

FAQ (Frequently asked questions) [ˌfriːkwəntli ɑːskt ˈkwestʃənz] „Häufig gestellte Fragen"
FAS [ˌef eɪ ˈes] Fetales Alkoholsyndrom
First World War (WWI) [ˌfɜːst ˌwɜːld ˈwɔː] Erster Weltkrieg (1914–1918)
Flashdance [ˈflæʃdɑːns] Musikfilm aus den 1980er Jahren
Fritz Bezeichnung für Deutsche

G

Great Southern Land [ˌɡreɪt ˌsʌðən ˈlænd] ursprüngliche Bezeichnung für Australien

H

Harbour Bridge [ˈhɑːbə brɪdʒ] Brücke in Sydney

I

Inuktitut [ɪnˈʊktəːtʊt] Sprache der Inuit
Iroquois [ˈɪrəkwɔɪ] Indianerstamm
ISS [ˌaɪ es ˈes] Internationale Raumstation

J

Jurassic Park [dʒuˈræsɪk pɑːk] Film von Steven Spielberg, Roman von Michael Crichton

K

Kawarau Bridge [ˈkɑːwəraʊ brɪdʒ] Brücke bei Queenstown, Schauplatz des ersten Bungeesprungs 1987
King Air CWO [ˈkɪŋ eə ˌsiː ˌdʌbl juː ˈəʊ] Flugzeugtyp

Kiwi Experience

Kiwi Experience [ˌkiːwiː ɪkˈspɪəriəns] Buspass-System in Neuseeland
Kunapipi [ˌkuːnəˈpiːpiː] Erdmutter bei den australischen Ureinwohnern

L

Lord of the Rings [ˌlɔːd əv ðə ˈrɪŋz] Roman von J.R.R. Tolkien

M

Mafia [ˈmæfiə] kriminelle Organisation
Mars [mɑːz] Mars
the Mickey Mouse Club [ðə ˌmɪki ˈmaʊs klʌb] am. Fernsehsendereihe für Kinder
the Milky Way [ˌmɪlki ˈweɪ] Milchstraße
Montreal Canadiens [ˌmɒntriˌɔːl kəˈneɪdiənz] Name einer kanad. Eishockeymannschaft
Mountain Time [ˈmaʊntən taɪm] Zeitzone in Kanada

N

National Geographic [ˌnæʃnəl ˌdʒiːəˈɡræfɪk] geografische Zeitschrift
National Hockey League [ˌnæʃnəl ˈhɒki liːɡ] nordam. Eishockeyliga
National Sorry Day [ˌnæʃnəl ˈsɒri deɪ] „Tag des Nationalen Bedauerns", Feiertag als offizielle Entschuldigung gegenüber den Ureinwohnern
New Scientist Magazine [ˌnjuː ˌsaɪəntɪst mæɡəziːn] naturwissenschaftliche Zeitschrift
Newfoundland Time [ˈnjuːfndlənd taɪm] Zeitzone in Kanada

O

oil crisis [ˈɔɪl ˌkraɪsɪs] Ölkrise (1973)
Ojibway [əʊˈdʒɪbweɪ] Indianerstamm
Orlando Magic [ɔːˌlændəʊ ˈmædʒɪk] Name einer Basketballmannschaft

P

Pacific Time [pəˈsɪfɪk taɪm] Zeitzone Kanadas
Pulitzer Prize [ˈpʊlɪtsə praɪz] am. Literaturpreis

R

Rabbit-Proof Fence [ˌræbɪt pruːf ˈfens] Titel eines austral. Films
Richter scale [ˈrɪktə skeɪl] Skala, mit der die Stärke von Erdbeben gemessen wird
Rock Around the Clock [ˌrɒk əraʊnd ðə ˈklɒk] erster großer Rock-'n'-Roll-Hit von Bill Haley
Royal Flying Doctor Service [ˌrɔɪəl ˌflaɪɪŋ ˈdɒktə sɜːvɪs] medizinischer Dienst in Australien
the Royal Ontario Museum [ðə ˌrɔɪəl ɒnˌteəriəʊ mjuːˈziːəm] Museum in Toronto

S

Schools of the Air [ˌskuːlz əv ði ˈeə] Fernkurse per Funk oder Internet für australische Kinder, die in abgelegenen Gegenden wohnen

List of names

Sears Tower ['sɪəz tauə] größtes Gebäude Nordamerikas in Chicago
Silicon Valley [,sɪlɪkən 'væli] Tal in Kalifornien, in dem viele Computer- und Elektronikfirmen ansässig sind
the Skydome [ðə 'skaɪdəum] Baseballstadion in Toronto
Skywalker Sound ['skaɪwɔːkə saund] Firma, die bei *Jurassic Park* für die Tontechnik verantwortlich war
South Sydney High School [,sauθ ,sɪdni 'haɪ skuːl] Schule in Maroubra bei Sydney
Soviet ['səuviət] Sowjetisch, Sowjet-
Stan Winston Studio [,stæn 'wɪnstən 'stuːdiəu] Filmstudio in Los Angeles
Star Trek ['staː trek] Science-Fiction-Serie
Survival [sə'vaɪvl] brit. Tiersendung
Sydney Opera House [,sɪdni 'ɒprə haus] Opernhaus in Sydney

T
The Mirror [ðə 'mɪrə] brit. Boulevardzeitung
the Simpsons [ðə 'sɪmpsnz] am. Comicserie
The Sun [ðə 'sʌn] brit. Boulevardzeitung
The Times [ðə 'taɪmz] seriöse brit. Tageszeitung
The Western Mail [ðə ,westən 'meɪl] regionale Tageszeitung
the Third World [ðə ,θɜːd 'wɜːld] die dritte Welt, Entwicklungsländer
Titanic [taɪ'tænɪk] am. Liebesfilm mit Kate Winslet und Leonardo Di Caprio
Tommy ['tɒmi] Bezeichnung für Briten
Toronto Blue Jays [tə,rɒntəu 'bluː dʒeɪz] kanad. Baseballmannschaft
Toronto Maple Leafs [tə,rɒntəu 'meɪpl liːfs] kanad. Eishockeymannschaft
Toronto Zoo [tə,rɒntəu 'zuː] zoologischer Garten in Toronto
Tourette Syndrome [tuə'ret ,sɪndrəum] Erkrankung des Nervensystems
the Tower of London [ðə ,tauər əv 'lʌndən] Befestigungsanlage in London
Trois Rivières [,twaː rivɪ'eə] Name eines Kernkraftwerks in Quebec, Kanada

U
United Nations (UN) [ju,naɪtɪd 'neɪʃnz] Vereinte Nationen
Universal Studios [ju:nɪvɜːsl 'stuːdiəuz] Filmstudios in Hollywood

V
Venus ['viːnəs] Venus
Vietnam War [,viːetnæm 'wɔː] Vietnamkrieg (1965–1975)
Volkswagen Beetle [,vɒlkswægən 'biːtl] VW Käfer

W
War and Peace [,wɔːr ən 'piːs] Oper von Prokofiev
War of the Worlds [,wɔːr əv ðə 'wɜːldz] Roman von H.G. Wells

Warner Brothers ['wɔːnə ,brʌðəz] Filmstudios in Los Angeles
Woodstock ['wudstɒk] Schauplatz eines berühmten Rockfestivals im Jahre 1969
World Trade Organisation [,wɜːld 'treɪd ɔːgənaɪzeɪʃn] Welthandels-organisation
World War II [,wɜːld wɔː 'tuː] Zweiter Weltkrieg (1939–1945)

X
XP [,eks 'piː] Xeroderma pigmentosum, genetisch bedingte Hautkrankheit

Places

A
Ajawaan Lake ['ædʒuwɔːn ,leɪk] See im Prince Albert Nationalpark in Saskatchewan, Kanada
Alaska [ə'læskə] Bundesstaat der USA
Alberta [æl'bɜːtə] Provinz in Kanada
Alice Springs [,ælɪs 'sprɪŋz] Stadt in Zentralaustralien
Amazon rainforest [,æməzən 'reɪnfɒrɪst] Regenwald am Amazonas
Arran ['ærən] schott. Insel
Auckland ['ɔːklənd] größte Stadt in Neuseeland
Australian Capital Territory (ACT) [ɒ,streɪliən ,kæpɪtl 'terətri] Region in New South Wales, in der die australische Hauptstadt Canberra liegt
Ayer's Rock [,eəz 'rɒk] Bezeichnung der weißen Australier für Uluru

B
Baffin Island [,bæfɪn 'aɪlənd] Insel in der kanadischen Provinz Nunavut
Bay Street ['beɪ striːt] Straße in Toronto
Beijing [,beɪ 'dʒɪŋ] Hauptstadt von China, Peking
Bombay [,bɒm'beɪ] Stadt in Indien, Mumbai
Bondi Beach [,bɒndaɪ 'biːtʃ] Strand in der Nähe von Sydney
British Columbia [,brɪtɪʃ kə'lʌmbiə] Provinz in Kanada

C
California [,kælə'fɔːniə] Bundesstaat der USA an der Pazifikküste
Cambridge ['keɪmbrɪdʒ] Universitätsstadt in England
Canberra ['kænbərə] Hauptstadt Australiens
Carnaby Street ['kaːnəbi striːt] kleine Straße in London, die in den 1960ern wegen ihrer Läden und Boutiquen berühmt wurde
Cathkin ['kæθkɪn] Ort in Schottland
Chicago [ʃɪ'kaːgəu] Stadt in den USA
Chinatown ['tʃaɪnətaun] Stadtteil von Toronto mit chinesischer Bevölkerung

Christchurch ['kraɪsttʃɜːtʃ] Stadt auf der Südinsel Neuseelands
Congo River [,kɒŋgəu 'rɪvə] Fluss in Afrika
Cornwall ['kɔːnwəl] beliebtes Urlaubsgebiet im äußersten Südwesten Englands

D
Darwin ['daːwɪn] Stadt im Northern Territory, Australien
Dunedin [dʌn'iːdɪn] Stadt auf der Südinsel Neuseelands

E
the Earth [ði 'ɜːθ] die Erde
Edinburgh ['edɪnbərə] Hauptstadt Schottlands

F
Florence ['flɒrəns] Stadt in Italien
Florida ['flɒrɪdə] Bundesstaat der USA
Fox glacier ['fɒks ,glæsiə] Gletscher in den Südalpen Neuseelands
Franz Joseph glacier [,frænts 'dʒəuzɪf ,glæsiə] Gletscher in den Südalpen Neuseelands

G
Georgia ['dʒɔːdʒə] Bundesstaat der USA
Gisborne ['gɪzbən] Stadt auf der Nordinsel Neuseelands
Glasgow ['glaːsgəu] Stadt in Westschottland
Greektown ['griːktaun] Stadtteil von Toronto mit griechischer Bevölkerung
Greenland ['griːnlənd] Grönland
Greymouth ['greɪməθ] Stadt auf der Südinsel Neuseelands
Grimstone ['grɪmstən] Stadt in England
Guildford ['gɪlfəd] Stadt in England

H
Hastings ['heɪstɪŋz] Stadt an der Südostküste Englands; in der Nähe fand die Battle of Hastings (1066) statt
Hawaii [hə'waɪi] Bundesstaat der USA
Heathrow (Airport) [,hiːθrəu 'eəpɔːt] Flughafen in der Nähe von London
Holloway ['hɒləweɪ] Stadtteil von London
Hollywood ['hɒliwud] Stadt und Filmzentrum in den USA
Hyde Park [,haɪd 'paːk] großer Londoner Park
Hyde Park Corner [,haɪd paːk 'kɔːnə] Platz und U-Bahnstation in London

I
Iqaluit [ɪ'kælu:ɪt] Hauptstadt der Inuit auf Baffin Island
Istanbul [,ɪstæn'bul] Stadt in der Türkei

K
Kalgoorlie [kæl'guəli] Stadt in Westaustralien
Kauai ['kauɪ] Insel, die zu Hawaii gehört

one hundred and forty-nine   **149**

List of names

Kawarau River ['kɑːwərəʊ rɪvə] Fluss bei Queenstown, Neuseeland
Kentish Town [,kentɪʃ 'taʊn] Stadtteil von London
Kingston ['kɪŋstən] Ort in Ontario, Kanada

L

Los Angeles (LA) [lɒs 'ændʒəliːz] Stadt in Kalifornien, USA
Lake Michigan [leɪk 'mɪʃɪgən] Michigansee
Lake Ontario [,leɪk ɒn'tæriəʊ] Ontariosee
Lake Rotorua [,leɪk ,rəʊtə'ruːə] See auf der Nordinsel Neuseelands
Lake Taupo [leɪk 'taʊpo] Kratersee auf der Nordinsel Neuseelands
Lake Wakatipu [leɪk wakə'tɪpuː] See bei Queenstown, Neuseeland
Leslieville ['lezlivɪl] Stadtviertel in Toronto
Limerick ['lɪmərɪk] Stadt und Verwaltungsbezirk im Südwesten Irlands
Lincoln Park ['lɪŋkən pɑːk] Park in Chicago, USA
Little India [,lɪtl 'ɪndiə] indisches Viertel von Toronto
Little Italy [lɪtl 'ɪtəli] italienisches Viertel von Toronto
London ['lʌndən] Hauptstadt von Großbritannien

M

Mackay [mə'kaɪ] Ort an der Küste von Queensland, Australien
Manitoba [,mænɪ'təʊbə] Provinz in Kanada
Maroubra [mə'ruːbrə] Strand und Ort in der Nähe von Sydney
Mediterranean [,medɪtə'reɪniən] Mittelmeer
Melbourne ['melbɔːn] Stadt in Victoria, Australien
Memphis ['memfɪs] Stadt in Tennessee, USA
Mexico ['meksɪkəʊ] Staat in Mittelamerika
Milford Sound [,mɪlfɔːd 'saʊnd] Fjordlandschaft im Süden Neuseelands
Montreal [,mɒntri'ɔːl] Stadt in Quebec, Kanada

N

Napier ['neɪpiə] Stadt auf der Nordinsel Neuseelands
Narogin ['nɑːrəgɪn] Ort in Australien
New Brunswick [nju: 'brʌnzwɪk] Provinz in Kanada
Newfoundland ['njuːfndlənd] Neufundland, Provinz in Kanada
New Hampshire [nju: 'hæmpʃə] Bundesstaat der USA
New Jersey [nju: 'dʒɜːzi] Bundesstaat der USA
New Mexico [,nju: 'meksɪkəʊ] Bundesstaat im Süden der USA

New South Wales [,nju: saʊθ 'weɪlz] Bundesstaat in Australien
New York (City) [,nju: jɔːk 'sɪti] größte Stadt in den USA
North Island [,nɔːθ 'aɪlənd] Nordinsel Neuseelands
the North Sea [ðə ,nɔːθ 'siː] Nordsee
Northern Territory [,nɔːðən 'terətri] Bundesstaat in Australien
Northwest Territories [,nɔːθwest 'terətrɪz] Provinz in Kanada
Norwich ['nɒrɪdʒ] Stadt in England
Nova Scotia [,nəʊvə 'skəʊʃə] Provinz in Kanada
Nunavut ['nʌnəvʌt] kanad. Provinz und Gebiet der Inuit in Nordkanada

O

Ontario [ɒn'teəriəʊ] Provinz in Kanada
Orlando [ɔː'lændəʊ] Stadt in Florida
Ottawa ['ɒtəwə] Stadt in Ontario, Kanada
Oxford Circus [,ɒksfəd 'sɜːkəs] Platz in London

P

Paddington Station [,pædɪŋtən 'steɪʃn] Bahnhof in London
Perth [pɜːθ] Stadt in Western Australia
Pohutu [po'huːtu] bekanntester Geysir in Rotorua, Neuseeland
Polynesia [,pɒlɪ'niːziə] Polynesien, östlichste der Kulturregionen Ozeaniens
Prince Albert National Park [prɪns 'ælbət ,næʃnəl 'pɑːk] Nationalpark in Saskatchewan, Kanada
Prince Edward Island [prɪns 'edwəd ,aɪlənd] Provinz in Kanada

Q

Quebec [kwɪ'bek] Provinz in Kanada
Quebec (City) [kwɪ,bek 'sɪti] Stadt in Quebec, Kanada
Queen Street East [,kwiːn striːt 'iːst] Straße in Toronto, Kanada
Queensland ['kwiːnzlənd] Bundesstaat in Australien
Queenstown ['kwiːnztaʊn] Stadt auf der Südinsel Neuseelands

R

the River Amazon [ðə ,rɪvə 'æməzən] Amazonas
Roswell ['rɒzwel] Ort in New Mexico, USA
Rotorua [,rəʊtə'ruːə] Stadt auf der Nordinsel Neuseelands, die durch ihre Thermalquellen bekannt ist

S

Saskatchewan [sæ'skætʃəwən] Provinz in Kanada
Seattle [si'ætl] Stadt in den USA
Shanghai [,ʃæŋ'haɪ] Stadt in China
Shiskine ['ʃɪskɪn] Ortschaft auf der schott. Insel Arran
Siberia [saɪ'bɪəriə] Sibirien
South Australia [,saʊθ ɒ'streɪliə] Bundesstaat in Australien

South Island [,saʊθ 'aɪlənd] Südinsel Neuseelands
South Pacific Ocean [,saʊθ pə,sɪfɪk 'əʊʃn] Südpazifik
South-East Asia [,saʊθiːst 'eɪʃə] Südostasien
Southern Alps [,sʌðn 'ælps] längste und höchste Bergkette auf der Südinsel Neuseelands
Southern Cross [,sʌðn 'krɒs] Ort in New South Wales, Australien
St Austell [snt 'ɒstl] Ort in Cornwall, England
St John's [snt 'dʒɒnz] Ort in Neufundland
Stewart Island ['stjuːət ,aɪlənd] neuseeländ. Insel
Sydney ['sɪdni] Stadt in Australien

T

Tasman Sea [,tæzmən 'siː] Meer zwischen Neuseeland und Australien
Tennessee [,tenə'siː] Bundesstaat der USA
Thames [temz] Englands bedeutendster Fluss
Tiwi Islands ['tiːwi: 'aɪləndz] Inseln nördlich von Darwin, Australien
Toronto [tə'rɒntəʊ] Stadt in Ontario, Kanada
Toronto Islands [tə,rɒntəʊ 'aɪləndz] Inseln bei Toronto, beliebt als Freizeitgelände
Torquay [,tɔː'kiː] Ort im Südwesten Englands
Trinidad ['trɪnɪdæd] karibische Insel
Turkey ['tɜːki] Türkei

U

Uluru [u'luːruː] größter Monolith der Welt im Zentrum Australiens, siehe Ayer's Rock

V

Vancouver [væn'kuːvə] Stadt in British Columbia, Kanada
Victoria [vɪk'tɔːriə] Bundesstaat in Australien

W

Wadebridge ['weɪdbrɪdʒ] Ort in Cornwall
Waskesiu [wɔːs'keɪsuː] See und Dorf im Prince Albert National Park, Kanada
Wellington ['welɪŋtən] Stadt auf der Nordinsel Neuseelands
Western Australia [,westən ɒ'streɪliə] Bundesstaat in Australien
Winnipeg ['wɪnɪpeg] Stadt in Manitoba, Kanada
Winter Park ['wɪntə pɑːk] Kleinstadt in Florida, USA

Y

Yukon ['juːkɒn] Provinz in Kanada
Yulara [yu'lɑːrə] Fremdenverkehrsort in der Nähe von Uluru

List of names

Geographical names

Country	Adjective	Language	People
Africa Afrika	African		African
America Amerika	American	American English	American
Asia Asien	Asian		Asian
Austria Österreich	Austrian	German	Austrian
Australia Australien	Australian	English	Australian
Bavaria Bayern	Bavarian	German	Bavarian
Belgium Belgien	Belgian	French /Flemish	Belgian
Brazil Brasilien	Brazilian	Portuguese	Brazilian
(Great) Britain Großbritannien	British	(British) English	Briton *pl.* the British
Canada Kanada	Canadian	English	Canadian
China China	Chinese	Chinese	Chinese (man/woman), *pl.* the Chinese
Costa Rica Costa Rica	Costa Rican	Spanish	Costa Rican
Cuba Kuba	Cuban	Spanish	Cuban
Czech Republic (the) Tschechische Republik	Czech	Czech	Czech
Denmark Dänemark	Danish	Danish	Dane
El Salvador El Salvador	Salvadorean	Spanish	Salvadorean
England England	English	English	Englishman/woman, *pl.* the English
Europe Europa	European		European
France Frankreich	French	French	Frenchman/woman, *pl.* the French
Germany Deutschland	German	German	German
Greece Griechenland	Greek	Greek	Greek
Hungary Ungarn	Hungarian	Hungarian	Hungarian
India Indien	Indian	Hindi, Urdu, English	Indian
Indonesia Indonesien	Indonesian	Bahasa Indonesia	Indonesian
Iran Iran	Iranian	Persian (Farsi)	Iranian
Iraq Irak	Iraqi	Kurdish, Arabic	Iraqi
(the Republic of) Ireland Irland	Irish	Irish Gaelic, English	Irishman/woman, *pl.* the Irish
Israel Israel	Israeli	Hebrew	Israeli
Italy Italien	Italian	Italian	Italian
Jamaica Jamaika	Jamaican	English	Jamaican
Japan Japan	Japanese	Japanese	Japanese (man/woman), *pl.* the Japanese
Korea Korea	Korean	Korean	Korean
Lebanon Libanon	Lebanese	Lebanese	Lebanese
Malaysia Malaysia	Malaysian	Malay, Chinese, English	Malaysian
Mexico Mexiko	Mexican	Spanish	Mexican
Netherlands (the) (die) Niederlande	Dutch	Dutch	Dutchman/woman, *pl.* the Dutch
New Zealand Neuseeland	New Zealand	English	New Zealander
Northern Ireland Nordirland	Northern Irish	English	Northern Irishman/woman
Norway Norwegen	Norwegian	Norwegian	Norwegian
Pakistan Pakistan	Pakistani	Urdu, English	Pakistani
Philippines (the) (die) Philippinen	Philippine	Filipino (Tagalog), English	Filipino
Poland Polen	Polish	Polish	Pole
Portugal Portugal	Portuguese	Portuguese	Portuguese (man/woman), *pl.* the Portuguese
Russia Russland	Russian	Russian	Russian
Scandinavia Skandinavien	Scandinavian		Scandinavian
Scotland Schottland	Scottish	Scots, Gaelic	Scot (Scotsman/woman), *pl.* the Scots, the Scottish
(the Republic of) South Africa (Republik) Südafrika	South African	English, Afrikaans	South African
Spain Spanien	Spanish	Spanish	Spaniard, *pl.* the Spanish
Sri Lanka Sri Lanka	Sri Lankan	Sinhala, English, Tamil	Sri Lankan
Sweden Schweden	Swedish	Swedish	Swede
Switzerland Schweiz	Swiss	German, French, Italian Swiss	Swiss
Tahiti Tahiti	Tahitian	Tahitian, English, French	Tahitian
Turkey Türkei	Turkish	Turkish	Turk
United States of America (the) Vereinigte Staaten von Amerika	American	American English	American
Vietnam Vietnam	Vietnamese	Vietnamese	Vietnamese, *pl.* the Vietnamese
Wales Wales	Welsh	Welsh	Welshman / Welsh woman, *pl.* the Welsh
West Indies Westindische Inseln	West Indian	English	West Indian

one hundred and fifty-one 151

INDEX

Aa

a, an ein, eine, ein **5-U0**, D
abbey Abtei, Kloster(kirche)**7-U4**, Ex7
abbreviation Abkürzung **10-U1**, Ex11
ability Fähigkeit **10-U3**, Read
able: be able to können, in der Lage sein **8-U1**, Sit1
abolish abschaffen **8-U3**, WP
Aboriginal Aborigine-**10-Lit**
Aborigine Ureinwohner/in **10-U1**, WP
about über **5-U2**, T2; ungefähr **5-U7**, T2
  be about to do sth im Begriff sein, etw zu tun **10-U2**, Read
above oberhalb, über **6-U4**, T2
abroad im Ausland, ins Ausland **9-U2**, T1
absolute absolut **7-U3**, T2
absolutely völlig **7-U3**, T1
accept annehmen, akzeptieren **9-U4**, T2
accident Unfall **5-U6**, T1
accidental zufällig, unbeabsichtigt **9-U3**, Read
accommodation Unterkunft **9-U3**, T1
achieve erreichen, schaffen, **9-U2**, Read
acrobat Akrobat/in **9-U1**, WP
across über, hinüber **6-U4**, T1
act spielen, aufführen **5-U6**, Ex9; handeln, tätig sein **9-U2**, Read
  act on handeln nach, sich richten nach **9-U3**, T2
  act out durchspielen, aufführen **7-U1**, Ex16
action Handlung **5-U6**, Ex6
activity Aktivität, Tätigkeit, Beschäftigung **5-U5**, Sit2
actor Schauspieler **6-U6**, WPB
actress Schauspielerin **9-Proj1**
actually tatsächlich **7-U1**, T1
add hinzufügen **5-U5**, Ex5
address Adresse **6-U3**, T1
administration Verwaltung **9-U2**, T1
admire bewundern **9-U3**, TYE
admit zugeben, eingestehen **7-U2**, T2
adopt adoptieren **10-U3**, T2
adoption agency Adoptionsvermitt- lungsstelle **10-U3**, T2
adult Erwachsene(r); erwachsen **7-U5**, Ex6
advanced fortgeschritten **9-U2**, Ex11
advantage Vorteil **9-U2**, WP
  advantage of doing sth Vorteil, etw zu tun **9-U2**, T1
adventure Abenteuer **7-U2**, T2
adventurous abenteuerlich **9-TP**
advert Anzeige, Reklame, Werbespot **10-U1**, Ex10
advertise Werbung machen (für) **8-U2**, T2
advertisement Reklame **6-U1**, Ex14
advice Rat **8-U4**, T2
advise den Rat geben, raten **9-U2**, Sit2
aeroplane Flugzeug **9-U3**, TYE
affair Affäre; Angelegenheit **7-U4**, T2
afford sich leisten **9-U4**, WP
afraid: be afraid Angst haben **6-U2**, Sit4
  I'm afraid ich fürchte, leider **7-U1**, Com

African afrikanisch; Afrikaner/in **9-U4**, T2
after nach, hinter, danach **5-U5**, WPA
  after all schließlich; doch **10-U2**, Read
afternoon Nachmittag **5-U1**, Sit6
afterwards danach **7-U2**, Sit3
again wieder, noch einmal **5-U5**, T1
against gegen **6-U2**, Ex10
age Alter **5-U1**, PYE6
aged im Alter von **7-U3**, T2
agent Agent/in, Detektiv/in **8-U1**, Read
ago vor **6-U2**, T1
agree zustimmen, einwilligen **7-U3**, T1
  it doesn't agree with sb etw bekommt jdm nicht **9-U2**, T1
ahead (of) voraus, vor **6-U4**, T2
aid Hilfe **7-U5**, WP
AIDS Aids **9-U4**, TYE
aim Ziel **8-U2**, Ex12
ain't *umgangssprachlich Kurzform von* am/is/are not *und* has/have not **10-U4**, Song
air Luft **6-U2**, WPB
air conditioning Klimaanlage **8-U4**, T2
aircraft Flugzeug **9-U3**, TYE
airfield Flugplatz **8-Rev1**
air force Luftwaffe **7-U3**, Read
airport Flughafen **5-U7**, Sit5
airstrip Rollbahn, Piste **10-U1**, TYE
aisle Mittelgang, Gang **8-U3**, T2
alarm Alarm **8-U1**, Read
alarm (clock) Wecker **10-U2**, T1
alcohol Alkohol **8-U1**, T2
alive lebendig, am Leben **7-U5**, Rev
all alle **5-U4**, WPB
  all over überall in, auf **7-U3**, WP
  all right in Ordnung **5-U3**, T2
alligator Alligator **8-U4**, T1
allow erlauben **10-U3**, Ex3
  be allowed to do sth etw tun dürfen **8-U1**, Sit3
almost beinahe **6-U6**, T1
alone: be alone allein sein **7-U3**, TYE
along entlang **6-U2**, T1
  along with zusammen mit **7-U5**, Read
aloud laut **9-Rev8**
alphabet Alphabet **5-U7**, Ex5
already schon **6-U4**, Sit3
also auch **5-U4**, Sit5
alternative alternativ **10-U1**, Ex10
although obwohl **7-U4**, Read
altogether insgesamt, im Ganzen **8-U2**, Sit1
always immer **5-U1**, T2
A.M./a.m./am vor 12 Uhr **8-U1**, Ex10
amazed erstaunt **7-U3**, Sit4
amazing erstaunlich **10-U1**, T2
ambassador Botschafter/in **7-U1**, TYE
ambition Ehrgeiz, Ziel **9-U3**, T2
ambitious ehrgeizig **9-Rev7**
ambulance Krankenwagen **6-U2**, T2
American Amerikaner/in; amerikanisch **5-U0**, A
among zwischen, unter **8-U2**, T2
amount Betrag; Menge **8-U2**, Sit3

amusement park Vergnügungspark **8-U2**, Read
amusing lustig, amüsant **10-Rev9**
and und **5-U0**, A
  and so on und so weiter **6-U3**, T1
angel Engel **10-U3**, Read
Angles: the Angles die Angeln **7-U2**, WP
angry wütend, verärgert **5-U6**, T2
animal Tier **6-U2**, WPA
announce ansagen, bekannt geben **10-U3**, Ex7
annoying ärgerlich **7-U3**, T1
annual jährlich; Jahres- **8-U2**, T1
another ein(e) andere(r, s), noch ein(e, es) **6-U4**, WPC
answer Antwort **5-U2**, Sit2
answer antworten, beantworten **7-U1**, Ex10
ant Ameise **8-U1**, T2
antenna Antenne **10-U4**, T1
any (irgend)eine(r, s) **6-U4**, Sit4
anything irgendetwas **7-U1**, Read
anyway jedenfalls **7-U5**, Sit2
anywhere irgendwo **7-U5**, Ex12
apartheid Rassentrennung **9-U4**, TYE
apartment Wohnung **8-U1**, WP
apologize (to sb) for sth sich (bei jdm) für etw entschuldigen **10-U1**, T1
apparent offensichtlich, scheinbar **10-U3**, Read
apparently anscheinend, offensichtlich **10-U3**, Read
appear erscheinen, scheinen **7-U3**, T2
appetite Appetit **6-U4**, T2
apple Apfel **5-U0**, D
application Bewerbung **9-TP**
apply to sb for sth sich bei jdm bewerben um, für **9-U2**, WP
apprentice Auszubildende/r **9-U2**, WP
apprenticeship Lehrzeit, Lehre **9-U3**, T2
April April **5-U4**, Sit5
apron Schürze **7-U5**, Sket2
arcade Spielhalle, Arkade **5-U7**, WPA; Einkaufspassage **7-U5**, Ex13
arch Bogen (Gebäude) **8-U4**, WP
archery Bogenschießen **7-U2**, T1
area Gebiet; Bereich **8-U1**, Ex7
argue streiten, argumentieren **7-U5**, T2
argument Streit **6-U1**, T1
arm Arm **5-U5**, T1
armour Rüstung **7-U2**, T2
army Armee **7-U4**, WP
around herum, umher **5-U3**, WPA
arrange vereinbaren; anordnen **8-U1**, Ex16
arrest festnehmen **7-U1**, T2
arrest: be under arrest verhaftet sein **8-U3**, T2
arrival Ankunft **8-U1**, Ex10
arrive ankommen **6-U5**, T1
arrow Pfeil **7-U4**, T1
art Kunst, Kunsterziehung **7-U3**, TYE
article Artikel, Beitrag **8-U2**, Ex2
artificial künstlich, Kunst- **9-U3**, Sit1
artist Künstler/in **9-Proj3**
as als, während **6-U6**, T1; da **10-U1**, Sit4

152

Index

as ... as so ... wie **6-U1**, Sit5
as if als ob, als wenn **10-U2**, T2
as soon as sobald **10-U2**, T1
as well as ebenso wie, sowohl ... als auch **10-U2**, Sit4
ashes Asche **10-Lit**
Asian asiatisch; Asiate, Asiatin **7-U5**, TYE
ask fragen; bitten **5-U2**, T2
ask out einladen, ausführen (in ein Lokal) **9-U1**, Sit2
asleep: be asleep schlafen **9-U3**, T2
fall asleep einschlafen **10-U1**, Sit1
aspect Aspekt, Seite **9-Proj4**
aspirin Aspirin **8-U4**, Ex11
assassin Mörder/in, Attentäter/in **10-Lit**
assistant Assistent/in, Verkäufer/in **9-U2**, WP
asteroid Asteroid **9-U3**, Sit2
astronaut Raumfahrer/in; Astronaut/in **9-U3**, Ex2
at an, auf, in **5-U1**, WPB
at (nine o'clock) um (neun Uhr) **5-U1**, Ex10
athlete (Leicht)athlet/in, Sportler/in **7-U3**, Read
atlas Atlas **8-U4**, WP
atmosphere Atmosphäre, Stimmung **8-U4**, Read
atom Atom **10-U2**, Ex22
attach anfügen, befestigen, verbinden mit **9-U3**, T2
attack angreifen **7-U4**, T1
attack Angriff **8-U3**, Read
attempt Versuch **10-U3**, Read
attend besuchen (Schule), teilnehmen **9-U2**, T1
attendant Aufseher/in, Wärter/in **9-U3**, Ex3
attention Aufmerksamkeit **7-U3**, TYE
attitude Haltung, Einstellung **9-U4**, T1
attract anziehen, reizen **9-Rev8**
attraction Attraktion, Anziehung **7-U4**, Ex10
audience Zuschauer, Publikum **7-U3**, Sit1
August August **5-U4**, Sit5
aunt Tante **6-U1**, Sit1
auntie Tante **5-U1**, Song
Australian Australier/in; australisch **10-U1**, WP
auto Auto **8-Proj2**
autobiographical autobiografisch **10-Lit**
automobile Auto, Automobil **8-U2**, TYE
autumn Herbst **6-U4**, WPB
available verfügbar **9-U2**, T2
avenue Boulevard, breite Straße, Allee **8-U1**, Ex7
average Durchschnitt(s-) **8-U4**, WP
on average im Durchschnitt **10-U1**, T1
avoid (ver)meiden **10-U1**, Sit1
awake wach **7-U5**, T2
award Auszeichnung, Preis **7-U5**, WP
aware: be aware (of) sich einer Sache bewusst sein **10-U2**, Read
away weg, fort **5-U1**, Sit6

awful schrecklich **5-U1**, Sit2
axe Axt **7-U4**, T1

Bb

baby Baby **5-U3**, Sit3
back zurück **5-U3**, T2
back Rückseite **5-U6**, Ex4; Rücken **6-U2**, T2
background Hintergrund **9-U1**, TYE
backpack Rucksack **7-U5**, T1
back-up (copy) Sicherungskopie, Backup **10-U3**, Sit4
backwards rückwärts **8-U2**, Ex12
backyard Hinterhof **7-U1**, Read
bad schlecht **5-U2**, Ex17
badger Dachs **6-U2**, T1
badminton Badminton **10-U4**, Sit2
bad-tempered schlecht gelaunt **9-U1**, Read
bag Tasche **5-U0**, D
ball Ball **5-U6**, T1
bamboo Bambus **10-U2**, T2
banana Banane **5-U6**, Sit4
band Band, Musikgruppe **5-U2**, T2
bank Bank(haus) **5-U2**, T1; Ufer **8-U4**, T2
banker Bankier, Bankfachmann/ -frau **9-TP**
banking Bankbranche **9-U2**, T1
barbecue Grillparty; Grillgericht **6-U7**, T1
barbed wire Stacheldraht **9-Rev5**
bareback ohne Sattel **7-U1**, Read
barefoot barfuß **10-U1**, T1
bargain Schnäppchen, guter Kauf **9-U3**, T1
bar mitzvah Bar-Mizwa **7-U3**, T2
barrel Fass **6-U4**, T1
barrier Schranke, Barriere **9-U2**, Ex21
baseball Baseball **5-U6**, Sit3
based: be based on sich stützen auf, basieren auf **8-Lit**
basement Kellergeschoss **9-U3**, WP
basket Korb **5-U6**, Ex4
basketball Basketball **5-U2**, Ex12
bastard Mistkerl, Schwein **10-U4**, Read
bat Fledermaus **8-Rev10**
bath Bad **7-U2**, WP
bathroom Badezimmer **5-U1**, T2
batter Schlagmann **6-U7**, Sit3
battery Batterie **9-U3**, Sit3
battle Schlacht **7-U2**, T1
battlefield Schlachtfeld **7-U4**, T1
be sein **5-U0**, F
beach Strand **5-U7**, WPA
bean Bohne **6-U5**, Sit2
beard Bart **7-U4**, Com
beat schlagen; klopfen **8-U2**, Sit4; übertreffen **10-U1**, WP
beautiful schön, hübsch **7-U2**, T1
because weil **5-U7**, Sit4
because of wegen **8-U2**, T2
become werden **6-U6**, WPC
bed Bett **5-U1**, Sit6
bedroom Schlafzimmer **5-U2**, WPB
beep piepen, hupen **10-U2**, T1
beer Bier **7-U1**, Read

beetle Käfer **10-U3**, T1
before vor, vorher, bevor **5-U5**, Sit2
begin anfangen **7-U4**, WP
beginner Anfänger/in **8-U2**, Ex18
beginning Anfang, Beginn **7-U3**, Ex1
behave sich verhalten, sich benehmen **9-U4**, Fol
behaviour Benehmen, Verhalten **9-U1**, Sit4
behind hinter **5-U2**, WPA
belief Glaube **9-U4**, Fol
believe (in) glauben (an) **7-U2**, Sit2
bell Glocke, Klingel **6-U1**, WPA
bell-bottom trousers Schlaghosen **10-U3**, WP
belly Bauch **9-U1**, Read
belong to gehören **5-U5**, T2
beloved Geliebte/r **10-Lit**
below unten, unterhalb **6-U7**, Song
bend Kurve, Biegung **8-U2**, Read
bend biegen; sich bücken **8-U4**, Read
berry Beere **7-U4**, T1
beside neben **10-U4**, T1
best beste(r, s) **5-U3**, PYE3
best-known bekannteste(r, s) **8-Rev8**
best-selling verkauft sich am besten **8-Rev8**
bet wetten **9-U4**, Read
better besser **6-U1**, Sit4
between zwischen **6-U6**, T1
bicycle Fahrrad **9-U3**, Sit4
big groß **5-U5**, T2
bike Rad **5-U2**, Sit3
biker Radfahrer/in **8-U4**, Com
bill Rechnung **9-U2**, T1
billion Milliarde **9-U3**, T1
bin Mülleimer, Abfalleimer **7-U3**, T1
biology Biologie **5-U2**, Sit2
biome Biotop, Lebensraum; Biom **10-U2**, T2
bird Vogel **6-U2**, WPB
birth Geburt **9-U1**, Sit4
birthday Geburtstag **5-U0**, G
birthplace Geburtsort **9-U4**, Fol
biscuit Keks **5-U4**, WPA
bit: a bit etwas, ein wenig **6-U4**, WPB
bite beißen **8-U3**, Read
black schwarz **5-U0**, C
blanket Decke, Wolldecke **10-U4**, Read
blast off in den Weltraum schießen **9-U3**, Sit2
bleed bluten **10-U4**, Song
bless segnen **10-U3**, T2
blind blind **8-U4**, Ex17
blister Blase **7-U5**, T1
blizzard Schneesturm **8-U4**, Read
bloated aufgedunsen **9-U2**, Read
block Block **7-U1**, WP; Häuser-, Wohnblock **8-U1**, Ex7
blonde blond (Frau) **9-U2**, Read
blood Blut **10-Dict**
blouse Bluse **9-U4**, Read
blow blasen, wehen **8-U4**, Read
blow up in die Luft jagen, explodieren **6-U4**, WPA

153

Index

blue blau **5-U0**, C
blues Blues (Musikrichtung) **10-U3**, WP
board Brett **10-U1**, Ex12
board (Wand-)Tafel **5-U0**, D; Kommission, Gremium, Aufsichtsrat **7-U1**, WP
board game Brettspiel **10-Proj2**
boat Boot, Schiff **5-U7**, WPD
body Leiche; Körper **7-U4**, T1
boil sieden, kochen **9-U4**, T1
bomb Bombe **8-U2**, Ex10
bone Knochen **10-U1**, Read
bonfire Freudenfeuer, Guy-Fawkes-Feuer **6-U4**, WPA
book Buch **5-U0**, D
book buchen **8-U1**, Sit2
bookshop Buchhandlung **5-U6**, WPB
boot Stiefel **9-U2**, Read
border Grenze **8-U4**, WP
bored gelangweilt **6-U2**, T2
boring langweilig **6-U1**, Sit5
born: be born geboren werden **7-U1**, TYE
borough (Stadt-)Bezirk **8-U1**, WP
borrow sich ausleihen, borgen **5-U7**, Ex14
boss Chef/in **9-U2**, T2
both beide **6-U2**, Sit5
  both ... and ... sowohl ... als auch ... **10-U1**, T1
bother (with/about sth) sich (um etw) kümmern **10-U2**, Read
bottle Flasche **5-U5**, PYE4
bottom Boden, Fuß (Berg) **5-U7**, T2
bounce aufprallen lassen **8-U2**, Ex12; federn (lassen), hüpfen **10-U1**, T2
bowling Bowling, Kegeln **6-U7**, T1
box Kiste, Schachtel, Kasten **5-U5**, T2
boxing Boxen, Box- **8-U2**, T1
box office Theater-, Kinokasse **9-U1**, WP
boy Junge **5-U1**, WPA
boycott Boykott **8-U3**, T2
boyfriend fester Freund **5-U1**, WPC
bracket Klammer **7-U1**, TYE4
brain Gehirn **10-U2**, Sit1
brake Bremse **9-U3**, Sit4
branch Ast **10-U4**, Read
bread Brot **6-U5**, Sit2
break Chance **7-U3**, T1; Pause **10-U2**, T1
break brechen **7-U1**, T1
  break in einbrechen **7-U1**, T1
break-dancing Breakdancing **8-U1**, T2
breakfast Frühstück **5-U4**, WPB
break-in Einbruch **7-U1**, T2
breathe (ein)atmen **9-TP**
breeze Brise **8-U2**, Sit1
brick Ziegelstein **6-U1**, Song
bridge Brücke **6-U1**, WPA
bright hell; strahlend, klar **8-U1**, T2
brilliant großartig, strahlend **10-U3**, Sit1
bring bringen **5-U4**, Ex6
  bring out herausbringen **7-U1**, Sit5
  bring up großziehen, erziehen **10-U1**, Read
British britisch **7-U3**, TYE
  British Isles Britische Inseln **9-Lit**

Briton Brite, Britin **7-U2**, WP
broken zerbrochen, kaputt **6-U5**, T2
bronze Bronze **7-U5**, WP
brooch Brosche **7-U5**, Sket1
broomstick Besen(stiel) **7-U2**, Read
brother Bruder **5-U0**, I
brown braun **5-U4**, Ex16
browser Browser **9-U2**, T2
brush bürsten, putzen **8-U2**, Read
budgie Wellensittich **5-U3**, WPB
buffalo Bison, Büffel **8-U3**, Ex7
buffalo chips getrockneter Büffelmist **8-U3**, Read
build bauen **6-U1**, Song
building Gebäude **6-U7**, T2
bulb Glühbirne, -lampe **9-U3**, Sit3
bullet Kugel, Geschoss **10-U3**, TYE
bully Mobber/in **10-U3**, Sit3
bungee jumping Bungeejumping **10-U1**, Sit3
burger Hamburger **6-U7**, T1
burn Verbrennung **10-U4**, Read
burn verbrennen, brennen **6-U4**, WPA
  burn down niederbrennen **7-U3**, TYE
bury begraben **8-U3**, Read
bus Bus **5-U0**, D
bush Busch, Strauch **5-U3**, T1
business Geschäft; Betrieb **8-U1**, Ex7
businessman Geschäftsmann **9-U3**, T1
bus service Busverbindung **8-U1**, Ex10
bus station Busbahnhof **5-U6**, WPA
bus-stop Bushaltestelle **5-U3**, Sit3
busy beschäftigt, belebt **6-U1**, T1
but aber **5-U1**, Sit2
butcher Metzger, Fleischer **9-U4**, Read
butter Butter **6-U5**, Sit2
buy kaufen **5-U4**, WPA
by an, bei, neben **6-U1**, WPA; mit **8-U4**, Ex16; bis (spätestens) **10-U2**, T1
bye Tschüss **5-U0**, B

Cc

cabinet Kabinett **9-U4**, T2
cable car Straßenbahn (in San Francisco) **6-U7**, T2
café Imbiss, Café **5-U6**, WPA
cafeteria Cafeteria **8-U2**, T1
cage Käfig **5-U3**, WPA
cake Kuchen **5-U4**, WPC
calculate rechnen **7-U5**, Read
calculator Taschenrechner **10-U2**, Com
calendar Kalender **8-U2**, WP
call Ruf, Anruf **7-U1**, T2
call rufen, anrufen **7-U2**, T1
  be called heißen **5-U3**, WPA
calm ruhig, still **9-U4**, Read
calypso Calypso **9-U4**, Sit4
camera Fotoapparat, Kamera **5-U2**, WPC
camp Lager **5-U7**, WPD
camp zelten **5-U7**, Ex14
campaign Kampagne, Aktion **8-U3**, T2
camping Camping, Zelten **6-U7**, T1
camp site Campingplatz **5-U7**, WPD
can Dose **7-U1**, Read

can können **5-U0**, F
canal Kanal **5-U6**, Ex16
candle Kerze **6-U4**, WPB
cannon Kanone **9-U1**, T2
cap Mütze **6-U7**, T1
capital Hauptstadt **8-U1**, Sit1
captain Kapitän **8-Rev15**
capture gefangen nehmen **8-U3**, T1
car Auto **5-U1**, Sit6
caravan Wohnwagen **5-U7**, WPB
carbon dioxide Kohlendioxid **10-U2**, Sit3
card Karte **6-U3**, Ex4
care Sorge, Sorgfalt, Pflege, Obhut **9-U4**, Sit2
care about sich kümmern, sich Sorgen machen um **9-U4**, T2
career Laufbahn, Karriere **9-U1**, T2
careful vorsichtig, sorgfältig **5-U5**, T1
Caribbean Karibik; karibisch **9-U1**, WP
carnival Volksfest; Karneval, Fasching **8-U2**, WP
car park Parkplatz, Parkhaus **5-U5**, T2
carry tragen **6-U2**, T2
  carry out aus-, durchführen **9-U3**, T1
cart Wagen, Karren **7-U5**, Sket2
cartoon Zeichentrickfilm **6-U6**, WPA
carve schnitzen **8-U3**, Read
case Koffer **5-U7**, T1; Fall **9-U3**, Sit3
  in case für den Fall, dass **10-U3**, T2
cash Bargeld **10-Rev17**
cassette Kassette **6-U5**, T2
cast Gipsverband **9-U3**, T2
caste Kaste **9-U1**, TYE
castle Schloss, Burg **6-U4**, T2
cat Katze **5-U0**, E
catch fangen **5-U3**, T2
  catch a bus einen Bus erreichen **6-U2**, Ex9
  catch fire Feuer fangen **9-U1**, T2
catcher Fänger/in **6-U7**, T1
cathedral Dom, Kathedrale **7-U5**, Ex13
Catholic katholisch; Katholik/in **6-U4**, T1
cattle Vieh, Rinder **7-U5**, Sket2
cause Ursache **10-U3**, Sit3
cause verursachen, hervorrufen **10-Rev17**
cave in einstürzen, nachgeben **10-U4**, Read
CD CD **5-U2**, T2
CD player CD-Spieler **7-U1**, Sit5
céilí irische Tanzveranstaltung **7-U1**, T1
celebrate feiern **8-U2**, WP
cellar Keller **6-U4**, T1
cellphone Handy, Mobiltelefon **8-U4**, Sit4
Celsius/C Celsius **8-U4**, WP
Celt Kelte, Keltin **7-U2**, WP
cent Cent **8-U2**, T1
centimetre Zentimeter **9-U3**, Read
central zentral **6-U1**, WPB
central heating Zentralheizung **9-U3**, Ex10
centre Zentrum **6-U1**, WPA
century Jahrhundert **7-U4**, WP
cereal Getreideflocken **10-U3**, Read
cerebral palsy zerebrale Bewegungsstörung **9-U3**, T2
ceremony Zeremonie **10-Lit**

Index

certain sicher **8-U1**, Sit2
certainly sicherlich **8-U1**, Sit2
certificate Urkunde **9-U2**, T1
chain-link fence Maschendrahtzaun **8-U2**, Read
chair Stuhl **5-U0**, D
chalk Kreide **7-U2**, WP
challenge Herausforderung **10-U2**, T1
chamber of horrors Gruselkabinett **6-U1**, T1
champion Meister/in, Champion **10-U1**, T1
championship Meisterschaft **8-U2**, T2
chance Chance **7-U3**, Sit1
change Änderung **9-U2**, Sit2
change (ver)ändern **7-U1**, WP; umsteigen **8-U1**, T; wechseln **9-U1**, Read
  change one's mind seine Meinung ändern **9-U1**, Sit3
changing room Umkleideraum **9-U3**, Read
channel Programm, Kanal **6-U6**, T2
chaos Chaos, Durcheinander **10-Lit**
character Figur, Charakter **6-U6**, WPA
charge anstürmen, angreifen **7-U4**, T1
charity Wohltätigkeit, wohltätige Organisation **8-U4**, Ex3
charming charmant, bezaubernd **8-U1**, Read
chase verfolgen **10-U4**, T2
chat plaudern **9-U1**, T1
chat room Chatroom (Internet) **8-U2**, Ex2
chat show Talkshow **9-U1**, Ex4
cheap billig **6-U1**, Sit2
cheat mogeln, betrügen **10-U4**, T1
check überprüfen **5-U5**, Ex17
cheek Wange, Backe **9-U4**, Read
cheeky frech **7-U3**, T2
cheer zujubeln, bejubeln, anfeuern **7-U3**, T1
cheerleader Cheerleader **8-U2**, T1
cheese Käse **5-U4**, WPB
cheeseburger Cheeseburger **10-U3**, Sit4
chemical chemisch **9-Rev1**
chemistry Chemie **9-U3**, WP
chess Schach **5-U5**, WPB
chief Häuptling **8-U3**, WP
child Kind **5-U3**, Sit3
childhood Kindheit **10-U1**, Read
chimney Schornstein **7-U5**, Sit1
Chinese chinesisch; Chinese, Chinesin **8-U1**, WP
chips Pommes frites **5-U4**, WPA
chiropractor Chiropraktiker/in **10-U4**, Read
chocolate Schokolade **5-U4**, Song
choice Entscheidung; Wahl **10-U4**, Song
choke on sth sich an etw verschlucken **10-U2**, Sit2
choose wählen **7-U2**, Proj
Christian christlich; Christ/in **9-U4**, T1
Christmas Weihnachten **5-U4**, Sit5
church Kirche **7-U2**, WP
cigarette Zigarette **10-U3**, Ex9
cinema Kino **5-U3**, PYE3
circle Kreis **6-U1**, WPB

circus Zirkus **9-U1**, T1
citizen (Staats-)bürger/in **10-Lit**
city Stadt, Großstadt **6-U1**, WPA
civil rights Bürgerrechte **8-U3**, T2
civil war Bürgerkrieg **8-U3**, WP
class Klasse; Unterrichtsstunde **5-U1**, WPB
classmate Klassenkamerad/in **8-U1**, T2
classroom Klassenzimmer **5-U0**, D
clay Lehm **6-U1**, Song
claypit Tongrube **10-U2**, T2
clean sauber **6-U5**, WPB
clean sauber machen **8-U1**, Ex13
cleaner Raumpfleger/in **9-U4**, Ex16
clear klar **7-U3**, T2
clear räumen; abholzen **10-U2**, Sit4
clever klug **7-U2**, T1
click on anklicken **6-U3**, WPB
cliff Kliff, Klippe **8-U4**, WP
climate Klima **8-U4**, T2
climb klettern **7-U5**, T1
cling to sth kleben, haften an etw; sich an etw klammern **10-U4**, Read
clock Uhr **9-U3**, WP
clone geklontes Wesen **9-U1**, WP
clone klonen **10-U2**, WP
close schließen **5-U0**, F
close knapp **8-U2**, T2
  close (to) nahe, in der Nähe von **8-U4**, T1
cloth Tuch **9-U4**, T1
clothes Kleidung **6-U5**, WPB
clothing Bekleidung, Kleidung **8-U1**, Sit1
cloud Wolke **5-U7**, T2
cloudy wolkig, bewölkt **7-U5**, T1
clown Clown **8-U4**, T1
club Club **5-U5**, WPB; Schläger **10-TP**
clue Hinweis **10-Rev5**
clumsy unhandlich; ungeschickt **10-U3**, Ex16
coal Kohle **9-U3**, Ex10
coal-mine Kohlebergwerk **9-U3**, Ex18
coast Küste **6-U2**, T1
coat Mantel **6-U5**, Sit2
code Code, Chiffre **7-U2**, Read
coffee Kaffee **5-U4**, WPA
coffin Sarg **10-Lit**
coin Münze **10-U3**, Ex9
cola Cola **5-U4**, WPC
cold kalt **5-U7**, WPD
collapse zusammenbrechen, einen Kollaps erleiden **9-U3**, Read
colleague Kollege, Kollegin **9-U2**, T1
collect sammeln, einsammeln **7-U5**, Rev
collection Sammlung **9-TP**
college College **7-U1**, T1
colonist Kolonist/in **8-U3**, Sit1
colony Kolonie **8-U3**, WP
colour Farbe **5-U0**, C
column Spalte; Säule **10-U4**, Ex23
combine zusammenfügen, verbinden **9-U1**, Ex10
come kommen **5-U0**, F
  come across zufällig finden/ treffen **10-U2**, Sit1

come on komm! komm schon! **5-U4**, Sit1; sei vernünftig, komm schon! **9-U1**, T1
come up to sb auf jdn zukommen **10-U1**, Sit3
comedian Komiker/in, Witzbold **8-Rev15**
comedy Komödie **6-U6**, WPA
comfortable bequem, angenehm **9-U3**, T2
comic Comic **6-U4**, Sit4
commander Kommandant/in **9-U3**, T1
comment Bemerkung, Kommentar **9-U1**, T2
commercial Werbespot **8-U2**, T2; kommerziell **10-U1**, T2
common: have sth in common etw gemein haben mit **9-U4**, Read
communicate in Verbindung stehen **9-U1**, Ex21
communication Kommunikation, Verständigung **5-U1**, Com
community Bevölkerungsgruppe; Gemeinde **7-U1**, T1
community centre Gemeindezentrum **7-U1**, T1
companion Begleiter/in, Gefährte, Gefährtin **10-U1**, Read
company Firma **5-U2**, T1
compare vergleichen **7-U5**, Rev
comparison Vergleich **10-U4**, T1
compete with, against konkurrieren mit, kämpfen gegen **9-U2**, Ex21
competition Wettbewerb **9-U3**, Sit4
competitor Konkurrent/in **9-U2**, T2
complain sich beschweren **7-U3**, T2
complete vollständig **7-U5**, Read
complete vervollständigen **5-U5**, Ex1
complex zusammengesetzt, komplex **10-U4**, TYE4
complicated kompliziert **9-U1**, T2
computer Computer **5-U1**, Sit7
concentrate (on) sich konzentrieren (auf) **9-U1**, T2
concert Konzert **6-U4**, Ex13
concrete Beton **7-U5**, TYE
condition Bedingung, Verhältnisse, Zustand **8-U1**, WP
conference Konferenz, Besprechung **10-U3**, Read
confident zuversichtlich, selbstsicher **8-U2**, T2
confuse verwechseln, durcheinanderbringen **7-U5**, Read
congratulations Glückwünsche, ich gratuliere **9-U3**, Sit4
congress Kongress **9-U4**, TYE
connect verbinden **9-U2**, T2
connection Verbindung, Zusammenhang **9-U4**, Read
conquer erobern **7-U2**, WP
consult fragen, konsultieren **10-U3**, Read
contain enthalten, beinhalten **10-U2**, Sit4
container Behälter, Gefäß, Container **9-U3**, Read

155

Index

contaminate verseuchen, verunreinigen **10-U4**, T2

contemporary zeitgenössisch; Zeit-genosse/-genossin **10-Lit**

context Kontext, Textzusammenhang **9-TP**

continent Erdteil, Kontinent **8-U3**, T1

continue weitermachen, fortfahren mit **9-U1**, Ex1

contract Vertrag **7-U3**, Sit1

contrast Gegensatz, Kontrast **10-U1**, WP

control Kontrolle **5-U7**, Sit5

control beherrschen, steuern **9-U4**, WP

conversation Gespräch **6-U2**, Ex13

cook kochen **7-U5**, T1

cool kühl **6-U2**, T1

cool down (sich) abkühlen; sich beruhigen **10-U2**, WP

cope with fertigwerden mit **9-U4**, Sit3

copper Kupfer; kupfern **8-U1**, T1

copy Kopie, Exemplar **9-U2**, Sit2

copy kopieren, abschreiben **6-U4**, Ex17

cork Kork(en) **8-U2**, Read

corn Mais **8-U4**, Read

corner Ecke **8-U1**, T1

cornflakes Cornflakes **5-U1**, Sit2

correct richtig **5-U5**, Ex15

correct verbessern, korrigieren **8-U1**, T2

corrupt bestechlich, korrupt **8-U2**, TYE4

cosmonaut Kosmonaut/in **9-U3**, T1

cost Kosten **8-U2**, Sit5

cost kosten **5-U5**, Sit4

costume Kostüm **7-U2**, Sit4

cot death plötzlicher Kindstod **9-U3**, T2

cottage Hütte, kleines Landhaus **6-U2**, WPA

could konnte **8-U1**, Sit1; könnte **8-U2**, Com

could do with könnte brauchen **10-U2**, Com

council Rat(sversammlung) **10-U2**, Read

count zählen **7-U5**, Sket1

counter Ladentisch, Tresen **8-U2**, Sit1

country Land **6-U2**, WPA; Land, Staat **7-U1**, WP

countryside Landschaft **9-Rev5**

county Verwaltungsbezirk, Grafschaft **7-U1**, T1

couple Paar, Ehepaar **7-U4**, WP

a couple of ein paar **7-U4**, WP

courage Mut **8-U1**, T1

course Kurs, Lehrgang **7-U3**, Ex11

off course nicht auf Kurs **9-U3**, Sit2

court Gericht, Gerichtshof **8-U3**, T2

cousin Cousin, Cousine **6-U1**, Sit1

cover bedecken **8-U3**, Read

cow Kuh **6-U2**, WPA

cowboy Cowboy **7-U1**, Read

cowgirl Cowgirl **7-U1**, Read

crampon Steigeisen **10-U1**, T2

crane Kran **7-U4**, TYE

crash Krach(en) **7-U1**, T2

crash abstürzen (Computer) **9-U1**, Com

crate Kiste **8-U4**, T1

crawl kriechen, krabbeln **9-U2**, Read

crazy verrückt; wütend **7-U1**, Read

creaking knarrend, quietschend **7-U4**, Read

cream Sahne, Rahm **10-U3**, Ex9

create (er)schaffen, hervorbringen; verursachen **8-U1**, Ex16

credit Kredit **9-U2**, T1

crew Besatzung, Mannschaft, Crew **9-U3**, T1

cricket Cricket **7-U1**, TYE

crime Verbrechen, Kriminalität **7-U5**, TYE

criminal Verbrecher/in **6-U1**, T2

crisis Krise **10-U3**, T1

crisps Kartoffelchips **5-U4**, T2

crocodile Krokodil **10-Rev13**

crop Feldfrüchte; Ernte **8-U3**, Read

cross überqueren **6-U1**, Sit3

crossroads Kreuzung **7-U5**, Com

crowd Menge **7-U2**, T2

crowded voll, überfüllt **8-U1**, T1

crown Krone **8-U1**, T1

cruel grausam **8-Lit**

cruise Kreuzfahrt **10-U1**, Ex8

crunch knirschen **10-U1**, T2

cry weinen, schreien **7-U2**, Read

cultural kulturell **10-U4**, T1

culture Kultur **10-U1**, T1

cup Tasse; Pokal **6-U4**, Sit1

cupboard Schrank **6-U5**, T2

cure heilen **10-U3**, Sit3

curly lockig, kraus **10-U3**, Sit1

customer Kunde **9-U2**, WP

customs Zoll(behörde) **10-Rev12**

curriculum vitae Lebenslauf **9-U2**, Ex11

cut schneiden, zerschneiden **7-U4**, Sit5

cut off abschneiden **7-U4**, Sit5

cut out ausschneiden **8-U2**, Ex8

CV Lebenslauf **9-U2**, WP

cycle Rad fahren **7-U5**, WP

cyclist Radfahrer/in **9-U3**, Read

Dd

dad Vati, Papa **5-U1**, WPC

daily täglich; Tages- **8-U2**, Sit5

damage beschädigen **10-U1**, T1

damn verflucht, verdammt **6-U5**, T1

dance Tanz, Tanzen; Tanzveranstaltung **8-U2**, T1

dance tanzen **5-U4**, Ex2

dancer Tänzer/in **10-U3**, Sit1

danger Gefahr **8-U3**, Sit4

dangerous gefährlich **5-U5**, T1

dark dunkel **6-U2**, T1

darkness Dunkelheit, Finsternis **10-U3**, Read

dash flitzen, sich beeilen **9-U3**, Com

database Datenbank **9-Rev6**

date Datum **5-U4**, Ex13

daughter Tochter **6-U1**, Sit1

day Tag **5-U1**, Sit4

the day after tomorrow übermorgen **9-U1**, Sit3

the day before yesterday vorgestern **9-U1**, Sit3

day-dream Tagtraum **6-U2**, Sit2

daylight Tageslicht **10-U4**, TYE

dead tot **7-U4**, T1

dead end Sackgasse **6-U6**, T1

deadline (letzter) Termin **10-U2**, T1

deal with sich beschäftigen mit **10-Rev13**

dear lieber, liebe, liebes **5-U4**, Sit4

death Tod **6-U4**, T1

decade Jahrzehnt **10-U3**, WP

December Dezember **5-U4**, Sit5

decide entscheiden, beschließen **6-U6**, WPC

decision Entscheidung **10-SP**

declare erklären; verzollen **9-Rev5**

decorate schmücken; tapezieren **8-U2**, T1

deep tief **8-U4**, Read

deer Reh, Hirsch **6-U2**, WPB

defeat (völlig) besiegen, eine Niederlage zufügen **7-U4**, WP

defend verteidigen **8-U4**, WP

defense Verteidigung **8-U2**, T2

defensive defensiv; Verteidigungs- **8-Proj5**

definite sicher, bestimmt, entschieden **10-U1**, Sit4

definitely bestimmt, absolut **10-U1**, Sit4

definition Definition **7-U4**, Ex11

degree Grad **8-U4**, WP

delay verzögern, aufschieben **9-Rev4**

delay Verzögerung, Aufschub **9-U3**, T1

delete löschen (Computer); streichen **10-U4**, Sit4

deliver (aus)liefern, austragen **6-U5**, WPA

demanding anstrengend, anspruchsvoll **10-U2**, T1

democracy Demokratie **9-U4**, WP

demolish zerstören, vernichten **10-U2**, Read

demolition Zerstörung, Vernichtung **10-U2**, Read

demonstration Demonstration **10-U3**, TYE

demo tape Demoband, Musterband **7-U3**, T1

dentist Zahnarzt, Zahnärztin **10-U3**, Ex9

deny bestreiten, leugnen **8-U2**, T2

department Abteilung **9-U2**, WP

department store Kaufhaus, Warenhaus **10-U1**, Ex9

departure Abfahrt, Abreise **8-U1**, Ex10

depth Tiefe **8-Lit**

descendant Nachfahre, Abkömmling **8-Lit**

describe beschreiben **6-U6**, Com

description Beschreibung **10-U4**, Ex23

desert Wüste **6-U7**, WPA

deserve verdienen **10-U2**, Sit3

design entwerfen, konstruieren **9-U1**, Ex8

designer Designer/in **9-U2**, WP

desire Verlangen, Wunsch, Begierde **9-U3**, Sit3

desk Schülertisch, Schreibtisch **5-U0**, D

desk clerk Empfangschef/in **8-U1**, Ex8

despite trotz **10-U3**, Sit4

Index

destination Bestimmungsort, Ziel
8-U3, Read
destroy zerstören **9-U2**, TYE
detail Einzelheit, Detail **8-U1**, Ex15
detective Detektiv/in **7-U2**, Com
determined entschlossen **9-Proj1**
develop (sich) entwickeln **8-U2**, T2
development Entwicklung **9-U2**, TYE
device Gerät, Vorrichtung **9-U3**, Sit3
diagnosis Diagnose **10-Lit**
dial wählen (Telefonnummer) **6-U6**, T2
dialect Dialekt **9-U4**, Ex19
dialogue Dialog **5-U5**, Ex8
diary Tagebuch **6-U2**, Sit2
dictation Diktat **10-Proj2**
dictatorship Diktatur **9-Lit**
dictionary Wörterbuch **9-Proj4**
die sterben **7-U2**, T1
  die out aussterben **10-U4**, TYE4
differ sich unterscheiden, verschieden sein
10-U3, Ex7
difference Unterschied **8-U4**, Ex16
difference engine mechanische Rechen-
maschine zur Lösung von Differen-
zialgleichungen **9-U3**, WP
different verschieden, anders **5-U6**, Ex16
difficult schwierig **5-U7**, T1
difficulty Schwierigkeit **9-SP**
dig graben **6-U4**, T1
dime Zehncentstück **10-U4**, Song
dining-room Esszimmer **5-U2**, WPB
dinner Hauptmahlzeit **8-U3**, Sit1
dinosaur Dinosaurier **6-U6**, WPB
dip (ein)tauchen **10-U1**, T2
diploma Diplom **9-U2**, WP
direct direkt **9-U2**, Com
direct Regie führen **8-Rev8**
direction Richtung **8-U1**, T1
director Regisseur/in; Direktor/in
9-U1, TYE3
dirt Schmutz, Dreck **8-U4**, T2
dirty schmutzig **6-U5**, WPB
disability Behinderung **10-U3**, T2
disabled behindert **7-U5**, Sit1
disagree sich mit jdm nicht einig sein
9-U2, Com
disappear verschwinden **7-U5**, Read
disappoint enttäuschen **10-U1**, T1
disappointed enttäuscht **10-U1**, Com
disaster Katastrophe **8-Rev15**
disc Disk, Diskette **6-U3**, WPB
disco Disco **5-U1**, Ex16
discover entdecken **8-U2**, WP
discrimination Diskriminierung **8-U3**, T2
discuss besprechen, diskutieren **8-U1**, T2
discussion Diskussion, Besprechung
9-U2, T1
disease Krankheit **7-U1**, Read
disk drive Diskettenlaufwerk **7-U5**, Read
dislike nicht mögen, nicht gern haben
10-U1, Read
display Ausstellung, Vorführung **7-U1**, Proj
  on display ausgestellt **10-U2**, Read

distance Entfernung **7-U4**, T1
district Bezirk, Stadtviertel **8-U1**, Ex7
disturb stören **7-U4**, Read
dive einen Kopfsprung machen, tauchen
10-U1, T2
diverse unterschiedlich, vielfältig
10-U4, WP
diversity Vielfalt **10-U4**, T1
divide teilen, aufteilen; trennen **8-U1**, Ex7
divorce sich scheiden lassen **7-U4**, T2
DJ Discjockey **8-U2**, T1
do tun **5-U1**, Sit6
  by doing sth indem man etw macht
10-U3, Sit4
dock andocken, koppeln **9-U3**, Sit2
doctor Arzt, Ärztin **6-U4**, T2
documentary Dokumentarfilm **6-U6**, WPB
dog Hund **5-U1**, WPA
doll Puppe **8-U3**, T1
dollar Dollar **8-U1**, Sit1
dome Kuppel **6-U1**, WPA
domino Dominospiel **9-Proj3**
donkey Esel **9-U4**, Read
door Tür **5-U0**, D
doorway Eingang **7-U4**, Read
double doppelt **5-U1**, PYE6
doubt Zweifel **9-U4**, Com
doubt bezweifeln **9-U4**, T2
dough Teig **7-U5**, Read
doughnut Berliner, Krapfen **5-U4**, WPA
down unten, nach unten **5-U0**, F
download herunterladen **6-U3**, T1
downstairs unten, die Treppe hinunter
9-U1, T1
downtown (im/ins) Stadtzentrum **8-U1**, Ex7
dozen: a dozen (ein) Dutzend **7-U5**, Read
drama Schauspiel **5-U5**, Sit2
dramatic dramatisch **9-Proj1**
draw zeichnen **5-U4**, Sit2
dream Traum **6-U6**, Ex2
dream (of) träumen (von) **9-U1**, WP
dreamtime Traumzeit **10-U1**, T1
dress Kleid **5-U0**, C
drink trinken **5-U4**, WPB
  drink up austrinken **10-U2**, Read
drink Getränk **6-U5**, T2
drive Aktion, Kampagne **8-U2**, T1
drive fahren **5-U1**, Sit7; (an)treiben
9-U1, T2
drive-in Drive-in **10-U4**, Song
driver Fahrer/in **6-U5**, WPC
driveway Einfahrt, Zufahrt **10-U4**, Read
drop fallen lassen, fallen **6-U4**, T1
  drop out of (die Schule o. Ä.) abbrechen
9-U2, Ex14
drown ertrinken, überschwemmt werden
9-U4, Sit4
drug Droge; Medikament **7-U1**, Read
Druid Druide **7-U2**, TYE
drum Fass (Öl), Tonne **10-U4**, Sit3
drums Schlagzeug **7-U3**, T1
dry trocken **9-U1**, Ex18
duck Ente **6-U4**, Ex18

duke Herzog **7-U2**, T1
dump abladen (Müll), versenken
10-U4, Sit3
dung Mist, Dung **10-U2**, TYE
dunno = don't know weiß nicht **9-U4**, Read
during während **7-U5**, T2
dust Staub **10-U2**, Sit4
Dutch holländisch; Holländer/in
8-U2, TYE
DVD DVD **6-U3**, WPB

Ee

each jeder, jede, jedes **5-U5**, Ex18
  each other einander, gegenseitig **8-U3**, Sit5
ear Ohr **6-U6**, Com
early früh **7-U4**, WP
earn verdienen **6-U5**, WPB
earth Erde **8-U4**, T1
earthquake Erdbeben **8-Proj1**
east Osten **6-U1**, WPA
Easter Ostern **5-U4**, Sit5
eastern östlich, Ost- **8-U1**, TYE
eastward ostwärts, nach Osten **8-U3**, TYE
easy einfach, leicht **5-U6**, T1
eat essen **5-U3**, WPA
economic wirtschaftlich, Wirtschafts-
10-U3, T1
economical wirtschaftlich, sparsam **9-Rev3**
economy Wirtschaft **10-U3**, T1
Ecstasy Ecstasy (Droge) **10-U3**, T1
edge Rand, Kante **10-U1**, Sit4
educate unterrichten, erziehen **9-Lit**
education Erziehung **9-U2**, Sit1
effect Wirkung, Effekt **9-U3**, T1
efficient leistungsfähig, effizient **9-U2**, Ex21
effort Anstrengung, Bemühung **10-U1**, Sit4
e.g. z.B. **9-SP**
egg Ei **10-U1**, Sit4
eight acht **5-U0**, G
eighteen achtzehn **5-U0**, G
eighty achtzig **5-U4**, WPA
either ... or entweder ... oder **10-U3**, Read
elder Stammesälteste/r **10-U1**, Read
electric elektrisch **8-U1**, Read
electrical elektrisch, Elektro- **9-U2**, Sit1
electric-orange signalorange **10-U1**, TYE
electrify elektrifizieren **9-TP**
electro Electro (Musikrichtung) **9-U1**, T1
electronic elektronisch **8-U4**, Ex17
elephant Elefant **6-U3**, WPA
elevator Aufzug, Lift **8-U1**, T1
eleven elf **5-U0**, G
else sonst **7-U1**, T1
e-mail E-Mail **6-U3**, WPC
embarrassing peinlich **10-U3**, Sit3
emergency Notfall; Not- **10-U4**, T2
emotion Gefühl, Emotion **9-U1**, Com
emperor Kaiser **7-U2**, WP
empire Reich, Imperium **8-U1**, WP
employ beschäftigen **8-U3**, TYE
employee Arbeitnehmer/in, Beschäftigte/r
9-Lit
employer Arbeitgeber/in **9-U1**, Sit4

157

Index

empty leer **6-U4**, T1
empty leeren, ausleeren **9-U4**, Read
enable befähigen, ermöglichen **9-U4**, Sit2
encourage ermutigen **9-U3**, T2
encyclopedia Lexikon, Enzyklopädie
 6-U4, PYE4
end Ende **5-U1**, Song
end beenden **6-U2**, Ex6
ending Endung, Ende **8-U1**, Ex14
endless endlos **6-U7**, Song
enemy Feind/in **7-U2**, Proj
engine Motor **8-Rev11**
engineer Ingenieur/in **8-U3**, TYE1
engineering Technik **9-U2**, WP
English englisch; Engländer/in **5-U0**, A
enjoy gern haben, genießen **5-U7**, WPC
 enjoy yourself! Viel Spaß! **8-U3**, Sit4
enormous gewaltig, enorm groß **10-U4**, WP
enough genug **6-U4**, Ex11
enter eintreten (in) **8-U1**, Ex9
entertainment Unterhaltung **8-U2**, T2
entrance Eingang **6-U4**, T2
envelope Briefumschlag, Kuvert **8-Rev12**
envy beneiden **9-U1**, T1
equal gleich **8-U3**, WP
equipment Ausrüstung **6-U7**, T1
error Irrtum, Fehler, Versehen **9-U3**, Read
escape flüchten, entkommen **8-U3**, Sit3
especially besonders **7-U3**, T1
establish gründen, einrichten **9-U4**, T1
etc usw. **6-U5**, Ex12
ethnic ethnisch, Volks- **10-U4**, WP
European europäisch; Europäer/in
 8-U2, WP
evacuate evakuieren, verlassen **10-TP**
even sogar **7-U4**, TYE; noch **10-U2**, T1
 even if selbst wenn **10-U2**, Ex20
 even though obwohl **8-U1**, T2
evening Abend **5-U1**, Sit6
event Ereignis, Veranstaltung **8-U2**, Sit3
eventually schließlich, endlich **9-Lit**
ever jemals **6-U5**, Sit4
every jeder, jede, jedes **5-U1**, Sit6
everybody jede(r), alle **7-U3**, Com
everyday alltäglich, Alltags- **9-U3**, WP
everyone jede(r), alle **6-U2**, Sit2
everything alles **6-U3**, WPC
everywhere überall **6-U2**, Song
evil böse, schlecht, übel **9-U4**, Fol
exact genau **6-U7**, T2
exam Prüfung **9-U2**, Sit1
examination Prüfung; Untersuchung
 10-U1, Ex10
examine untersuchen **8-U1**, TYE
example (of) Beispiel (für) **8-U2**, Ex17
 for example zum Beispiel **7-U4**, T2
excellent ausgezeichnet **9-U1**, Ex11
except außer **7-U1**, WP
exchange austauschen **8-Proj2**
excited aufgeregt, begeistert **7-U2**, T2
excitement Aufregung **8-U4**, T1
exciting spannend, aufregend **6-U1**, WPA
excuse Entschuldigung **7-U2**, Ex3

excuse: excuse me Entschuldigung
 5-U6, WPB
execute hinrichten, exekutieren **7-U4**, T2
exercise Übung **5-U1**, Ex1
exercise book Schulheft **5-U0**, D
exhausted erschöpft **7-U5**, T1
exist existieren, vorhanden sein **6-U5**, T1
existing vorhanden, existierend **9-U2**, T2
exit Ausgang **10-U3**, Ex9
expect erwarten **6-U6**, Sit1
expedition Expedition, Forschungsreise
 7-U5, WP
expensive teuer **5-U7**, WPA
experience erleben, erfahren **8-U4**, T1
experience Erfahrung **9-U2**, WP
experiment Experiment **9-U3**, WP
experiment with sth mit etw experimentieren
 10-Lit
expert Experte, Expertin **7-U5**, Sket1
explain erklären **6-U2**, T2
explanation Erklärung **6-U7**, Com
explode explodieren **9-U3**, Read
exploit ausnutzen, ausbeuten **10-U2**, T1
explore erforschen, erkunden **8-U3**, Sit1
explorer Forscher/in, Forschungsreisende/r
 10-U1, WP
export ausführen, exportieren **7-U1**, WP
express ausdrücken **8-U3**, Ex8
expressway Autobahn **8-U2**, Read
extra zusätzlich **6-U5**, WPB
extract Auszug, Extrakt **10-U1**, Read
extreme extrem, äußerst **10-U4**, WP
eye Auge **6-U6**, Com
eyelash Augenwimper **10-U4**, Read

Ff

fable Fabel **9-Lit**
face Gesicht **6-U6**, Com
face sth vor etw stehen; gegenüber sein
 10-Proj1
fact Tatsache, Faktum **8-U4**, T1
 in fact eigentlich, tatsächlich **8-U1**, T2
factory Fabrik **6-U5**, WPA
Fahrenheit Fahrenheit **10-U4**, T1
fail scheitern, keinen Erfolg haben
 7-U3, Read
failure Scheitern **9-U3**, Read
fair fair, gerecht **6-U5**, T1; schön,
 liebreizend **6-U1**, Song
fairground Rummelplatz **7-U5**, Sit1
fair(-haired) blond **7-U4**, Com
fairly ziemlich, relativ **10-U4**, Sit2
fake unecht; Fälschung **8-U1**, Read
fall fallen **5-U5**, T1
 fall in love (with) sich verlieben (in)
 7-U2, T1
 fall off herunterfallen **6-U2**, T2
 fall over hinfallen, umkippen **8-U1**, Sit1
false falsch, unrichtig **8-U1**, Ex12
familiar (with) gewohnt, bekannt,
 vertraut (mit) **9-Proj4**
family Familie **5-U1**, WPA
famous berühmt **6-U1**, WPA

fan Anhänger/in, Fan **5-U2**, T2
fancy mögen **6-U3**, T2
fantastic wundervoll **5-U2**, T1
far weit **5-U5**, T1
farm Bauernhof **6-U2**, WPA
farmer Bauer, Bäuerin **5-U3**, Song
farmhouse Bauernhaus **8-U4**, Read
farming Landwirtschaft **9-U3**, WP
fascinated: be fascinated by fasziniert sein
 von **10-U3**, Com
fascinating faszinierend, fesselnd **9-U3**, WP
fashion Mode **7-U3**, T1
fast schnell **5-U5**, WPA
fat dick, fett **7-U4**, T2
fatal tödlich, mit tödlichem Ausgang
 9-U2, Read
father Vater **5-U2**, Sit4
fault Fehler **6-U6**, T2
favour Gefallen **6-U6**, T2
favourite Lieblings- **5-U1**, Sit2
fear fürchten, befürchten **10-Dict**
February Februar **5-U4**, Sit5
Federal Bureau of Investigation/FBI FBI
 8-U1, Read
fed: be fed up die Nase voll haben **6-U1**, T2
feed füttern **5-U3**, WPA
feel (sich) fühlen **6-U2**, T1
feeling Gefühl **7-U2**, T2
fellow Kumpel, Kamerad **9-Proj4**
female weiblich **7-U3**, Read
fence Zaun **5-U3**, T1
ferry Fähre **10-U4**, T1
festival Fest, Festival **6-U4**, WPB
fetal fetal, Fetal- **10-U3**, T2
fetch holen **7-U5**, T2
fever Fieber **8-U3**, Read
few: a few ein paar **6-U4**, Sit2
fiction Erzählliteratur **9-Lit**; Fiktion
 10-U2, WP
field Feld **7-U1**, WP
fifteen fünfzehn **5-U0**, G
fifty fünfzig **5-U1**, Sit5
fight Kampf, Streit **8-U3**, Sit2
fight kämpfen **7-U2**, WP
file Datei; Akte **9-U2**, TYE
fill füllen **8-U3**, T2
 fill in ausfüllen **10-U2**, TYE5
film Film **5-U1**, Sit1
film filmen **9-Proj1**
filthy dreckig **7-U5**, T1
final letzte(r,s), endgültig **7-U4**, T2; Finale,
 Endspiel **10-U1**, T1
finally schließlich **7-U4**, T2
financial finanziell **9-U1**, T2
find finden **5-U0**, J
 find out herausfinden **6-U3**,
fine gut, schön **5-U0**, B
fine Bußgeld verhängen **8-U3**, T2
finger Finger **10-U3**, Ex9
finish beenden **5-U4**, WPA
fire Feuer **6-U4**, WPA
fire feuern, schießen **6-U4**, T2
fire-eater Feuerschlucker **6-U1**, WPA

Index

firefighter Feuerwehrmann, Feuerwehrfrau **10-U3**, T2
fire truck Feuerwehrauto **10-U3**, T2
firewood Brennholz **8-U3**, Read
fireworks Feuerwerk **6-U4**, WPA
first erste, erster, erstes **5-U1**, Sit3
 at first zuerst **8-U3**, Sit1
first aid erste Hilfe **7-U5**, WP
first-class erstklassig **10**-Dict
first floor erster Stock **5-U2**, WPB
fish Fisch **7-U5**, Ex6
fish fischen, angeln **8-U3**, Sit1
fishing boat Fischerboot **8-U3**, Sit1
fit fit, geeignet **7-U5**, Rev; einbauen, ausrüsten mit **9-U3**, Sit4; passen **9-U3**, Ex17
five fünf **5-U0**, G
five and dime billiger Laden **10-U4**, Song
fix befestigen **6-U5**, T2; reparieren **8-U3**, Ex8
flag Flagge **8-U2**, WP
flame Flamme **9-U1**, T2
flared ausgestellt **10-U3**, WP
flashing blinkend, blitzend **8-U1**, T2
flat Wohnung **5-U2**, WPA
flat flach **8-U2**, Read
fleet Flotte **7-U4**, TYE
flight Flug **5-U7**, Ex2
flipper Flosse, Schwimmflosse **8-U4**, TYE
float treiben, schwimmen, schweben **10-U4**, T1
flood Flut, Überschwemmung **10-U2**, Sit3
floor (Fuß-)Boden **5-U5**, Sit1; Stockwerk, Etage **8-U1**, T1
flower Blume **6-U2**, WPB
flu Grippe **10-U1**, T1
flute Flöte **7-U3**, Ex11
fly fliegen **5-U1**, Sit8
fly Fliege **10-U2**, TYE
follow folgen **6-U6**, T1
 follow sth up etw nachgehen, etw weiter verfolgen **10-U4**, T2
follower Anhäger/in **9-U4**, T1
following folgend **9-U2**, Ex5
follow-up Fortsetzungs- **9**-Proj1
fond: be fond of mögen, gern haben **10-U3**, T2
food Essen, Lebensmittel **5-U4**, WPC
fool Narr, Dummkopf **6-U4**, WPD
fool zum Narren halten **8-U1**, Read
foot Fuß **5-U5**, T1
 on foot zu Fuß **7-U5**, Sit3
football Fußball **5-U1**, Ex10
footballer Fußballspieler/in **6-U1**, Ex2
for für **5-U1**, WPB; seit **7-U1**, Sit4
 what for? wozu? **7-U1**, Read
forbid verbieten, untersagen **7-U1**, Read
force Macht, Kraft **10-U3**, Read
force sb to do sth jdn zwingen, etw zu tun **9-U4**, Sit2
forecast Vorhersage **6-U3**, Sit1
forecast voraussagen, vorhersehen **9-U3**, Sit1

foreigner Ausländer/in **9-U2**, T1
foreign language Fremdsprache **8**-Rev4
foreleg Vorderbein **7-U1**, Read
forest Wald, Forst **6-U2**, Sit3
forever für immer **9**-Rev10
forget vergessen **5-U4**, T2
fork Gabel **10-U3**, Ex9
form Form **6-U1**, Ex4; Formular **10-U2**, T1
form formen, bilden **8-U1**, Read
formal Tanzveranstaltung **8-U2**, T1
formation Bildung; Formation **8-U4**, T2
former ehemalig **10-U1**, Ex9
Formula One Formel 1 **5-U2**, T1
fort Festung, Fort **8-U4**, Ex7
fortunately glücklicherweise **9-U1**, T1
forty vierzig **5-U1**, Sit5
forward(s) vorwärts **7-U1**, Ex3
found (be)gründen **8**-Lit
foundation Stiftung; Gründung **7-U3**, Read
four vier **5-U0**, G
fourteen vierzehn **5-U0**, G
fraction Bruchteil **10-U3**, Read
frame Rahmen **10-U2**, T2
free kostenlos, frei **5-U7**, Sit1
free freilassen, befreien **10**-Lit
freedom Freiheit **8-U1**, Sit3
free fall freier Fall **10-U1**, T2
freeway (gebührenfreie) Autobahn **8-U2**, Read
freeze frieren, gefrieren **8-U4**, Read
freezing kalt, frierend **7-U5**, T1
French Französisch, französisch **5-U1**, Sit3
french fries Pommes frites **6-U7**, Ex1
frequent häufig **10-U3**, Sit3
fresh frisch **7-U1**, Read
freshman Student/in im ersten Studienjahr **8**-Proj2
Friday Freitag **5-U1**, Sit4
friend Freund/in **5-U1**,
friendly freundlich **6-U7**, T2
frighten jdn erschrecken **8-U4**, T2
 be frightened of Angst haben vor **10**-Rev15
frog Frosch **10**-Rev12
from von, aus **5-U0**, A
front Vorderseite **6-U2**, T1
 in front of vor **5-U2**, WPA
frontier Grenze, Grenzgebiet **8**-Lit
frown (at sth/sb) die Stirn runzeln (über etw/jdn) **10-U2**, Read
frozen gefroren, tiefgefroren **7-U5**, T1
fruit Frucht, Obst **10-U1**, Ex18
full voll **5-U7**, T2
full-time Vollzeit-, ganztags **10-U2**, T1
fun Spaß **6-U4**, WPD
funnel Trichter **9-U3**, Read
funny witzig, komisch, seltsam **5-U7**, T2
furious wütend **7-U4**, T2
further weiter **8**-Lit
fury Wut **10-U3**, Read
fuss Wirbel, Aufhebens, Theater **10-U2**, Read
future Zukunft **6-U5**, Sit1

Gg

Gaeltacht Gebiet, in dem Gälisch gesprochen wird **7-U1**, T1
gain sich verschaffen, bekommen, gewinnen **10-U2**, T1
galactic galaktisch **10-U2**, Read
galaxy Sternsystem **10-U2**, Read
game Spiel **5-U1**, Sit7
gang Bande, Gang **8-U1**, Read
gangster Gangster, Verbrecher **8-U1**, T2
gap Lücke, Spalt, Abstand **10-U3**, T1
garage Garage **5-U2**, WPA
garbage Müll, Abfall **6-U7**, Sit4
garden Garten **5-U2**, WPA
garment Kleidungsstück **9-U3**, T2
gas Benzin **6-U7**, Ex1; Gas **10-U2**, WP
gate Tor **6-U5**, T2
gather sich (ver)sammeln **10**-Lit
GCSE General Certificate of Secondary Education **9-U2**, Sit1
general allgemein, General-; ungefähr **10-U4**, WP
generally gewöhnlich; allgemein **10-U4**, WP
generation Generation **10-U1**, Sit2
generation gap Unterschied zwischen den Generationen **10-U3**, T1
genetic genetisch **10-U2**, WP
gentle sanft **8-U4**, Read
genuine echt, unverfälscht **7-U4**, Ex10
geography Geografie **8-U2**, Read
German Deutsch; deutsch; Deutsche/r **5-U0**, A
get holen **5-U3**, T1; bekommen, werden **6-U3**, T2
 get clean sauber machen, sauber bringen **6-U5**, WPB
 get home heimkommen **5-U2**, T1
 get in einsteigen (in) **5-U1**, T2
 get mad with sb mit jdm böse werden **8-U3**, Sit2
 get married heiraten **10-U3**, T2
 get on sb's nerves jdm auf die Nerven gehen **9-U2**, T1
 get on with auskommen mit **7-U3**, T2
 get out (of) aussteigen, herauskommen **7-U1**, T2
 get ready vorbereiten **6-U5**, Sit2
 get through sth etw erledigen **10-U2**, T1
 get to gehen zu, kommen zu **6-U6**, T1
 get to know kennen lernen **9-U2**, T1
 get up aufstehen **5-U1**, Sit6
 get used to sich gewöhnen an **8-U4**, T2
geyser Geysir, Geiser **10-U1**, Sit3
ghetto Getto, abgesondertes Wohnviertel **7-U1**, Read
ghost Geist, Gespenst **6-U6**, WPA
giant Riese, Riesin **9**-Lit
gibber stammeln, brabbeln **9-U1**, Read
gift Geschenk **8-U3**, Sit2
gig Konzert, Auftritt **7-U3**, Sit1
girl Mädchen **5-U1**, WPA
girlfriend Freundin **5-U1**, Song
girlie mädchenhaft **9-U2**, Read

159

Index

give geben **5-U3**, Sit1
  give as good as you get sich kräftig wehren **9-U2**, Read
  give away abgeben, verschenken **8-U2**, T2
  give in nachgeben **8-U3**, T2
  give sb a lift jdn im Auto mitnehmen **7-U4**, Sit3
  give up aufgeben, verzichten auf **8-U3**, T2
glacier Gletscher **10-U1**, T2
glad froh **6-U4**, T2
glass Glas **6-U3**, Ex14
glasses Brille **7-U4**, Com
glimpse flüchtiger Blick **9-U3**, WP
global weltweit, global **9-U2**, T2
globalization Globalisierung **9-U2**, T2
global warming Erwärmung der Erdatmosphäre **10-U2**, Sit3
globe Kugel, Erdball, Globus **9-U1**, Sit4
glove Handschuh **10-U1**, T2
go gehen **5-U0**, A
  go on weitermachen, weitergehen **8-U3**, T2; vor sich gehen, passieren **9-U1**, T1
goal Tor **7-U3**, Read
goalkeeper Torwart **8-U2**, Ex12
God Gott **6-U4**, T1
going: be going to werden **6-U3**, Sit1
go-kart Gokart **5-U7**, Sit4
gold Gold **7-U5**, WP
golden golden, aus Gold **6-U7**
golf Golf **8-U4**, T1
golfer Golfspieler/in **10-TP**
good gut **5-U1**, Sit2
  be good at doing sth gut sein in; etw gut können **8-U2**, TYE
goodbye auf Wiedersehen **5-U0**, B
Goth Gothic (Musikrichtung) **10-U3**, T1
government Regierung **8-U3**, Sit2
gown Robe, Talar **7-U2**, TYE
grade Note (Schule) **10-U2**, T1
graduate die Abschlussprüfung bestehen **8-U2**, T1
graffiti Graffiti **8-U1**, T1
grammar Grammatik **9-TP**
grandad Opa **5-U5**, Sit3
grandma Oma **6-U3**, Sit1
grandmother Großmutter **9-U4**, TYE5
grandparents Großeltern **6-U2**, WPA
grandson Enkel(sohn) **7-U3**, T2
grape Traube **10-U2**, T2
graphic design grafisches Design **10-U2**, T1
grass Gras **5-U3**, WPA
grateful dankbar **8-U4**, Read
great großartig **5-U1**, Sit2
great-grandfather Urgroßvater **8-U1**, TYE3
great-great-grandfather Ururgroßvater **8-U1**, TYE3
greedy habgierig, gierig **10-U3**, Read
green grün **5-U0**, C
green card Aufenthaltsgenehmigung **9-U2**, T2
greenhouse Gewächshaus **10-U2**, WP
grey grau **7-U4**, Com

grip (er)greifen **10-U1**, T2
grizzly bear Grizzlybär **5-U0**, Song
grocery (store) Lebensmittel(geschäft) **8-U1**, Read
ground Grund, Boden **6-U2**, WPB
ground floor Erdgeschoss **5-U2**, WPB
group Gruppe **5-U1**, Ex4
grow anbauen; wachsen **8-U3**, T1; werden **9-U4**, T2
  grow up aufwachsen, erwachsen werden **9-U2**, T2
grudging widerwillig, unwillig **10-U3**, Read
guard Polizist **7-U1**, T2
guard rail Leitplanke; Schutzgeländer **10-U4**, Read
guess raten, schätzen **6-U2**, Ex7
guest Gast **6-U6**, WPA
guest house Gästehaus, Pension **7-U1**, Sit1
guidance counselor Schulberater/in **8-Proj2**
guide Führer/in **6-U2**, T1
guitar Gitarre **5-U0**, E
gulf Golf **6-U7**, Song
gun Schusswaffe **5-U3**, Song
gunpowder Schießpulver **6-U4**, T1
guy Typ, Bursche **6-U4**, WPA

Hh

hacker Computerhacker **9-U2**, TYE
had better, you du solltest besser **9-U1**, T1
hair Haar **6-U2**, Sit2
hairdresser Friseur/in **9-U2**, Ex9
half halb **5-U1**, Sit5
half past (ten) halb (elf) **5-U1**, Sit5
half-term Schulferien **5-U4**, Sit5
halfway auf halbem Weg; die halbe Strecke **8-U3**, TYE
hall Flur **5-U2**, WPB
ham Schinken **7-U5**, T1
hamburger Hamburger **5-U4**, WPA
hamster Hamster **5-U3**, WPA
hand Hand **5-U6**, T1
handful Handvoll **10-U1**, Read
handsome gut aussehend **8-U1**, Read
handy praktisch, nützlich, handlich **10-U4**, T1
hang aufhängen; erhängen **8-U3**, Sit3
  hang around herumlungern, herumhängen **7-U1**, Read
  hang out sich rumtreiben, rumhängen **10-U3**, T2
happen passieren, geschehen **6-U2**, Ex3
happy glücklich, froh **5-U0**, G
  Happy birthday! Herzlichen Glückwunsch zum Geburtstag! **5-U0**, G
harbour Hafen **9-U1**, TYE4
hard hart, schwer, schwierig **5-U6**, T1
hardly kaum **7-U5**, T1
hat Hut **10-U1**, Read
hate Hass **9-Lit**
hate hassen, gar nicht mögen **5-U5**, Sit2
haunted Spuk- **7-U4**, Read
have got haben, besitzen **5-U0**, E
have to müssen **6-U6**, T1

he er **5-U1**, WPA
head Kopf, Oberhaupt **6-U2**, Ex7
head end Kopfende **9-U1**, Read
headache Kopfschmerzen **7-U1**, Ex14
heading Überschrift **8-U2**, Ex14
headlights Scheinwerfer (Auto) **8-Rev1**
headline Schlagzeile **8-U2**, Ex11
headmaster Schuldirektor **9-Rev7**
health Gesundheit(szustand) **10-U2**, T1
healthy gesund **8-U3**, T1
hear hören **5-U7**, T1
hearing Hören, Gehör **9-U3**, Read
heart Herz; Zentrum **9-U4**, WP
  by heart auswendig **9-SP**
heart attack Herzanfall, Herzinfarkt **10-U3**, T1
heat Hitze **8-U3**, Read
heating Heizung **9-U3**, Ex10
heater Heizofen **10-U4**, Read
heavy schwer **7-U2**, TYE
heavy metal Heavy Metal **8-U1**, Sit1
hedge Hecke **6-U6**, T1
height Höhe **10-U2**, Sit4
helicopter Hubschrauber **9-U2**, Read
hell Hölle **10-Rev13**
hello hallo **5-U0**, A
helmet Helm, Schutzhelm **10-U3**, T2
help Hilfe **6-U5**, Sit2
help helfen **5-U3**, Com
  I can't help it ich kann nicht anders **10-U3**, Sit3
hen Henne, Huhn **6-U2**, WPA
her ihr, ihre, ihr **5-U1**, T1; sie, ihr **5-U2**, Sit5
here hier; hierher **5-U0**, F
hero Held **7-U3**, Proj
hers ihr(e, s) **6-U3**, Sit2
herself sich; selbst **8-U3**, Sit3
hexagon Sechseck **10-U2**, T2
hexagonal sechseckig **10-U2**, T2
hi hallo **5-U0**, A
hide (sich) verstecken **7-U1**, Read
high hoch **5-U7**, T2
high flier Senkrechtstarter/in, Hochbegabte/r **9-U2**, Read
high school Oberschule **6-U3**, T2
highway Hauptverkehrsstraße **6-U7**, Song
hill Hügel **6-U7**, WPA
him ihn, ihm **5-U2**, Sit5
himself sich; selbst **8-U3**, Sit3
Hindi Hindi (Sprache in Indien) **9-U4**, WP
Hindu Hindu **6-U4**, WPB
hip hop Hip-Hop **8-U1**, T2
hippie Hippie **10-U3**, T1
hire mieten, jdn anstellen **8-U3**, Read
his sein, seine, sein **5-U1**, WPB
Hispanic hispanisch; Hispano-Amerikaner/in **8-U1**, WP
hiss zischen; fauchen **8-U4**, T2
history Geschichte **6-U3**, WPE
hit Hit **7-U3**, T1
hit schlagen, treffen **6-U7**, Sit3
  hit the headlines Schlagzeilen machen **10-U3**, TYE

Index

hitchhiker Anhalter/in, Tramper/in **10-U2**, Read
hi-tech technisch hoch entwickelt **9-U2**, T2
hobby Hobby **9-U4**, Sit1
hockey Hockey **5-U5**, Sit2
hold halten **5-U4**, T1; enthalten, fassen **8-U1**, T1
hole Loch **5-U3**, T1
holiday Ferien, Urlaub **5-U4**, Sit5
holy heilig **9-U4**, Fol
home Heim, Zuhause **5-U1**, Sit6
homeless obdachlos **7-U5**, TYE
home town Heimatort **10-SP**
homework Hausaufgaben **5-U1**, Sit6
honey Honig **6-U5**, WPA
hoot hupen (Auto); rufen (Eule) **7-U2**, Read
hope Hoffnung **9-U4**, Fol
hope hoffen **5-U2**, T2
hopeful optimistisch, voller Hoffnung **7-U3**, T2
hopeless hoffnungslos **6-U1**, T1
horn Hupe; Horn **10-U3**, T2
horrible fürchterlich, schrecklich **6-U1**, T2
horror Horror **7-U4**, T1
horse Pferd **6-U2**, WPA
hospital Krankenhaus **5-U6**, WPA
host Gastgeber/in; Gast; Moderator/in **8-U2**, T2
hostel Wohnheim **9-U4**, T2
hot heiß **5-U7**, WPD
hot-air balloon Heißluftballon **7-U5**, Rev
hotel Hotel **5-U7**, WPD
hot pants Hotpants **10-U3**, T1
hour Stunde **5-U5**, Sit3
house Haus **5-U0**, G
household Haushalt **9-U2**, T2
household name Name, den jeder kennt **9-U3**, TYE
housework Hausarbeit **9-U3**, Ex11
housing Unterbringung, Wohnungen **8-U3**, T2
how wie **5-U0**, B
  how about ...? wie wär's mit ...? **8-U2**, Ex9
  how many ...? Wie viele ...? **5-U0**, H
  how much ...? Wie viel ...? **5-U6**, Sit3
however jedoch **8-U2**, T2
huge riesig **6-U7**, WPA
human Menschen-; menschlich **8-U4**, TYE
humid feucht **10-U2**, Sit4
hundred hundert **5-U4**, WPA
hungry hungrig **5-U4**, WPA
hunt jagen **8-U3**, T1
hunter Jäger/in **8-U3**, TYE3
hurricane Wirbelsturm **8-U4**, T1
hurry Eile **7-U1**, T2
  in a hurry in Eile **7-U1**, T2
hurry eilen, sich beeilen **5-U1**, Sit6
  hurry (up) sich beeilen **5-U1**, T2
hurt schmerzen, weh tun **5-U6**, T1
husband Ehemann **6-U1**, Sit1
hutch Kaninchenstall **5-U3**, WPA
hydroelectric hydroelektrisch, Wasserkraft- **10-U4**, T2

hygiene Hygiene, Gesundheitspflege **9-U1**, Sit4
hyperspace Hyperraum **10-U2**, Read

Ii

I ich **5-U0**, A
ice Eis **10-U1**, T2
ice age Eiszeit **10-U2**, WP
iceberg Eisberg **7-U3**, WP
ice-cream (Speise-)Eis **5-U4**, WPA
ice-rink Eisbahn **7-U5**, TYE
icy eisig **10-U4**, T2
idea Idee **5-U4**, T2
identify identifizieren **10-U2**, TYE5
idiom Redewendung, idiomatischer Ausdruck **9-U2**, Ex8
idiot Dummkopf, Idiot **5-U6**, T2
if wenn, falls **6-U1**, Sit2; ob **7-U2**, T1
  if only wenn ... nur **10-U2**, Ex20
  what if ...? was ist, wenn ...? **8-U4**, T2
ignorant unwissend **9-U4**, T2
ill krank **6-U2**, Ex1
illegal ungesetzlich, illegal **10-U4**, T2
illuminated beleuchtet **10-U2**, TYE
imaginary frei erfunden, eingebildet **9-U1**, Ex18
imagination Fantasie **10-U1**, Read
imagine sich vorstellen **5-U7**, WPD
immediate sofortig, umgehend **9-U3**, TYE
immediately sofort **9-U3**, TYE
immigrant Einwanderer **8-U1**, TYE
immigration Einwanderung **8-U1**, TYE
importance Bedeutung **9-U2**, T2
important wichtig, bedeutend **7-U2**, T1
impossible unmöglich **9-U4**, T1
impress beeindrucken **8-U4**, Ex15
improve verbessern, sich bessern **9-U2**, T1
in in **5-U0**, A
inch Inch, Zoll **7-U5**, Read
include einschließen, beinhalten **7-U5**, Read
including einschließlich, inbegriffen **9-U3**, T1
incorrect falsch, unrichtig **9-U3**, Ex7
increase zunehmen, anwachsen **8-U2**, Sit5
independence Unabhängigkeit **8-U2**, WP
independent (of/from) unabhängig (von) **8-U3**, Sit5
Indian Indianer/in; Inder/in **8-U2**, Ex7
individual einzeln, individuell **8-U2**, Sit5
industry Industrie **9-U1**, TYE
inferior minderwertig, unterlegen **10-U4**, T1
influence beeinflussen **10-Lit**
influence (on) Einfluss (auf), Auswirkung **9-U1**, TYE
Influenza Grippe **10-U1**, Ex10
info box Infobox **9-U3**, Ex5
informal umgangssprachlich; ungezwungen **10-U3**, Com
information Information(en) **5-U7**, Ex3
inhabit bewohnen **10-U4**, WP
inhabitant Bewohner/in **10-Proj1**
inhospitable unwirtlich **10-U4**, TYE

injure verletzen **8-U2**, Sit2
injury Verletzung **9-U2**, Read
in-line skates Inlineskates, Rollerblades **5-U5**, WPA
inn Gasthaus **7-U2**, T2
insect Insekt **10-U2**, Sit4
inside innen, drinnen **6-U6**, T1
insist on doing sth darauf bestehen, etw zu tun **10-U1**, Sit1
instant sofort, augenblicklich **9-U2**, T2
instead of anstatt **8-U1**, Ex1
institute Institut **9-U3**, T2
instructor Lehrer/in, Ausbilder/in **10-U1**, Sit3
instrument Instrument **10-Proj1**
insurance Versicherung **10-U2**, T1
intelligent intelligent **10-U2**, WP
intend to do sth beabsichtigen, etw zu tun **10-U2**, Sit2
interest Interesse **7-U2**, Com
interested: be interested in interessiert sein (an) **6-U3**, T2
interesting interessant **6-U1**, WPA
internal innerlich, innere(r, s) **9-U2**, Read
international international **7-U5**, TYE
internet Internet **6-U3**, WPC
interpreter Dolmetscher/in **8-U1**, TYE2
interrupt unterbrechen **10-U2**, T1
inter-school zwischen Schulen **8-U3**, Sit3
intersection Kreuzung, Autobahnkreuz **8-U2**, Read
interview Gespräch, Interview **9-U2**, Sit1
interview interviewen **6-U2**, Ex9
interviewer Interviewer/in **8-U3**, Com
into hinein, in **6-U2**, T1
  be into sth auf etw stehen, auf etw abfahren **10-U3**, Com
introduce einführen **9-U4**, T1
  introduce sb (to sb) jdn (jdm) vorstellen **10-U1**, Sit3
introduction Einführung **5-U1**, Intro
Inuit Inuit **10-U4**, WP
invade einmarschieren in, eindringen in **7-U4**, WP
invader Eindringling, Angreifer/in **7-U4**, WP
invent erfinden **8-U2**, TYE
invention Erfindung **8-U2**, TYE
inventor Erfinder/in **9-U3**, Sit3
investigate nachforschen, Ermittlungen anstellen **9-U4**, T2
invisible unsichtbar **7-U5**, Read
invitation Einladung **7-U1**, Com
invite einladen **6-U6**, WPC
involve mit sich bringen, zur Folge haben **10-U2**, T1
Irish irisch **7-U1**, WP
iron Eisen **7-U4**, T1
irrigate bewässern **9-U3**, Read
irritate ärgern, reizen **10-U4**, T1
island Insel **6-U7**, Song
issue Frage, Thema; Ausgabe (Zeitung) **10-U3**, TYE

161

Index

it es **5-U0**, B

  it's fun es macht Spaß **6-U4**, WPD

  it's my turn Ich bin dran. Ich bin an der Reihe. **5-U1**, T2

  it's no good es ist sinnlos **9-U1**, Ex18

Italian italienisch; Italiener/in **8-U1**, TYE4

italics Kursivdruck **7-U1**, Ex6

itch jucken, brennen **9-U3**, T2

item Punkt (auf einer Liste); Meldung; Artikel, Gegenstand **10-U2**, Ex9

its sein, seine, sein, ihr, ihre, ihr **5-U3**, Sit1

itself sich; selbst **8-U3**, Sit3

Jj

jack Wagenheber, Winde **10-U1**, TYE

jacket Jacke, Jackett **5-U4**, Ex16

jail Gefängnis **8-U1**, Read

jam Marmelade, Konfitüre **6-U5**, WPA

January Januar **5-U4**, Sit5

jar Krug, Gefäß, Marmeladenglas **9-U1**, Read

jeans Jeans **6-U6**, Com

jelly Götterspeise, Gelee **10-U1**, T2

jet lag Jetlag **6-U7**, T1

Jew Jude, Jüdin **8-U1**, WP

jewel Juwel **9-U4**, T1

jewelry Schmuck, Juwelen **8-U2**, TYE

job Job, Arbeitsplatz **5-U2**, T1

jockey Jockey **7-U1**, Read

jog joggen **10-U3**, Ex11

join verbinden, sich anschließen **7-U2**, Sit4

joke Witz, Scherz **6-U1**, Sit4

joke Witze machen, scherzen **10-U3**, T2

joker Spaßvogel **10-U3**, T2

journey Reise **5-U7**, WPC

joy Freude **10-Lit**

judo Judo **5-U5**, WPB

juggler Jongleur/in **6-U1**, WPA

July Juli **5-U4**, Sit5

jumble sale Wohltätigkeitsbasar, Flohmarkt **10-SP**

jump springen **5-U5**, WPA

jumpsuit Overall **9-U2**, Read

junction Straßenkreuzung **8-U2**, Read

June Juni **5-U4**, Sit5

jungle Dschungel; *hier:* Jungle (Musikrichtung) **9-U4**, Sit4

junior Student/in im vorletzten Studienjahr **8-U2**, T1

just nur, bloß **5-U4**, T1; genau, gerade **6-U4**, Sit3

Kk

kangaroo Känguru **10-U1**, WP

keen: be keen on doing sth/to do sth darauf wild sein, etw zu tun, gern mögen **10-U3**, T1

keep halten, behalten **6-U5**, WPC

  keep an eye on sb/sth auf jdn/etw aufpassen **10-U3**, T2

  keep back zurückbleiben, zurückhalten **6-U2**, T2

keep out fernhalten, nicht hereinlassen **7-U2**, WP

kerosine Petroleum, Kerosin **10-U4**, Read

key Schlüssel **7-U2**, Read

keyboard Keyboard (Musikinstrument) **7-U3**, T2

kick (mit dem Fuß) treten **7-U1**, T2

kid Kind **5-U5**, WPB

kid Spaß machen, jdn aufziehen **8-U4**, Sit1

kill töten, umbringen **7-U2**, T1

killer Mörder/in **8-U1**, Read

kind (of) Art, Sorte, Gattung (von) **9-U1**, Ex1

king König **6-U1**, T2

kingdom Königreich **7-U1**, WP

kiss Kuss **6-U7**, T2

kitchen Küche **5-U1**, T2

kiwi Neuseeländer/in (*umg*); Kiwi (Vogel); Kiwifrucht **10-U1**, T2

knee Knie **7-U5**, T1

kneel knien **10-U1**, Read

knife Messer **7-U2**, T2

knight Ritter **7-U2**, WP

knock klopfen **7-U4**, Read

know wissen, kennen **5-U2**, Sit2

knowledge Wissen, Kenntnis **10-U2**, T1

koala bear Koalabär **10-U1**, WP

Ll

label Etikett, Schildchen **6-U5**, Ex17

laboratory Laboratorium, Labor **9-U3**, Sit2

labourer: (farm) labourer (Land-)Arbeiter/in, Tagelöhner/in **10-U1**, Sit2

labour ward Kreißsaal **9-U1**, Read

lady Dame **6-U1**, Song

lake See **5-U7**, T2

lamp Lampe, Leuchte **9-U3**, Ex10

land Land, Boden **6-U7**, Song

land landen **6-U2**, T2

landing Landung **9- Rev5**

landlord Wirt; Vermieter **7-U4**, Read

lane Feldweg, Gasse **7-U1**, T2

language Sprache **7-U3**, Sit3

  bad language Kraftausdrücke, unanständige Ausdrücke **7-U3**, Sit3

lap Runde **10-U1**, T1

large groß **5-U4**, Sit4

laser Laser **10-U2**, Ex22

last dauern, andauern **10-U1**, T1

last letzte(r, s) **6-U2**, Sit2

  at last endlich **5-U7**, T1

late spät **5-U1**, Sit1

lately in letzter Zeit, vor kurzem **10-U4**, Sit1

later später **5-U7**, T1

Latin Latein, Lateinisch **9-U1**, Sit4

laugh (at) lachen (über) **6-U4**, T2

launch abschießen (Rakete); vom Stapel lassen (Schiff) **8-U4**, T1

law Gesetz, Recht **7-U1**, Read

lawyer Rechtsanwalt/-anwältin **9-U2**, T2

lay legen; verlegen **8-U3**, T1

  lay the table den Tisch decken **6-U4**, Sit3

layout Anordnung, Layout **10-U2**, T1

lead führen, leiten **8-U2**, T1

leader Führer/in, Anführer/in **8-U3**, T1

leaf Blatt **10-U4**, WP

league Bündnis, Liga **6-U3**, T1

leak undichte Stelle, Leck **10-U3**, Ex9

learn lernen, erfahren **5-U1**, Sit8

least: at least zumindest, mindestens **7-U3**, WP

leather Leder **10-U1**, Read

leave verlassen, weggehen, abfahren **5-U1**, Sit6; lassen, liegen lassen **5-U5**, Sit1

lecture Vortrag; Standpauke **10-U2**, Sit3

left links **5-U6**, WPB

left: be left übrig sein **7-U3**, Sit1

leg Bein **5-U5**, T1

legend Legende **10-U3**, WP

leggings Leggings **10-U3**, T1

lemon Zitrone **10-U2**, T2

lemonade Zitronenlimonade **6-U5**, T2

lend leihen **6-U4**, Sit4

less weniger **8-U3**, Sit2

lesson Unterrichtsstunde **5-U1**, Ex4

let lassen **8-U3**, T2

  let's Lass(t) uns **5-U0**, A

  let go (of) loslassen **9-U1**, Read

  let out hinauslassen, herauslassen **5-U3**, WPA

letter Brief **5-U6**, Sit1; Buchstabe **6-U1**, Ex19

level Stand, Höhe; Niveau; Ebene **10-U2**, WP

level eben, gerade **10-U1**, T2

lezzie Lesbierin **9-U4**, Read

liberty Freiheit **8-U1**, WP

library Bibliothek, Bücherei **5-U5**, T2

license Erlaubnis; Führerschein **8-U1**, Sit3

lie Lüge **7-U5**, Read

lie liegen **6-U2**, WPB

life Leben **5-U6**, T1

lifestyle Lebensstil **10-U3**, T1

lift Mitfahrgelegenheit **7-U4**, Sit3; Aufzug, Lift **9-U1**, Read

lift hochheben **6-U2**, T2

light Licht **6-U2**, T1

light anzünden **6-U4**, WPA

light leicht **9-U3**, T2

light year Lichtjahr **10-U2**, WP

like mögen **5-U1**, Sit7

like wie **5-U7**, WPD

likely wahrscheinlich **9-U1**, Ex7

limousine Limousine **8-Rev11**

line Linie, Zeile **6-U1**, WPB; Reihe, Schlange **8-U1**, T1

link Link, Verknüpfung im Internet **8-Proj4**

link verbinden **10-U2**, Ex12

lion Löwe **7-U1**, TYE

lip Lippe **8-U4**, T2

list Liste **5-U5**, PYE6

listener Zuhörer/in **10-U2**, TYE4

listen (to) zuhören **5-U1**, Sit8

liter Liter **8-U4**, T1

literature Literatur **10-Lit**

Index

litter Abfall **8-U1**, T1
little klein **5-U0**, Song; wenig **8-U2**, Read
live live, lebend **9-U1**, WP
live leben, wohnen **5-U0**, A
lively lebendig, rege, lebhaft **6-U1**, WPA
living Lebensunterhalt **9-U4**, WP
living-room Wohnzimmer **5-U2**, WPB
lizard Eidechse **10-U2**, Sit4
load laden, beladen **6-U4**, PYE2
local örtlich, am Ort, Lokal- **8-U2**, Sit3
located, be gelegen sein **10-U2**, Sit4
lock Schloss (Tür) **10-U3**, Read
locked verschlossen **7-U2**, T2
locust (Wander-)Heuschrecke **10-U2**, Sit4
Londoner Londoner **7-U5**, TYE3
lonely einsam **10-U1**, Read
long lang **5-U1**, T2
longer: no longer nicht mehr, nicht länger **10-U1**, Read
long-term langfristig, Langzeit- **9-U3**, T1
look schauen **5-U2**, Sit5; aussehen **6-U1**, T2
  look after sich kümmern um **6-U1**, T1
  look for suchen **5-U6**, WPB
  look forward to sich freuen auf **6-U1**, Ex5
  look forward to doing sth sich darauf freuen, etw zu tun **9-U1**, Ex11
  look out aufpassen **5-U5**, T1
  look round sich umschauen **6-U3**, Sit1
  look: have a look (etw) ansehen **8-U1**, T1
Lord Lord **6-U4**, T1
lorry LKW **6-U7**, Ex1
lose verlieren **6-U4**, Sit1
lost: get lost sich verlaufen **6-U6**, T1
lot: a lot of eine Menge, viel **6-U1**, Sit2
  lots of viel **6-U7**, Sit2
loud laut **8-U1**, Sit1
loudspeaker Lautsprecher **10-U2**, TYE
love Liebe **5-U5**, PYE4
  love herzliche Grüße **5-U4**, T2
love lieben **6-U2**, T1
lovely schön, hübsch **6-U2**, WPB
lover Liebhaber/in, Geliebte/r **10-U1**, T2
low niedrig **9-U4**, T1
lower sinken lassen, (sich) senken **10-U1**, Read
LP Langspielplatte **10-U3**, T1
luck Glück **6-U7**, T2
lucky Glück haben **5-U1**, T1
luggage Gepäck **9-U3**, T1
lunar module Mondfähre **9-U3**, Ex2
lunch Mittagessen **5-U3**, WPA
lunchtime Mittagsstunde **5-U3**, WPA
lynch lynchen **8-U3**, T2
lyrics Songtext **9-Proj3**

Mm
machine Maschine **6-U5**, WPD
machinery Maschinen-, Maschinenbau **9-U4**, WP
madam meine Dame, gnädige Frau **5-U7**, Sit5
magazine Zeitschrift **5-U5**, WPB
magic Magie, Zauberkunst **7-U2**, T1

magical magisch, zauberhaft **10-U1**, WP
magician Zauberer, Magier **7-U2**, T1
magnificent prächtig, großartig **7-U5**, Read
mail schicken, aufgeben **6-U7**, Ex1
mailbox Briefkasten **10-U4**, Read
main Haupt-, hauptsächlich **6-U6**, T1
mainland Festland **9-U1**, TYE4
major Major **8-U3**, Read
major größer, bedeutend **6-U3**, T1
make machen **5-U4**, Sit1
  make sure sicherstellen, sorgen für **7-U4**, WP
make-up artist Visagist/in **9-U2**, Ex9
male männlich **10-Lit**
mama Mama **9-U4**, Read
man Mann **5-U3**, Sit3
manager Geschäftsführer, Manager, Filialleiter/in **6-U5**, WPA
manage to do sth es schaffen, es fertig-bringen, etw zu tun **9-U1**, T2
manatee Seekuh **8-U4**, TYE
man-eater Menschenfresser **8-Rev10**
mango Mango **10-U2**, T2
manners Manieren, Umgangsformen **9-Lit**
many viele **5-U7**, Sit4
Maori Maori **10-U1**, Sit4
map Landkarte **5-U7**, T1
maple Ahorn **10-U4**, WP
march Marsch **9-U4**, T1
March März **5-U4**, Sit5
marcher Teilnehmer/in eines Marsches **9-U4**, T1
Mardi Gras Mardi Gras (Karneval) **8-U2**, WP
marital status Familienstand **9-U2**, Ex11
mark Kratzer, Markierung; Note **9-Rev9**
market Markt **6-U5**, WPB
marmalade Marmelade aus Zitrusfrüchten **6-U5**, WPA
marriage Ehe, Hochzeit **7-U4**, T2
marry heiraten **7-U2**, T1
marvellous fabelhaft **7-U2**, T2
master Meister, Herr **7-U5**, Read
match passend zusammenfügen, zusammenpassen **7-U4**, Ex5
material Material, Stoff **9-U3**, WP
math Mathematik (*AE*) **8-U1**, Ex11
mathematics Mathematik **9-Lit**
maths Mathematik (*BE*) **5-U1**, Ex4
matinee Nachmittagsvorstellung, Matinee **9-U1**, WP
matter Angelegenheit **6-U4**, T1
  a matter of opinion Ansichtssache **9-U2**, Com
  what's the matter? was ist los? **7-U2**, Read
matter von Bedeutung sein **9-U2**, Read
mattress Matratze **10-U1**, TYE
maximum Höchst-; maximal **10-Rev12**
May Mai **5-U4**, Sit5
may: may I? darf ich? **5-U7**, Sit5
maybe vielleicht **5-U7**, T2
mayor Bürgermeister/in **9-U1**, T2
maze Labyrinth **6-U6**, T1

me mich, mir **5-U2**, Sit5
meal Mahlzeit **5-U4**, WPB
mean meinen, sagen wollen **5-U6**, T2; bedeuten **7-U1**, T1
mean gemein, geizig **6-U6**, T2
meaning Bedeutung **7-U5**, Ex4
meanwhile inzwischen **6-U7**, T1
measure messen **8-Lit**
meat Fleisch **7-U5**, Sket2
mechanic Mechaniker/in **9-U2**, WP
medal Medaille **10-U1**, T1
media Medien **7-U3**, TYE
medical medizinisch **8-Rev8**
medicine Medizin **9-U3**, WP
medium mittelgroß **5-U4**, Sit4
meet treffen **6-U6**, WPA
meeting Treffen, Zusammenkunft **9-U2**, Ex17
melt schmelzen **10-U1**, T2
member Mitglied **6-U3**, T1
memory Erinnerung, Gedächtnis; Arbeitsspeicher **7-U5**, Read
mental hospital Heil-und Pflegeanstalt für psychisch Kranke **10-Lit**
mention erwähnen **8-U2**, TYE1
menu Speisekarte **5-U4**, WPA
mess Durcheinander **7-U5**, T2
  in a mess durcheinander **7-U5**, T2
  make a mess of verkorksen, verpfuschen, Mist bauen **7-U3**, T2
message Mitteilung, Nachricht, Botschaft **6-U3**, WPC
metal Metall **8-U1**, Sit1
method Methode, Verfahren **9-U1**, T2
metre Meter **5-U7**, T2
microwave Mikrowelle **7-U5**, Read
middle Mitte **6-U6**, T1
midnight Mitternacht **8-U1**, T2
midsummer Mittsommer **9-Lit**
midtown Manhattan Stadtteil von Manhattan **8-U1**, T1
might könnte (vielleicht) **7-U3**, T1
mile Meile **5-U1**, Sit6
military Militär, militärisch **9-U2**, TYE
milk Milch **5-U4**, WPA
milk melken **8-U2**, Ex1
millennium Jahrtausend, Millennium **6-U1**, WPA
million Million **6-U3**, WPC
millionaire Millionär **6-U6**, WPC
mimic nachahmen, imitieren **10-U3**, Sit3
mind Verstand, Geist **10-U1**, T1
mind etw einzuwenden haben gegen **9-U1**, T1
  mind your own business kümmere dich um deine Angelegenheiten **9-U4**, T2
mine meine(r, s) **6-U3**, Sit2
mine Bergbau betreiben, abbauen (Erz, Gold, ...) **10-U2**, WP
minibus Kleinbus **7-U5**, T1
mini-golf Minigolf **5-U2**, Sit1
miniskirt Minirock **10-U3**, T1
minister Minister/in **7-U4**, T2

163

Index

minus minus **8-U4**, WP
minute Minute **5-U1**, Sit1
mirror Spiegel **8-U3**, Sit5
miserable elend, furchtbar, armselig **10-Lit**
miss verpassen **6-U6**, T1; vermissen **9-U2**, T1
missing fehlend, nicht vorhanden **6-U1**, Ex8
mission Mission, Auftrag; Missionsstation **6-U7**, WPA
mistake Fehler **7-U3**, Ex12
mixed gemischt, vermischt **10-U1**, Sit2
mixed-up konfus, zerstreut, durcheinander **9-U1**, Sit3
mixture Mischung, Gemisch **7-U1**, Proj
mobile (phone) tragbares Telefon, Handy **6-U2**, T2
model Modell; Fotomodell **6-U1**, Ex20
modern modern **7-U5**, TYE
modernize modernisieren **9-TP**
mom Mama **6-U7**, T1
moment Moment **6-U2**, T1
Monday Montag **5-U1**, Sit4
money Geld **5-U4**, Sit3
monster Ungeheuer, Scheusal **7-U4**, T2
month Monat **5-U4**, Sit5
mood Laune, Stimmung **9-U4**, Read
moon Mond **8-U3**, WP
more mehr **6-U1**, Com
morning Morgen **5-U1**, Sit6
mosaic Mosaik **10-U4**,
mosque Moschee **9-U4**, Fol
most meiste (r,s) **5-U6**, T1
mostly hauptsächlich **8-U4**, T1
motel Motel **8-U4**, Sit3
mother Mutter **5-U2**, Sit2
motionless regungslos, unbeweglich **10-U2**, Read
motor Motor, Auto- **8-U4**, WP
motorbike Motorrad **8-U4**, Ex7
motorist Autofahrer/in **10-U3**, T2
motorized motorisiert **9-U3**, Read
motor-racing Autorennen **7-U3**, Read
motorway Autobahn **10-U2**, Ex17
mountain Berg **5-U2**, Song
mountain bike Mountainbike **8-U4**, Sit1
mourn betrauern, beklagen **10-U3**, Read
mouse Maus **5-U3**, WPB
mousetrap Mausefalle **9-Lit**
mouth Mund **6-U6**, Com; Mündung (Fluss) **8-U3**, T1
move (sich) bewegen, umziehen **5-U5**, T2
movement Bewegung **8-U1**, TYE
movie Film **6-U7**, WPA
Mr Herr **5-U0**, F
Mrs Frau **5-U0**, B
Ms Anrede für verheiratete oder ledige Frau **9-U2**, Ex10
much viel **5-U5**, Sit3
mud Schlamm, Matsch, Dreck **10-U1**, Sit4
muddy schlammig, matschig **10-U2**, Ex20
mug überfallen und ausrauben **8-U1**, Read
multiply multiplizieren, malnehmen **10-U3**, T2

mum Mutti, Mama **5-U1**, WPC
murder Mord **8-U2**, TYE4
murder ermorden **10-Rev17**
museum Museum **6-U1**, Sit2
music Musik **5-U1**, Sit3
musical Musical **7-U1**, T1
musical instrument Musikinstrument **6-U6**, Ex2
musician Musiker/in **9-Proj3**
Muslim muslimisch, Muslim/in **9-U4**, T1
must müssen **5-U6**, Sit1
  mustn't nicht dürfen **7-U5**, Sit3
my mein, meine, mein **5-U0**, A
myself mich, mir; selbst **8-U3**, Sit3
mythology Mythologie **10-Lit**

Nn

nachos Nachos **8-U1**, T2
nail Nagel **9-U3**, Read
naked nackt **9-U3**, Read
name Name **5-U0**, A
name nennen **7-U1**, TYE1
narrow eng, schmal **9-U3**, T2
nasty ekelhaft, scheußlich **9-Lit**
nation Nation **9-U4**, WP
national national, National- **6-U7**, WPA
nationality Staatsangehörigkeit, Nationalität **9-U2**, Ex11
native gebürtig; eingeboren; Eingeborene/r **8-U3**, WP
natural history Naturkunde, Naturgeschichte **8-U1**, Ex7
nature Natur **10-U1**, T1
navigator Navigator/in **9-U3**, TYE
navy Marine, Kriegsmarine **9-Rev10**
near nah **5-U1**, Sit6
nearly fast, beinahe **10-U3**, Sit2
neat ordentlich, sauber, gepflegt **7-U5**, Read
necessary notwendig **8-Rev14**
necessity Notwendigkeit, Bedürfnis **9-U3**, Sit3
neck Hals **9-U2**, Read
need Bedürfnis **10-U1**, Read
need brauchen **5-U4**, Sit1
  need to do sth etw tun müssen **7-U1**, Com
  needn't nicht müssen, nicht brauchen **7-U5**, Sit3
needle Nadel **7-U1**, Read
negative negativ **7-U2**, Sit1
neighbour Nachbar/in **5-U3**, Sit1
neither auch nicht **9-U1**, Sit1; keine(r, s) von beiden **10-Rev13**
nephew Neffe **9-U1**, Read
nervous nervös **6-U6**, Ex9
network Sendenetz (TV, Radio) **8-U2**, T2
never niemals **5-U5**, Sit2
  never mind macht nichts, vergiss es **6-U1**, T2
new neu **5-U0**, E
news Neuigkeit(en), Nachricht(en) **6-U3**, WPC
newspaper Tageszeitung **6-U3**, WPD

next nächster, nächste, nächstes **5-U3**, T1
nice nett, schön, hübsch **5-U1**, Sit2
nigger Nigger (*abwertend*) **9-U4**, T2
night Nacht **5-U1**, Sit1
nightmare Albtraum **9-U1**, Read
nine neun **5-U0**, G
nineteen neunzehn **5-U0**, G
ninety neunzig **5-U4**, WPA
no nein **5-U0**, B; kein(e) **6-U1**, T1
nobody niemand **7-U2**, Read
nod nicken **9-U4**, Read
noise Lärm **6-U2**, T1
nomadic nomadisch; Nomaden- **10-U4**, TYE
none keine(r, s) **9-U2**, T2
nonsense Unsinn **10-U2**, Sit1
non-stop ohne Zwischenlandung, pausenlos, Nonstop- **9-U3**, TYE
non-violent gewaltfrei, gewaltlos **9-U4**, T1
non-white farbig; Farbige/r **7-U5**, TYE
noon Mittag **8-Rev9**
no one niemand **7-U1**, T2
nor auch nicht **9-U1**, Sit1
normal normal **9-U1**, Read
Norman normannisch; Normanne, Normannin **7-U4**, WP
north Norden **5-U7**, T1
northern nördlich, Nord- **7-U1**, WP
nose Nase **6-U6**, Com
not nicht **5-U0**, B
not ... at all überhaupt nicht **9-U4**, T2
note Notiz **7-U3**, Ex14; Banknote, Geldschein **9-U1**, Read
note down notieren, aufschreiben **8-U1**, Ex11
not ... either auch nicht **8-U3**, WP
nothing nichts **6-U2**, T2
notice Zettel, Notiz **7-U5**, Sket1
notice bemerken **7-U2**, T2
novel Roman **9-Lit**
November November **5-U4**, Sit5
now jetzt **5-U0**, F
nowadays heutzutage, heute **10-U1**, WP
nowhere nirgendwo **7-U3**, T2
nuclear nuklear, atomar, Atom-, Kern- **9-U3**, WP
nuisance Ärgernis, Quälgeist **7-U3**, Sit2
number Zahl **5-U0**, G
nurse Krankenschwester, Krankenpfleger **9-U1**, Read
nursery Kindertagesstätte **9-U2**, WP

Oo

oasis Oase **8-U4**, T2
obey gehorchen **9-U4**, T1
object Gegenstand **10-U2**, TYE5
obscene obszön; widerlich **10-U3**, Read
observatory Sternwarte, Observatorium **7-U2**, TYE
obsolete veraltet **7-U5**, Read
obtain erhalten, sich verschaffen, erzielen **9-U2**, Ex11
occur geschehen **7-U3**, Ex1

Index

ocean Meer, Ozean **6-U7**, WPB
o'clock Uhr **5-U1**, Sit5
October Oktober **5-U1**, Sit5
odd: odd jobs anfallende Arbeiten **10-U3**, T2
  odd word out Wort, das anders ist **6-U2**, Ex16
of von **5-U1**, Sit2
  of course natürlich **5-U1**, Sit8
off von ... herunter, weg **6-U2**, T2; aus, abgestellt **10-U4**, Read
offensive beleidigend, kränkend **8-U3**, T1
offensive offensiv; Angriff(s-) **8-Proj5**
offer anbieten **7-U3**, T2
office Büro **6-U5**, WPD
office block Bürogebäude, Bürokomplex **7-U1**, WP
officer Beamte, Beamtin **5-U7**, Sit5
official offiziell **9-U4**, WP
official Beamte/r, Beamtin **9-U4**, WP
often häufig, oft **5-U3**, PYE3
oil Öl **8-U4**, WP
OK OK **5-U0**, B
old alt **5-U0**, G
olive Olive **10-U2**, T2
Olympic olympisch **10-U1**, T1
on auf **5-U1**, T2
  on (Monday) am (Montag) **5-U1**, Sit4
once einmal **6-U5**, Sit4
oncoming aus der Gegenrichtung **9-U2**, Read
one eins **5-U0**, G; Wort, das anstelle eines Substantivs stehen kann **7-U2**, Sit5
online online **9-U1**, WP
only nur, bloß **5-U5**, Sit3; einzige(r, s) **10-U4**, T1
onto auf ... (hinauf) **6-U3**, Ex7
open offen, geöffnet **7-U1**, TYE
open öffnen **5-U0**, F
  open up sich auftun, sich erschließen **9-U4**, Sit2
opera Oper **9-U1**, Ex8
operating system Betriebssystem **9-U2**, T2
operation Operation **9-U3**, T2
opinion Meinung **7-U3**, T2
opportunity Gelegenheit, Chance **8-U1**, Sit1
oppose sich widersetzen **10-U3**, TYE
opposite Gegenteil **5-U5**, Ex16
opposition Opposition **10-U3**, TYE
or oder **5-U0**, I
  or so ungefähr **7-U4**, Read
orange Orange, Apfelsine **5-U6**, Sit4; orange **9-U2**, Read
orange juice Orangensaft **5-U4**, WPA
orbit Umlaufbahn **9-U3**, Ex1
orbit umkreisen **9-U3**, Sit1
order Reihenfolge **5-U7**, Ex9 Befehl **9-U2**, Sit2
order bestellen **9-U4**, Read
ordinary normal, gewöhnlich **7-U3**, WP
organization Organisation **8-U3**, Sit4
organize organisieren **7-U3**, Sit1

organizer Veranstalter/in, Organisator/in **10-U3**, Ex8
origin Ursprung, Herkunft **7-U5**, TYE
original ursprünglich, Original- **10-U2**, Sit4
other andere(r, s) **5-U4**, Ex6
ought to sollte **7-U4**, T1
our unser, unsere, unser **5-U3**, Sit1
ours unsere(r, s) **6-U3**, Sit3
ourselves uns; selbst **8-U3**, Sit3
outback australisches Hinterland **10-U1**, WP
outdoor Außen-, im Freien **10-U1**, Sit3
outlaw Gesetzlose/r **7-U5**, Sket2
outlying abgelegen, entlegen **10-U2**, Read
out (of) hinaus **5-U1**, Sit7
outside draußen **6-U1**, Sit4; außerhalb **7-U2**, Ex6
over über **5-U3**, T1; zu Ende **7-U1**, T2; über, mehr als **7-U1**, TYE
  over and over (again) immer wieder **8-U4**, T2
over there dort drüben **6-U1**, T2
overnight über Nacht, ganz plötzlich **7-U3**, Sit1
owl Eule **7-U2**, Read
own besitzen **9-U4**, WP
own eigen **6-U2**, WPB
owner Besitzer/in, Eigentümer/in **7-U5**, Rev
ox Ochse **8-U3**, Read

Pp

pack (ver)packen, einpacken **7-U5**, T2
packet Paket **5-U5**, PYE4
page Seite **5-U1**, Ex1
pain Schmerz **7-U5**, T1
  the pains die Wehen **9-U1**, Read
paint malen, streichen **6-U5**, T2
painter Maler **7-U4**, TYE4
pair Paar **6-U4**, Ex1
palace Palast **6-U1**, WPA
palm (tree) Palme **10-U2**, T2
panic Panik **10-U2**, TYE4
panic in Panik geraten **10-U2**, Read
pant keuchen, hecheln **9-U1**, Read
papa Papa **9-U4**, Read
paper Papier **6-U5**, T2; Zeitung **9-U1**, T1
parachute Fallschirm **9-Rev5**
parade Umzug, Festzug, Parade **8-U2**, WP
paradise Paradies **9-U3**, T1
paragliding Drachenfliegen **7-U5**, WP
paragraph Absatz, Abschnitt **6-U6**, Ex8
paramedic Rettungsassistent/in **6-U2**, T2
paraphrase umschreiben, paraphrasieren **10-U2**, TYE2
pardon? Verzeihung? **7-U5**, T2
parents Eltern **5-U2**, T1
park Park **5-U2**, Sit3
park parken **8-U1**, T1
parka Parka **10-U3**, T1
parliament Parlament **6-U1**, WPA
part Teil **6-U1**, T1; Rolle **7-U2**, Sit4
partly teilweise, zum Teil **9-U1**, T2

partner Partner/in **5-U5**, WPB
part-time Teilzeit-, halbtags **10-U2**, T1
party Party, Feier **5-U4**, WPC; Partei **10-U3**, TYE
pass bestehen (Prüfung) **8-U1**, Sit3; vorbeigehen, vorbeifahren **9-U1**, Read; durchfließen, durchgehen **9-U3**, Read
  pass a law ein Gesetz verabschieden **9-U4**, T1
passenger Fahrgast, Passagier/in **8-U1**, TYE
passport Reisepass **5-U7**, Sit3
past Vergangenheit **6-U2**, Sit2
past nach **5-U1**, Sit5; an ... vorbei **10-U2**, T2
path Fußweg, Pfad **5-U5**, T1
patience Geduld **10-U3**, Read
patient Patient/in **9-U2**, Read; geduldig **10-U4**, Sit1
pattern Muster **8-U1**, Ex7
pavement Gehsteig **8-U1**, Ex15
pay zahlen **6-U5**, T2
peace Friede **8-U3**, T1
pen Füllfederhalter, Füller **5-U0**, D
pencil Bleistift **5-U0**, D
penfriend Brieffreund/in **9-U3**, Ex20
penguin Pinguin **9-Proj4**
penny Penny **5-U4**, WPA
pen pal Brieffreund/in **8-U2**, T1
people Leute **5-U3**, Sit3
per cent Prozent **9-U2**, T2
perfect perfekt **9-U1**, T1
perform spielen, vorführen **7-U3**, Sit3
performance Aufführung, Vorstellung **9-U1**, T1
perhaps vielleicht **7-U2**, Sit2
period (Unterrichts-)Stunde **8-U2**, Sit2; Zeit, Zeitraum **10-U3**, Ex20
permission Erlaubnis **9-U1**, Read
person Person **5-U1**, T1
personal persönlich **9-U2**, T2
personality Persönlichkeit **10-U2**, WP
persuade sb to do sth jdn überreden, etw zu tun **9-U4**, Sit2
pet Haustier **5-U3**, WPA
petrol Benzin **6-U7**, Ex1
petrol station Tankstelle **5-U2**, T1
pet shop Tierhandlung **5-U6**, WPB
phone telefonieren **5-U5**, PYE4
phone box Telefonzelle **7-U1**, T2
phonograph Phonograph **9-U3**, WP
photo Foto **5-U1**, Sit2
photocopy fotokopieren **7-U4**, Proj
photograph fotografieren **8-U4**, T1
photography Fotografieren **9-U3**, WP
phrase Ausdruck, Satzglied **6-U3**, WPC
physical körperlich **9-U2**, Read
physics Physik **8-U2**, Sit2
physiology Physiologie **9-U2**, Read
piano Klavier **5-U1**, Sit8
pick Spitzhacke **10-U4**, Read
pick pflücken, auswählen **7-U4**, T1
  pick up aufheben, aufsammeln **8-U3**, T2
pickpocket Taschendieb **9-Lit**
picnic Picknick **7-U5**, Ex6

165

Index

picture Bild **5-U1**, WP
pie Pastete, Obstkuchen **7-U5**, Read
piece Stück, Teil **6-U5**, T2
piercing Piercing **10-U3**, T1
pig Schwein **6-U1**, Ex19
pilgrim Pilger/in **8-U3**, Sit1
pilot Pilot/in **9-U2**, Read
pink rosarot **8-U4**, T1
pioneer Pionier/in, **9-U3**, TYE
pipeline Rohrleitung, Pipeline **9-U3**, Read
pitcher Werfer **6-U7**, Sit3
pity: it's a pity schade **6-U5**, Com
pizza Pizza **5-U4**, WPA
place Ort, Platz **5-U6**, WPA
plan Plan **5-U2**, WPB
plan planen **8-U1**, Sit2
plane Flugzeug **5-U7**, WPC
planet Planet **9-U3**, Sit1
plant Pflanze **8-U4**, TYE; Werk, Fabrik
    10-U4, T2
plant pflanzen **8-U3**, Read
plantation Pflanzung, Plantage **8-U3**, WP
plastic Plastik, Kunststoff **7-U4**, Com
plate Teller **5-U4**, WPA
platform Plattform; Bahnsteig **10-U1**, T2
play (Schau-)Spiel **7-U2**, Com
play spielen **5-U1**, Sit7
player Spieler/in **6-U7**, T1
playground Spielplatz **5-U6**, Sit2
play-off Entscheidungsspiel **8-U2**, T2
pleasant angenehm, erfreulich **9-TP**
please bitte **5-U0**, F
pleased erfreut **9-U1**, Read
plenty of eine Menge, viel **8-U4**, T1
plot Komplott, Verschwörung **6-U4**, T1;
    Handlung (Film, Literatur) **9-U1**, T2
plotter Verschwörer/in **6-U4**, T1
plug Stecker, Stöpsel **7-U1**, Sit5
plus plus **9-U3**, T1
P.M./p.m./pm nach 12 Uhr **8-U1**, T1
pocket Tasche **6-U1**, T1
poem Gedicht **8-Lit**
poetry Lyrik, Dichtung **9-Lit**
point Punkt **8-U2**, T2; Sinn, Zweck
    10-U2, Read
point zeigen **7-U5**, Sket1
    point sth out auf etw hinweisen **10-U4**, T1
pointless sinnlos, zwecklos **10-U3**, Read
poison Gift **9-U1**, T2
poisonous giftig **8-U4**, T2
police Polizei **7-U1**, T2
policeman Polizist **5-U5**, T1
polite höflich **6-U1**, Com
political politisch **10-U3**, TYE
politician Politiker/in **9-U4**, TYE
politics Politik **9-U4**, T2
pollute verschmutzen **10-Rev17**
pollution Umweltverschmutzung
    10-Rev17
polo Polo **7-U1**, TYE
pony Pony **6-U2**, WPA
pool Teich; Pfütze, Lache **8-U4**, T2
poor arm **5-U3**, T1

Pope Papst **7-U4**, WP
pop (music) Popmusik **5-U1**, Sit7
popular beliebt **6-U1**, Sit2
population Bevölkerung **8-U2**, WP
porch Veranda; Vorbau, Portal
    10-U4, Song
posh chic, vornehm, nobel **7-U3**, WP
position Stellung, Lage **6-U7**, T1
positive positiv **7-U2**, Sit1
possibility Möglichkeit **10-U2**, WP
possible möglich **7-U5**, WP
post Post(sendung) **10-U3**, Read
post zur Post bringen, aufgeben **5-U6**, Sit1
postcard Postkarte **5-U7**, WPD
poster Poster **5-U0**, D
postman Postbote **5-U2**, T1
post office Postamt **5-U6**, WPA
potato Kartoffel **6-U5**, T1
pothole Schlagloch **10-U4**, T2
pound Pfund **5-U4**, WPA
pour gießen, sich ergießen **7-U5**, Sit1
poverty Armut **9-U4**, WP
power Macht, Kraft, Fähigkeit **9-U2**, Ex21
power antreiben, betreiben **9-U3**, T2
power cut Stromsperre, Stromausfall
    8-U4, Read
powerful stark; mächtig **8-Rev3**
practical praktisch **9-U2**, T1
practice Training, Übung **7-U5**, T1
practise üben **5-U1**, PYE
prairie Prärie, Grassteppe **8-U3**, Ex7
pray beten **8-U3**, Read
predict vorhersagen **10-U2**, Sit2
prediction Vorhersage **10-U2**, TYE
prefer vorziehen, lieber haben **9-U1**, Ex9
pregnant schwanger **10-U3**, T2
prejudice Vorurteil **9-Lit**
prejudiced voreingenommen, befangen, mit
    vorgefasster Meinung **9-U4**, T2
premier bedeutendste(r) **7-U5**, Read
prepare zubereiten **9-U1**, T2
present Geschenk **5-U3**, Sit5; Gegenwart
    6-U5, Ex6
presentation Präsentation, Vorstellung
    8-Proj4
presenter Moderator/in **6-U1**, T2
president Präsident/in **6-U1**, T2
pretend so tun als ob, etw vorgeben **10-SP**
pretty ziemlich **7-U5**, Read; hübsch
    8-U3, Read
prevent sb from doing sth jdn daran hindern,
    etw zu tun **10-U2**, T1
price Preis **6-U5**, T1
pride Stolz **9-Lit**
priest Priester/in **7-U2**, TYE
primary hauptsächlich, primär **9-U4**, Sit2
prime minister Premierminister/in **9-U4**, T2
primitive primitiv, urzeitlich **9-U2**, T2
prince Prinz; Fürst **7-U3**, T1
princess Prinzessin **6-U1**, T2
principal Rektor/in **8-Proj2**
print (out) (aus)drucken **6-U3**, WPB
prison Gefängnis **6-U1**, WPA

prisoner Gefangene/r, Häftling **7-U4**, Sit5
private privat **10-Rev14**
prize Preis, Gewinn **6-U4**, Ex3
probably wahrscheinlich **6-U6**, T1
problem Problem **5-U1**, T2
produce produzieren, herstellen **8-U4**, WP
producer Produzent/in **9-U2**, T2
product Produkt **8-U2**, Sit1
production Herstellung, Produktion
    8-U2, T1
professional Berufs-, Fach-, Profi- **8-U2**, T2
program Computerprogramm **8-Rev3**
program programmieren **10-U2**, T1
programme Sendung **6-U6**, WPA
programmer Programmierer/in **10-U2**, Sit2
project Projekt **6-U2**, Sit2
promise Versprechen **10-U1**, Ex14
promise sth (to sb) (jdm) etw versprechen
    10-U3, Ex3
promote werben (für); auf den Markt
    bringen **8-U4**, Ex3
prompt Stichwort, Stimulus **9-SP**
pronunciation Aussprache **10-Dict**
...-proof (against) sicher vor, gefeit gegen
    10-U1, Sit1
propeller Schiffsschraube; Propeller
    8-U4, TYE
proper hinreichend, gebührend, richtig
    7-U1, Read
protect beschützen **8-U4**, TYE
protest Protest **9-U4**, T1
protest protestieren **8-U3**, T2
protester Demonstrant/in **10-U3**, TYE
proud (of) stolz (auf) **7-U1**, Read
prove beweisen **10-U4**, T2
proverb Sprichwort **9-U3**, Ex12
provide (with) versorgen (mit) **10-U1**, TYE
province Provinz **10-U4**, WP
pub Kneipe, Pub **7-U3**, Read
public öffentlich **5-U5**, T1
public address system Lautsprecheranlage,
    Verstärkeranlage **10-U2**, Read
public house Kneipe, Gastwirtschaft
    10-U1, Ex10
pull ziehen **7-U2**, T1
    pull down abreißen, einreißen **7-U5**, TYE
pullover Pullover **10-U2**, T2
pump Pumpe **9-U3**, T2
punish bestrafen **8-U3**, Sit3
punk Punk **10-U3**, T1
pupil Schüler/in **5-U1**, WPB
purple purpurrot **9-U1**, Read
purpose Zweck, Ziel, Absicht **8-U1**, Ex6
purse Geldbeutel **6-U5**, Sit2; Handtasche
    8-U3, T1
push schieben, anrempeln **5-U6**, T1
put setzen, stellen, legen **5-U3**, T1
    put in einstecken, einlegen **7-U1**, Sit5
    put on anmachen, auflegen (CD)
    7-U1, Sit5; anziehen **8-U4**, T2
    put out löschen, ausmachen **9-U1**, T2
    put together zusammensetzen,
    zusammenlegen **8-U4**, Sit2

166

Index

puzzle Rätsel, Geduldsspiel **6-U5**, Ex2
puzzle Rätsel aufgeben, verwirren **10-U3**, T2
pyjamas Schlafanzug **10-TP**

Qq

qualification Qualifikation **9-U2**, Sit1
quarter Viertel **5-U1**, Sit5
queen Königin **6-U1**, WPA
question Frage **5-U2**, Sit2
questionnaire Fragebogen **7-U5**, Sket1
queue Warteschlange **6-U1**, Sit2
quick schnell **5-U3**, T1
quiet ruhig, still **5-U1**, T2
quit aufhören mit; verlassen **10-U3**, T2
quite ziemlich **7-U4**, Com
quiz Quiz **5-U5**, Sit3
quote Zitat **10-U3**, Ex1

Rr

rabbit Kaninchen **5-U3**, WPA
race Rennen **5-U5**, T2; Rasse **9-U4**, Sit4
race jagen, rasen **9-U1**, WP
racism Rassismus **9-U4**, Sit3
racist rassistisch; Rassist/in **9-U4**, T2
racket Tennisschläger **5-U2**, WPC
radio Radio **5-U1**, T2
railroad Eisenbahn **8-U3**, Sit4
railway Eisenbahn **9-U3**, Com
rain regnen **5-U4**, Sit1
rain Regen **6-U1**, Ex13
rainbow Regenbogen **10-U1**, T1
rainforest Regenwald **10-U1**, T2
raise sammeln (Geld) **10-U2**, Sit4
ramp Rampe **7-U2**, TYE
rap Rap **8-U1**, T2
rare selten **10-Lit**
rather ziemlich **10-U3**, T2
rather than eher als, statt **10-U1**, Ex6
rattler Klapperschlange **8-U4**, T2
rattlesnake Klapperschlange **8-U3**, Read
rave Rave-Party **10-U3**, T1
raven Rabe **7-U1**, Sit2
ravine Schlucht **10-U1**, T2
reach erreichen **8-U1**, T1
react reagieren **9-SP**
read lesen **5-U1**, Sit7
reader Leser/in; Lesebuch, Lektüre **9-Lit**
ready fertig, bereit **5-U1**, T1
real echt **5-U3**, Sit4
realize erkennen, begreifen, klar werden **8-U2**, Read
really wirklich **5-U5**, Sit3
reason Grund, Begründung **8-Lit**
reassure beruhigen, versichern **9-U1**, Com
receipt Quittung, Kassenbon **10-U1**, Ex9
receive erhalten, empfangen **10-U1**, Sit2
recent jüngst, aktuell **10-U3**, Read
recently vor kurzem, neulich **10-U3**, Read
reception Empfang, Rezeption **10-U1**, T2; Empfang (TV, Radio) **10-U4**, T1
reckless leichtsinnig, unbesonnen, rücksichtslos **10-U4**, Song

recognize erkennen, anerkennen **8-U1**, Read
recommend empfehlen **10-U1**, Ex9
record Schallplatte; Rekord **10-U3**, Sit1
record aufnehmen **6-U6**, T2
recruitment agency Arbeitsvermittlung **9-U2**, WP
recycle wieder aufbereiten, wieder verwerten **6-U7**, Sit4
red rot **5-U0**, C
redback spider australische Witwenspinne **10-U1**, WP
reduce vermindern, reduzieren **9-U3**, Sit4
redwood Redwood **6-U7**, WPA
refugee Flüchtling **10-Lit**
refuse sich weigern **8-U2**, TYE
regard as betrachten (als), halten (für) **9-U3**, Sit3
reggae Reggae (Musikrichtung) **9-U1**, T1
region Gebiet, Region **8-U3**, Sit1
regret bedauern, bereuen **9-U2**, T1
reject zurückweisen, ablehnen **10-U1**, T1
related to verwandt (mit), zusammenhängend **9-Proj3**
relations Beziehungen **10-Lit**
relationship Beziehung, Verbindung, Verwandtschaft **9-Lit**
relative Verwandte/r **5-U7**, WPC
relative relativ, verhältnismäßig **9-U4**, WP
relax sich erholen **7-U1**, T1
relief Erleichterung **9-U1**, Com
relieved erleichtert **10-U1**, T2
religion Religion **8-U1**, TYE
remember sich erinnern **5-U6**, Ex6
remind erinnern **7-U3**, T1
remote abgelegen, entlegen, fern **10-U1**, Sit2
remove wegnehmen, entfernen **10-U1**, Sit2
rent Miete **10-U3**, Ex9
rent mieten, vermieten **8-U4**, T2
repair reparieren **7-U5**, Rev
repeat wiederholen **5-U5**, Ex17
replace ersetzen **9-U3**, Sit4
replica Nachbildung, Rekonstruktion **9-U1**, T2
reply Antwort **10-U4**, T1
report Bericht **6-U3**, T1
report berichten **9-U2**, Sit1
reportage Reportage **10-Lit**
reporter Reporter/in **7-U2**, Ex3
reptile Reptil **10-Rev12**
republic Republik **7-U1**, WP
request Aufforderung, Bitte **8-U4**, Com
require benötigen, erfordern **9-U2**, WP
required verlangt, gefordert, erforderlich **9-U2**, WP
rescue Rettung **9-U2**, Read
rescue retten **10-Rev17**
research Forschung, wissenschaftliche Untersuchung **9-U3**, T1
reservation Reservat; Reservierung **8-U3**, Ex7
residence Residenz, Amtssitz **7-U1**, TYE
resident Bewohner/in, Einwohner/in **9-U3**, T1

resist widerstehen; sich widersetzen **8-U4**, Sit3
resolution Vorsatz, Beschluss **6-U3**, Ex2
resort Ferienort **6-U7**, WPA
respect Respekt, Achtung **10-U1**, T1
respond (to) reagieren (auf), antworten **10-SP**
responsible (for) verantwortlich (für) **10-U1**, T1
rest Rest **6-U6**, Ex14; Ruhe **7-U4**, T1
rest ausruhen **8-U3**, Read
restaurant Restaurant **10-U2**, Ex21
result Ergebnis **6-U3**, WPC
return zurückkehren **8-U1**, T2; zurückgeben **9-Rev6**
return ticket Rückfahrkarte **9-U3**, T1
reunification Wiedervereinigung **10-U3**, T1
revenge Rache **9-U1**, T2
review Rezension, Kritik **9-Proj1**
revise (Lehrstoff) wiederholen **10-SP**
revolt Aufstand, Aufruhr, Revolte **6-U3**, Sit3
rewrite umschreiben, neu schreiben **7-U1**, Ex6
rhyme (sich) reimen **7-U3**, T1
rice Reis **10-U2**, Sit4
rich reich **6-U6**, WPC
ride Karussell, Fahrt **5-U7**, Sit4
ride fahren **5-U2**, Sit3
rider Reiter/in; Radfahrer/in **8-U3**, TYE3
ridge Bergkamm, Grat **6-U7**, WPA
riding accident Reitunfall **5-U6**, T1
right Recht **8-U3**, WP
right rechts **5-U6**, WPB; richtig **5-U1**, T1; genau **7-U5**, T2
ring anrufen **6-U2**, T2
ring Ring **9-U1**, WP
riot Aufstand, Aufruhr **9-U4**, Sit4
rise sich erheben; aufgehen; (an)steigen **10-U1**, T1
rival Konkurrenz-, Rivale/Rivalin **9-U2**, T2
river Fluss, Strom **6-U1**, WPA
road Straße **5-U1**, Sit6
rob berauben, ausrauben **8-U1**, Read
robber Räuber/in **8-U1**, Read
robot Roboter **6-U5**, Sit1
rock Fels(en), Stein **10-U1**, WP; Rock (Musikrichtung) **10-U3**, WP
rocket Rakete **8-U4**, T1
rock'n'roll Rock 'n' Roll (Musikrichtung) **9-U1**, WP
roll Brötchen **7-U5**, T1
roll rollen **7-U5**, T2
roll up zusammenrollen, aufrollen **7-U5**, T2
roller coaster Achterbahn **8-U4**, Ex7
Roman römisch; Römer/in **7-U2**, WP
romance Romanze, Liebesgeschichte **9-U1**, TYE
romantic romantisch **10-U3**, T1
roof Dach **9-U1**, T2
room Zimmer **5-U1**, Ex4

167

Index

rope Seil, Tau **7-U2**, TYE
rose Rose **9**-Rev10
rotten verdorben, faul **10-U1**, Sit4
rough uneben, rau **5-U5**, T2
round Runde **6-U6**, WPC; umher, um …
  herum **5-U2**, Song; rund **7-U2**, T2;
route Route, Strecke **8-U4**, Read
royal königlich **6-U1**, T2
rubber Gummi **10-U2**, T2
rubbish Abfall, Müll **6-U5**, T2
rucksack Rucksack **10-U2**, T2
rugby Rugby **10-U1**, WP
ruin Ruine **7-U2**, Sit1
rule Regel **6-U1**, Ex10; Herrschaft **9-U4**, T1
rule herrschen über, beherrschen **9-U4**, WP
ruler Lineal **5-U0**, D; Herrscher/in **9**-Lit
run laufen **5-U3**, WPA; leiten, führen
  7-U1, Sit1
runner Läufer/in **10-U1**, T1
rupture Bruch, Riss **9-U2**, Read
rush fließen, stürzen; eilen, hetzen
  10-U2, T2
rush hour Hauptverkehrszeit, Stoßzeit
  10-U1, Ex9
Russian russisch; Russe, Russin **9-U3**, Sit1

Ss

sad traurig **6-U2**, T2
saddle Sattel **9-U3**, Read
safari Safari **6-U6**, WPA
safe sicher **7-U2**, T1
safety Sicherheit **9**-Rev5
sail Segel **10-U1**, Ex12
sail segeln **7-U4**, Sit1
sake: for Christ's sake um Gottes willen!
  8-U2, Read
salad Salat **5-U4**, WPA
sale Verkauf, Ausverkauf **6-U5**, T2
  for sale zu verkaufen **7-U4**, Read
salt Salz **9-U4**, T1
samba Samba (Tanz) **9-U1**, WP
same gleich **5-U1**, Sit6
sample Kostprobe, Muster **8-U2**, Sit1
sand Sand **8-U4**, T2
sandwich Sandwich, belegtes Brot **5-U1**, T2
sari Sari (Kleidungsstück) **9-U4**, Read
satellite Satellit **9-U3**, WP
Saturday Samstag, Sonnabend **5-U1**, Sit4
sausage Wurst **5-U4**, WPA
save sparen **6-U5**, T1; retten **7-U1**, Read
Saxon sächsisch; Sachse, Sächsin **7-U2**, WP
say sagen **5-U2**, Sit2
scandal Skandal(geschichte) **10-U4**, T2
scared: be scared (of) Angst haben (vor)
  7-U4, T1
scary unheimlich, gruselig **10-U1**, T2
scene Szene **6-U1**, T2
scenery (schöne) Landschaft **8-U4**, WP
schedule Stundenplan, Zeitplan **8-U2**, T1
schedule sth (for sth) etw (für etw) ansetzen,
  planen **10-U2**, Read
scholarship Stipendium **9-U2**, T1
school Schule **5-U1**, WPB

at school in der Schule **5-U1**, WPB
science (Natur-)Wissenschaft **6-U6**, WPA
science fiction Science-Fiction **9-U3**, T1
scientific (natur)wissenschaftlich **9-U3**, WP
scientist Naturwissenschaftler/in
  9-U2, TYE
scissors Schere **9-U3**, Ex8
score Punktestand, Spielstand **10-U3**, T2
score erzielen **7-U3**, Read
scratch kratzen **8-U4**, T2
scream schreien **10-U1**, T2
screen Bildschirm, Leinwand **6-U3**, WPB
screw up your face das Gesicht verziehen
  9-U1, Read
sea Meer, die See **6-U2**, Sit3
seafood Meeresfrüchte **8-U2**, T1
seal Robbe, Seehund **10-U4**, TYE
search (for) suchen (nach) **6-U3**, WPC
seaside Meeresküste **5-U7**, WPB
season Jahreszeit; Saison **8-U2**, T1
season ticket Dauerkarte **8-U2**, Sit5
seat Sitz, Sitzplatz **5-U7**, T2
second Sekunde **9**-Rev3
second-hand gebraucht, aus zweiter Hand
  10-U3, T1
secret geheim **7-U1**, T2
secret Geheimnis **9**-Rev6
secretary Sekretär/in **10-U3**, Ex9
see sehen **5-U0**, B
  see you bis dann!, tschüss! **5-U0**, B
seem scheinen **7-U3**, T2
  seem to do etw zu tun scheinen **7-U3**, T2
segregation Trennung **8-U3**, T2
seize packen, ergreifen **10-U1**, Read
seizure Anfall **10-U3**, T2
sell verkaufen **6-U5**, WPB
seller Verkäufer/in **7-U5**, Rev
send schicken **6-U3**, WPC
senior Student/in im letzten Studienjahr
  8-U2, T1
sensation Aufsehen **8-U3**, T1
sense Sinn, Gefühl, Verstand **9**-Lit
sensibility Empfindsamkeit **9**-Lit
sensitive (about/to) empfindlich, sensibel
  (gegenüber) **10-U4**, T1
sentence Satz **5-U5**, Ex1; Strafe, Urteil
  10-Rev12
separate (sich) trennen **9-U1**, Read
separate getrennt **7-U1**, WP
September September **5-U4**, Sit5
series Serie **6-U6**, WPA
serious ernst **6-U3**, T2
servant Diener/in, Dienstmädchen **9-U4**, WP
serve servieren, bedienen **8-U2**, Sit1
service Dienst **8-U1**, Ex10
set: set fire to anzünden, in Brand stecken
  9-U4, Read
  be set (in) spielen in (Handlung)
  10-U4, T1
  set up gründen, eröffnen **9-U1**, T2
settle sich ansiedeln, sich niederlassen
  8-U2, TYE
settlement Siedlung **10-U1**, Sit4

settler Siedler/in **8-U2**, WP
seven sieben **5-U0**, G
seventeen siebzehn **5-U0**, G
seventy siebzig **5-U4**, WPA
several mehrere, einige **7-U4**, T2
sew nähen **7-U5**, Read
sex Sex, Geschlechtsverkehr; Geschlecht
  10-U3, Sit1
shack Hütte, Baracke **9-U4**, TYE
shake schütteln; zittern **10-U1**, Read
shall sollen **10-U4**, Sit3
shape Form **10-U2**, Sit4
share teilen, gemeinsam haben **7-U5**, T2
shark Hai **8-U4**, T1
she sie **5-U1**, Sit2
shed Schuppen, Stall **5-U3**, T2
sheep Schaf **6-U2**, WPA
shelf Regal, Ablage **5-U5**, Sit1
sheriff Sheriff **7-U5**, Sket2
shield (Schutz-)Schild **7-U2**, Sit5
shine glänzen, scheinen **10-U3**, Read
ship Schiff **7-U3**, WP
ship versenden, verschiffen **9-U2**, WP
shirt Hemd **5-U0**, C
shit Scheiße **9-U4**, T2
shock Schock **6-U2**, T2
shock schockieren **10-U3**, WP1
shocked erschüttert, entsetzt **10-U1**, TYE2
shoe Schuh **5-U3**, Sit2
shoot schießen **7-U1**, Read
shop Geschäft **5-U4**, Sit1
shop einkaufen (gehen), Einkäufe machen
  8-U1, Sit2
shopping centre Einkaufszentrum
  5-U6, WPB
shopping mall Einkaufszentrum **10-U4**, Sit1
shore Strand, Ufer **7-U4**, TYE
short kurz **6-U1**, Ex3
shorten (ver)kürzen **10-U1**, Ex10
shorts kurze Hose, Shorts **9-U3**, T1
shot Schuss **8-U1**, Read
should sollte **6-U6**, T2
shoulder Schulter **9-U2**, Read
shout schreien, rufen **5-U6**, T2
shovel schaufeln **10-U4**, Read
show Sendung **5-U5**, Sit3
show zeigen **6-U1**, Ex21
shower Regenschauer; Dusche **8-U3**, Read
shrug mit den Achseln zucken **10-U2**, Read
shut schließen **10-U4**, Ex1
  shut up den Mund halten **7-U1**, T1
shy schüchtern, scheu **7-U3**, TYE
sick krank **8-U3**, Read
side Seite **6-U2**, T1
sidewalk Gehsteig, Bürgersteig **8-U1**, T1
sigh Seufzer **9-U1**, Read
sight Sehenswürdigkeit **6-U1**, WPA
sighting Sichten **10-U2**, TYE5
sightseeing Stadtbesichtigung **6-U4**, PYE6
sign Schild, Zeichen **5-U7**, T1
signal Signal **6-U4**, T2
signal signalisieren, Zeichen geben
  9-U1, Com

Index

signpost Wegweiser **8-U2**, Read
silicon Silizium **6-U7**, WPA
silly albern **5-U1**, T1
silver Silber **7-U5**, WP
similar ähnlich **9-U2**, Ex10
simple einfach, schlicht **6-U5**, Ex13
since seit **7-U1**, Sit4
sing singen **5-U1**, Ex13
singer Sänger/in **6-U1**, T2
single einzeln, Einzel- **8-U1**, Com;
   alleinstehend, unverheiratet
   9-U2, Read
sink sinken, untergehen **7-U3**, WP
Sir mein Herr **5-U1**, Ex7
sister Schwester **5-U0**, I
sit (down) sitzen; sich hinsetzen **5-U0**, F
site Stelle, Platz **5-U7**, WPD
situation Situation **5-U1**, Sit1
six sechs **5-U0**, G
sixteen sechzehn **5-U0**, G
sixty sechzig **5-U4**, WPA
size Größe **5-U4**, Sit4
skate Rollschuh laufen **5-U5**, WPA
skateboard Skateboard **10-U3**, T1
skate park Skatinggelände **5-U5**, T1
ski Ski fahren **6-U7**, WPA
skill Fertigkeit, Geschicklichkeit **9-U2**, WP
skin Haut, Fell **8-U3**, T1
skinny dürr **9-U1**, Read
skirt Rock **6-U6**, Ex3
sky Himmel **5-U7**, T2
skydiving Skydiving, Freifallen **10-U1**, Sit3
skyline Silhouette, Skyline **8-U1**, WP
skyscraper Wolkenkratzer **8-U1**, T1
skyway Himmelsweg **6-U7**, Song
slave Sklave, Sklavin **8-U3**, WP
slavery Sklaverei **8-U3**, WP
sled Schlitten **10-U4**, TYE
sleep schlafen **6-U2**, Sit4
sleep Schlaf **9-U3**, T2
sleeping bag Schlafsack **7-U5**, T1
sleeve Ärmel **9-U4**, Read
slide gleiten, rutschen **10-U1**, T2
slight gering, klein, leicht **10-U2**, Read
slightly ein bisschen, etwas **10-U2**, Read
slogan Parole, Wahlspruch **6-U1**, Ex14
slope Gefälle, Hang **7-U4**, T1
slow langsam **5-U5**, Ex1
slow down (sich) verlangsamen, langsamer
   werden **9-U3**, Sit4
slums Elendsviertel **7-U1**, Read
slush Schneematsch **10-U4**, Read
smack einen Klaps geben **10-U1**, Read
small klein **5-U2**, WPA
smallpox Pocken **10-U1**, T1
smart schick, elegant, flott **7-U1**, WP;
   clever, raffiniert **10-U1**, Read
smartcard Smartcard **9-Rev8**
smell Geruch, Gestank **9-U1**, Ex15
smell riechen **5-U3**, WPB
smile Lächeln **10-U4**, T1
smile lächeln **6-U1**, T2
smoke Rauch **7-U5**, Sit1

smoke rauchen **10-U3**, Ex9
smooth glatt, sanft **10-U4**, T2
smuggle (into) (ein)schmuggeln (in)
   8-U1, Read
snack Imbiss **5-U5**, PYE5
snake Schlange **7-U2**, Read
sneakers Turnschuhe **10-U3**, T2
snow Schnee **8-U2**, T1
snow schneien **8-U4**, Read
snow bank Schneeverwehung **10-U4**, T2
snowblind schneeblind **10-U4**, Read
snowflake Schneeflocke **8-U4**, Read
snowmobile Schneemobil **10-U4**, TYE
snowplough Schneepflug **10-U4**, Read
snowstorm Schneesturm **8-U3**, Read
so so **5-U7**, Sit4; auch **9-U1**, Sit1
   so that sodass, damit **8-U1**, Sit1
   so what? na und? **7-U3**, T1
soap Seife **10-U1**, Ex9
soap opera Seifenoper **6-U6**, WPA
soccer Fußball **7-U3**, Read
so-called so genannt **10-U2**, Sit2
social sozial; Sozial- **8-Proj2**
society Gesellschaft, Verein **9-Lit**
sock Socke **7-U2**, Ex9
soda Soda(wasser) **8-U1**, T2
soft weich, zart **6-U4**, T2
softball Softball **6-U3**, T2
software Software **7-U1**, WP
solar panel Sonnenkollektor **9-U3**, Sit2
solar system Sonnensystem **10-U2**, WP
soldier Soldat/in **6-U4**, T1
sold: be sold out ausverkauft sein
   10-U3, Sit2
solo Solo-, allein **9-U3**, TYE
solution Lösung **9-U3**, Sit4
solve lösen **9-U3**, Sit4
some etwas, ein wenig; einige, ein paar
   5-U4, Sit1
somebody jemand **7-U3**, Sit1
somehow irgendwie **8-U1**, T2
someone jemand **6-U2**, Sit2
someplace irgendwo, irgendwohin
   8-U4, Sit1
something etwas **5-U4**, Sit3
sometimes manchmal **5-U1**, T1
somewhere irgendwo **7-U1**, T1
son Sohn **6-U1**, Sit1
song Lied **5-U0**, J
songwriter Liedermacher/in,
   Songschreiber/in **10-U3**, Sit1
soon bald **6-U5**, T1
sophomore Student/in im zweiten
   Studienjahr **8-Proj2**
sorry tut mir leid **5-U1**, Sit1
sort of Art, Sorte von **10-U2**, Read
soul Soul (Musikrichtung) **9-U1**, Ex9;
   Seele **9-U4**, T1
sound Klang, Laut **5-U5**, Ex17
sound klingen **6-U7**, T1
soup Suppe **7-U5**, T1
south Süden **6-U1**, WPA
southern südlich, Süd- **8-U1**, WP

souvenir Andenken, Souvenir **8-U2**, TYE
sow säen **7-U5**, Read
space Lücke, Raum, Platz **5-U5**, Ex18;
   Weltraum **10-U2**, WP
space capsule Raumkapsel **9-U3**, WP
spacecraft Raumfahrzeug, -schiff
   9-U3, Ex2
spaceship Raumschiff **7-U2**, Ex3
space shuttle Raumfähre **9-U3**, T1
spacesuit Raumanzug **9-U3**, T1
spaghetti Spaghetti **9-U1**, Read
spare part Ersatzteil **10-U4**, T2
spare time Freizeit **5-U5**, WPA
speak sprechen **5-U1**, Sit8
speaker Sprecher/in, Redner/in **7-U1**, Ex4
special spezial, besondere(r, s) **6-U4**,
spectator Zuschauer/in **10-U1**, T1
spectacular sensationell, atemberaubend
   8-U1, T1
speech Rede **9-SP**
speed Geschwindigkeit **9-TP**
speedway (track) Speedway-,
   Aschenrennbahn **8-U4**, Ex7
spell buchstabieren **5-U0**, J
spelling Rechtschreibung **6-U7**, Sit1
spend ausgeben (Geld) **7-U4**, T2; verbrin-
   gen (Zeit) **9-U2**, T1
spider Spinne **6-U4**, WPD
spill verschütten, vergießen **7-U1**, Sit3
spin spinnen **9-U4**, T1; schleudern (Wäsche)
   10-U2, TYE5
splash bespritzen, platschen **6-U7**, T2
spoil verwöhnen; verderben **10-U3**, Read
spokesman Sprecher, Wortführer
   9-U3, Read
sponsor finanziell unterstützen **6-U5**, Com
spoon Löffel **7-U5**, T2
sport Sport **5-U2**, Sit1
sporting Sport(s)-, sportlich **7-U3**, Proj
sports car Sportwagen **8-Rev11**
spot Fleck(en) **5-U7**, Ex13
spray Sprühnebel, Spray **10-U2**, T2
spray (be)sprühen **7-U4**, TYE
spread (sich) verbreiten, (sich) ausbreiten
   10-U3, WP
spring Frühling, Frühjahr **6-U4**, T1; Quelle
   10-U1, Sit4
spy Spion/in **9-TP**
spy (on) nachspionieren, bespitzeln
   9-U3, Sit1
squad car Streifenwagen **8-U3**, T2
square Platz **6-U7**, T2
squeeze sich quetschen, drängen, drücken
   10-U1, T2
stab (nieder)stechen, erstechen **9-U4**, Read
stadium Stadion **10-U4**, T1
stage Bühne **9-U1**, WP
stamp Briefmarke **5-U6**, Sit1
stamp stampfen **7-U3**, T2
stand stehen; sich hinstellen **5-U0**, F
   stand for sth für etw stehen **10-U4**, T1
   stand up aufstehen **5-U0**, F

169

Index

standard of living Lebensstandard **8-U3**, WP

standby: on standby in Bereitschaft **9-U2**, Read

star (Film-)star **5-U1**, Sit2; Stern **7-U3**, Com

star (in) eine Hauptrolle spielen (in) **7-U3**, WP

stare at anstarren **9-U1**, Read

start Start **7-U1**, Ex3

start anfangen **5-U4**, WPA

state Staat, Bundesstaat; Zustand **6-U7**, WP

station Bahnhof, Station **5-U7**, T2

statue Statue **8-U1**, WP

stay Aufenthalt **8-U1**, T2

stay bleiben, wohnen **5-U7**, Sit1

steal stehlen **6-U5**, T1

steam (Wasser-)Dampf **9-U3**, WP

steel Stahl **9-U1**, WP

steep steil **6-U7**, WPA

step Stufe; Schritt **8-U1**, T1

step gehen, treten **7-U1**, Read

stepbrother Stiefbruder **7-U3**, T1

stereo Stereogerät **5-U2**, WPC

stew Eintopf **5-U3**, Song

stick Stecken, Stock **8-U4**, T2

still ruhig **6-U2**, T2; (immer) noch **7-U1**, WP

stilt Pfahl, Stelze **10-U4**, TYE

stink stinken **10-U4**, Read

stolen gestohlen **7-U1**, T2

stomach Magen **9-U2**, Read

stone Stein **6-U1**, Song

stop Halt(en), Haltestelle; Aufenthalt **8-U1**, T1

stop anhalten, aufhören **6-U2**, Sit2

store Laden, Geschäft **8-U1**, Sit1

storey Stockwerk **10-U2**, T2

storm Sturm **7-U4**, WP

story Geschichte **6-U2**, Ex5

stove Ofen, Herd **8-U3**, Read

straight gerade **7-U5**, Com

   straight ahead geradeaus **5-U6**, WPB

   straight on geradeaus **7-U5**, Com

strange merkwürdig **6-U2**, T2

stranger Fremder, Fremde **7-U4**, WP

strawberry Erdbeere **7-U1**, Sit3

stream Bach **6-U2**, WPB

street Straße **6-U1**, WPB

stretcher Tragbahre **6-U2**, T2

strict streng **8-Lit**

string Saite (Musikinstrument) **10-U4**, Song

stripe Streifen **8-U4**, WP

strong stark **7-U2**, T1

struggle Kampf, Auseinandersetzung **8-Lit**

struggle kämpfen, sich abmühen **9-Proj1**

stuck stecken geblieben **8-U4**, Read

student Schüler/in, Student/in **10-Dict**

studies Studium **9-U2**, Ex11

studio Studio **8-U1**, T2

study studieren; sich genau ansehen **8-Rev8**

stuff Zeug, Sachen; Material **9-U1**, T1

stupid dumm, blöd **5-U3**, T2

style Stil **8-U4**, Read

subject Schulfach **5-U6**, T1

substitute Ersatz(form) **10-Rev11**

subtract abziehen, subtrahieren **10-U3**, Ex9

suburb Vorort **8-Rev8**

suburbia die Vororte **10-Lit**

subway U-Bahn **8-U1**, T1

succeed (in) gelingen, Erfolg haben (mit) **7-U3**, Sit1

success Erfolg **9-U1**, T2

successful erfolgreich **8-Rev1**

such solche(r,s), so, derartig **9-U1**, T2

such as wie zum Beispiel **9-U3**, Ex9

suddenly plötzlich **6-U2**, T2

suffer (from) leiden (an), erleiden **9-U4**, Sit4

sugar Zucker **5-U4**, Sit1

suggest vorschlagen **9-U2**, T1

suggestion Vorschlag **5-U5**, Ex18

suicide Selbstmord **10-U4**, TYE

suit Anzug **10-U3**, T1

suit stehen (Kleidung, Farben) **10-U4**, Sit1

suitable passend, geeignet **10-SP**

suitcase Koffer **9-U1**, Read

summary Zusammenfassung **8-U1**, Ex5

summer Sommer **5-U4**, Sit5

sun Sonne **6-U2**, Sit3

sun cream Sonnencreme **10-U1**, Ex9

Sunday Sonntag **5-U1**, Sit4

sunglasses Sonnenbrille **9-U3**, Ex8

sunlight Sonnenlicht **10-U3**, Ex16

sunny sonnig **7-U5**, T1

sunset Sonnenuntergang **8-U4**, T1

sunshine Sonnenschein **8-U4**, Sit1

Super Bowl Super Bowl **8-U2**, T2

supermarket Supermarkt **5-U2**, Sit4

supermodel Supermodel **7-U3**, TYE

superstar Superstar **7-U3**, T2

support Unterstützung, Hilfe **10-U3**, TYE

support unterstützen **5-U2**, T1

suppose annehmen, vermuten **9-U3**, Read

supposed: be supposed to do tun sollen **9-Lit**

Supreme Court Oberster Gerichtshof **8-U3**, T2

sure sicher **5-U1**, Sit3

surf surfen **7-U5**, Ex7

surface Oberfläche **9-U3**, Sit1

surfing Surfen **6-U7**, WPA

surname Familienname **10-SP**

surprised überrascht **7-U3**, Sit4

surround umzingeln, umgeben **8-U1**, Read

surroundings Umgebung **10-U4**, Ex23

survival Überleben **9-U2**, Read

survive überleben **8-U2**, WP

suspect vermuten; misstrauen, verdächtigen **10-U4**, T1

swallow Schwalbe **6-U2**, WPB

swampland Sumpfgebiet **10-U4**, T2

swap tauschen **5-U2**, Ex1

swear fluchen **10-U3**, T1

sweater Pullover **5-U0**, C

sweep fegen **9-U4**, Sit3

sweets Süßigkeiten **6-U4**, T2

sweet talk Schmeicheleien, schöne Worte **7-U1**, Proj

sweet-talk jdm schmeicheln **7-U1**, Proj

swim schwimmen **5-U1**, Sit8

swimmer Schwimmer/in **8-U4**, TYE1

swimming-pool Schwimmbad **5-U6**, WPA

swimsuit Badeanzug **10-U1**, Sit4

swing Schaukel **5-U3**, T1

swing schwingen **7-U4**, T1

switch off abschalten **9-U2**, Ex19

switch on anschalten, einschalten **6-U3**, T2

sword Schwert **7-U2**, T1

sympathy Mitgefühl, Mitleid, Verständnis **9-U4**, T1

syndrome Syndrom **10-U3**, Sit3

synonym Synonym, Wort mit ähnlicher Bedeutung **10-Proj2**

synthesizer Synthesizer **10-U3**, T1

system System **9-U3**, T1

Tt

table Tisch **5-U1**, T2

taboo Tabu **10-Proj2**

tackle angreifen **8-U2**, Ex12

tactic Taktik, taktischer Zug **9-U2**, T2

tail Schwanz **8-U4**, TYE

take nehmen **5-U4**, WPA; dauern, Zeit in Anspruch nehmen **6-U5**, Ex2

   take a photo ein Foto machen **5-U5**, WPB

   take notice of sth etw beachten, etw zur Kenntnis nehmen **10-U3**, TYE

   take off abnehmen, ausziehen **8-U4**, T2; (gut) anlaufen, durchstarten **10-U1**, Sit4

   take out herausnehmen, herausziehen **7-U1**, Sit5

   take over übernehmen **10-U2**, Sit1

   take part (in) teilnehmen (an) **8-U2**, T1

   take place stattfinden **8-U2**, T2

tale Geschichte, Erzählung **9-Lit**

talk reden **5-U2**, T2

tall groß **6-U6**, Com

tap (Wasser-)Hahn **9-U4**, TYE

tape Tonband, Videoband **6-U6**, T2

tapestry Wandbehang, Wandteppich **7-U4**, WP

task Aufgabe **8-Proj5**

taste schmecken **7-U5**, Sit1

tattoo Tätowierung **9-Rev10**

tax Steuer **9-U1**, TYE

taxi Taxi **5-U7**, Ex6

tea Abendessen **5-U3**, Sit1; (schwarzer) Tee **5-U4**, WPA

teach unterrichten **6-U3**, T1

teacher Lehrer/in **5-U0**, D

team Team, Mannschaft **5-U1**, Ex17

tear Träne **10-U1**, T2

tech house Tech House (Musikrichtung) **9-U1**, T1

technician Techniker/in **7-U1**, Sit1

techno Techno (Musikrichtung) **10-U3**, T2

technology Technik **6-U3**, T1

teenager Teenager **6-U6**, WPA

Index

telecommunications Telekommunikation **9-U3**, WP
telephone Telefon **5-U1**, PYE6
(tele)phone box Telefonzelle **7-U1**, T2
telesales Verkauf per Telefon **9-U2**, Ex20
telescope Teleskop **9-U3**, Ex18
television Fernsehen **5-U1**, Sit6
tell erzählen, mitteilen **5-U5**, WPB
temper Laune, Stimmung, Wesensart **7-U4**, T2
temperate gemäßigt **10-U2**, Sit4
temperature Temperatur **8-U4**, WP
temple Tempel, Kultstätte **6-U4**, WPB
ten zehn **5-U0**, G
tennis Tennis **5-U2**, WPC
tension Anspannung, Spannung **8-U2**, T2
tent Zelt **7-U5**, T1
terabyte Terabyte **7-U5**, Read
term Semester, Trimester **5-U4**, Sit5
terrible schrecklich **5-U6**, T2
terrified: be terrified (of) schreckliche Angst haben (vor) **10-U1**, Read
terrifying Furcht erregend, schrecklich **10-U1**, Read
territory Gebiet **10-U1**, Ex3
terror panische Angst, Schrecken **10-U2**, Read
test Test **6-U5**, Com
test testen, ausprobieren **6-U6**, WPA
text Text **5-U1**, T1
textbook Lehrbuch **5-U3**, Ex11
textile Textil-, Stoff- **9-U4**, WP
than als **6-U1**, Sit3
thank: thank sb for doing sth jdm. danken, etw getan zu haben **9-U1**, Ex11
  thank you danke **5-U0**, B
thanks danke **5-U0**, B
Thanksgiving Erntedankfest **8-U2**, WP
that der, die, das (dort) **5-U0**, D
thatched strohgedeckt **9-U1**, T2
the der, die, das **5-U0**, D
theatre Theater **7-U4**, WP
their ihr, ihre, ihr **5-U1**, WPB
theirs ihre(r, s) **6-U3**, Sit3
them sie, ihnen **5-U2**, Sit5
theme Thema; Motto **8-U2**, T1
theme park Freizeitpark **8-U4**, T1
themselves sich; selbst **8-U3**, Sit3
then dann **5-U1**, Sit7; also, nun **5-U3**, Sit1
therapy Therapie, Behandlung **9-U3**, T2
there dort **5-U1**, Ex4
  there are es gibt, es sind vorhanden **5-U1**, WPA
  there is es gibt, es ist vorhanden **5-U1**, WPA
thermal Thermal-, thermisch **10-U1**, Sit4
these diese **5-U3**, Sit2
they sie **5-U1**, WPB
thick dick, dicht **7-U5**, Sit1
thief Dieb/in **7-U5**, T2
thin dünn **7-U4**, Com
thing Sache, Gegenstand **5-U4**, T2
think denken, meinen **5-U1**, T2

thirsty durstig **7-U5**, T1
thirteen dreizehn **5-U0**, G
thirty dreißig **5-U1**, Sit5
this dieser, diese, dieses, dies **5-U0**, D
those jene **5-U3**, Sit2
though doch, jedoch, trotzdem **10-U4**, Sit1
thought Gedanke **9-U3**, T1
thousand tausend **5-U7**, T2
three drei **5-U0**, G
thriller Thriller, Krimi **9-Lit**
throne Thron **9-U1**, T2
through durch **6-U2**, T1
throw werfen **5-U6**, Ex4
thunder Donner **8-U3**, Read
Thursday Donnerstag **5-U1**, Sit4
tic Zucken, Tick **10-U3**, Sit3
ticket Fahrkarte; Eintrittskarte **6-U1**, T1
tidy ordentlich **7-U1**, Sit2
tidy aufräumen **5-U5**, Sit1
tie Krawatte **9-U4**, Read
tiger Tiger **6-U3**, Ex3
tight eng(anliegend) **10-U3**, T1
till bis **8-U1**, Sit2
time Zeit **5-U0**, B
  hit/be the big time ganz groß rauskommen, ganz oben sein **7-U3**, WP
  on time pünktlich **5-U1**, Sit6
  the next time das nächste Mal **7-U5**, TYE4
  take time off sich freinehmen **10-U1**, Sit3
timeline Zeitleiste **9-Rev6**
times mal **7-U2**, Ex7
timetable Stundenplan **5-U1**, PYE1
tin Büchse, Dose **6-U5**, Sit2
tiny winzig **9-Lit**
tip Tipp, nützlicher Hinweis **7-U3**, Sit1
tired müde **5-U6**, T1
  tired of doing sth, be es satt haben, etw zu tun **8-U3**, T2
title Titel **7-U1**, Ex3
to zu **5-U0**, B
toast Toast **5-U4**, WPB
tobacco Tabak **8-U3**, T1
today heute **5-U0**, G
toe Zehe **10-U4**, Read
together zusammen **5-U5**, Ex6
toilet Toilette **9-U3**, Read
tomato Tomate **7-U5**, T1
tomorrow morgen **6-U2**, Sit2
ton Tonne **7-U2**, TYE
tonight heute Abend **6-U4**, Ex2
tonne (metrische) Tonne **10-U4**, T2
too auch **5-U0**, G; zu **5-U5**, Ex1
tooth Zahn **8-U2**, Read
top Spitze, Gipfel **5-U7**, T2; Oberteil, Top **7-U1**, Sit1
  on top of auf, über, obendrauf **8-U4**, T2
topic Thema **9-Proj1**
torch Fackel **7-U2**, TYE
torture Folter, Qual **6-U1**, T2
total (End-)Summe, Gesamtmenge **8-U2**, T1; völlig, absolut **10-U4**, Ex3
total zu Schrott fahren **10-U4**, Read

touch berühren **8-U2**, Ex12
touchdown Versuch **8-U2**, Ex12
tough robust, hart, zäh **6-U4**, T2
tour Rundfahrt, Führung **6-U1**, WPA
tourism Tourismus, Fremdenverkehr **9-U2**, Sit3
tourist Tourist/in **6-U1**, Sit2
towards auf ... zu, in Richtung, gegen **10-U1**, T2
towel Handtuch **9-Rev9**
tower Turm **6-U1**, WPA
town Stadt **5-U6**, WPA
town hall Rathaus **7-U5**, Ex13
township Township (Südafrika) **9-U4**, TYE
toy Spielzeug **6-U5**, T2
track Gleisstrecke **8-U3**, TYE; Pfad, Weg **10-U1**, T2
tractor Traktor, Zugmaschine **8-U4**, Read
trade Handel **8-U1**, Ex7
trade Handel treiben, handeln **8-U3**, T1
tradition Tradition, Brauch **8-U3**, Sit1
traditional traditionell **7-U1**, WP
traffic Verkehr **6-U6**, T2
tragedy Tragödie **8-U4**, Sit4
trail Weg, Pfad; Spur **8-U3**, Read
train Zug **5-U7**, WPA
train trainieren, schulen **9-U2**, WP
training Ausbildung, Schulung **9-U2**, WP
tram Tram, Straßenbahn **7-U5**, Sit1
trampolining Trampolin springen **6-U5**, Sit4
translate übersetzen **7-U3**, TYE4
translation Übersetzung **8-U3**, Ex16
trapped gefangen, eingeschlossen **9-U2**, Read
travel reisen **5-U7**, WPA
travel agency Reisebüro **9-U2**, WP
traveller Reisende/r **9-Lit**
treat behandeln **8-U2**, Sit3
tree Baum **5-U3**, PYE2
tree-lined baumbestanden **10-U4**, T1
trek anstrengende Wanderung **8-Rev4**
trendy modisch, schick **8-U4**, T1
trial and error Ausprobieren **10-U2**, T1
tribe Stamm **8-U3**, T1
trick Trick **10-U4**, Read
trigger auslösen **9-U3**, Sit4
trip Reise **6-U4**, PYE6
tropical tropisch **10-U2**, Sit4
tropics: the tropics die Tropen **10-U2**, T2
trouble Mühe, Umstände **8-U1**, Sit2
  in trouble in Schwierigkeiten **7-U3**, Sit1
trousers Hose **9-U1**, Ex12
truck LKW, Truck **6-U7**, Ex1
true wahr **7-U2**, Sit1
truth Wahrheit **7-U2**, Read
try versuchen **5-U5**, T1
  try on anprobieren **10-U1**, Ex9
  try to do sth versuchen, etw zu tun **7-U1**, Ex3
T-shirt T-Shirt **5-U4**, Sit3
tube U-Bahn **6-U1**, WPB; Röhre, Röhrchen, Schlauch **9-U3**, T2
Tuesday Dienstag **5-U1**, Sit4

171

Index

tunnel Tunnel **6-U4**, T1
turkey Truthahn **8-U2**, WP
turn Kurve, Abzweigung **8-U2**, Read
  take turns etw abwechselnd tun, sich
    abwechseln mit **10-SP**
turn einbiegen **5-U6**, WPB; drehen **6-U6**, T1
  turn off ausschalten **9-U2**, T2
  turn on anschalten **9-U2**, T2
  turn to/into verwandeln in **10-U4**, Read
turning Abzweigung **6-U6**, T1
tutor Betreuungslehrer/in, Klassenlehrer/in
  5-U1, WPB
TV Fernsehen **5-U6**, Ex9
twelve zwölf **5-U0**, G
twenty zwanzig **5-U0**, G
twice zweimal **6-U5**, Sit4
twin Zwilling **6-U6**, WPA
twist sich winden; biegen; verdrehen
  10-U2, T2
twitter zwitschern **10-U2**, T2
two zwei **5-U0**, G
two-way radio Funksprechgerät
  10-U1, TYE6
type Typ **7-U1**, T1
type (in) (ein)tippen **6-U3**, WPC
typewriter Schreibmaschine **8-Rev3**
typical (of) typisch (für) **8-U2**, Sit1
tyre Reifen **10-U4**, Read

Uu

ultimate perfekt, vollendet **8-U2**, T2
umbrella Regenschirm **5-U0**, D
unable: be unable to do sth unfähig, nicht in
  der Lage sein, etw zu tun **10-Lit**
uncle Onkel **5-U1**, Song
uncomfortable unbequem **7-U5**, T1
unconscious bewusstlos **10-TP**
uncountable unzählbar **10-Dict**
under unter **5-U3**, T1
underground U-Bahn **6-U1**, WPB
understand verstehen **6-U6**, Sit1
underwear Unterwäsche **10-U3**, T1
undoubtedly zweifellos **7-U5**, Read
unemployed arbeitslos **9-U4**, T2
unemployment Arbeitslosigkeit **9-U4**, TYE
unfair unfair, ungerecht **9-U2**, Ex17
unfortunate unglücklich, bedauerlich
  10-U1, T1
unfortunately unglücklicherweise **8-Rev4**
unfriendly unfreundlich **9-U4**, T2
unhappy unglücklich **10-U3**, Read
unidentified unbekannt, nicht identifiziert
  10-U2, TYE5
uniform Uniform **5-U1**, WPB
unit Unit, Lektion **5-U1**,
United Kingdom Vereinigtes Königreich,
  UK **7-U1**, WP
university Universität **8-Rev8**
unless wenn nicht, es sei denn **10-U2**, Sit2
unpleasant unangenehm, unerfreulich
  10-Dict
unreal unwirklich **10-U4**, T2
untidy unordentlich **9-U1**, Read

until bis **6-U5**, Sit2
untouchable Unberührbare/r **9-U4**, T1
unwind abschalten, sich entspannen
  10-U4, Song
up hinauf, herauf, nach oben **5-U0**, F
  up to bis zu **10-U1**, Sit2
update Aktualisierung, neueste Version
  10-U1, Sit1
update aktualisieren, auf den neuesten
  Stand bringen **9-U2**, T2
upper obere(r, s) **9-Lit**
uprising Aufstand, Volkserhebung
  9-U4, TYE
ups and downs Höhen und Tiefen (des
  Lebens) **9-U2**, T1
upset aufgebracht **7-U5**, T2
upside down verkehrt herum, auf dem Kopf
  stehend **9-U1**, Read
upstairs oben **9-U1**, T1
up-to-date aktuell, modern **6-U3**, WPD
urban städtisch, Stadt- **7-U1**, Read
urgent dringend **7-U1**, T2
us uns **5-U2**, Sit5
use Gebrauch, Verwendung **10-U4**, T1
use gebrauchen, verwenden **5-U5**, WPB
  no use doing sth, it's (es hat) keinen Sinn,
    etw zu tun **9-U1**, T1
used to etw früher getan haben **9-U3**, T1
useful nützlich **7-U5**, WP
user Benutzer/in **8-Rev3**
usually gewöhnlich **5-U5**, WPB
U-turn: no U-turn Wenden verboten
  8-U2, Read

Vv

vacation Ferien **6-U7**, Sit1
vague vage, ungenau **9-U1**, Ex7
valley Tal **6-U7**, WPA
van Lieferwagen **7-U1**, T2
variant Variante **10-Dict**
various verschieden, unterschiedlich **9-TP**
vary variieren, sich verändern **9-U3**, T1
vegetable Gemüse **8-U3**, T1
vehicle Fahrzeug **10-U1**, TYE
Velcro Klettband **9-U3**, T2
ventilate belüften, ventilieren **9-U3**, T2
verb Verb, Tunwort **5-U5**, Ex1
version Version, Fassung **9-U3**, Ex1
very sehr **5-U1**, Sit1
vet Tierarzt, Tierärztin **6-U5**, WPD
veterinary tierärztlich, Veterinär- **9-U2**, WP
vice versa umgekehrt **10-U4**, Ex10
victim Opfer **10-Rev17**
victory Sieg **8-U3**, T2
video(cassette) Videokassette **5-U4**, T2
video recorder Videorekorder **7-U3**, Sit2
view Ausblick **5-U7**, T2
Viking Wikinger/in **7-U4**, Sit1
village Dorf **6-U2**, Sit3
vintage car Oldtimer **8-Rev11**
violence Gewalt **8-U1**, T2
violent gewalttätig **8-U1**, T2
violin Geige **7-U5**, Read

virgin Jungfrau; jungfräulich **9-U4**, Read
virtual virtuell **9-U3**, WP
visa Visum, Sichtvermerk **8-U1**, Ex9
visit Besuch **7-U1**, TYE5
visit besuchen, besichtigen **5-U3**, Ex16
visitor Besucher/in **6-U6**, WPD
visual visuell **10-SP**
vocational Berufs- **9-U2**, Ex11
voice Stimme **6-U2**, T2
volleyball Volleyball **8-U2**, T1
volt Volt **9-U3**, T2
vote wählen, Stimme abgeben für **8-U3**, WP
voyage Seereise **8-U1**, TYE4

Ww

wage(s) Lohn **10-U4**, TYE
wagon Wagen, Planwagen **8-U3**, TYE
wait warten **5-U5**, T2
wait Warten, Wartezeit **8-U1**, T1
waiting room Wartesaal, Wartezimmer
  9-U4, T1
waitress Kellnerin **9-U2**, Ex11
wake up aufwachen, aufwecken **7-U3**, T2
walk Wanderung **7-U5**, T1
walk gehen, wandern **5-U2**, Sit3
  walk on weiterlaufen, weitergehen
    10-U4, T2
walkman Walkman **5-U4**, T1
wall Mauer, Wand **5-U2**, T2
wall chart Wandkarte **8-Proj2**
wander wandern, schlendern **10-Rev9**
want wollen **5-U2**, T2
war Krieg **7-U3**, Com
wardrobe (Kleider-)Schrank **5-U2**, WPC
warm warm **6-U3**, Sit1
warm warm werden, (sich) erwärmen
  10-U2, WP
warn warnen **6-U4**, T2
wash (sich) waschen **6-U2**, Sit2
  wash away wegspülen **6-U1**, Song
  wash up abspülen **6-U4**, Ex11
washing machine Waschmaschine
  9-U3, Ex8
waste Abfall, Exkrement **9-U3**, Read
waste vergeuden, verschwenden **9-U3**, T1
watch Uhr **5-U1**, T2
watch sehen, beobachten **5-U1**, Sit6
water Wasser **5-U4**, WPA
water canon Wasserwerfer **10-U3**, TYE1
waterfall Wasserfall **6-U7**, WPA
waterproof Regenmantel, wasserundurch-
  lässiges Kleidungsstück **10-U1**, T2
wave Welle, Woge **9-U4**, T2
wave winken **10-U1**, T2
wax Wachs **7-U1**, TYE5
waxwork Wachsfigur **6-U1**, Sit2
way Weg **5-U1**, Sit7; Art u. Weise **6-U1**, Ex4
  no way! kommt überhaupt nicht in Frage!
    9-U1, T1
  way of doing sth Art und Weise, etw zu tun
    8-U2, Com
  way of life Lebensart, Lebensweise
    8-U1, T2

172

Index

we wir **5-U1**, Sit1
wealthy reich, wohlhabend **10**-Dict
weapon Waffe **7-U2**, T2
wear tragen **5-U4**, Sit3
weather Wetter **5-U7**, WPD
weather wetterfest sein, überstehen
    7-U5, Read
web Netz **9-U2**, WP
webmaster Webmaster **10-U2**, T1
website Website **6-U3**, WPC
wedding Hochzeit(stag) **7-U5**, Sket2
Wednesday Mittwoch **5-U1**, Sit4
week Woche **5-U1**, Sit3
weekday Wochentag **10-U3**, T2
weekend Wochenende **5-U1**, Sit4
weep weinen **10-U1**, Read
weigh wiegen **7-U2**, TYE
weight Gewicht **7-U5**, Sit3
weightlessness Schwerelosigkeit **9-U3**, T1
welcome willkommen **6-U7**, T1
well nun **5-U1**, Sit8; gut **6-U6**, Sit3
well-known berühmt **8**-Lit
well off wohlhabend, reich, gut dran
    9-U2, Ex21
Welsh Waliser/in; walisisch **5-U7**, T1
west Westen **6-U1**, Sit1
western westlich, West- **7-U5**, Ex16
West Indian westindisch **7-U5**, TYE
westward westwärts, nach Westen
    8-U3, TYE
wet nass, feucht **7-U4**, TYE
whale Wal **10-U2**, WP
what was **5-U0**, A
  what about? wie wär's mit …? **5-U2**, WPA
  what's was ist **5-U0**, A
  what's on? was läuft (im Kino/Theater)?
    9-U1, WP
  what's up Was ist los? **9-U4**, Read
whatever was auch immer **7-U5**, Read
wheel Rad **5-U3**, WPA
wheelchair Rollstuhl **5-U6**, T1
when wann **5-U4**, Ex14;ls **5-U6**, T1;
    (immer) wenn **5-U7**, Sit4
where wo **5-U0**, J
whether ob **7-U5**, Read
which welche(r, s) **6-U1**, WPB; der, die, das,
    welcher, welche, welches **7-U4**, Sit1
while Weile **10-U4**, Sit3
while während **7-U1**, T2
whisper flüstern **8-U4**, T2
white weiß **5-U0**, C
white-water rafting Wildwasserfahren
    10-U1, Sit3
whiz-kid Wunderkind, Genie **10-U2**, T1
who wer **5-U1**, T2
whole ganz **7-U2**, Ex8
whore Hure **10-U1**, Read
whose deren, dessen **7-U4**, Sit3
whose wessen **5-U6**, Sit3
why warum **5-U4**, T1
wide groß, weit **8-U3**, WP
widow Witwe **7-U4**, T2
wife Ehefrau **6-U1**, Sit1

wild wild, ungezügelt **6-U2**, T1
wildlife Tierwelt **9**-Proj4
will werden **6-U5**, Sit1
willing bereitwillig, gewillt **9-U2**, T1
win gewinnen **5-U4**, Sit1
wind Wind **8-U4**, T2
window Fenster **5-U0**, D
window-cleaner Fensterputzer/in **7-U5**, Rev
windshield Windschutzscheibe **8-U4**, Read
windsurfing Windsurfen **8-U4**, Sit1
windy windig **10-U4**, Ex23
wine Wein **6-U7**, WPA
wing Flügel **7-U2**, Read
wink blinzeln, zwinkern **9-U4**, Read
winner Gewinner/in **8-U2**, T2
winter Winter **6-U4**, T2
wipe (ab)wischen **9-U4**, Read
wish wünschen **9**-Rev9
witch Hexe **7-U2**, Read
with mit **5-U1**, Sit2
within innerhalb **10-U4**, T2
without ohne **6-U5**, T1
witness Zeuge, Zeugin **8-U2**, TYE4
witness Zeuge sein von **8-U2**, TYE4
woman Frau **5-U3**, Sit3
women's refuge Frauenhaus **10-U3**, Read
wonder Wunder **8-U2**, Read
wonder sich fragen, gerne wissen wollen
    9-U1, Sit3
wonderful wunderbar **5-U7**, WPD
wood Holz **6-U1**, Song
wooden hölzern, aus Holz **8-U3**, TYE
word Wort **5-U0**, J
work Arbeit **5-U1**, Sit7
work arbeiten **5-U2**, Sit4
worker Arbeiter/in **9-U1**, WP
workhouse Armenhaus **9**-Lit
workman Handwerker **8-U3**, TYE
world Welt **6-U1**, T1
worldwide weltweit **8-U2**, T2
worried besorgt **7-U5**, T2
worry sich sorgen **6-U1**, T1
worse schlechter **6-U1**, Sit4
worship (an)beten, **9-U4**, Fol
worst am schlechtesten **6-U1**, Sit4
worth wert **6-U6**, T2
  it's worth doing sich lohnen zu tun
    9-U1, T1
would würde **8-U4**, Sit4
  would like möchte gern **5-U4**, WPA
  would like /love to do sth möchte gerne etw
    tun **7-U1**, Com
  would rather möchte lieber **9-U1**, T1
wound verwunden **10-U4**, Read
write schreiben **5-U3**, Com
writer Schriftsteller/in **8-U4**, T1
wrong falsch **5-U2**, Ex5
wrote schrieb **6-U3**, T2

Xx
X-ray Röntgenaufnahme **9-U3**, Read
XXXL übergroß, XXXL **10-U3**, T1

Yy
yeah ja **9-U2**, T1
year Jahr **5-U1**, Sit3
yearbook Jahrbuch **8-U2**, T1
yell brüllen, laut schreien **8-U4**, T2
yellow gelb **5-U0**, C
yes ja **5-U0**, B
yesterday gestern **6-U2**, Sit1
yet: not... yet noch nicht **6-U4**, Sit3
  yet, ... yet? schon **6-U4**, Sit3
yoghurt Joghurt **5-U4**, WPA
you du, ihr, Sie **5-U0**, A
young jung **6-U2**, WPB
your dein, deine, dein, ihr, ihre, ihr **5-U0**, A
yours deine(r, s) **6-U3**, Sit2
yourself dich, dir; selbst **8-U3**, Sit3
yourselves euch; selbst **8-U3**, Sit3
Yours faithfully/sincerely Mit freundlichen
    Grüßen (Brief) **9-U2**, Ex10
youth Jugend **9-U4**, Sit1
yummy lecker, schmackhaft **8-U2**, Sit1
yuppie Yuppie **10-U3**, T1

Zz
zero Null **10-U3**, Ex9
zone Zone, Bereich **8-U4**, Sit2
zoo Zoo, Tierpark **5-U3**, Ex16

173

Extra Pages

Unit 1 Extra Pages

to **slap** [slæp]	(drauf)klatschen
to **wrap (up)** [ˌræp ˈʌp]	einwickeln
outdoors [ˌaʊtˈdɔːz]	im Freien
protective [prəˈtektɪv]	Schutz-
anti [ˈænti]	gegen, anti-
ultraviolet [ˌʌltrəˈvaɪələt]	ultraviolett
burn time [ˈbɜːn taɪm]	Verweildauer in der Sonne
fair [feə]	hell (Haut)
to **risk** [rɪsk]	riskieren
shade [ʃeɪd]	Schatten
few [fjuː]	wenige
pollution [pəˈluːʃn]	Umweltverschmutzung
to **shine** [ʃaɪn]	glänzen; scheinen
acid rain [ˌæsɪd ˈreɪn]	saurer Regen
solar [ˈsəʊlə]	Sonnen-, Solar-
radiation [ˌreɪdiˈeɪʃn]	Strahlung
asthma [ˈæsmə]	Asthma
ozone [ˈəʊzəʊn]	Ozon
layer [ˈleɪə]	Schicht
cancer [ˈkænsə]	Krebs
crocodile [ˈkrɒkədaɪl]	Krokodil
meerkat [ˈmɪəkæt]	Erdmännchen
to **slip on** [ˌslɪp ˈɒn]	hineinschlüpfen, überstreifen
slop [slɒp]	kippen, überschwappen
bump [bʌmp]	Beule
hay [heɪ]	Heu
oxygen [ˈɒksɪdʒən]	Sauerstoff
chemical [ˈkemɪkl]	Chemikalie
CFC [ˌsiː ef ˈsiː]	FCKW
fridge [frɪdʒ]	Kühlschrank

Ex2

sunshade [ˈsʌnʃeɪd]	Sonnenschirm

Ex3

freckles [ˈfreklz]	Sommersprossen
tan [tæn]	bräunen
SPF/ sun protection factor [ˌes piː ˈef]	Lichtschutzfaktor
table [ˈteɪbl]	Tabelle
to **multiply** [ˈmʌltɪplaɪ]	vervielfältigen
to **sunbathe** [ˈsʌnbeɪð]	sonnenbaden
minerals [ˈmɪnərəls]	Mineralien

Unit 2 Extra Pages

lifelike [ˈlaɪflaɪk]	lebensecht
to **wow** [waʊ]	begeistern, umhauen
DNA [ˌdiː en ˈeɪ]	DNS
grandchild [ˈɡræntʃaɪld]	Enkel(kind)
maker [ˈmeɪkə]	Macher/in, Produzent/in, Hersteller/in
puppet [ˈpʌpɪt]	Puppe, Handpuppe
full-size [ˈfʊl saɪz]	in Originalgröße, lebensgroß
mechanical [mɪˈkænɪkl]	mechanisch
graphics [ˈɡræfɪks]	Grafiken
tyrannosaurus rex [tɪˌrænəsɔːrəs ˈreks]	Tyrannosaurus rex

fibreglass [ˈfaɪbəɡlɑːs]	Glasfaser
kilo [ˈkiːləʊ]	Kilo(gramm)
latex [ˈleɪteks]	Latex; Milchsaft
hydraulic [haɪˈdrɔːlɪk]	hydraulisch
mechanism [ˈmekənɪzəm]	Mechanismus
to **instruct** [ɪnˈstrʌkt]	anweisen, instruieren
radio [ˈreɪdiəʊ]	Funk
close-up [ˈkləʊs ʌp]	Nahaufnahme
velociraptor [vəˌlɒsɪˈræptə]	Velociraptor
high-tech [ˌhaɪ ˈtek]	hoch technisiert
wire [ˈwaɪə]	Draht
creature [ˈkriːtʃə]	Geschöpf, Lebewesen
herd [hɜːd]	Herde
animation [ˌænɪˈmeɪʃn]	Animation
image [ˈɪmɪdʒ]	Bild
industrial [ɪnˈdʌstriəl]	industriell
to **scan** [skæn]	(ein)scannen
digital [ˈdɪdʒɪtl]	digital, Digital-
to **animate** [ˈænɪmeɪt]	animieren, beleben
to **dry off** [ˌdraɪ ˈɒf]	abtrocknen
realistic [ˌriːəˈlɪstɪk]	naturgetreu
element [ˈelɪmənt]	Element
editor [ˈedɪtə]	Redakteur/in, Herausgeber/in
dolphin [ˈdɒlfɪn]	Delfin
goose [ɡuːs] pl **geese**	Gans
penguin [ˈpeŋɡwɪn]	Pinguin

Unit 3 Extra Pages

conspiracy [kənˈspɪrəsi]	Verschwörung
wreckage [ˈrekɪdʒ]	Trümmer
saucer [ˈsɔːsə]	Untertasse
to **crash** [kræʃ]	abstürzen, einen Unfall haben
balloon [bəˈluːn]	Ballon
untrue [ʌnˈtruː]	unwahr, falsch
to **claim** [kleɪm]	behaupten; beanspruchen
alien [ˈeɪliən]	außerirdisches Wesen; Ausländer(in)
increase [ˈɪnkriːs]	Zunahme, Steigerung
contact [ˈkɒntækt]	Kontakt
encounter [ɪnˈkaʊntə]	Begegnung
common [ˈkɒmən]	häufig, allgemein
alien [ˈeɪliən]	außerirdisch
abduction [æbˈdʌkʃn]	Entführung
survey [ˈsɜːveɪ]	(Meinungs-)Umfrage
to **abduct** [æbˈdʌkt]	entführen
hypnosis [hɪpˈnəʊsɪs]	Hypnose
gray [ɡreɪ] *AE*	grau
to **stick** [stɪk]	stecken; kleben
victim [ˈvɪktɪm]	Opfer
vivid [ˈvɪvɪd]	lebhaft
evidence [ˈevɪdəns]	Beweis, Indiz
public [ˈpʌblɪk]	Öffentlichkeit
humanity [hjuːˈmænəti]	Menschheit
DNA [ˌdiː en ˈeɪ]	DNS

Extra Pages

hybrid ['haɪbrɪd] — Kreuzung, Hybride
theory ['θɪəri] — Theorie
amusing [ə'mjuːzɪŋ] — lustig, amüsant
ridiculous [rɪ'dɪkjələs] — lächerlich

Ex1
to decrease [di'kriːs] — zurückgehen, abnehmen

responsibility [rɪˌspɒnsə'bɪləti] — Verantwortung
Ex3
intelligence [ɪn'telɪdʒəns] — *hier*: Geheimdienst
dictator [dɪk'teɪtə] — Diktator/in
Ex4
scale [skeɪl] — Maßstab, Skala
standard ['stændəd] — Standard-, Normal-
geological [ˌdʒiːə'lɒdʒɪkl] — geologisch
to fear [fɪə] — fürchten, befürchten
to come true [ˌkʌm 'truː] — wahr werden
to ridicule ['rɪdɪkjuːl] — verspotten
magnetic [mæg'netɪk] — magnetisch
energy ['enədʒi] — Energie
damage ['dæmɪdʒ] — Schaden
islander ['aɪləndə] — Inselbewohner/in
tabloid ['tæblɔɪd] — Boulevardblatt
broadsheet ['brɔːdʃiːt] — seriöse Tageszeitung
to quote [kwəʊt] — zitieren
regional ['riːdʒənl] — regional, Regional-

Unit 4 Extra Pages
cabin ['kæbɪn] — Hütte
canoe [kə'nuː] — Kanu
beaver ['biːvə] — Biber
to turn your back on sb/sth [tɜːn jɔː 'bæk ɒn] — sich von jdm/etw abwenden
to trap [træp] — mit einer Falle fangen
conservation [ˌkɒnsə'veɪʃn] — Erhaltung, Schutz
wilderness ['wɪldənəs] — Wildnis
extinction [ɪk'stɪŋkʃn] — Ausrottung
to beg [beg] — betteln, bitten
to trick [trɪk] — täuschen, hereinlegen
fantasy ['fæntəsi] — Fantasie
to wander ['wɒndə] — wandern, schlendern
wood(s) [wʊdz] — Wald
timber yard ['tɪmbə jɑːd] — Holzlager
to handle ['hændl] — umgehen mit
sunburnt ['sʌnbɜːnt] — von der Sonne verbrannt

elk [elk] — Elch
fur [fɜː] — Pelz, Fell
environment [ɪn'vaɪrənmənt] — Umwelt
hunting ground ['hʌntɪŋ graʊnd] — Jagdrevier
trap [træp] — Falle
obvious ['ɒbviəs] — offensichtlich, klar
fraud [frɔːd] — Betrug, Schwindel

Song
to preach [priːtʃ] — predigen
to do without [ˌduː wɪ'ðaʊt] — ohne jdn/etw auskommen

trouble ['trʌbl] — Ärger, Schwierigkeit
to make up your mind [ˌmeɪk ʌp jɔː 'maɪnd] — sich entscheiden
to raise a family [reɪz ə 'fæməli] — Kinder großziehen
sacrifice ['sækrɪfaɪs] — Opfer
to live it up [ˌlɪv ɪt 'ʌp] — sich ein schönes Leben machen

Poem (Green)
launderette [ˌlɔːnd'ret] — Waschsalon
washing ['wɒʃɪŋ] — Wäsche
to whirl [wɜːl] — (herum)wirbeln
to dry [draɪ] — trocknen, abtrocknen
vivid ['vɪvɪd] — lebhaft
speck [spek] — Pünktchen, Fleck
rink [rɪŋk] — Schlittschuhbahn; Rollschuhbahn

date [deɪt] — Verabredung
to swear [sweə] — schwören

Poem (Tug of War)
tug of war [ˌtʌg əv 'wɔː] — Tauziehen
latest ['leɪtɪst] — neueste(r,s)
puppy ['pʌpi] — junger Hund, Welpe
pictures ['pɪktʃəz] — Kino
rag [ræg] — Lappen, Fetzen
bull [bʊl] — Bulle, Stier
tightrope ['taɪtrəʊp] — Drahtseil
to bear [beə] — ertragen, aushalten
tug [tʌg] — Ziehen
pull [pʊl] — Zerren, Ziehen

Story
hell [hel] — Hölle
to reach [riːtʃ] — sich erstrecken
wound [wuːnd] — Wunde, Verletzung
machine gun [mə'ʃiːngʌn] — Maschinengewehr
devil ['devl] — Teufel
headquarters [ˌhed'kwɔːtəz] — Hauptquartier
as well [əz 'wel] — auch
psycho ['saɪkəʊ] — verrückt; Verrückte/r
to murder ['mɜːdə] — ermorden
murderer ['mɜːdərə] — Mörder/in
propaganda [ˌprɒpə'gændə] — Propaganda
ceasefire ['siːsfaɪə] — Waffenruhe
Christmas Eve [ˌkrɪsməs 'iːv] — Heiligabend
the Milky Way [ˌmɪlki 'weɪ] — die Milchstraße
ugly ['ʌgli] — häßlich
silent ['saɪlənt] — stumm, still
Christmas carol [ˌkrɪsməs 'kærəl] — Weihnachtslied
accent ['æksent] — Akzent
woollen ['wʊlən] — wollen, Woll-
to take care of [teɪk 'keər əv] — sich kümmern um
sense of humour [ˌsens əv 'hjuːmə] — Humor

175

Umschlag	U1: Corbis: *J. Feingersh*; **Renate Grieshaber**; U4: Corbis: *Anders Ryman*
Innenumschlag vorn	Australian Tourist Commission (3); Corbis: *D. Lehmann, R. Essel, RF, S. Westmorland, R. Holmes, N. Rains, P.A. Souders*; **S. Priggemeyer**; **Wildlife**: *M. Harvey*; **zefa**: *F. Kamphues, R. I. Loyd, T. Allofs*; **Getty Images**: *D. Bayer*; **Photolibrary.com**: *R. Loopers*
Innenumschlag hinten	Canadian Tourist Commission (16); zefa: *Masterfile-A. Pytlowany, B. Brooks*

Fotos

AJHackett Bungy, Queenstown: S. 14; **APEX Photo Agency, Devon**: S. 30, 31, 32; **Allan Cash Photolibrary**: S. 62, 63, 64, 65; Australia Tourist Commission: S. 3, 5 *(5)*, 6, 8; **K. Barnett**: S. 44; **Klaus Berold**: S. 94; **Canadian Tourist Commission**: S. 53 *(6)*, 66 *(2)*, 68, 79; **COMSTOCK**: S. 45; **Corbis, Düsseldorf**: S. 3 *S. Houston*, S. 4 *C. Trotman – New Sport, Kent News & Picture – Sygma*, S. 5 *J. Klee* (Cricket), S. 8 *Duomo*, S. 9 *P.A. Souders*, S. 12 *C. Lovell*, S. 13 *A. Ryman*, S. 21 *Images.com – Sanford Agliolo, Pete Saloutos*, S. 23 *Charles O'Rear*, S. 24 *Andrew Brookes, Herrmann Starke*, S. 26 *John van Hasselt – Sygma, Wolfgang Kaehler*, S. 28 *Galen Rowell*, S. 29 *Collart Herve – Sygma, Michael&Patricia Fogden*, S. 35 *Bettmann (2)*, S. 37 *Wally McNamee, Lynn Goldsmith*, S. 38 *Frank Tapper (2), Ethan Miller, Rune Hellestad*, S. 39 *David Berman*, S. 40 *Frank Tapper, Bettmann (2), Corbis*, S. 41 *Scott Houston, John van Hasselt, Robert Essel, RF*, S. 42 *Pennie Tweedie*, S. 45 *Helen King*, S. 50 *Bettmann*, S. 54 *Reed Kaestner (2), Bob Krist*, S. 55, *Reed Kaestner*, S. 57, *Alan Schein Photography*, S. 66, *Richard A. Cooke*, S. 67, *Wolfgang Kaehler, Lowell Georgia*, S. 73 *Murray Close – Sygma*, S. 75 *Digital Arts*, S. 76 *AINACO*, S. 78 *Kent News&Picture – Sygma*, S. 79 *Hulton Deutsch Collection*, S. 88 *David Aubrey*, S. 90 *C. McPherson (2)*, S. 91 *R. Hellestad*; **COREL Library**: S. 5, 12, 53; **Das Fotoarchiv, Essen**: S. 12 *M. Schwerberger*; **Deutscher Fernsehdienst, Hamburg**: S. 3 (Robocop), S. 7 (Rabbit-Proof Fence) *(2)*, S. 22 (Terminator II), S. 73, 74 (Jurassic Park), S. 94 (Notting Hill, Herr der Ringe Teil 3), **E-Lance Media, München**: S. 10, 53(Eishockey), 91; **Emap, London**: S. 44; **Getty Images, München**: S. 6 *D. Durfee*, S. 2 *Gamma Ray Studio/Dennis Hallinan*, S. 25, *Aja Productions*, S. 37, *James Henry (2)*, *FPG*, S. 59, *Lisa Peardon, Lawrence Lucier*; **David Graham Picturefile**: S. 22, 23, 28, 35, 46, 50, 60 *(3)*, 61, 64, 65, 69, 82, 85, 87, 95 *(12)*; **R. Grieshaber**: S. 15, 16, 84; **S. Gröne**: S.8; **Imperial War Museum, London**: S. 4, 82, 83;**Mary Evans Photo Library, London**: S. 34; **New Zealand Tourist Board**: S. 12, 13, 16 *(2)*, 84; **Orlando Sentinel**: S.46, 47, 48 *AngelaPeterson*; **Picture-Alliance/dpa, Frankfurt/M.**: S. 9, S. 90 *(4)*, S. 91 *(2)*; **S. Priggemeyer**: S. 9; **Prof. Dr. Jürgen Albrecht, Berlin**: S. 88; **Royal Flying Doctor Service**: S. 18; **The Estate of Bessie Head**: S. 91 (Mudrooroo); **Unionsverlag, Zürich**: S. 91 (Mudrooroo); **Universal Studios**: S. 72 (The Making of Jurassic Park); **WA Police Service**: S. 88; **Wildlife, Hamburg**: S. 11, **zefa, Düsseldorf**: S. 24, *Masterfile – Ron Fehling*, S. 25, *Masterfile – Ron Fehling*, S. 45, *Rick Gomez*, S. 56 *Masterfile – Scott Tysick, J.A. Kraulis*, S. 57 *Masterfile – Rommel*, S. 58 *Masterfile – Scott Tysick*, S. 60 *Masterfile – Robert Holmes*, S. 78 *Masterfile – Day, Benson*, S. 80 *Masterfile – Brian Sytnyk*; **E. Zahn**: S. 84

Illustrationen

Wendy Sinclair, Angus Montrose

Cartoons

Wendy Sinclair (Raben), Peter Muggleston

Buchumschläge

S. 20: *The Bone People* **MacMillan, London**; S. 36: *The Hitchhiker's Guide to the Galaxy* **1979** by **Douglas Adams**, Used by permission of **Harmony Books**, a division of **Random House, Inc.**; S. 52: *How to Be Good* **Penguin Books, 2001**; S. 90: *Angela's Ashes* **Harper Collins**; *The Buddha of Suburbia* **Faber & Faber**; *Midnight's Children* **Penguin**; *The Joy Luck Club* **Ivy Books**; *The English Patient* **Vintage Books**; *The Blind Assassin* **Anchor**; S. 91: *Bend in the River* **Penguin**; *When Rain Clouds Gather* **Heinemann International Literature & Textbooks**; *Beloved* **Vintage**; *An Angel At My Table* **The Womens Press**; *Aboriginal Mythology* **Thorsons Publishers** for **Harper Collins**; *The Falls* **St. Martin's Minotaur, 2003**

Texte

S. 18: *The flying doctor* adaptation from *The Wildflower Evacuation* **Royal Flying Doctor Service National Office, 2003**; S. 20: *The Bone People* by **Keri Hulme**, © Keri Hulme 1983, Penguin Books, 1986; S. 36: *The Hitchhiker's Guide to the Galaxy* **1979** by **Douglas Adams**, Used by permission of **Harmony Books**, a division of **Random House, Inc.**; S. 44: *Katie's Story* Emap élan, London, 2003; S. 46/47: from *A World of One* by Linda Shrieves, 30.5.2002, in *Orlando Sentinel*; S. 52: *How to Be Good* by Nick Hornby, Penguin Books, 2001 © Nick Hornby 2001; S. 59: *Summer of '69* Adams / Vallance / Irving Music Inc. / Adams Communications, Inc. Almo Music Corp., Rondor Musikverlag GmbH, Berlin; S. 68: *Diary of a South African* http://travel.iafrica.com; S. 81: *Papa don't preach* Ciccone, Madonna Louise / Elliot, Brian / Elliot Jacobsen Music Publ., Neue Welt Musikverlag, München; *Green* by Jennifer and Graeme Curry, *Glitter When You Jump* Fiona Waters **(Ed.)**, MacMillan Children's Books, MacMillan Publishers Ltd., 1996; *Tug of War* by **John Kitching**, *All In the Family* John Foster (Ed.), OUP, 1993; S. 82/83: *Christmas in Hell* Arthur Gordon, Kaleidoscope Publishers Ltd, 1987; S. 92: Reproduced by permission of **Oxford University Press: 1.** *Oxford Wordpower Dictionary* © OUP 2000; **2.** *Das Große Oxford Schulwörterbuch* © OUP 2003

Nicht alle Copyrightinhaber konnten ermittelt werden; deren Urheberrechte werden hiermit vorsorglich und ausdrücklich anerkannt.